The Random House Personal Finance Library

The Practical Law Manual to Consumer Legal Affairs

George Milko, Kay Ostberg &
Theresa Meehan Rudy

This work was originally published as three separate books, entitled
Everyday Contracts, Real Estate, and *Small Claims Court.*

RANDOM HOUSE
ELECTRONIC PUBLISHING

New York

This work was originally published as three separate books, entitled *Everyday Contracts* (1988), *Real Estate* (1990), and *Small Claims Court* (1990) by Random House, Inc.

Everyday Contracts: Katherine Lee and Allison Rottmann were contributing authors. Substantial assistance was provided by Richard Hebert.
Real Estate: Chip Greenwood, Paul Hasse, and Daniel Lewolt were contributing authors.
Small Claims Court: Paul Hasse and Chip Greenwood authored the original draft. Dennis St. George, Timothy J. Wall and Richard Hebert provided substantial assistance.

Halt—An Organization of Americans for Legal Reform, is a national nonprofit, nonpartisan, public-interest group with more than 150,000 members. Located at 1319 F. St. NW, Suite 300, Washington, DC 20004, its goals are to enable people to handle their legal affairs simply, affordably, and equitably. HALT's education and advocacy programs strive to improve the quality, reduce the cost, and increase the accessibility of the civil justice system. Its activities are funded by members' contributions.

New York, Toronto, London, Sydney, Auckland

CONTENTS

BOOK
I

EVERYDAY CONTRACTS

For Dianne

ACKNOWLEDGMENTS

I gratefully acknowledge the support of my family and particularly my wife, Dianne. I also want to express my appreciation for the assistance of: Ronald M. Legro and Constance Kilmark, who read the manuscript and provided valuable comments; my agent Oscar Collier; my editor Charlotte Mayerson and the other people at Random House; the dozens of lawyers and judges who have provided lessons in law and the operation of the legal system; and, most important, the thousands of people who have done me the honor of seeking out my advice and assistance and who, I fervently hope, have benefited from it. The responsibility for any errors is entirely mine.

Kenneth J. Doran

INTRODUCTION TO EVERYDAY CONTRACTS

Though we may not be aware of it, most of us frequently enter into contracts in our daily lives . . . with the bank, a home-improvement contractor, a landlord, an auto-repair shop.

We don't think about reviewing such arrangements with a lawyer or even about carefully reading the fine print, partly because it doesn't seem to be worth the trouble, partly because we reason that such people are unlikely to change the terms of their standard agreements anyhow, even if we do take the time or spend the money on a lawyer.

But what if something goes wrong? It is then that the contract language becomes all-important. You may learn to your surprise that you have agreed to *accelerate* your loan payments, or that the bathroom repairs won't be completed until three months after your son's wedding.

Everyday Contracts tells you what to watch for before signing an

5

agreement or verbally committing yourself to one. It explains what laws apply and translates the "boilerplate" used in standard contracts into plain language. It provides important tips on how to read a contract, how to negotiate the best deal, and how best to get it in writing. Finally, the book tells you what your rights are if you have a dispute over a contract and where you can turn for help.

A Word About Terms

This book, unlike other HALT material, is full of legal terms. That is because they are used in contracts and it is our goal to translate them for you into understandable language. The book also explains the "fine print" so you can understand the contracts in your life without heading to a lawyer or a law library. Each legal term is italicized and defined the first time it is used. You can also consult the Glossary on page 247, where major terms and their definitions appear again.

How to Use This Book

The first four chapters give basic information about all contracts. Chapters 1 and 2 explain basic contract language and laws, Chapter 3 gives basic consumer tips, and Chapter 4 explains avenues for resolving problems. After reading these, turn to the part that covers the agreement you're interested in.

Each part is devoted to one kind of contract or a "family" of contracts, with an explanation of the laws involved, tips about entering into the agreement, and a translation of standard contract terms into plain language. As appropriate, consumer-oriented provisions are suggested. Keep in mind, this is sample language; read it carefully before using it to be sure it's appropriate for the agreement you want.

Also listed are books, organizations, and dispute-resolution resources available if you need more help. Other resources are listed in the Bibliography, Appendix VI.

Contract Laws

It is often said that the basic right to make a deal, even a bad one, is found in the U.S. Constitution, and that we live in a "buyer beware" society. In fact, many laws do regulate our contracts. These range from "common law" principles, derived by our courts from early English precedents, to state laws that govern the buying and selling of goods and services, most of them variations of what's known as the Uniform Commercial Code. Several federal agencies, notably the Federal Trade Commission, the Federal Reserve Board, and the U.S. Department of Housing and Urban Development, also enforce laws that regulate contracts. These often also have state counterparts.

Knowing about these laws and agencies can make the difference between being taken advantage of and making good agreements with which you can live comfortably.

Professional Help

Everyday Contracts gives you information you need to feel confident preparing, negotiating, and signing a contract on your own, without professional legal help. Going it alone may be your only option if you need your car repaired today, are handed a lease to sign in a city with a housing crisis, or are getting a loan from the only bank in town. However, if possible, when considerable money is at stake or you are uncertain about a substantial part of the deal, consider hiring professional help. *But before you hire anyone, know your options.*

Decide, first, whether you want someone to help you negotiate the contract, draft it, or review an agreement that's already written. The more you want done, the higher the fee will be.

Investigate all your alternatives. You may not need a lawyer. Instead, a competent paralegal, experienced nonlawyer, or a consumer group may be able to help, particularly if you simply want someone to review a standard agreement. Whomever you hire, negotiate a fair fee. Ask others what they charge. A lawyer will probably quote an hourly fee, but you can try to negotiate a flat fee or an hourly fee with an agreed-upon maximum.

Be clear whether you want help in negotiating the contract or only a review of the agreement you're planning to sign. If you ask only for a review and can specify which clauses you want help with, it will keep your cost down. Whatever you agree on, remember: That's a contract, too. Get it in writing, including the work that will be done, when it will be done, how much you'll pay, and when you'll pay it.*

As you read this book, you will periodically encounter references to the software featured with this book, Home Lawyer. Home Lawyer is a personal legal software product that lets you create, change or update frequently-needed documents. Home Lawyer contains important documents from Hyatt Legal Services, the nation's largest general practice law firm. Hyatt Legal Services selected the documents used most often in protecting the rights of their clients.

Home Lawyer has several features that enhance the legal information in this book. Home Lawyer includes a Preventive Law Interview, designed to help you identify the documents you are most likely to need. When you answer the Preventative Law Interview questions, you'll be directed to the appropriate documents in the program.

You'll also be given directions to topics of interest in Home Lawyer's Personal Law Topics. The Advisor contains information about the law and its impact on many areas of your life, from home ownership to estate planning, from family law to buying and selling an automobile.

Home Lawyer also features a glossary of legal terms, and a list of state bar associations to contact when you need a lawyer.

*See *Using a Lawyer,* Kay Ostberg in association with HALT, Random House, 1990.

PART I

CONTRACTS IN GENERAL

CHAPTER

I

THE CONTRACT

Julie's car makes funny noises. She takes it to her neighborhood repair shop. A service representative estimates the job will cost $350. She leaves the car and arranges to pick it up at the end of the day.

Bill has finally agreed to sell Jim his stereo. Jim agrees to pay Bill $300 for it next payday.

Beth's mom agrees to let her live at home rent free for the rest of her life if Beth will take care of her when her health declines.

Mary's landlord doesn't want to renew her lease but says she can live in the house month-to-month on the same terms as in her previous lease. Mary agrees.

Andrew receives a mailed invitation to join a prepaid legal services plan before September 3. He signs the registration form and sends it on September 2.

In each of these examples, chances are a legally binding, valid contract* has been entered into. A contract is any agreement between two or more people. It involves a "meeting of the minds"

---

*In this book, the terms *contract*, *agreement*, and *deal* are used interchangeably.

expressed orally or in writing to do or not do something in exchange for something else.

It is a popular misconception that a contract must be signed or notarized to be valid or that you must pay at least one dollar to make a deal "stick." People even think that a contract must be in writing.

Although it's true some contracts must be in writing (explained later in this chapter), for the most part oral contracts are legal. However, although legal, they aren't usually smart. HALT strongly urges that you get any agreement in writing to protect against misunderstandings and later problems.

The underlying principle of the marketplace, still the cornerstone of contract law, is that once a bargain is made, it should be upheld. This promotes predictability and protects everyone's right to make a deal. As a result, judges still try hard to uphold any deal. In some instances, courts will uphold a contract even if it means filling in terms of the deal that were left out or vague. They will use tradition or what is customary in the business or industry to supply the missing information.

In recent decades, laws have been enacted to protect consumers' contract rights, a recognition that businesses and consumers often have unequal bargaining power. However, courts still rely on the basic principle that a contract should be upheld whether or not it reflects a fair bargain.

With this in mind, you have a valid contract if you have:

- An offer, counteroffer, and acceptance
- Consideration
- Itemized terms
- No valid defenses

Offer and Acceptance

An offer is an invitation to make a deal or an invitation to exchange promises. An offer might be someone stopping you on the street and telling you, "For only $10, you can be the proud owner of this genuine cut-glass fake ruby ring." Or it can be a newspaper advertisement promising a television set at the sale price of $400 to the first 10 buyers.

You can tell when an offer is made because all that's needed to clinch the agreement is your acceptance, signaled by your agreeing to the deal on the terms offered. This can be by oral acceptance, signing on the proverbial "dotted line," or, in the example of the ring, handing over $10 to the fellow on the street. Watch out for jokes, though. If it was not reasonable to believe an offer was really made, you have no contract.

Beware of something else, too. Sometimes all it takes for acceptance is your silence. Record and book clubs, for example, get you to "agree" that if they don't hear from you after notifying you of each month's selection, you have "accepted" the offer to buy that selection at the listed price.

In other cases, you accept by completing your side of the agreement (called *performance*). For example, your brother says, "If you paint the outside of my house this summer, I'll pay you $1,500 plus the cost of supplies." All you need to do to accept the arrangement is start painting the house.

An acceptance isn't a *counteroffer*. If you say, "Sure, I'll take that dynamite ring, but I'll only give you $7 for it," you've made a counteroffer, not an acceptance. A counteroffer is considered to cancel the original offer. No contract exists unless the counteroffer is accepted. Not only is the ring seller not obligated to sell you the ring for $7, once you've made your counteroffer, the seller is not even obligated to sell it to you for $10.

You also can withdraw an offer anytime before it is accepted. So, if the ring seller says, "Oops, I changed my mind. I don't want to sell you this fine ring," and you have not yet agreed to buy it or whipped out your $10, the offer is rescinded, and you have no right to buy the ring. (Some states make exceptions and prohibit businesses to rescind offers they have promised in writing to keep open for a specified time.)

Similarly, you have only a reasonable amount of time in which to accept an offer. Although what is considered a reasonable time varies, it's safe to say that if you accept an offer years after it was made, even though it was never formally rescinded, it's unlikely a contract was created by your acceptance.

Consideration

To have a valid contract, there must also be an exchange. Each side must give up something, called *consideration*. Consideration is the glue that binds a deal; it answers the question "What do I get out of it?" The most common consideration is money for goods or services, as in the sale of the ring. In that deal, one side gave up the ring and the other gave up the cash.

Consideration can also be a promise to do or not do something. In one of the examples at the beginning of this chapter, the consideration was a promise to care for an ill parent in return for free rent. Other forms of nonmonetary consideration might be a promise not to sue, or a promise to hold open an offer to sell property.

However, if your best friend says, "I'll take you to Paris if I win the lottery," and you agree, no contract exists because no exchange of consideration has taken place. You have not given up anything.

Also, if you agree to something you already previously agreed to or are already legally bound by, there is no consideration and therefore no contract. For example, if you call up a creditor and say, "I'll only pay you the $500 I owe you if you don't charge me the interest we had agreed upon," you are making an offer with no consideration. You already owe the money and the interest. Even if the creditor agrees, chances are you still legally owe the interest from the original deal.

Finally, the law does not require that the consideration be "fair" for the contract to be binding. To do so is considered interfering with the right to bargain. (Exceptions to this "right to make a bad bargain" are discussed later in the chapter.)

Terms

For a contract to be valid, it should also be clear who is making the contract and what property, time, place, price, and other pertinent details are involved. These material terms define each side's rights and obligations. Some states have laws that specifically address failure by a business to disclose the material terms of an agreement (see Chapter 5, Bank Loans).

If essential terms are missing or are so indefinite as to make the contract unclear, no "meeting of the minds" has occurred and, technically, no contract has been entered into. The contract is void. On the other hand, if many of the terms in a contested contract are clear, a court may try to fill in the missing or unclear terms with a "best guess" as to what both sides intended to agree on. A court will consider past usage in contracts of the industry or past contracts between both sides.

If the terms were mistakenly stated, the person who made the mistake can be held to it unless the mistake was obvious: for example, if a real ruby was offered and the quoted price was missing a few zeroes. If both sides made mistakes in defining the terms and either side wants to cancel the contract, the contract can be voided. (Please note the difference between *void* and *voidable*. If a contract is void, there is no contract. If a contract is voidable, there is a contract until one side or the other chooses to nullify it.)

Defenses

You have an offer, an acceptance, consideration, and clear terms, but you still do not have an enforceable contract if one side or the other has a valid defense against enforcing it. Be mindful, however, that basic public policy is to uphold contracts whenever possible, so it is usually stiff going to prove a defense.

Before explaining some valid defenses, it's worthwhile mentioning some that are not valid. A court will not let you out of a contract if you're challenging it because you:

- Failed to read the contract
- Changed your mind (see Chapter 3 for some exceptions)
- Can't pay
- Didn't have the agreement notarized

Valid defenses include: that a contract was entered into for illegal purposes; that one or both sides were not competent to enter into the contract; that the contract violates the state's Statute of Frauds; that one side was forced or tricked into signing; and that the contract includes "unconscionable" provisions. Each of these is discussed below.

Illegal Purpose

A contract with an illegal purpose is no contract at all. It's considered void. Thus, if you want to put terms in writing because you don't trust the arsonist you hired to burn down your financially failing business, don't bother. You won't create a contract, only evidence of your crime.

However, if, for example, you sign a loan agreement that obligates you to pay an illegally high interest rate (usury), a court might reduce the interest rate to the highest legal level before enforcing the contract. Although the consideration was illegal, the purpose of the contract was not, and the court will make its best effort to uphold the bargain. (This is called *reformation*).

Incompetence to Contract

The law identifies certain people as lacking the capacity to enter into a valid contract. They include minors (usually under age 18), the mentally unstable, and people who enter into an agreement while under the influence of drugs or alcohol. An incompetent person or that person's legal caretaker (*guardian*) has the right to cancel a contract, but a court will also try to correct any injustice the cancellation creates. If a parent cancels a child's purchase agreement for a stereo, for example, chances are good that a court will order the stereo returned to its previous owner.

A word of caution, however, to anyone planning to use the drug-and-alcohol defense: courts are reluctant to allow anyone to cancel a contract based on the defense of incapacitating intoxication. To plead this defense successfully, you'll need to show that when the deal was clinched, the other side knew about your intoxication and took advantage of you.

Statute of Frauds

Some contracts must be in writing. These are listed in each state's Statute of Frauds and Uniform Commercial Code. Although state laws differ, the most common contracts that must be in writing are for the sale of goods worth more than $500, the sale of land, the sale of securities, auto repairs, sales warranties, and consumer loans. Also, contracts that won't be fulfilled within one year must be in writing.

If you have one of these contracts and it's not in writing, either you or the other side may cancel it. Be mindful, however, that some courts may enforce an oral agreement if one side relied on the promises of the other and put up money or some other significant investment.

Fraud, Duress, and Undue Influence

A contract is voidable if you were forced or tricked into signing it, threatened with serious harm, or, while you were in a weakened condition, strongly pressured by someone in a financial or confidential relationship with you. Those considered to be in a financial or confidential relationship include your doctors, lawyers, accountants, clergy, and members of your family. Courts are reluctant to accept this defense, but if a gun was held to your head, or if you clearly were taken advantage of by someone close to you while you were ill, or if one side of the bargain was clearly misrepresented, most courts will hold the contract void.

Unconscionable Provisions

This defense is relatively new. It has been used successfully when the two people who made the deal have unequal bargaining power. Anyone subject to an unreasonable clause in a contract can ask the court to cancel that clause or, sometimes, even the entire deal. This defense has been allowed to protect people from having to live with one-sided "take it or leave it" contracts. However, terms that are considered "unconscionable" are usually defined by court precedents.

Some unconscionable provisions are: a clause in a hospital emergency admission form that waives all claims for medical malpractice against the hospital or doctors, and a clause that allows a retail store to take back *all* merchandise bought on credit even though most of it has been paid for. In such instances, a court may strike the unconscionable clause but uphold the rest of the contract.

Having a valid contract is no guarantee that problems won't develop, however. The other side may not stick to the deal, or you may change your mind about what you thought was a great deal when you signed. The next chapter explains your rights when a contract dispute arises and what can happen if you decide to back out of a legally binding agreement.

CHAPTER

2

ENFORCEMENT

When someone fails to live up to the terms of a contract, it's called a *breach*. When that happens, you can negotiate, mediate, or sue for damages. Knowing what a court might award in such cases can help you negotiate a settlement directly, go into mediation with some understanding of your legal rights, or assess whether it's worth your time and money to sue. It also will help you write into your contract explicit protections against breach.

Common-law principles developed to govern buying and selling in the marketplace. The underlying marketplace principle is that the side that breached the contract should pay for the losses caused by the breach, but not be additionally penalized for breaking the contract. A punishment payment is not required.

In deciding whether a breach has occurred, if the contract can still be upheld, and what might be owed, a court will not deviate greatly from custom and tradition for a given business unless the terms of your contract clearly specify otherwise.

With this in mind, if a breach occurs, you may get one or more of the following remedies. Each of the remedies discussed in later chapters fits under one or another of these categories.

Damages

The remedy most frequently awarded by a court is money to compensate for loss caused by the breach *(damages)*. For example, if you were one of the first ten buyers to arrive to pick up that television set for $400, as advertised, and you found all the sets already sold, the store "owes" you any amount above the $400 that you had to pay to buy the set somewhere else.

There are limits to what you can recover, however, even if you can show a loss. If your mother had a heart attack because she was worried when you didn't call her, you will probably not be able to recover her medical expenses from the telephone company by claiming it failed to hook up your service when promised.

You can get compensation only for losses that are a foreseeable result of the breach. In the example above, it is unlikely a court would find that the telephone company could have foreseen that connecting your telephone late would injure your mother. Damages are considered foreseeable if both sides know in advance that the damages are likely to occur because of the breach. You also need to keep in mind two other limits on damages.

Another limitation is that you have an obligation to try to avoid increasing the damages that result from a breach even though the other side caused the breach. If you have an opportunity to mitigate the damages and you don't, you may never recover for the loss.

Say your roofer failed to patch all the holes in your roof and your upstairs floor was ruined by a subsequent rain. You have a responsibility to mop up the water before it seeps through the ceiling and damages the floor below. If you don't, you may not be reimbursed for the damage to the lower floor.

Even if you write a clause into your contract setting out how much money will be owed to you if the contract is broken, the amount must be sensible in light of the losses likely to occur.

(Clauses that specify how much will be owed are called *liquidation* clauses.)

Excused Counterperformance

This is just a fancy way of saying that if the other side fails to live up to its side of a deal, you have no obligation to live up to yours: You are released from your part of the agreement. As a lawyer would say, you are excused from *performance*.

One caution, however: a court will not let you out of the contract if it finds that the breach was minor. So, if your brother agreed to pay you $1,200 for painting his house and you painted everything but the front porch, a court won't let your brother out of paying you. Chances are the court will instead award you the $1,200 minus reasonable costs to hire someone to finish the job.

Quasi-Contract

Even if, in the housepainting example, your contract explicitly stated that your brother would pay you only if the painting was completed exactly as specified, the court will still probably order your brother to pay you something. However, instead of looking at the contract to determine how much you're owed, the court will calculate the fair market value of the work you did complete. This is called suing in quasi-contract. In other words, the court will award money based not on the written contract, but on the principle that your brother should not unfairly benefit from your work by not paying anything for it. When a contract results from unequal bargaining power or the outcome doesn't seem fair in light of typical business practices, a court may use this principle to reform a contract.

Rescission and Restitution

If one side breaks a contract by not coming up with money or other promised consideration, the court may allow the other side to cancel the contract and get back anything that has already been paid. This is called *rescission*. For example, if you learn that the "new" piano you bought was really used, the seller has failed to come up with the promised consideration. A court will probably let you return the piano for a refund. Of course, if you played the piano for a year before returning it, the court has two choices: It may deduct a rental fee from that refund or decide that since you didn't discover the misrepresentation for a year, it couldn't have been serious. In that case, it will consider you to have affirmed the contract by using the piano.

Specific Performance

In rare instances, when a court doesn't think money can adequately repay you for a breach, it may order the other side to live up to the agreement. Courts will award such specific performance only if they think the contract was fair to start with and you can't replace the services reasonably elsewhere.

Tort Action

If a broken contract caused someone to be injured or property to be damaged (a *tort*), you may be able to sue for damages, but only if both sides could foresee that the breach might cause the injury. For example, you buy medication that's prepared incorrectly and as a result you suffer ill effects; a court will probably uphold your claim for damages from the manufacturer based on the misrepresentation and incorrect preparation of the medicine.

CHAPTER

3

BEFORE YOU SIGN

We suggest reading this chapter now and rereading it immediately before you enter into any contract. It contains practical suggestions about what to keep in mind when entering into an agreement.

Practical Rules

Get It in Writing. Many oral contracts are legal, but unless you want to risk a courtroom contest over whose word is more believable, get the agreement in writing. Many, if not most, contract disputes result from misunderstanding the terms of the agreement. Putting the terms in writing usually helps both sides understand them clearly. Also, it's easier to hold the other side to the agreement if it's in writing and you can point to it if problems develop.

Don't Sign Anything Unless You're Sure. Make sure you understand all the terms of an agreement before accepting it. Do not simply listen to a salesperson's description of the agreement; read it thoroughly. Although there may be instances when you have little choice but to sign immediately, you do this at some risk. Ask questions about language you don't understand. If you have doubts, ask to take the agreement home so you can go over it with someone you trust who has knowledge or experience in the subject area.

Change the Language to Fit the Terms. Make sure all the terms you are agreeing to are written into the contract. Don't let a salesperson tell you, "Oh, we never go by that clause, it's just standard language left over from before," or "The cost includes free delivery even though it's not listed in the agreement." Change the language to reflect the agreement. Whenever possible, cross out clauses that are incorrect, add new language, and have both signers initial in the margin next to each change.

Fill in the Blanks. Make sure all blank spaces in standard-form contracts are filled in or crossed out. Otherwise, they may be filled in later without your knowledge. Never sign a blank agreement.

Make Sure You Know the Payment Schedule. If the contract involves payments you'll owe, make sure you know the full amounts, all interest or other charges, when payments are due, and what happens if you fail to pay on time. Some state laws require banks and other lenders to give you a payment schedule if you ask for one. Always ask.

Keep a Copy of the Agreement. This is your evidence that a deal was made. Your copy should have original signatures, if at all possible. This is considered an "original." Keep the contract in a safe place.

Consider Adding a Mediation or Arbitration Clause. If you have a chance to change a contract or are drafting one, consider adding a provision that if problems arise that can't be solved directly, you will take them to either *mediation* or *arbitration.* These alternative dispute-resolution forums are quicker, less expensive, and less time-consuming than suing in court.

In mediation, you and the other side identify problems and discuss solutions with the guidance of a neutral mediator. Any agreement you make must be put into writing before it is legally binding. Once you sign the agreement, it has the legal force of any contract.

Arbitration is more formal than mediation. Rules of court do not apply; it is similar to a shortened, less formal court hearing. Each side submits a summary of its arguments to an arbitrator, who then makes a decision that is put in writing.

Special Laws

When signing any agreement, you should also know about two other kinds of laws that govern consumer contracts: rules that require a "cooling-off" period for some contracts and plain-language requirements.

The Cooling-Off Rule

If you sign a contract other than at the seller's normal place of business, such as in your home, chances are you have three days to change your mind and cancel it. This rule is intended primarily to prevent door-to-door salespeople from pushing you into expensive, unplanned purchases. When you sign the contract, the seller is also obligated to give you a cancellation form to use if you change your mind and choose to exercise your rights under this rule.

This cooling-off rule is enforced by the Federal Trade Commission and applies to any contract that meets all of these requirements:

- It is not made at the seller's normal place of business.
- It is not made by telephone or mail.
- It is for more than $25.
- It is not for real estate, insurance, or securities.
- It is not for emergency home repairs.

Plain-Language Laws

Some states require that all consumer contracts be written in clear, coherent, and nontechnical language. Many more states apply this requirement to insurance contracts. In states that have such plain-language laws, you can sue a business if you can show that because you did not understand confusing or technical language, you suffered a monetary or other loss. Contact your state or local Consumer Protection Agency (Appendix I) for further information about your state's plain-language laws.

CHAPTER

4

SOLVING PROBLEMS

If you have a problem with your contract—either before or after you sign—review this chapter as well as the problem-solving tips and resources in the chapters that discuss your subject area.

If you're having a contract problem, you have several standard options for solving it, no matter what kind of contract it is:

- Direct negotiation with the other side

- Filing a complaint with a government or private consumer agency

- Participating in arbitration or mediation

- Taking your complaint to court

Direct Negotiation

When you suspect you have a problem with your landlord, your home-improvement contractor, your bank, or someone else you have a contract with, try to sort it out first by direct contact. This is not only the least expensive option, it also lets you clear up problems that are simply misunderstandings.

Check your contract before you call or write. If you call, regardless of the outcome of your conversation, put your concerns in a letter to the other party to document the problem and any agreement you reached. This creates a "paper trail" that may be useful if you later have to take your complaint to arbitration.

If you can't solve the problem by talking to the other person involved, try that person's supervisor or the Consumer Affairs or Customer Relations Office of the business you've contracted with, if it has one. If it is a large company you are complaining to, it may have a toll-free "800" number you can use.

Local and State Agencies

If direct negotiation fails, try taking your complaint to a government or private agency. These typically offer help in resolving consumer problems at little or no expense. For almost all consumer complaints, you can get help from either a government-run Consumer Affairs Office or the privately operated Better Business Bureau (see Private Agencies, below). In some cases, you might want to contact a trade association or media-sponsored consumer "action line."

City and county Consumer Protection Agencies often act as neutral intermediaries to help resolve complaints. This can be effective because these agencies' staffs are usually familiar with the business practices and relevant laws in your area. The agencies typically limit the type of complaints they handle, however. For example, they do not usually handle landlord-tenant problems or problems with service professionals, such as lawyers.

If your city or county doesn't have a Consumer Protection Agency, contact your state agency (Appendix I). It will operate either as a separate Department of Consumer Affairs or as part of the office of the governor or attorney general. If the office nearest you doesn't handle your type of problem, it should be able to refer you to one that does.

Consumer Protection Agencies have authority to force businesses to respond to your complaint, and can even sue businesses on your behalf. However, because their resources are limited, they usually sue only businesses with serious patterns of illegal activity.

Filing a complaint with a government-run Consumer Protection Agency may lead in either direction—to a mediated resolution or to a bureaucratic shuffle that offers you little more than advice on whether or not you have a valid legal claim. To find out what you can expect from your agency, call and ask how they handle individual complaints.

U.S. Government Agencies

Although almost every area of consumer concern is the responsibility of one federal agency or another, these agencies usually work on overall regulation, such as by promulgating "Truth in Lending" rules, not on individual complaints. It's worthwhile, however, to ask the agency that deals with your area of concern what consumer information it has available and if it is one of the few that does investigate complaints.

Private Agencies

Better Business Bureaus (BBBs) are nonprofit, private organizations sponsored by local businesses. Currently, there are 170 BBB offices in the United States. (Their addresses are listed in Appendix II.) Besides compiling complaint records on local businesses, they usually try to resolve consumers' problems through direct negotiation with the business. Some also offer binding arbitration.

About 40,000 trade and professional organizations in the United States represent the interests of banks, insurers, medicine, other professional services, and every major industry and manufacturing group. Some trade associations run their own mediation or arbitration programs either directly or through a service council or consumer action program. If you decide to use one of these, make sure you know exactly what you are agreeing to and try to find out whether it has a reputation for fairness or bias toward the businesses it represents.

Many local radio and television stations and newspapers also sponsor consumer-mediation programs, typically called "action lines" or "hot lines." They use media exposure to pressure businesses into cooperating in dispute settlement. Some programs are selective in the complaints they take, reserving their resources for the "worst" cases. To learn what's available in your area, contact your local newspaper and radio or television stations.

The best way to register a complaint with any agency is by writing a letter. Include copies of your contract, bills, and any other documents relevant to the dispute. Remember to keep a copy for your files. Your letter should include:

- Your name, address, and telephone number where you can be reached both at home and at work

- The name and address of the business you are complaining about

- A *brief* description of the problem and supporting facts

- The amount of money involved, if any

- The resolution you want

Arbitration and Mediation

If federal, state, county, city, or private Consumer Protection Agencies can't help resolve your dispute, investigate using a public or private arbitration or mediation service. These *alternative dispute-resolution forums* are often less expensive than going to court and, in the case of mediation, emphasize cooperative resolution rather than pitting adversaries against each other. This is particularly important if you know that you will have future dealings with the other side.

As explained earlier, in *mediation* you and the other side identify problems and discuss solutions with the guidance of a neutral mediator. Mediation is not for every dispute, however. If either side is hostile or unwilling to talk to the other, mediation may not work.

Also, shop carefully for your mediator. This person can influence the process significantly. Any agreement you make must be put into writing before it is legally binding, at which time it has the legal force of any contract.

Shopping for a mediator is a little different from shopping for other service professionals because most mediators are not in private practice. Instead, most belong to a community group or court program. You'll probably end up interviewing the program administrator first and the particular mediator only later. When interviewing a mediator or program administrator, be sure to ask:

- Does the mediator specialize, for example, in consumer disputes?

- Where was the mediator trained?

- How long has the mediator been practicing?

- How many cases has the mediator handled? Were they similar to yours?

- How much will mediation cost? Are unforeseen increases in cost likely? Under what circumstances?

Arbitration is a more formal process than mediation. Although the rules of court do not apply, it is similar to a shortened, less formal court hearing. Each side submits a summary of its arguments to an arbitrator (or panel of arbitrators), who then makes a decision.

Before you agree to arbitrate, be sure you know whether the decision will be binding. If it is binding, the arbitrator's decision is enforceable in court. Although a binding process is final and therefore guarantees quick resolution, be sure you feel comfortable with the process, your arbitrator, and the people who run the program.

Ask your local courts if they run a mediation or arbitration program, and check the telephone directory for listings of private arbitrators or mediators. You might also contact the Society of Professionals in Dispute Resolution (SPIDR) or the American Bar Association Standing Committee on Dispute Resolution for more information and referrals. Both are located in Washington, D.C.

Suing in Court

If none of these alternatives works, consider suing. Keep in mind that this should be your last resort because of the expense, time, and frustration it usually entails. Before deciding to sue, carefully weigh the costs against your chances of winning and the amount you are likely to win.

If your dispute involves a small sum of money, you may be able to sue inexpensively in small claims court. This is far preferable to taking a claim to district or municipal court. Small claims courts offer a quick, informal, and fairly consumer-hospitable forum. Most do not take cases that involve more than $2,500, although the limits differ from state to state.* If your claim is for more than the small claims limit, consider filing suit in the next-highest court, usually municipal or district court, or sue for less so your claim can be handled in small claims court.

Taking a case through small claims court has many advantages over higher courts. The process is streamlined, you can represent yourself (in some states, lawyers aren't even allowed in the courtroom unless they're defending themselves), filing fees are lower, and you can usually get a hearing within 30 or 40 days.

If you represent yourself in a higher court, you'll be expected to know which court to file in, what the rules of procedure are, how to collect evidence, how to discern what evidence is and isn't admissible, when to file papers, what the different legal terms mean, and how to present your case to the judge. Also, don't be surprised by longer delays, higher filing fees, and a judge who isn't at all happy to see you there without a lawyer.

If you don't choose to represent yourself but decide to hire a lawyer to handle the suit, calculate how much you stand to win after deducting your lawyer's fees and expenses, including court fees.

*For state limits, see Appendix VI. Book 3, Small Claims Court, is a step-by-step guide that explains how to file papers, collect evidence, present your case to the judge, and enforce an award in court.

PART II

TAKING A LOAN

CHAPTER

5

BANK LOANS

Sally and Suzanne decide to open an office-cleaning business. They have customers and staff, but they need money to buy equipment. They talk to three banks. Their best loan offer is $20,000 at 10% interest to be repaid at $424.94 a month for five years.

Alan's three credit cards are "maxed out." He owes $3,000 on the first, $2,000 on the second, $5,000 on the third, and pays 18% interest on each. He checks with his local bank and decides to pay off his accounts with a loan for $10,000 at 14% interest, to be repaid in 36 monthly payments of $341.78.

Ellen is buying a car for $9,000, and because sales are slow, the dealer offers financing at 2% with no money down payable in 36 monthly payments of $257.78. After three years, she will have paid $9,280.08 for this loan—$9,000 for the car, and $280.08 for the interest.

Loans like these are agreements to lend money (the *principal*) in exchange for a fee, called *interest,* usually based on a percentage of the loaned amount. Bank loans typically involve standard forms, government regulations, and collateral—the property you "put up" as security that you'll forfeit if you don't pay back the loan.

Because most bank loans require collateral, they are considered *secured* loans.

Government Regulation

Consumer loans are regulated by several government agencies. The Federal Reserve Board, the Federal Trade Commission, and state and federal banking authorities all have a role in regulating and monitoring consumer lending. In addition, these agencies enforce laws to make sure that people are not denied credit on illegal grounds.

The regulations are intended to protect consumers by seeing to it that they are aware of all the terms of the loan and their full financial obligations. The agencies' roles, the laws they enforce, and how you can get redress if those laws and regulations are violated are all discussed later in this and the next chapter. First, you will find an overview of basic loan concepts, followed by consumer problem-solving tips and resources. The final chapter in this section offers a clause-by-clause analysis of a typical bank-loan contract. Secured loans from nonbank lenders, like finance companies, car dealerships, and furniture stores, often include identical clauses.

Basic Concepts

Most people who borrow use *installment* loans. That means they repay the loan over time in monthly or other periodic payments. In *consideration* for the loan, they agree to repay the principal and the interest. The length of time they have to pay back a loan is called its *term*.

How Interest Rates Are Set

All banks get their money from Federal Reserve Banks, operated by the Federal Reserve Board. This board, appointed by the president of the United States, controls the flow of the nation's money supply. One of its most important tools for doing this is the *discount* rate of interest that it charges its member banks for the money they borrow. The board sets that rate as a political and economic strategy to keep the economy healthy. Banks in turn base their rates on the discount rate, charging customers a little more than they themselves have to pay "the Fed."

The *prime rate* is the interest that the largest banks charge their preferred, or "prime," borrowers—typically huge corporations. All other interest rates are set higher than the prime, reflecting the banks' perception of their costs and the risks they take that the loans won't be repaid. Banks make consumer loans based on two types of interest rates: *fixed* and *fluctuating*.

Fixed-Rate Loans

A fixed-rate loan has the same interest rate applied throughout its life. Because fixed interest rates don't change, you can calculate before signing exactly what the loan will cost you each month and over its entire life.

Fluctuating-Rate Loans

The cost of a loan with a fluctuating interest rate varies over the life of the loan. The interest rate usually goes up or down with the prime rate, with a special rate set by the Office of Thrift Supervision for mortgages, or with the current interest being paid for U.S. Treasury bills, the money the U.S. government borrows.

Because fluctuating rates have many variations, you should call around and shop for the best deal. Things to look for when comparing fluctuating-rate loans include:

- How *often* your rate can be changed

- The limit on how many percentage points your rate can be adjusted at any one time (a *yearly* or *periodic* cap)

- The limit on how much your rate can be changed over the entire life of the loan (a *lifetime* cap)

For example, you might have a five-year loan for $5,000 at the prime rate plus 2%, with an annual adjustment, a 1% yearly cap and a lifetime cap of 3%. If the prime is at 10% at the start of the loan, your beginning interest rate will be 12%. At the first annual adjustment, that rate can go up to 13% or down to 11%. As the prime rate changes, so will your interest rate. However, your rate can go up only to 13% the first year, 14% the second, and 15% the third. The lifetime 3% cap means the highest rate you will ever have to pay on that loan is 15%. The cap also means the lowest interest rate you'll pay is 9%, the original 12% rate minus 3%, even if the prime goes below 7%. Some loans apply the cap to the maximum that can be charged but not to the minimum, a decided advantage for you if prevailing interest rates decline steadily or steeply.

Calculating Interest

Banks charge interest on the declining balance of the principal of your loan. At the start, the interest is assessed against the entire amount of the loan. A chunk of what you pay goes to interest, with only what's left over applied to reducing the principal. On your second payment, the interest is assessed on the entire amount of the original loan less that part of the first payment that was applied to lower the principal. Each time you make a payment, you reduce the principal more and thus also reduce the amount used to pay the interest. This is called *amortization*.

Say you take out a fixed loan of $13,000 for 9% interest payable over five years. Your first payment is $269.86. Banks divide each payment you make between principal and the interest. In this example, $172.36 of your first payment goes to pay off the principal and $97.50 ($13,000 times .09 annual interest divided by 12 months) goes to the interest (see box). At your second payment, the interest is based on the remaining principal ($12,827.64), applying $173.65 to the principal and $96.21 as interest. After five years, you'll have paid $3,191.60 in interest for borrowing $13,000. The example that follows covers only the first year of monthly payments on the $13,000 loan.

Amortization Table

Payment No.	Payment	Principal	Interest	Balance
1	269.86	172.36	97.50	12,827.64
2	269.86	173.65	96.21	12,653.99
3	269.86	174.96	94.91	12,479.00
4	269.86	176.27	93.59	12,302.77
5	269.86	177.59	92.27	12,125.18
6	269.86	178.92	90.94	11,946.26
7	269.86	180.26	89.60	11,765.99
8	269.86	181.62	88.25	11,584.38
9	269.86	182.98	86.88	11,401.40
10	269.86	184.35	85.51	11,217.05
11	269.86	185.73	84.13	11,031.32
12	269.86	187.13	82.74	10,844.19

The advantage of a fixed-rate loan is that regardless of how high other interest rates soar, your loan isn't affected. The disadvantage is that if other interest rates plummet during your repayment period, yours won't. Discuss your options with a number of lender banks.

Other Fees

Besides interest, you may also have to pay an application fee, a credit-check fee, and other miscellaneous fees for your loan. Ask about fees *before* applying for the loan. Some loans carry no fees. You could save a few hundred dollars by shopping around.

Collateral or Security

Few loans are made on the mere promise by the borrower that the money will be repaid with interest. Most loans are *secured,* which means you give the bank an ownership right in your property should you fail to make the loan payments *(default).* This is called your *collateral.*

Most borrowers put up collateral that is related to the loan. Sometimes that is the only way to get the loan or "financing." Thus, if you take out an auto loan, the car may be your collateral. If you fail to make the payments, the bank can repossess your car to sell it and repay the loan, the interest, and any fees you still owe. You may also use as collateral property you already own, such as a house, stocks, bonds, or your savings account.

If a bank makes you an *unsecured* loan, it can sue if you default. However, the bank must go through a legal process to get a court's judgment against you. It cannot simply "cash in" your collateral. Your chances of getting an unsecured loan are greater if:

* The loan principal is small

* The term of the loan is short

* You're willing to pay higher-than-average interest

* You are personally known to the bank officer

If you apply for an unsecured loan, you'll have to fill out a statement of financial worth. Also, the bank will not give you such a loan unless you are cleared by a national credit-reporting bureau, a company that keeps records of people's credit histories (see page 42).

To get other types of loans—for college tuition, home improvement, dental care, a vacation—many people use their home for collateral. When they make consumer loans, banks are reluctant to take anything but real property as collateral. In making commercial loans, however, they sometimes accept business assets as collateral.

Default

Your loan contract will have a default clause that explains rights or remedies if you miss payments or violate other provisions. Standard reasons banks resort to the default clause include:

- Lying on the loan application
- Declaring bankruptcy
- Failure to make a specified number of payments

Many default clauses include an *acceleration* provision that lets the bank sue you for the balance of the amount you owe if you are found in default. The logic is that you broke the agreement and, as a result, the bank wants out. It can ask a court to require you to pay in one lump sum all the money you owe. If you can't, the bank can sell the property you named as collateral and keep the money as repayment of the entire loan. When you negotiate a loan, therefore, it's important to understand how you can avoid default. If you ever find yourself in danger of defaulting, immediately inquire about your legal rights, including your right to a *grace period* in your contract and all the rights you have under the Fair Debt Collection Practices Act, discussed on page 41.

Prepayment

Some loan contracts include a prepayment penalty that allows the bank to charge you the full interest you would have owed for the entire life of the loan even if you pay it off early. If your contract includes such a prepayment penalty, you won't save interest and finance charges by prepaying the loan. It is to your advantage *not to* have this penalty clause.

Cosigning a Loan

Cosigners guarantee that they will pay off a loan if the principal borrower fails to pay. Cosigners are legally responsible for the full value of the loan, plus all late fees and penalties. In many states, lenders can even collect from cosigners whether or not they've tried to collect from the principal borrowers.

WARNING: Consider your full liability before you cosign any loan. The Federal Trade Commission found in 1986 that in three out of every four cosigned loans that defaulted, cosigners were asked to repay them. If you're considering cosigning a loan for someone else, have as much of the following language incorporated into your loan agreement as you can:

- Ask the lender to notify you if a payment is missed by the principal borrower.

- Get copies of all important documents, including the truth-in-lending disclosure statement (see page 39), the contract, and all attachments.

- Ask that your responsibility for the loan be limited to the principal only, thereby avoiding having to pay late charges, interest, and penalties.

Shopping for a Loan

When you shop for a loan, talk with loan officers at several banks. Be sure to tell them how much you need and your ideal repayment schedule so they can fashion the loan to meet your needs as closely as possible. For instance, one person may want low payments and a loan that is stretched out over 10 years. Someone else may want to pay off the loan in as few years as possible. Be specific about your needs.

The bank officer will estimate the terms of the loan and call you to complete the application. Only after you actually apply for the loan will the bank tell you the interest rate, how long you have to repay it, and the requirements for collateral. This is called *pricing* the loan.

Consumer Protections

Many consumer protection laws apply to loans. These include federal laws that prohibit discrimination and regulate debt collection practices, the Truth in Lending Act, and Federal Reserve Board regulations. States have enacted laws as well.

Truth in Lending

This law is contained within the *Consumer Credit Protection Act.* Under its provisions, whenever you apply for credit, whether it is a loan for home improvements, a mortgage, or a credit card, the lender is required to inform you in writing about certain terms and conditions *before you sign.* This allows you to evaluate different lenders' terms and assures that you know exactly how much you'll have to pay.

The law is extremely detailed. It specifies each term that must be disclosed and exactly how it must appear on the disclosure form. One of the two most important terms that must be disclosed to you under the law is the *finance charge,* the amount you pay to take out the loan. This includes the interest, service charges, and any appraisal charges (in the case of mortgages). The law also requires that this finance charge appear more conspicuously (in either boldfaced or larger type) than other items on the form.

The second important term is the *annual percentage rate* (APR). This translates the monthly interest you'll pay into the effective rate you'll be charged for an entire year. It, too, must be displayed more prominently than the other terms on the form.

For example: You borrow $1,000 for a year and pay a finance charge of $80. If you were to pay the whole loan off at once at the end of the year, your APR would be 8%, but loans rarely work this way. People usually pay loans back in equal monthly installments. In this case that would be $90 each month. This means you don't really get to "use" all of the $1,000 for the entire year but a declining amount of it each month, thereby in effect paying a higher interest rate—the APR. In this example, the APR would be 14.5%.

The Truth in Lending Act requires that consumers be given this information so they can more easily calculate and compare terms.

Another provision in the Consumer Credit Protection Act allows you to cancel your loan contract within three business days of signing it if you used your home as collateral. This "right of rescission," or "cooling-off" period, is to allow you to reconsider whether you want to risk your home as collateral. Any or no reason is enough for canceling the loan agreement. However, your cancellation has to be in writing. You may waive this right, but again, you must do so in writing.

Equal Credit Opportunity Act

Under this federal law, it is illegal to discriminate against loan applicants because of their sex, marital status, race, color, age, religion, national origin, or receipt of public assistance. For example, the law forbids loan officers to ask about a woman's childbearing intentions or to ignore alimony and child-support income in calculating her ability to repay a loan. The law also protects borrowers from retaliation when they exercise their rights under federal credit laws.

Under the Act, lenders *can* ask questions about your ability to repay, such as your wages, place of employment, occupation, how long you have been employed, your monthly expenses, your credit history, outstanding debts, and whether you pay your bills on time. They can also ask for a list of your assets. A lender who goes beyond this violates the law and can be taken to court by the state attorney general; or you can sue that lender for damages, a penalty, and your lawyer's fees.

Fair Debt Collection Practices Act

The law spells out the limits on what a "debt collector" can do in pressuring you to pay a debt. Prohibited tactics include threats of violence, repeated use of the telephone to harass you, publication of a debt, making false statements about your credit history, and discussing your debt with your neighbors or coworkers. Lawyers who engage in debt collection were exempt from this law until it was amended in 1986. Now, they, too, are covered. Violations should be reported to the Federal Trade Commission (Appendix III).

Credit Practices Rule

This rule applies to finance companies, department stores, car dealers, and others. It does not specifically apply to banks. Similar rules created by the Federal Reserve Board do, however, cover some banks. Administered by the Federal Trade Commission, they forbid lenders from adding certain anticonsumer provisions to credit agreements. For example, you cannot be asked to sign away your right to be notified of a court hearing in the event your creditor sues you for nonpayment (called a confession-of-judgment clause). Nor can you waive your right to keep personal belongings exempt from creditors under the bankruptcy laws. The law also identifies information that must be disclosed to cosigners of a loan and limits on the late fees that can be charged.

Fair Credit Reporting Act

If you have ever applied for credit, you have been protected by this law. Under its provisions, all institutions to which you apply for credit—banks, loan companies, department stores—prepare a "credit history" and send it to "credit bureaus." Credit bureaus keep computer files of these credit histories. Under this law, you have a right to a free copy of any credit report that has been used by any creditor as the basis for denying you credit. The law also requires that, with certain exceptions, unfavorable information must be eliminated from your record after seven years. You also have the right to correct any mistakes in the bureau's credit history of you. If the bureau still insists you have a credit "blemish," you can include in your file a letter of explanation that must be sent along with future credit inquiries to lenders.

Home Lawyer Tip

Home Lawyer will draft a Request for Credit Report. This letter is for requesting a credit report (also called a credit record or profile) from a local credit bureau. To draft a Request for Credit Report, select Credit and Collections from the Document submenu, then select Request for Credit Report. Point to "New," and then answer the questions that Home Lawyer asks.

If you find errors in your credit report, you have a right to have them corrected. Home Lawyer will draft a Request for Credit Report Correction. This letter is for requesting a local credit bureau to correct your credit report. To draft a Request for Credit Report Correction, select Credit and Collections from the Document submenu, then select Request for Credit Report Correction. Point to "New," and then answer the questions that Home Lawyer asks.

State Protections

Each state has its own official who regulates banks, typically called the Commissioner or Superintendent of Banking and Financial Institutions. State laws overlap federal laws, but if a conflict arises, usually federal law prevails.

State laws sometimes give more protection to borrowers than their federal counterparts. For example, some states' banking laws require lenders to exhaust all avenues of collection from the principal borrower before trying to collect from a cosigner. In some states, you cannot waive your right to exempt from collection certain pieces of property, such as your home and car. And in all states, you cannot waive your right to be notified of a court hearing if you're sued for nonpayment. Whenever state law gives you protections *in addition to* the federal laws, those protections will be upheld as well.

State banking authorities regulate interest rates and charges and penalties such as late fees. State Consumer Protection Agencies and attorneys general monitor discrimination in credit and often investigate illegal credit practices by finance and credit card companies and, occasionally, banks. They sue offenders as necessary.

These authorities and agencies can be helpful, especially with the laws unique to your state (see Appendix III). In particular, some state agencies offer pamphlets in several languages on banking laws. In California, for example, the superintendent of banks provides pamphlets in English, Chinese, and Spanish. Other states provide pamphlets in languages common in their areas.

CHAPTER
6

SOLVING PROBLEMS

Although many state and federal laws govern lending and credit, there are few places that will help in resolving a lending dispute. This section explains where you can go and discusses the two major federal agencies that investigate banks. Although these agencies do not handle individual complaints, they do investigate and penalize banks that break the law.

Common Problems

People have three common legal problems with lenders: being turned down for a loan for an illegal reason, finding out they owe much more than they anticipated because of inadequate loan disclosures, and illegal collection techniques.

Loan Rejection

If you have been turned down for a loan, ask your loan officer why. A responsible loan officer will show you the financial criteria used

to make the decision and even discuss with you the loan committee's denial. If the decision was based on incorrect information
about your credit record, ask to have the loan reconsidered. Submit
a letter explaining the error. Also, be sure to correct the information
if a credit bureau was involved.

If you suspect that the bank turned down the loan for an illegal
reason, such as your race or sex, talk to the loan officer's supervisor.
Any questions or discussion about your ethnic origin, marital status,
religion, or the like should be reported to the supervisor. If your
application is still denied, file a claim of discrimination with the
local, state, or federal agency that handles discrimination in credit.
You should also notify the bank's regulatory authority.

If you've been turned down for a loan, the Equal Credit Opportunity Act requires the lender to give you the name of the regulatory
agency that you can complain to.

Every state, many counties, and most major cities have an office
that handles individuals' credit-discrimination complaints. Each
one operates under a different law, and the laws overlap, but usually
state and local laws forbid more "bases" of discrimination. For
example, while a state or local law may prohibit discrimination
based on political affiliation, federal law does not, so if you've been
turned down because of your political-party registration, check with
local or state authorities; federal law won't help you.

Also, each agency has a different deadline by which you must file
a complaint after being turned down. Call your local Office of
Consumer Affairs to find out about deadlines, where to file your
complaint, and the rules and procedures that apply. If you're unsure
where to file, contact the Consumer Affairs Office of the Federal
Reserve Bank nearest you and ask for a referral (see Appendix III).

Agencies that investigate claims of discrimination will negotiate
with the bank and may hold a conference to determine if you have
been rejected illegally. Both you and the bank officials will have to
attend this conference, and although most people do not hire a
lawyer to represent them, if lots of money is at stake, you might
want to consider that course. If you win, depending on your state,
you can collect damages plus a penalty and your attorney's fees.

The law also requires you to exhaust your administrative remedies before litigating. That means you must take your claim to one of these agencies before you can sue in court.

Women and Credit Problems

Women have been frequent victims of credit discrimination. Lenders have refused to loan money to single women, women of childbearing age, and women who received alimony or child-support income. The Equal Credit Opportunity Act forbids such activities. If you find yourself the victim of discrimination because of your sex, follow the suggestions above and contact a local or national women's organization to ask where you can go for help locally.

Inadequate Disclosures

If the bank failed to give you the disclosures required by the federal Truth in Lending Act, you have two recourses: Get the bank to agree to the terms as you understood them or get out of the loan. Your local Consumer Affairs Office or the Consumer Affairs Division of your State Attorney General's Office may investigate such claims. If so, either one may have authority to negotiate an agreement with the bank on your behalf. If not, or if negotiation doesn't resolve the problem, your only recourse is to sue.

If the paperwork is in order, these cases are fairly simple. But, as in all court cases, they take time and can be expensive. If you win, you'll be able to collect damages plus a penalty.

Collection Problems

If your bank is using illegal collection methods, such as trying to accelerate the loan after only one missed payment, and it is unwilling to listen to reason, again you should complain to your local Consumer Affairs Office or the State Attorney General's Office. They will both be familiar with collection laws. Most such agencies also handle individual collection complaints. Again, if this doesn't solve the problem, you'll have to go to court.

Regulatory Agencies

Several federal and state agencies regulate banking and credit. Most of them can give you information about the law, some will refer you to agencies where you can file a formal complaint, and all of them keep records on violations of the banking and lending laws they enforce. If a bank shows a pattern of violating the law, these agencies can bring suit to stop the illegal behavior, impose fines, and, if the bank's illegal behavior persists, close it down.

If you complain to one of these agencies, it will contact the bank about the practice. This may be enough to get your complaint resolved informally.

The two major federal agencies that regulate lending and credit are the Federal Reserve Board and the Federal Trade Commission. If these don't handle your problem, they will refer you to the federal or state agency that does.

The Federal Reserve Board oversees its member banks' compliance with federal laws like Truth in Lending and the Credit Practices Rule. Most banks are members of the Federal Reserve System. If you complain to "the Fed" and learn that your bank is not a member, your complaint will be referred to the appropriate agency within 15 days. The Federal Reserve has free information on the laws that govern lending and credit (see Appendix III for regional offices).

The Federal Trade Commission (FTC) monitors compliance with federal laws by nonbank lenders, like credit unions and retail store credit departments. The FTC also has free literature about your rights under credit protection laws.

Finally, every bank is responsible to a federal government agency that monitors its activity. Although none of these agencies can resolve individual disputes, all of them can and will apply pressure when appropriate. A little pressure from one of them can make all the difference in the world. If you were turned down for a loan, you should have received one of these addresses from the lender. If you didn't, the lender is violating the Equal Credit Opportunity Act; ask your local Office of Consumer Protection or the Federal Reserve

Bank regional office nearest you what agency you should complain to. These include:

Comptroller of the Currency
Consumer Affairs Division
490 L'Enfant Plaza, E SW
Washington, DC 20219
(202) 447-1810
(For national banks)

Federal Deposit Insurance
  Corporation (FDIC)
Consumer Affairs Division
550 17th St. NW
Washington, DC 20429
(800) 424-5488
(For non–Federal Reserve state banks)

Office of Thrift Supervision (OTS)
Consumer Affairs Division
1700 G St. NW
Washington, DC 20552
(202) 906-6237
(For federally insured savings and
  loans)

National Credit Union
  Administration
Consumer Affairs Division
1776 G St NW, Suite 800
Washington, DC 20006
(202) 682-1900
(For Federal credit unions)

Resources

Many of these materials are offered free, some for a nominal fee. For best service, call or write for an order form and mail it in with your request.

From the Federal Trade Commission

Bureau of Consumer Protection, Washington, DC 20580. (202) 326-3650.

Buying and Borrowing: Cash in on the Facts

Credit Billing Errors? Use FCBA (Fair Credit Billing Act)

Credit Practices Rule, Facts for Consumers

Equal Credit Opportunity, Facts for Consumers

Fair Debt Collection, Facts for Consumers

Fair Credit Billing

Fair Credit Reporting

Fix Your Own Credit Problems and Save Money

Solving Credit Problems

From the Federal Reserve Board

Board of Governors, Federal Reserve, 20th and Constitution Ave. NW, Washington, DC 20551. (202) 452-3000.

A Guide to Federal Reserve Regulations

Consumer Credit Terminology Handbook

Consumer Handbook to Credit Protection Laws

Federal Reserve Glossary

The Story of Banks and Thrifts

Truth in Lending Simplified

What Truth in Lending Means to You

Other Materials

Tips on Saving and Investing, Tips on Consumer Credit. Council of Better Business Bureaus, Inc., Consumer Information Services, 1515 Wilson Blvd., Arlington, VA 22209. (703) 276-0100.

The Bank Book. Naphtali Hoffman and Stephen Brobeck. Consumer Federation of America, Harcourt Brace Jovanovich, 757 Third Ave., New York, NY 10017. (212) 614-3000. 1986. 222 pages.

CHAPTER

7

CONTRACT LANGUAGE

The contract explained in this chapter is for a standard, multipurpose loan from a bank. Other kinds of loans, such as those from finance companies that work through car dealers, large-appliance distributors, and mortgage companies, will have similar if not identical terms.

You cannot write your own loan contract with banks because, unfortunately, they will not accept it. You'll probably be stuck with a standard, single-page form that comes with five or six different-colored carbon copies. It will have a great deal of fine print, all of which is explained in this chapter. When presented with such a standard form, the best you will probably be able to negotiate is elimination of some provisions.

Because most loan forms are multipurpose, when complete, your form probably will have some blank spaces, where portions don't apply to your loan. Be sure to mark them clearly: "N/A," for "not applicable."

The "Magic Box"

The front of the loan form lists the financial terms of the contract: the costs of the loan, including principal, interest, fees, insurance costs, interest rate, late charges, prepayment options or penalties, security interest, and space for the signatures. These terms are usually contained in what is called the "Magic Box," set off from the rest of the contract. The Magic Box is intended to make sure these terms are "clear and conspicuous" and separated from the other items on the form, as required by the Truth in Lending Act.

This example includes only those items required by the law. Some lenders choose to add other information as well. The following list describes all of the items you are likely to find in the "Magic Box" on the loan contract you are offered—both those required and those not required.

Borrower(s)—This is you, your spouse, and anyone else who is a borrower, and your address.

Lender—The law requires that the lender's name be disclosed on the form. Most lenders also include their address. Under the law, lenders are permitted to call themselves either "creditor" or "lender."

Annual Percentage Rate
The cost of my credit as a yearly rate.
_____ %

Annual Percentage Rate (APR)—Your contract will include the words "Annual Percentage Rate." Required by law, this is the interest rate for the declining balance for each year of the loan. Remember, if you have a fluctuating interest rate, the APR will not remain the same throughout the life of the loan. In that case, the contract will state that the rate is "fluctuating." If it's a fixed rate, the percentage will be fixed for the period stated in the contract, typically one, two, or three years.

When calculating the APR of a fixed-rate loan, it's important to note that it is an *annual* interest rate, not a lifetime rate. This means

Annual Percentage Rate	Finance Charge	Amount Financed	Total of Payments
The cost of my credit as a yearly rate. ___ %	The dollar amount the credit will cost me. $	The amount of credit provided to me or on my behalf. $	The amount I will have paid after I have made all the payments as scheduled. $

My payment schedule will be:

Number of Payments	Amount of Payments	When Payments Are Due
	$	Monthly beginning ___
	$	

Security: (Applicable box(es) checked)

☐ I am giving you a security interest in my real estate located at:

Street _____ City _____ State _____ Zip _____

☐ I am giving you a security interest in my motor vehicle identified as follows:

Year ____ Make ____ Model ____ Body Type ____ Serial No. ____

Demand: If this box is checked ☐ , this obligation is payable on demand.

I acknowledge that the bank has a right of setoff against my accounts, except IRAs and Keogh accounts.

Filing Fees: $ _____ **Late Charge:** If a payment is more than fifteen (15) days late, I will be responsible for a late charge of 5% of the payment.

Prepayment: If I pay off early, I will not have to pay a penalty, and if I have already paid any prepaid finance charge, I will not be entitled to receive a refund of any or all of the prepaid finance charge.

I will purchase: ☐ Credit Life Insurance ☐ Credit Disability Insurance

I can see the contract documents for additional information about nonpayment, default, any required payment before the scheduled date, and prepayment refunds and penalties.

A Typical "Magic Box"

that if the loan is taken out at 10%, one twelfth of 10% interest of the unpaid principal is charged *each month,* turning your effective annual rate into considerably more than 10%.

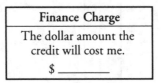

Finance Charge
The dollar amount the credit will cost me.
$ _____

Finance Charge—This section must show in dollars and cents the amount you will pay for the loan, including any costs, such as insurance "hidden" in your monthly payments. The law also requires a brief definition of terms. Most banks will use the phrase "The dollar amount the credit will cost me." This must be more conspicuously displayed than the other information, and lenders must use the exact words "Finance Charge." They usually put them in bold face and inside a border.

Amount Financed
The amount of credit provided to me or on my behalf.
$ _____

Amount Financed—This term must be used to describe the total amount of the loan and any other money the bank is lending you to pay for costs.

Total of Payments
The amount I will have paid after I have made all the payments as scheduled.
$ _____

Total of Payments—This is the total amount of money you will have paid after the loan is paid off. It includes finance charges, the principal, insurance, and all other costs. For a three-year, 10% interest loan of $12,000, the total of all payments is $13,939.56.

Number of Payments

Amount of Payments
$
$

When Payments Are Due
Monthly beginning

Payment Schedule—Here you will find: the total number of payments, the amount of those payments, and when they are due. Most banks do not list each payment separately unless the payment amounts vary.

Security: (*Applicable box(es) checked*)

I am giving you a security interest in my real estate located at:

Street:_____

City:_____ County:_____

State:_____ Zip:_____

   I am giving you a security interest in my motor vehicle identified as follows:

Year:_____ Make:_____

Model:_____ Body Type:_____

Serial Number:_____

   Other (describe)_____

_____

Security—The typical Magic Box also identifies any security or collateral you are putting up. If the loan is a secured loan, the property that is to serve as the collateral must be disclosed. If the loan is secured by the item being financed, the collateral will be described as "the property purchased in this transaction." If it is other property, it must be described in specific detail. Many creditors will be precise here to protect themselves. If a loan is unsecured, put "N/A" in these blanks.

> This obligation is payable on DEMAND ☐

Demand Feature—Check your agreement to see if it says your loan will be "payable on demand." If it does, the bank can legally require you to pay the full amount of the principal and interest you owe *any time it chooses.* If that's the case, the law requires the bank to inform you on the front of the loan. A bank officer usually checks a box for this purpose. If your loan is not payable on demand, be sure to write "N/A" in that box.

Most consumer loans are installment loans that do not include "payment on demand." However, a demand clause on the back of the agreement often gives the lender the right to "call in" the loan if you default on one or more payments. This is different from the payment-on-demand feature in the Magic Box, which must be disclosed.

> I acknowledge that the bank has a right of setoff against
> my accounts, except IRAs and Keogh accounts.

This sentence applies when the bank has a security interest that gives it the right to collect from accounts you have at the bank. Federal law forbids collecting from Individual Retirement Accounts (IRAs) and Keogh accounts (self-employment retirement accounts). These terms are spelled out in more detail on the back of the loan agreement.

> Filing Fees: ___*(amount of fee)*___

Filing Fees—Loan application fees and other such charges are listed here. Most other costs, such as interest, are already factored into the "Amount Financed" and are not included here. Frequently, application fees are nominal.

> Late Charge: If a payment is more than fifteen (15) days
> late, I will be responsible for a late charge of 5% of the
> payment.

Late Charge—Late fees must be explained here. Many states'
banking laws prescribe the maximum late charges that can be collected, usually a percentage ceiling, such as 5%. Grace periods are
common and almost all forms list them here, but the law doesn't
require it.

> Prepayment: If I pay off early, I will not have to pay a
> penalty, and if I have already paid any prepaid finance
> charge, I will not be entitled to receive a refund of any
> or all of the prepaid finance charge.

Prepayment—If a fee is charged when you make loan payments
early, it must be stated here. If no penalty is charged, that, too, must
be stated. Most consumer loans allow prepayment, but none of
them will refund that part of the finance charge that you've already
paid. Thus, if you pay off your loan early, you'll end up paying a
somewhat higher interest rate even if you aren't charged a penalty,
because your early payments included interest on the full term of the
loan.

> I will purchase: ☐ Credit Life Insurance
>   ☐ Credit Disability Insurance

Insurance—You may want, or be required by the lender, to buy
insurance that will pay off the balance of your loan if you die or
become disabled. Insurance isn't required by law, but your lender
may require it, especially from borrowers who make small down
payments on home mortgages. If you are buying insurance as a
hedge against default, either because the bank requires it or because
you want it, the law does require that it and its cost be listed on the
loan form.

If it isn't required by the lender, the decision of whether or not
to buy insurance should be based on your assessment of the risk. If

yours is a two-income household and either of you earns enough to pay all monthly bills including the loan, you probably don't need insurance. If the death or disability of one spouse would spell financial ruin, however, you may want to consider it.

> I can see the contract documents for additional information about nonpayment, default, any required payment before the scheduled date, and prepayment refunds and penalties.

This is called the contract reference section. The lender must cite the other documents or other parts of the contract wherever relevant. For instance, if you are giving collateral, the security agreement must be mentioned next to the identification of the collateral on the loan form.

Itemization of Amount Financed—Lenders are required by law to give notice on the loan form that borrowers can request a written

ITEMIZED LIST

Itemization of Amount Financed:	
Amount paid directly to me	$ _____
Amount paid to others for me	_____
Credit life insurance	_____
Credit accident and health insurance	_____
Credit report fee	_____
Title examination fee	_____
Appraisal fee	_____
Title insurance	_____
Recording fees	_____
Notary fee	_____
Automobile license, title and registration	_____
Other	_____
Subtotal	$ _____
Less prepaid amounts (paid by me— application fee, finance charge)	$ _____
TOTAL	$ _____

itemization of payments. Most lenders, however, go beyond this minimum disclosure requirement and print the itemization directly on the agreement. Many of the blanks on the itemization section are for specific kinds of loans, such as mortgages, car loans, or home-improvement loans. Make sure the appropriate blanks are completed on your form and the others marked "N/A."

Back of the Form

The back of your loan form is probably wall-to-wall "fine print." This is where the lender describes fully the specific terms of the loan. As noted earlier, many if not all of the terms on the front of the form are legally required. Few federal and state laws apply to the loan terms on the back, however. As you read them, notice that now, many lenders at least try to use plain language, compared to what was true only a few years ago.

> Definitions or Meanings of Words—The words "I," "me," "we," and "my" mean all borrowers to this agreement and all guarantors. "You" and "your" mean the bank and its successors and assigns.

All contracts have a definitions section. The term *borrower* is used to mean all signers except the witnesses and the bank. When a loan is guaranteed by someone other than the borrower, that *guarantor* is considered to be your legal backer. If you don't pay, your guarantor owes the money.

Real estate mortgages are often *sold.* When a bank sells your loan, the new owner (called the *successor* or *assign*) steps into the shoes of the original lender and takes on the same rights and obligations as that original lender.

> Applicable Law—This note shall be governed by the laws of the state in which it is signed. Terms which do not comply with the laws of that state shall not be effective. If a term shall be deemed invalid, it shall not affect the validity of the remainder of this agreement.

This adds nothing to the contract. It merely tells you that the contract must obey state laws. It notifies you that if the bank has agreed to a term that's illegal in your state, that term is void, but not the rest of the contract.

> Payments—I agree to pay all the principal and interest of this loan as set forth in the payment schedule. I agree that each scheduled payment I make shall be applied against the unpaid balance as described in the amortization schedule provided. In addition, I agree that payments made by me shall be applied first to late payments or penalties, if any, then to interest and then to principal.

This obligates you to make payments according to the payment schedule in the loan. Most loans include a payment schedule in the agreement. This language also tells you how much of each scheduled payment is applied to the interest. For large loans, early payments are applied almost entirely to paying off the interest, with only a small portion to the principal.

The bank will probably supply you a schedule of payments. If it doesn't, ask for one. This itemizes the interest and principal you will pay at each step along the way. It can be especially useful in calculating income-tax deductions for the mortgage interest you pay.

> Default—I will be in default if: (1) I fail to make any payment when it is due under this agreement, (2) any representation or statement made by me under this agreement is false, (3) I file for bankruptcy or insolvency, or receivership proceedings are begun against me or any other collection attempts are made against any of my property, whether through legal process or not, (4) I die or am declared incompetent, (5) I violate any security agreement by selling or transferring any of the property of which you have been given a security interest without your permission, (6) I fail to keep any other promise in the agreement, (7) a judgment of any kind is obtained against me.

This is standard default language, and all of the listed reasons for default are typical. They define when the bank can find that you have broken the loan agreement and what the bank can do about it. Most banks will not negotiate any changes in this section.

Be sure you know exactly what you are agreeing to. Pay particular attention to how default is defined and what the bank may do if you are found in default. However, the bank has the option of triggering the default clause; whether it does so or not is up to the bank.

Typically, failing to make one payment is not enough to cause a bank to find you in default. More likely, you'll be charged a late fee. Most banks prefer that you pay back the loan as agreed, so they will wait through the grace period, or even longer, before moving for default. However, if you lie or omit to tell part of the truth on your loan application, especially about your credit history, the bank may well start default proceedings if you miss one or more payments. If you file for bankruptcy or are successfully sued by another creditor for default, this, too, will cause a bank to consider your loan in default.

In this agreement, as is standard, you are in default if you die. All payments become the property of your estate and beneficiaries, and your heirs may want to negotiate with the bank to continue to pay in installments. Some loans are forgiven or canceled at death, but most are not, unless you purchased life insurance that pays off your loan in full.

This section also allows default if a court declares you mentally incompetent, but you should be aware that this has been successfully challenged in some states, based on laws that prohibit discrimination against the mentally disabled.

If you sign a security agreement, it's standard for the bank to require that you agree not to sell or give away whatever property you've put up as collateral for the loan. If you do sell or give it away, the bank has the right to move for default.

Most banks also include a catchall statement that you can be found in default if you don't live up to the terms of the loan contract.

Finally, if a judgment is entered against you—that is, if another creditor to whom you owe money sues you and wins—the bank will be able to have you declared in default.

In the event of my default, you may do any of the following:

Acceleration—You may accelerate the loan, declaring all unpaid sums under the loan immediately due,

Collection—You may take any legal action to collect the loan and charge me for all court costs and reasonable attorneys' fees,

Set-off—You may offset any amounts that I owe against any account that I maintain with you, with the exception of tax-deferred retirement accounts. In addition, you shall not be liable for dishonor of a check for insufficient funds in the event you exercise this right, or

Exercise any other rights you have under the law.

If you are in default of the loan, the bank can use the *acceleration clause* to make the entire loan due immediately. However, if you make one or two late payments, that's usually not enough to cause the bank to accelerate your loan. If it tries, contact the loan officer to correct the mistake.

If the lender sues you to collect the loan, this language requires that, if you lose, you'll have to pay the lender's attorneys' fees. That's standard, but if you can get a loan without this language, do so; you will save yourself money even if you default.

If the lender wins a court judgment finding you in default, it can sell any of your secured property, seize any bank accounts you have in its banks (except tax-sheltered retirement accounts), garnish and attach your wages, even try to seize other property of yours to pay off the debt. If the bank seizes money in your account, you are responsible for any costs that result, such as bounced-check charges. But banks can't pressure you to deposit your savings in their banks simply so they can exercise this right. If one does pressure you, report it to a Consumer Affairs Office.

Prepayment—I may prepay all or part of this loan at any time. Prepayment will not change any of the dates due or amount of payments. There will be no prepayment penalty and no refund of prepaid finance charges.

This prepayment language is standard. If you pay double on one monthly payment, you still must make the full payment next month, but you'll be lowering the total interest you'll eventually pay.

As noted earlier, prepayment clauses define your responsibility if you wish to pay off the loan early. In this contract, you aren't required to pay additional interest or other charges if you prepay. Many loans, like this one, do allow you to prepay with no penalties, but even so you won't get any refund of any charges already paid (excepting payment for insurance, as noted below). Also, your effective annual interest will be higher because your early payments were for interest across the entire life of the loan.

> Late Payments—I agree to pay a late charge of 5% if any payment is received by you more than fifteen (15) days after the payment due date.

This gives you a 15-day "grace" period for late payments, with no late fee. State law commonly requires such a penalty-free period. Be sure your loan includes such a grace period and let the bank officer know what time of the month is most convenient for you to make your payments.

> Insurance—I agree to purchase credit life insurance, if required by you for this loan as described in the itemization of the amount financed. This purchase shall be made through a company licensed to do business in this state and approved by you. Such insurance will cover only those person(s) signing this note. Insurance coverage shall begin when this note is signed and shall expire on the original maturity date of this note, unless there is a prepayment. In the event of prepayment, I shall be entitled to a refund of a portion of the insurance premium.

Some lenders require you to take out "credit life insurance" that pays off the loan if you die or, in some cases, are severely disabled. Some loans, like student loans, are canceled if the borrower dies. Most, however, become the debt of the person's heirs unless paid off by insurance. If you're required to get insurance, expect to be urged to buy it from a company of the lender's choosing, but you are free to buy it from any licensed insurer or agent. In fact, you probably can save a little money by shopping around. Insurance can add anywhere from $5 to $50 a month to your payments, depending on the size of the loan insured.

Credit life-insurance premiums are computed as part of the loan repayment. Federal law requires that the Magic Box on the front of the loan form include a disclosure of the cost of the insurance.

Lenders usually require insurance for an unsecured loan and for mortgage loans when the down payment is small.

You may be able to convince your lender not to require credit life insurance. Ask your loan officer what criteria are used to determine who must buy it. Remember: It is illegal to make this decision based on your race, age, sex, national origin, marital status, or source of income. It is legal, however, to make it based on your credit record, your income, or other objective evidence of your ability to pay. If you feel you are being discriminated against, talk to a state or local Office of Consumer Affairs or Human Rights.

> Borrowers' Waivers—I waive presentment, demand, notice of dishonor, and protest except where prohibited by applicable law.

Every loan contains this condition. Waiving "presentment and demand" means relinquishing your right to be billed separately for each payment. Instead, lenders often provide a coupon book with tear-out coupons for each payment. When your loan is due at the bank's discretion (*demand* loans), this clause isn't included.

Waiving notice of "dishonor and protest" means giving up your right to be notified that you are late with your payments or have otherwise violated the agreement and that the lender intends to collect the full balance due.

> My signature on the reverse side of this note acknowledges that I have read this note and all the disclosures required by law and that I agree to all its conditions.

This is a statement by you that you have read and agree to all the terms of the loan. If you have signed the loan agreement, or *note*, there is a legal presumption that you know and understand all its terms. This language is simply the bank's way of reinforcing this presumption and putting you on notice of its effect.

> Confession of Judgment—I authorize an attorney that you designate to appear on behalf of me in court in the event I default, and obtain a judgment for the unpaid balance of this loan. I waive any right I may have

to notice and authorize you, upon obtaining such judgment, to immediately execute such judgment.

This statement is *illegal* under the federal Credit Practices Rule for consumer loans. If it appears in your agreement, it is void. Once popular with lenders, such a provision waives your right to defend against a lawsuit if you violate the default clause. It allows the lender to have any attorney it chooses go to court in your place and accept a judgment against you. This in turn allows the lender to take your property without even informing you that you're being sued. *Any lender who needs to be reminded that this provision is illegal should be avoided at all costs.*

Security Agreement

I grant you a security interest in the collateral described on the front of this agreement to secure the loan obligation arising from the loan.

This explains that if you fail to pay or otherwise violate the agreement, you are allowing the bank to sell the property you've put up as collateral and listed as such in this agreement.

Protection of the Property/Purpose—I agree to keep the collateral in good order and repair and will not use it in violation of the law. I shall not permit others to use the collateral in violation of the law or this agreement. I understand that the collateral is to be used for consumer purposes only and any other use shall be a violation of this agreement.

This protects the bank's interest in your collateral. It requires that you keep the collateral—be it a home or a car or a pleasure boat—in good repair and not use it for business purposes, unless, of course, that use is permitted in the contract. Obviously, the collateral will be no good to the bank if it is damaged or lost.

Use and Maintenance—I will not sell, lease or otherwise dispose of the collateral without your written prior approval. I agree to keep the property in the jurisdiction where I reside, except if the collateral is an automobile, I may use it outside the jurisdiction for temporary periods of normal usage.

I agree that I shall abide by the terms of any insurance to which the collateral is subject.

This is more typical language to protect the bank's interest in the collateral. It requires you to get the bank's written approval before you do anything that changes your control over the collateral, by selling it, for example. This doesn't mean you can never sell or lease your collateral. You can, as long as the bank agrees or you pay off the loan immediately and thus settle your debt. Any substitution of collateral will have to be approved by the lender in writing and in advance.

This also obliges you to keep the collateral in the state where you live, except in the case of automobiles, which are allowed to be used outside the state for normal purposes.

Payment of Taxes and Fees—I agree to pay all taxes, fees or other charges which come due on the property. If I fail to pay taxes and fees due on the collateral, you have the right under this agreement to make these payments for me and I will become immediately obligated to reimburse you for these costs. These amounts shall become an additional debt secured by the collateral and as such will immediately begin to accrue interest.

This allows the bank to protect its interest in the collateral by paying any fees or taxes that are due on it and to bill you, with interest, for reimbursement. If you are using your car as collateral, the bank may pay your insurance or registration fees. If your collateral is a condominium unit, the bank may step in and pay any fees that, if they weren't paid, could cause the loss of the unit or cause a lien to be placed against it. Don't confuse the "fees" referred to here with those, like application fees, due on the loan itself.

The bank will add to your loan payments any fees it pays and charge you interest on this additional "loan." Make sure that if you are refusing to pay a bill intentionally, the lender is told in writing and doesn't pay it against your wishes. For example, if the government is overcharging you because of a mixup in your property taxes, notify your lender in writing that you are withholding your payment and why.

Insurance—I agree to keep the collateral insured for the full value against damage or loss with an insurance company approved by you. I shall make a copy of this policy available to you. Such policy shall designate you as the loss payee. I shall pay all premiums when they are due. If I fail to purchase insurance or fail to make timely payments, you have the right to make them and add such costs to the loan secured by this agreement. These costs shall accrue interest from the first day.

If the collateral is damaged or lost, you may, at your option, use any insurance proceeds to repair or replace the collateral and I will be responsible to repay, if any, the remaining amount of the loan.

Yet more standard language to protect the lender's interest in your collateral property: It requires you to insure the collateral using a policy approved by the bank. The bank will usually suggest insurers it is used to dealing with, but remember that you are free to get your own. If the collateral is damaged or stolen, the bank can collect the insurance payment. Here, you are also agreeing that if you fail to pay the premiums, the bank can do so and add it to the cost of the loan.

The insurance payment replaces the damaged or stolen collateral, which may turn out to be less than the amount of the loan. If the insurance payment is not enough to reimburse the bank completely, you'll have to make up the difference.

Inspection—I agree to permit you to inspect the collateral at any reasonable time.

Banks rarely inspect collateral. However, if the bank has reason to believe the property is lost or damaged, it may do so under this provision, as long as it is during normal business hours and you are given advance notice. If you feel you are being subjected to an unfair inspection, report it to the nearest Consumer Affairs Office and appropriate banking authority.

Remedies—If I default, you may, in addition to remedies listed above, take any of the following actions:

Repossess and repair the collateral without notice to me and without legal proceedings.

Require me to deliver the collateral to a place of your choosing.

Sell the collateral after providing me with 15 days' notice. Notice, for the purposes of this agreement, shall be considered given when it is put in the U.S. Mail, postage prepaid, addressed to anyone signing this agreement.

I shall be responsible for the costs of repossession and resale of the collateral and such costs shall be added to this obligation and interest shall accrue thereon. I shall also be responsible for any deficiency that results from a sale of the collateral.

This is also standard. It sets out the lender's rights to your collateral if you are found in default and allows the bank to sell the collateral without suing you or getting a court judgment. If you are in default, the lender may take the collateral from you, give you 15 days' notice, and sell it if you don't pay the balance of the loan within that 15 days.

Each state has a "repossession" law that sets out what procedures a lender can use to sell the collateral. In the District of Columbia, for example, you must be given 10 days' notice before your collateral can be taken, and another 15 days in which to bring your payments up to date before it can be sold. You must also be given the right to buy back the collateral any time before the actual sale.

Each state's law describes how lenders can seize the collateral (for example, they can't "disturb the peace") and how many days' notice they must give you before they can sell it (typically 15). Your local or state Consumer Affairs Office will be familiar with your state's "repo" law.

If you owe more than the lender can get from selling the repossessed collateral, you may be sued for the "deficiency." Many suits are for such repossession or deficiency judgments.

Notice of Your Right to Cancel

I am entering into a transaction that will result in a mortgage or security interest on my home. I have a legal right under federal law to cancel this transaction, without cost, within three business days from whichever of the following events occurs last:

(1) The date of the transaction, which is _____, or
(2) The date I received my disclosures under the Truth in Lending law,
(3) The date I received this notice of the right to cancel.

If I cancel this transaction, the mortgage or security interest is also cancelled. Within 20 calendar days after you receive notice, you must take the steps necessary to reflect the fact that the mortgage or security interest on my home has been cancelled, and you must return to me any money or property I have given to you or to anyone else in connection with this transaction.

If I decide to cancel this transaction, I may do so by notifying you in writing, at *(mailing address of lender)*.

I may use any written statement that is signed and dated by me and states my intention to cancel, or I may use this notice by dating and signing below.

If I cancel by mail or telegram, I must send the notice no later than midnight of *(date)*. If I send or deliver written notice to cancel some other way, it must be delivered to the above address no later than that time.

I Wish to Cancel

_____ *(Your Name)*   _____
Consumer's Signature   Date

The Borrower should keep one copy of this notice because it contains important information about the Borrower's rights.

If your loan is secured by your residence, the Truth in Lending Act requires that you be given a three-day "cooling-off" period after you sign a loan and be told about it by your lender. This gives you 72 hours to cancel it for any reason. Canceling means you also end any right the lender has to your home.

Because of this law, lenders prefer to wait three days before turning the money over to you and completing the paperwork. If you can't wait, you can waive the "cooling-off" period, but you must do so in writing.

Home Lawyer Tip

Home Lawyer will draft a Promissory Note. This document will obligate one party (the Maker) to pay money to another (the Payee). To draft a Promissory Note, select Credit and Collections from the Document submenu, then select Promissory Note. Point to "New," and then answer the questions that Home Lawyer asks.

PART III

IMPROVING YOUR HOME

Tom wants to replace his bathroom fixtures. He obtains four bids: two high, one low, and one in between.

Each morning at 6:00, Joan hears banging, sawing, and drilling from the house next door. She warns her neighbor to do something about the noise or she'll complain to the police.

Kate wants to install a swimming pool. A neighbor offers to do the work for half what a professional contractor would charge if Kate will buy the materials and get the building permit. Kate agrees and seals the deal with a handshake.

Undertaking major home improvements like these allows you to do something creative and personal with your environment, increases the value of your property, and can be less expensive than moving.

If you don't know what you're doing, however, or if you get stuck with an incompetent contractor, your home "improvement" can quickly turn into a home nightmare, spiraling you into debt, wreaking havoc in your life, and making you wish you'd spent the money on a trip to Bali instead. That's why it's important to make the effort to find a contractor who's well qualified, financially stable, and willing to sign a contract that spells out the specifics—what you want done, how much it's going to cost, and when it's going to be completed.

Americans spent more than $94 billion on home remodeling in 1987. Each job involved a legal contract, and many ended in problems: That year, according to the Better Business Bureau, 45,750 complaints were filed against home-improvement companies and contractors, making it the fourth-most-frequent kind of complaint lodged with the BBB. Most complaints were that the job wasn't finished on time or correctly. That's why it's so important that you have complete information about contractors and home-improvement agreements *before* starting a job.

A Case Study

Connie and David Wade, of Sacramento, California, never dreamed when they hired a general contractor to oversee construction of their new home that so many problems could be caused by one person.

After they fired him, they filed papers listing a new general contractor's name with their title company. Too late, they discovered the title company could not record the new papers because a *mechanic's lien* for $125,000 had been filed against their property by the first contractor. This lien froze their construction loan until they paid what the contractor demanded.

Desperate, the Wades tried to get insurance to cover the lien. That required coming up with one-and-a-half times the amount of the lien in cash. They turned to the state's licensing board for help but found it had a three-month backlog. To free up money so construction could proceed, the Wades were forced to pay the shoddy contractor $5,000 in cash to dismiss the lien.

If the Wades had had correct information, they could have prevented the nightmare in a number of ways. The contractor could have been prosecuted for breach of contract if the Wades had thought to include written deadlines in their contract. Or, they could have required the contractor to sign a *lien waiver* form before each payment.

Contractors

Don't let the Wades' example frighten you. Many contractors are hardworking, honest, and talented tradespeople interested in doing good work. Their biggest motivation (as in any business) is making money. That's an important incentive, so if you're trying to get a sun deck installed for the cost of the materials alone, don't be surprised if no one's interested in the job.

Several types of contractors do home improvement work: general contractors, independent contractors, and subcontractors. Both general and independent contractors offer building services, and both are responsible for overseeing and being legally responsible for the entire project. The independent is in business alone, whereas general contractors may employ other contractors as well as sell their own services. Subcontractors are specialists hired to do specific tasks, such as electrical or plumbing work.

Before deciding to act as your own general contractor, you should know that you'll be undertaking a multitude of responsibilities:

- Buying supplies
- Obtaining permits
- Making sure renovations meet code or apartment building requirements
- Hiring and paying subcontractors
- Supervising the work

If something goes wrong, you, the general contractor, will be the one responsible. Make sure the money you save by not hiring a general contractor outweighs the headaches of being responsible for the work and the outcome of the project.

When should you act as the general contractor? It depends on the size and complexity of the job and how much free time you have.

You can easily act as general contractor if the project is simple and won't take much time: installing a bay window, laying an oak floor, building a wall cabinet, or lowering a ceiling. If, however, you're authorizing a more complex home improvement—adding a room, for example—that requires hiring and working with a variety of people (carpenter, electrician, plasterer, and roofer), you'll need plenty of time and knowledge about how the improvement can best be done.

This chapter assumes you'll hire and work with an independent contractor.

Independents and "Subs"

Most people hire *independent contractors* to oversee the entire project, including drafting the work plans, hiring and paying subcontractors for specific tasks, arranging building permits and inspections, and providing workers' compensation and general liability insurance.

When you hire an independent, the contractor does not legally become your employee, and legal obligations normally imposed on employers do not apply. For example, you are not required to provide the contractor with workers' and unemployment compensation, tax withholding, or the like. Once given your instructions, the contractor has complete control to direct what, when, and how things are to be done. Your "control" is limited to approving the finished product.

You *are* legally responsible as an employer, however, if you hire someone from down the street to paint your house and that person doesn't maintain a separate business, relies on you for tools, works at your location, and is closely supervised by you. Such a worker is considered your employee under the law, so you would be legally responsible for insurance against job-related injuries.

A subcontractor, referred to in the trade as a *sub,* is a specialist hired by an independent contractor to do a specific job or jobs on your home improvement. Electricians, plumbers, plasterers, drywall contractors, and painters are examples.

Basic Concepts

Qualifications

The most important qualification to consider when shopping for a contractor is experience. If you're having a bathroom installed, try to find someone who has experience with the kinds of work involved—plumbing, tiling, and the like. Many people in this field are "jacks-of-all-trades" and can competently handle a variety of home improvements, but you'll probably get what you want done more quickly and with less trouble if you hire someone who has demonstrated an ability in the area you need.

The *legal* qualifications for being a contractor vary. The contractor you hire may be licensed, certified, registered, or none of these. It all depends on where you live. According to a 1988 study by the National Association of Home Builders (NAHB), 22 states have licensing requirements for home remodelers, and nearly all states license electricians and plumbers. Getting a license in most states requires a specific amount of work experience and passing an exam. The licensing requirements in California, Florida, and Maryland are among the nation's most stringent.

Seven states (Arkansas, Connecticut, Georgia, Kansas, Nebraska, New Jersey, and West Virginia) have *registration* requirements for home remodelers. To register, contractors simply file their name and address with the appropriate state agency before practicing their trade. They may also have to pay a registration fee, but nothing else is required.

A few states also have certification, in addition to licensing. The certification program is designed for those who want special recognition for their skill. It requires passing another exam and paying yet another fee.

If you're having extensive work done, using a licensed contractor can have three advantages. First, a licensed contractor typically is required to carry insurance. This protects you if your property is damaged or the people working on it are injured. Second, many licensed contractors belong to trade associations that can help you settle disputes or disagreements if they arise. Finally, a licensed contractor may be more willing than someone else to try to resolve problems, especially if the license is at stake.

For information on the licensing requirements in your state, contact your state's licensing agency, usually called the Contractors Licensing Board, or the State Licensing Board for General Contractors.

Bonds

Most states require licensed contractors to be bonded. A *bond* is insurance that compensates you, up to a certain amount, for shoddy work by a contractor. If contractors aren't required to be licensed or registered in your state, it's particularly important to make sure they're bonded. Ask to see their insurance papers. If the contractor you're hiring balks at that request, be wary. Good contractors can find insurance easily and quickly.

A *surety* or *performance bond* issued by an insurance company guarantees that if the contractor goes bankrupt or otherwise fails to live up to the contract, any money owed to you, subcontractors, or suppliers will be taken care of, up to a specified limit.

Find out what the bond covers and for how much before hiring a contractor. Some bonds protect you only against substandard work that doesn't comply with the building code. As a result, you may have to live with work that doesn't violate the code but is shoddy nonetheless.

Permits, Codes, and Inspections

A *building permit* is required when structural work is involved or a home's basic living area is to be changed. For example, if you're turning a garage into a family room or an attic into a bedroom, you need a building permit because you're changing the amount of "livable" space in your home. By getting a building permit, you notify the city or county of your project, allowing the building inspector to schedule *inspections* throughout the course of construction to make sure it meets code requirements. All contractors should know state and local requirements for *building permits, inspections,* and *codes.*

The contractor should obtain the necessary permit from your town or county Building Inspector's Office before beginning work. Whoever applies for the building permit is the one ultimately responsible if the work doesn't comply with building codes, so unless you've taken on the responsibility as general contractor, let the contractor apply for the permit. The contractor must display the permit in a public area. The cost of permits and inspections is usually included in the contractor's bid.

Obtaining a *building permit* is usually not difficult, unless your plans encroach on someone else's property or violate your local government's zoning regulations. It's the contractor's responsibility to notify the inspector when the job is at the half or three-quarter point, the stages when inspections are usually done.

Building codes set minimum safety standards. Remember that a contractor can meet these minimum safety requirements and still botch the appearance of the final job. You can get a copy of the code at your town hall.

Mechanic's Lien

If you don't pay contractors, subcontractors, or suppliers, state laws allow them to place a *mechanic's lien* on your property, giving them the right to sell it to pay the debt owed them.

Even if you've paid in full, the subcontractors and suppliers can file a mechanic's lien against your home if they haven't been paid by your general contractor. Unfair as it seems, this could force you to pay your bill twice. To protect yourself, ask the general contractor to provide proof that workers and suppliers are being paid with each installment and include a *release of lien* in your contract. This puts all workers and suppliers on notice that, before receiving payment, they will have to sign a lien *waiver* form. The waiver states that they cannot place a lien on your property if they've accepted payment. Ask your contractor for a waiver form.

To protect yourself further from liens by subcontractors and suppliers, make your payments jointly payable. Write a check to both the contractor and supplier, or to both the contractor and the sub. That way, all parties involved will have to endorse your check.

Late or Poor Work

Delays occur for many reasons: unavailable materials, weather problems, absent subs. Delays can also occur if your contractor doesn't take the job seriously or isn't told when certain stages of the construction are expected to be completed.

All home improvement contracts should state specific deadlines for completion. For example: foundation in by August 2, framing by September 3, and roofing by November 25. In addition, if you're concerned about a contractor falling behind schedule, include a provision that *"time is of the essence."* This language is primarily used when timing is critical—for example, getting the roof on your house before the rainy season.

"Time is of the essence" is a legal phrase interpreted by courts to mean that completion dates are important to you. If the contractor is late, you can be compensated either by having your bill reduced each day the job is not done or by requiring the contractor to pay for damages caused by the lateness. Damage done to your hardwood floor by rain that came through the incomplete roof repair is one example.

The best protection you can get against poor or incomplete work is by spelling out in your contract your right to inspect the work before you make the final payment.

If the contractor disagrees with you about the quality of the work, a court will determine whether the contractor complied with the material terms of the contract. If a judge or arbitrator decides that the contractor did comply, you'll be ordered to pay the balance due on the contract, perhaps minus a reasonable amount you'll need to hire someone to complete work not done to your satisfaction. If it's ruled that the contractor didn't live up to the contracted terms, you'll probably owe nothing more.

Environmental Toxins

State and federal laws regulate the detection, treatment, and removal of environmental toxins, such as asbestos fibers and lead paint. Contractors are required to obtain special licenses and permits before handling these substances.

Today, many contractors are including in their contracts language that releases them from liability for refusing to work with or to be exposed to toxins. Before signing a contract that has such a provision, ask the contractor to investigate and test the premises for hazardous substances. Contractors are required by law to provide this service free. If toxic substances are detected, you can decide how to proceed and make sure your contractor has the proper qualifications to handle them.

CHAPTER

9

BEFORE YOU SIGN

Before hiring a contractor and agreeing on what will be done and for how much, you need to prepare yourself with some preliminary decisions.

Know What You Want Done

To get the most satisfactory results, take an active role in the project. It's not enough to say you want the kitchen remodeled without giving the contractor your ideas on layout, design, and materials. For example, offer ideas about:

- The size of the kitchen

- Placement of doors and windows

- Size and placement of cabinets

- Placement of stove, sink, and refrigerator

- Tile, Formica, or other surface materials

- Built-in cutting boards, lazy Susan, or microwave shelf

- Electrical and plumbing needs
- Wall coverings, moldings, or ceiling beams

When you know what you want done and exactly what's involved to complete the work, you can make better decisions about hiring and how to achieve the home improvements with minimum disruption of your family, lifestyle, and pocketbook.

Establish a Budget

Knowing how much you can afford will help you decide the size and quality of the project. Before talking to contractors, estimate how much you want to spend.

This helps potential contractors calculate how best to meet your budget requirements. If most contractors can't meet your budget without cutting corners or using cheap materials, you may have to scale down the size of the renovation or rethink the project entirely.

Find Financing

If you own a home, condo, co-op, or an apartment building, you can finance improvements in a number of ways. The best for you depends on how much money you need and how quickly the work has to be done. A common way is through bank or credit union loans. *Construction loans* (money specifically lent to finance a building project) are offered by most lending institutions (see Chapter 5).

When you apply for a loan, ask for 10% to 20% more than the contractor estimated the job will cost. If the money runs out before the project is complete, you may not have time to refinance. You'll avoid the headaches later by giving the bank a high estimate now.

You may be eligible for a Federal Housing Administration (FHA) loan insured through the U.S. Department of Housing and Urban Development (HUD). HUD offers a variety of home-improvement loans, including an FHA Title 1 loan of up to $17,500 (in 1989) for any home improvement that makes a single-family unit, individual condo or co-op, or apartment unit you own more livable or useful. Several restrictions apply, however. For example, you can't use the money to buy luxury items like swimming pools or saunas or to improve the outside of a condominium or co-op building. You can, however, install a dishwasher, refrigerator, built-in oven, and the like to improve the quality of your living environment. For more information on Title 1 and other FHA loans, contact a HUD regional office (Appendix IV).

Although more difficult to find, some cities and counties offer one-time home improvement *grants* to people who want to renovate homes in certain neighborhoods. These grants do not have to be paid back. If grants are available in your area, the Mayor's or City Council Office should be able to tell you how to apply.

Prepare Work Plans, Specifications

The *work plans* and *specifications* explain in words and drawings the measurements and materials to be used in your renovation. They also show how the project will look when it's finished. Typically, the contractor or an architect draws up the plans. You can, however, provide ideas about what you want done by giving contractors an initial sketch. Don't worry if your sketch is not to scale. You'll probably give a much better idea of what you want done with a drawing than you can with only words, regardless of how amateurish the drawing is. In turn, the contractor can add suggestions or make corrections and give you a detailed drawing done to scale.

If you don't feel comfortable about drawing your own plans, make sure you check the contractor's or architect's draft design. Don't hand over the entire project with a "talk to me when it's over" attitude, unless you're willing to take virtually any result you get.

For specific design suggestions or ideas, check home-improvement books and magazines available in most bookstores. Magazines, in particular, can keep you up to date on the latest in materials, designs, and building techniques.

Hiring a Contractor

Shopping

The best way to find a reliable and competent contractor is to do comparative shopping. Ask for recommendations from people who have already had similar work done. Also, get names of reliable contractors from people who frequently do business with them: bankers, supply stores, trade associations, and local building inspectors.

Although you must carefully check advertised facts, the Yellow Pages or the advertisement section of a local newspaper can also put you in touch with qualified contractors.

Before considering an unsolicited contractor, check references and ask about the contractor's license, bond, and trade-association membership, if any. Then, if you think it's necessary, get a second or even third opinion on the repairs the soliciting contractor is suggesting. Above all, don't rush into anything.

Sometimes contractors will come looking for you. Some who do this are disreputable and cheat homeowners out of thousands of dollars each year. A common tactic is to convince victims that their homes need unnecessary repairs—a new roof, gutter, or paint job.

A Case Study

Two dishonest contractors, brothers, recently bilked more than $300,000 from Katherine Fink, a 77-year-old resident of Baltimore, Maryland. Among other charges, she was billed $6,000 to replace a toilet, $9,000 to replace a kitchen radiator, and $8,000 each for five other radiators in her house. The contractors splashed water on the walls and floors to convince her that repairs were needed to avoid water damage. They also pulled out electrical wires that were in perfect condition and punched a hole in the pipe leading to her gas range to create yet more work. Their licenses were later suspended. Ms. Fink, who was able to recover only $20,000 from a Guarantee

Fund of the Maryland Home Improvement Commission, now faces years of litigation to try to collect the rest of her loss.

The Interview

Whether you find them or they find you, you should interview at least three contractors if yours is a large job. If you need to scale down your list, do it by making a few telephone calls first. You can easily eliminate some names over the telephone: Some won't be taking on additional work, others won't be available when you need them, and still others won't be in your price range.

When you've narrowed your list, it's time to set up in-person interviews. You need to know the contractor's training and experience, how much you'll be charged, and how long the project will take. The contractor can supply you with time and cost estimates in writing after getting the chance to look over the place you want renovated or the space you want added onto.

Before the interview, send all contractors the same information about the project, your budget, and any work sketches you have. Some questions to ask at the interview:

When Did You Get Into This Business? How Many Jobs Do You Have Going? What Type of Remodeling Work Do You Typically Do? Answers to these questions will help you determine if this is someone you want to hire. A person who has only a few jobs going may just be starting out and willing to charge less. Someone who is extremely busy might be a good catch but hard to hold.

Are You Licensed and Bonded? Not all states require this, but if they do, ask to see the license and get the license number, then check to see if the license is current. Consider checking the contractor's status with the state's licensing board. Also, ask the bonding company what the bond covers and what its maximum payout is.

Do You Belong to a Trade Association? If the answer is yes, ask which one, and call to make sure the membership is current. Two of the largest trade associations are the Remodelers Council of the National Association of Home Builders (NAHB) and the National

Association of the Remodeling Industry (NARI). Both promote the professional remodeling and rehabilitation industries, providing their members business and technical support.

If your contractor belongs to such an association, ask if it will act as intermediary between you and the contractor if things go wrong.

Do You Carry Liability and Workers' Compensation Insurance? This insurance protects you, your neighbors, passers-by, and all workers in case of an accident. Ask to see Certificates of Insurance or check coverage by asking the contractor's insurance carrier.

Is There a Warranty on Your Work? Materials? For How Long? Make sure you get all warranties in writing. A warranty is a promise or guarantee by the contractor or manufacturer of the supplier's products to stand behind its service or product if something goes wrong.

Ask if the quality of both the work and the materials is covered by warranty, and who will make good on it if there's trouble. How long is the warranty good for? Is it a *full* or *limited* warranty? If it's a full warranty, all products found to be faulty will have to be repaired or replaced or your full purchase price will be refunded. If it's a limited warranty, some limitations will apply on the repair or replacement. Ask what these are.

Will You Put Your Fees in Writing? The law requires that contracts that involve more than $500 must be in writing. That includes home-improvement contracts. Once signed, the contract cannot be changed unless otherwise provided for in the contract itself or unless you approve the changes.

Are You Willing to Be Paid in Installments and to Accept Final Payment Only after the Job Is Completed by the Terms of Our Agreement? It's common practice to reserve 10% or more of the fee to be paid only after you and a local government inspector have examined the work and you've signed a certificate of completion.

If during the interview the contractor is difficult to talk to or uses language you don't understand, chances are communication will get worse once construction starts. You need to feel comfortable and confident about both the contractor's skills and personality. After all, if major repairs are planned, the contractor may be in your home for weeks or months.

Ask the contractor to supply you with a bid (a written estimate of how much materials and labor will cost) as soon as possible after the interview.

Evaluating Bids

Make sure each bid is based on the same work and includes the same-quality materials. A contractor who is under the impression you want custom-designed or imported materials is obviously going to quote you a higher bid than the one who gives you an estimate on less expensive materials. A contractor's bid should include:

- A description of the work to be done

- Approximate starting and completion dates

- The estimated cost of materials, labor, and building permits

The "quoted" bid is usually good for 30 days. Some contractors will submit a bid on a preprinted form that becomes your contract if you agree to it. These forms have contract language that tends to favor the contractor, much as preprinted leases favor landlords. If you plan to accept a bid, make sure you read the fine print and understand everything in it before signing. Once signed, it's a legally enforceable contract. If you think it's necessary, ask to make changes and to add or strike provisions. Be sure to check our translations and advice in the next chapter.

Initial any changes you make on the preprinted form. If the contractor doesn't agree to them, find someone who will. Remember, you can accept the estimate but do not have to accept the contract it's written on. You can use a different form or write your own. As long as you're reasonable and not expecting the contractor to work for nothing, the contractor shouldn't mind drafting a contract that meets with your approval.

References

Ask the contractors you're most interested in to give you the names of past clients and suppliers. When you've narrowed your choices, you'll have several more ways to measure them. You can check firsthand the quality of their finished work by visiting past clients, and you can see if they pay bills on time by checking with their suppliers. A third check is to ask the Better Business Bureau or your local Office of Consumer Affairs if any complaints have been registered against the contractor. Both organizations usually will let you know.

In 1987 alone, the Better Business Bureau received 897,600 requests for information about home-improvement companies and contractors. Take advantage of the information they collect by calling the bureau nearest you. They're listed in Appendix II.

Making Payments

The amount you pay the contractor at any given stage is also important. You want to give enough money so work can proceed but not so much that the contractor doesn't have a continuing incentive to finish the job. With minor jobs, a small deposit upon signing the contract or after materials are bought is typical, with the balance paid upon completion.

Large home improvements will require several installments. You and the contractor may have conflicting interests here. You will want to make payments as stages are completed, while the contractor will want money before stages are begun. The best way to get around this is to start with a reasonable deposit of 10% to 20%, smaller payments during construction, and slightly less than half (about 40%) upon completion. Being owed a substantial part of the money near the end gives the contractor incentive to finish. Make sure you do not make your final payment until the project is completed, the releases of liens are signed and handed in by subs and suppliers, the building authorities have completed their inspections satisfactorily, and all warranties are in your hands: Then and only then should you sign the last check.

CHAPTER

10

SOLVING PROBLEMS

This section briefly describes your options for resolving disputes with home-improvement contractors and should be read with the general problem-solving information in Chapter 4. A well-written contract will prevent misunderstandings and help you resolve disputes through direct negotiation. However, if attempts at negotiation fail, several agencies may be able to help you resolve your problem at little or no expense.

Licensing Authorities

If your contractor is licensed, start by contacting the licensing authority. This agency keeps current records about work and home addresses of its contractors and will be able to track yours down more easily. Also, you can usually get the agency to investigate your complaint and, if applicable, forward it to the bonding company. Getting a bonding company to pay up on a claim is not always easy, unless the contractor readily admits guilt. Otherwise, you'll have to prove the contractor's guilt, probably in court, before your claim will be paid.

The amount of help a state's licensing board will give varies. Some state agencies have authority not only to license contractors, but to investigate complaints and, if necessary, suspend or revoke their licenses.

At least one state, Maryland, goes a step further and requires contractors to pay $50 into a restitution fund used to reimburse victims of fraudulent or incompetent work. This is called the Guaranteed Fund of the Home Improvement Commission, operated by the Maryland Department of Licensing and Regulation. It holds hearings to determine if complaints are valid and then reimburses complainants up to $10,000 per homeowner or $50,000 per contractor. Consumers can receive as much as $2,500 from the fund without attending a hearing, more than that if they win their case in arbitration or receive a nondefault court judgment against the contractor.

Don't expect too much from licensing agencies, however. Many are criticized for siding with the construction industry in their decisions and for not being aggressive enough in compensating victimized consumers. Even Maryland's Guaranteed Fund has come under attack.

Trade Associations

If you're dealing with a licensed contractor, chances are you're also dealing with someone who belongs to a trade association. If the licensing board in your area isn't helpful, try the contractor's trade association. Many, like the National Association of Home Builders (NAHB) and the National Association of the Remodeling Industry (NARI), will contact the contractor on your behalf to help resolve the dispute.

Consumer Affairs Offices, Better Business Bureaus

If you still can't get adequate help, the next step is to complain in writing to a government Consumer Affairs Office or Better Business Bureau. Both handle consumer complaints and, depending on the office, may specialize in dealing with complaints against contractors. (For more information on these agencies, see Chapter 4.)

Formal Dispute Resolution

If informal methods of resolving your dispute don't work, consider mediation, arbitration, or a lawsuit. All are discussed in Chapter 4. Be advised, however, that *construction* arbitration can sometimes be as expensive and complicated as litigation, especially if a lot of money is at stake. Expert testimony, witnesses, and thorough documentation will probably be required.

The American Arbitration Association (AAA) is a private organization that offers arbitration of construction disputes. It requires lengthy application forms and a filing fee—up to 3% of the amount in the dispute, with a $300 minimum—to be paid before arbitration begins.

Explore all your arbitration alternatives if you go this route. Some jurisdictions may offer court-annexed arbitration, and that may be less expensive than the AAA's services. Ask at your local court clerk's office.

Resources

For more information, contractor referrals, and sample home-improvement contracts, contact the following trade associations:

American Homeowners Foundation
1724 S. Quincy St.
Arlington, VA 22205

National Association of the Remodeling Industry
1901 N. Moore St., Suite 808
Arlington, VA 22209

Remodelers Council of the National Association of Home Builders
15th and M Sts. NW
Washington, DC 20005

Home Owner's Warranty Corporation (HOW)
2000 L St. NW
Washington, DC 20036

American Institute of Architects
1735 New York Ave. NW
Washington, DC 20006

The following free brochures, of five to 10 pages each, offer advice on shopping for a contractor, writing contracts, and getting help with problems.

Choosing a Professional Remodeling Contractor. Prepared by U.S. Office of Consumer Affairs, Better Business Bureau, the National Association of Consumer Agency Administrators and the Remodelers Council of the National Association of Home Builders.

Home Help: How to Get It & Who Can Do It. My Home Magazine Referral Network, 6715 Lowell Ave., Suite 2, McLean, VA 22101.

Home Improvements and Repairs. Wisconsin Department of Justice, Office of Consumer Protection, 123 W. Washington Ave., Madison, WI 53707.

How to Choose a Remodeler Who's on the Level. Send self-addressed, stamped envelope to the Remodelers Council of the National Association of Home Builders at the address above.

Selecting a Professional Remodeling Contractor. National Association of the Remodeling Industry (address above).

Simple Home Repairs Inside. Consumer Information Center—E, P.O. Box 100, Pueblo, CO 81002.

Tips on Home Improvements. Better Business Bureau, 1515 Wilson Blvd., Arlington, VA 22209.

CHAPTER

II

CONTRACT LANGUAGE

For your protection, your agreement with your contractor should be in writing. It should describe the job the contractor is to complete, the materials to be used, the total price, and the payment schedule. Your contract should also include a provision for arbitration of unforeseen disputes.

If you authorize home improvements without a written agreement, or if you simply sign a preprinted bid from the contractor, you run the risk of costly mistakes.

You have several options: You can use a standard building-contract form and modify it to fit the work you want done; you can revise the contractor's suggested contract; or you can write your own.

Writing your own contract for simple home improvements is not difficult, though the contractor is certain to scrutinize it before signing. To avoid disagreements, discuss major provisions you want to include with the contractor in advance—for example, provisions

for making payments, approving work, storing equipment, or settling disputes.

If you don't feel comfortable writing your own contract and don't
want to pay a lawyer to do it for you, think about using a preprinted
form. Such forms, complete with instructions, are offered by several
building-trade associations, including those listed at the end of
Chapter 10.

In this chapter, we've drafted a pro-consumer agreement that
contains the most important elements of a home improvement
contract. For additional items, you may wish to consult page 106,
Other Important Clauses.

Home Lawyer Tip

Home Lawyer will draft an Independent Contractor Agreement. Although this document is primarily for situations
where one individual will serve as an independent contractor
or consultant for a business organization, you may prefer to use
the Home Lawyer to draft your contract for home improvement contractors. If you do, you can edit the agreement as you
desire on your word processor, using the "Shell to WP . . ."
function.

To draft an Independent Contractor Agreement, select
Credit and Collections from the Document submenu, then
select Independent Contractor Agreement. Point to "New,"
and then answer the questions that Home Lawyer asks.

To edit the agreement, you must have first set up the word
processor under System Setup. After you have specified your
word processing program under System Setup, select Shell to
WP from the Edit submenu. When you exit your word processor, you will automatically return to the Home Lawyer Main
Menu.

HOME IMPROVEMENT CONTRACT

On this, the _____ day of _____, 19___,

_____ (Owner)

residing at _____

and_____ (Contractor)

doing business at _____

agree as follows:

1. Work to Be Performed.
   At the following address,_____
   _____contractor will:_____
   _____
   _____
   _____

   _____. For a detailed description of the work involved, parties will refer to the attached drawings and specifications which are incorporated into this agreement by this reference.

First, fill in the date, your name and address, and the name and address of the contractor.

In Clause 1, in the space provided, you should note a brief description of your project—basement refinishing, room addition, kitchen remodeling, etc.—and the address of the property to be remodeled.

The "drawings and specifications" are the *work plans* discussed in Chapter 9. They are the illustrations and written instructions of your project and are an important part of every home improvement agreement. If a disagreement arises over materials, labor, or design, you'll need to refer to these drawings and specifications for direction, so make sure they are specific, accurate, and attached to this document.

2. Starting and Completion Dates.
   The contractor shall start work on _____, 19___ and subject to authorized time adjustments, complete work no later than _____, 19___.

A clause explaining when work is to begin and when it must be completed is extremely important. Many home-improvement contracts state when a project is to begin but not when it is to be finished. If a final date is missing from the contract you receive, make sure it's added. This is the date when *all* the work, without exception, must be finished.

3. Date of Substantial Completion.
   Work will be substantially completed, subject to authorized time adjustments, on _____, 19___.
   If work is not substantially completed by _____, 19___, contractor will owe owner $___ for each day beyond the date of substantial completion.

In this clause, insert the date by which most of the work (substantial completion) should be done. Although not defined, substantial completion is considered the point at which the space or area can be used for its intended purpose. Dates when other phases of the work have to be completed, if necessary, can be written into a separate clause (see page 109, Time Is of the Essence).

A provision that will compensate you if the contractor fails to meet the substantial completion date is important. You and the contractor should agree upon a "good faith" estimate of how much you will get if the contractor is late.

Some contracts actually list what the amount will be, for example, $50 or $100 per day. If you get such a contract and do not agree with the stated penalty amount, try to get the contractor to change it before you sign. If you don't and a dispute later ensues, a court or arbitrator (depending on what your contract states about resolving disputes) will decide what a reasonable estimate should have been at the time the contract was signed.

4. Price.
   Owner agrees to pay contractor in cash, certified check or money order, a sum total of $_____, subject to authorized additions or deductions of that price.

This clause lists the total amount you'll pay (Price) for the entire project. That price may eventually go up or down depending on any changes you authorize once construction is under way. For example, if you change your mind and substitute a Superduper Deluxe washing machine for a Wash-O-Matic by Wring 'n' Rinse, the total price will probably increase. Or, if the contractor can't find the exact materials you requested and needs to use substitutes (as often happens), that will affect the total cost.

5. Schedule of Payments.
   Owner agrees to reimburse contractor for the total cost of the contract, including labor, materials and equipment, upon receiving a written request for payment and a satisfactory work inspection, as follows:
   10% payable upon signing of this contract.
   15% payable after ____ weeks.
   15% payable after ____ weeks.
   20% payable upon date of substantial completion.
   40% payable upon completion.

   If a payment is not received within ____ days of being due, the owner shall pay contractor an additional ____% of the total amount overdue.

Paying the contractor in installments (or "draws," as progress payments are sometimes called in the construction business) is standard. Under this clause, two things need to occur before each payment will be made: The work has to pass inspection (by the town inspector or whomever you've chosen to conduct inspections) and the contractor has to provide you with a written request for payment.

To make sure you hold up your end of the bargain, a late charge is assessed if you do not make payments within the time line given. You and the contractor must decide when payments are due and how much will be charged if they're late.

This clause also allows you to reserve 40% of the pay till the end. Some contractors may balk at this (and you may have to compromise), but leaving a substantial amount to be paid on completion helps to prevent contractors from leaving a job unfinished.

6. Final Payment.
   Final payment, the entire unpaid balance of the amount due, shall be paid by the owner to the contractor when the work has been completed, the contract has been fully performed, the work has passed inspection and the owner has given final approval.

Most home improvement contracts make final payment contingent on something. This one makes final payment contingent on the work being completed, passing inspection, and receiving final approval from you.

Allowing you to give final approval is *not* standard, and you will probably not see anything like it in a preprinted form. It is included here to give you leverage, within reason, but is not meant to give you an easy way out of paying what you owe. Contractors may allow you to write a contract or revise a final-payment provision in a way that gives you final approval, but they won't hesitate to take you to court if they think they've met their obligations but you haven't paid. If a judge or arbitrator has to decide this type of dispute, expect the doctrine of substantial performance to be used in determining whether or not you owe more money (see Glossary, Appendix V).

> 7. Acknowledgment of Payment and Waiver of Mechanic's Lien.
> The owner will require the contractor to attach to each request for partial or final payment, an acknowledgment of payment, and all subcontractors' acknowledgments of payment, for work done and materials, equipment and fixtures furnished through the date covered by the previous payment. Concurrently with the final payment, the owner will require the contractor to execute a waiver or release of lien for all work performed and materials furnished hereunder and to obtain similar waivers or releases from all subcontractors and suppliers.

This is an important protection for you. It requires the contractor to give you a document called an Acknowledgment of Payment each time you make a payment for labor or materials, to serve as proof that your bills are being paid.

Each year, hundreds of consumers are cheated by contractors who don't pay their subcontractors or suppliers with the funds they've been entrusted with. This language prevents such abuse by also requiring contractors, subcontractors, and suppliers to sign a "waiver of mechanic's liens" before you make your final payment. If this waiver *isn't* signed and your contractor doesn't pay off the subs or suppliers, a mechanic's lien might be attached to your property and stop you from selling or mortgaging it, even though you've already paid the contractor.

Because you're ultimately responsible for all debts incurred, we strongly urge you to make *sure* this language is included in your home-improvement contract. Be aware, however, that many contract forms include language similar to this but use the word "may" instead of "will" ("The owner may require . . ."). The stronger, more definite language we suggest allows no room for misunderstanding. While some contractors may fuss about it, such language will certainly not be new to them.

8. Supplying Materials.
   The contractor shall provide all materials and equipment required to carry out the terms of the contract.

This language places responsibility on the contractor to supply all materials and all equipment needed to get the job done. It can be changed to fit your circumstances. For example, you may prefer that the contractor save you money by installing used parts. Or you may want to be responsible for buying the materials or supplying equipment if you believe you can save money that way.

9. Warranty.
   The contractor warrants that all materials will be new unless otherwise specified, and that all materials will be of good quality and covered by manufacturers' warranties. The contractor will supply the owner with copies of all manufacturers' warranties. The contractor also warrants that the work, including work done by subcontractors, will be of good quality, free from faults and defects in workership for a period of _____ from the date the work is completed.

This requires the contractor to guarantee (warrant) that the materials are new and to give you copies of warranties for all materials covered by manufacturer's warranty. It also requires the contractor to guarantee the work for a specified time after the job is completed: If the work is found to be faulty (for example, if the toilet begins to leak) within the time specified, you can call the contractor back to correct the work without charge. You have the right to expect the contractor to guarantee work for a reasonable length of time. The current market standard is 12 months.

10. Change in Plans.
The owner, without invalidating the contract, may order changes in the work within the general scope of the contract consisting of additions, deletions or other revisions. The contract price and the contract time will be adjusted accordingly. All such changes in the work shall be in writing, and signed by the contractor and owner and attached to this document.

Change orders (sometimes referred to as "addenda" or "modifications") are papers that specify changes you authorize in the original agreement before or after work has started. For example, if the agreed-upon completion date has to be pushed back because of inclement weather, draft a change order that states the new date. It should be dated and signed by you and the contractor. Once signed, change orders become official parts of your agreement and should be attached to it. If you're having a large job done, adding a room or remodeling a kitchen, for example, expect a number of change orders.

Change orders typically include:

- The name of the project (e.g., refinishing basement)

- The date of the change

- A precise description of the change

- A detailed description of necessary materials, including brand names

- Additional charges or deductions caused by the change

- Deadline changes

- Signatures of both the contractor and you

11. Noise, Cleanup, Storing Equipment.
The contractor at all times shall keep the premises free from accumulation of waste materials or rubbish caused by the operations. At the completion of the work each day, the contractor shall remove all waste materials and rubbish from and about the project and store all construction equipment, machinery and surplus materials.

If the contractor fails to clean up or store equipment at the completion of work each day, the owner may do so and be credited $_____ against the contract price for each day the owner takes care of cleanup.

> To prevent neighbors from being unduly bothered by construction noise, contractor agrees to perform work between the hours of _____ A.M. and _____ P.M., on the following days of the week: _____.

Spelling out who will clean up and store equipment is especially important to include in your contract when large renovations are being done. It ensures that the work area is clean and safe at the end of each day. If you need the contractor to haul away large volumes of debris or large items like a refrigerator during or at the end of construction, you can expect to be charged extra for that.

A good "cleanup" credit you can ask for is $25 for each day you have to clear away debris or put away the contractor's tools and equipment. Disruptions cannot be entirely prevented, but they can be reduced.

Days of the week and hours of work should be spelled out, particularly because some communities have specific regulations about this. Specify "Monday through Friday only," if that is the agreement.

> 12. Arbitration.
>   All claims, disputes and other matters in question between the contractor and owner arising out of or relating to the contract documents or the breach thereof, and not resolved by referring to the contract documents, shall be decided by arbitration in accordance with the construction industry arbitration rules of the American Arbitration Association, unless the parties mutually agree to resolve the dispute otherwise.

Arbitration clauses are common in consumer contracts. If you don't have such a provision, you run the risk of having to settle disputes in court, and that can be time-consuming and expensive. In arbitration, it's simple, less expensive, and quicker: You and the contractor meet with a neutral third party who listens to your testimony, reviews the evidence, and renders a final and binding decision.

This language suggests that your dispute be decided by an American Arbitration Association (AAA) arbitrator. AAA has been arbitrating construction disputes for years. However, the organization, a private corporation based in New York, has been criticized by some as pro-business. If you decide to use AAA, find out what arbitrator will be assigned your case, get a copy of the rules, and go into the meeting prepared with documented evidence of work plans, schedules, drawings, payments, photographs of the work in question, and any other pertinent materials. If you prefer, rewrite the contract language in the clause we've suggested by using the name of a different dispute resolution company or agency. Always check qualifications of the companies and individuals offering arbitration. You can find some in the telephone directory's Yellow Pages.

_____   _____
Owner   Contractor

Date: _____   Date: _____

Make sure to sign the contract, date it, and see that the contractor does the same.

Other Important Clauses

The following provisions from a variety of other home-improvement contracts cover some of the other pro-consumer clauses a home-improvement contract could include.

Relationship of Parties

The parties intend that an independent contractor-owner relationship will be created by this contract. Owner is interested only in the results to be achieved. The conduct and control of the work will lie solely with contractor. It is understood that contractor is free to perform similar services for other customers while under contract with owner.

An independent contractor may use language like this to explain how your relationship with the contractor is to be conducted, though usually it is taken as "a given" and is not written in.

Legally, independent contractors have complete control over how the work is to be done. They make decisions about process, what tools to use, and how to do the work. They also hire and pay subcontractors, unless otherwise specified in your contract. (See

Chapter 8 for the legal differences between "independent contractors" and "employees.") One way to make sure you don't lose total control of what's happening in your home is to substitute the following clause when you find this "Relationship of Parties" language in a contract you've been offered:

Owner's Right of Supervision and Inspection

In the performance of the work described in the contract, contractor is an independent contractor with the authority to control and direct the performance of the details of the work, owner being interested only in the results obtained. However, the work contemplated herein must meet the approval of owner and will be subject to owner's general right of inspection and supervision to secure his or her complete satisfaction.

You may or may not find this language in your home-improvement agreement. It makes two important points: that the independent contractor has total control over how the project will be done and that the finished product must get your approval.

This clause does not give you any new rights; it simply reinforces your right to stay involved, to inspect the work, and to offer comments if you think something should be done differently. Your right is limited to inspections and comments. The contractor is free to accept or reject your suggestions, but is reminded here that the work must get your approval, so it's probably wise to listen to you.

Subcontractors

All or any portion of the work covered by this contract may be subcontracted by contractor, but any subcontract shall specify that there will be no contractual relationship between the owner and subcontractors, nor will the subcontracting of all or any portion of the work in any way relieve contractor of obligations to the owner under this contract.

This makes it clear that your independent contractor is solely responsible for hiring, supervising, and paying all subcontractors—electricians, plumbers, and carpenters, for example. If problems occur with a sub, the independent contractor will be responsible for settling it—for example, by firing a sub who consistently fails to report to work on time. The contractor cannot use the behavior or performance of a sub as an excuse for not fulfilling contract obligations to you, nor can the contractor involve you in any agreement she or he has with the sub.

Although independent contractors automatically assume responsibility over subs, your contract should include language that makes this clear. If you want the responsibility of hiring, supervising, and paying subs, substitute this language:

All or any part of the work covered by this contract may be subcontracted by owner. Owner will assume responsibility for hiring, paying and supervising subcontractors.

or

All or any part of the work covered by this contract may be subcontracted by owner. Owner will assume responsibility for hiring and paying subcontractors but contractor will assume responsibility for their supervision.

Indemnity of Owner

All work under this contract will be performed entirely at contractor's risk, and contractor assumes all responsibility for the condition of tools and equipment used in its performance. Contractor will carry, for the duration of this contract, general liability insurance in an amount acceptable to the owner. Contractor agrees to indemnify owner for any and all liability or loss arising in any way out of the performance of this contract.

This gives the contractor the responsibility of dealing with all injuries to people or property from the performance of the contract. It also requires the contractor to carry liability insurance to cover any claims that are made because of those injuries. (This does not apply to workers on the job, however, as they are covered under workers' compensation provisions.)

It makes sense to select a contractor who carries liability insurance. It's especially important, however, if you're having extensive repairs or renovations done. Say, for example, that a neighbor visits your house while it's under construction and is injured by a falling brick. If your contractor doesn't carry liability insurance, paying for your neighbor's injury will have to come out of your pocket or from your homeowner's insurance. If the contractor carries liability insurance, however, your neighbor could file directly with the contractor's insurance company.

Time is of the Essence

Contractor is notified that time is of the essence and will make every effort to complete the job by the agreed-upon completion date. If most of the work is substantially completed by the agreed-upon date, that is cause enough for owner to continue making payments.

Delays, however, will be considered a serious breach, allowing the owner to be compensated as provided for in Clause 3.

If you have a specific and demonstrable reason to need work done by a certain date, include this language. For instance, say your basement floods easily and you need work done before the rainy season begins. Include language stating the importance of having the job completed on time. This language works, however, only if you have a clause that specifically states when the work is to be finished.

Also, if you include this clause without a good reason, a court is not likely to enforce it. If a court does enforce a time-is-of-the-essence clause, you will be compensated for the delays according to your substantial completion date provisions (see Clause 3).

Termination

Contractor may end this contract if, through no fault of the contractor, the owner fails to make payments according to the time provisions stipulated in this contract. All disagreements over payments due and owing will be resolved in arbitration as provided for in Clause 12.

Owner may end this contract if the contractor's work is unsatisfactory. All disagreements over payments due and owing will be resolved in arbitration as provided for in Clause 12.

A provision like this, allowing either side to break the contract, appears in many home-improvement agreements. This one allows the contractor to stop work if the owner fails to meet the deadlines set by the "schedule of payments" provision. Other contracts include language even less hospitable to consumers, allowing the contractor to get out of his or her obligations if the work is stopped through no fault of the contractor's (e.g., a court order, or inclement weather that lasts 30 or more days). In the sample provision, if the contractor ends the agreement, he or she will have to turn to arbitration to resolve the money disputes that led to the termination of the contract.

The second paragraph turns the tables: It allows you to break the agreement if the contractor doesn't do the work or fails to do it correctly. Again, disputes between you and the contractor will have to be resolved through arbitration.

Protection from Weather

Contractor will take special precaution to protect work during inclement weather. No mortar, concrete, plaster, paint and the like shall be used during inclement weather unless proper and special precaution is taken to prevent damage. Contractor will also provide protective coverings.

If your project might be exposed to and damaged by bad weather, include this language. Contractors do not usually mind taking these extra precautions, because they'll require you to pay for any extra work or materials they need to fulfill the obligation.

Getting Out of a Contract

If you sign a contract and then realize you've made a mistake, don't panic. The Federal Trade Commission requires contractors to give you a cancellation form, sometimes called "A Right of Rescission Notice," at the time the contract is signed. It gives you the right to cancel the contract within three days of signing it. If you don't get such a form, ask the contractor for it or add such a statement to the end of your contract.

PART IV

REPAIRING YOUR CAR

CHAPTER

12

AUTO REPAIRS

Dick dropped off his car for a tune-up and oil change. The mechanic gave an oral estimate of $89.95 and told him to pick up his car after 5:00 P.M. When he arrived to get the car, he found his bill exceeded the estimate by $50.

On a friend's advice, Pam marked the parts in her car that needed to be replaced: the tailpipe, muffler, and radiator. When the work was completed, she found that the radiator hadn't been replaced, even though she had been charged for it.

Debbie is proud of her ability as a backyard mechanic, but when her attempt to fix the carburetor failed, she decided to take her car to a nearby garage. The mechanic later called to suggest an engine overhaul. Debbie agreed without hesitating.

All three instances above involved auto repair contracts and the special rules that govern them. Getting your car repaired shouldn't be a traumatic experience, but for many of us it is. According to the Council of Better Business Bureaus, 28,100 complaints were filed with its affiliate offices against auto repair shops in 1987, ranking that group fifth nationally. In reality, the problem is even larger: In California alone, during the 1987–88 fiscal year, 25,367 complaints were registered with the Bureau of Automotive Repair in the State Department of Consumer Affairs.

Legal Considerations

The most frequent complaints against auto repair shops are those alleging charges for unnecessary repairs and repairs that were never done; used parts sold as new; and advertised "specials" that resulted in more expensive repairs.

A typical scam, confirmed by the California bureau, is a repair shop's suggestion that an engine overhaul is needed when the car already has a perfectly good engine. Never intending to do the work suggested, the shop simply steam-cleans the existing engine and spray-paints it to look new. The cost to the garage is minimal, but the customer winds up paying about $1,000.

Regulation

Less than a dozen states have laws that require licensing of auto-repair shops. According to the most recent study by the Automotive Parts and Accessories Association (APAA), by 1982 only six states (California, Connecticut, Hawaii, Michigan, New York, and Rhode Island) and the District of Columbia had laws that required licensing of repair shops. The agency responsible for licensing these shops varies from state to state, but in most it's the Attorney General's Office, the Department of Motor Vehicles (DMV), or the Office of Consumer Affairs. The kind of help you may get from these agencies varies and is described in Chapter 4.

Disclosure Laws

More than half the states and the District of Columbia have "truth in auto repair" or "good-faith disclosure" laws. Such laws require repair shops to give consumers written estimates, to notify them in advance if the estimate will be exceeded, to return replaced parts, and to itemize repair bills, stating whether the parts installed were used, new, or repaired.

Disclosure laws vary. In Maryland, written estimates are required only on repairs that exceed $50, and a customer can be charged up to 10% more than the estimate without being contacted in advance.

In California, however, customers must get written estimates on *all* repairs before any work is done; they cannot be charged more than the estimate unless they have approved the charge in advance.

The best way to protect yourself is to know what the laws are in your state. For more information, call your local or state Office of Consumer Affairs (Appendix I). Most of these offices offer basic advice and distribute pamphlets that describe your state's laws regulating auto repairs.

Lemon Laws

New-car owners who find themselves with unexpected and numerous repair bills can also find help. As of 1989, 45 states and the District of Columbia have *lemon laws* that require manufacturers to make their cars conform to warranty within a prescribed time or replace the vehicle entirely. These are described in Chapter 13.

Armed with correct information, you should be able to get competent, quality auto care without being overcharged. This and the next two chapters describe auto repair shops, offering advice on how to find a good one; what to look for in a mechanic; how to review a "repair order"; and your options if something goes wrong.

Repair Shops

Where you go depends on what you need done, your budget, the kind of personal service you're accustomed to or want, and, of course, the location of the repair shop. Repair shops belong to national chains, new-car dealerships, and independent garages. Each has advantages and disadvantages.

Chains

Large discount department stores like Zayres, Sears, K mart, and Montgomery Ward now operate auto-service centers. They offer routine services, like muffler installation, batteries, tune-ups, oil changes, tire mountings, front-end alignments, and brake work.

Discount chains offer both brand-name parts and lower-cost parts sold under their own house labels.

Tire Outlets

Tire manufacturers, such as Goodyear and Firestone, and tire stores, like Merchant's Tire and Auto Centers, have also entered the auto repair business. Their primary enterprise is selling tires, so they limit the type of repair services they offer, typically to computerized tire balancing, complete front-end alignment, disc and drum brake repairs, and shock absorbers. Some also work on radiators, battery installation, and air conditioners.

The major difference between tire manufacturers and tire stores is in the parts they sell. Tire manufacturers sell their own brand-name parts, and tire stores sell a variety of both brand names and discount parts.

Specialty Franchises

Nationwide companies, such as AAMCO Transmissions and Midas Muffler Shops, specialize in specific repairs—rebuilt transmissions, muffler installations, exhaust-system work. Despite their televised advertisement claims, however, these specialty franchises tend to charge as much as 20% or 30% more for their work than the market rate. In return, customers get a full guarantee on both parts and labor and can count on getting their cars back quickly.

Service Stations

Like the "garages" of yesteryear, service stations still offer a variety of services, from oil changes and tune-ups to major engine work. Some services are offered free to regular customers, for example, adding oil that you supply, checking your tires' pressure, or adding water to the radiator. Other service, if simple (taping a leaky hose, for instance), might be handled by a station attendant at a smaller cost than if the station's mechanic had to do it.

If personalized service is what you want, find a local station you like and use it whenever you have repair needs it can handle. Repeat customers get much better service in this shrinking market.

If your car needs heavier work done and your station's mechanic can't handle it, ask to be referred to an independent garage.

Dealerships

If your car is still under warranty, the dealer you bought it from is the best place to go. You may be able to get the repairs done free under the warranty. Also, the dealer will be familiar with the type of car and have most if not all the necessary parts in stock. If the repair you need is at all complex, the dealership may be the only place to take it.

On the other hand, if all you need is routine work not covered by your warranty, you can probably get a better deal outside. This is because dealerships' per-hour labor charges tend to be high to cover overhead. Once the new-car warranty expires, people seldom return to their dealership for minor repairs.

Independents

Taking your car to an independent garage can be the best or worst thing you do. If you don't do homework in advance to learn how a garage and its mechanics operate, you could be headed for trouble.

Like service stations and store chains, independents' services vary. Some work only on domestic cars, others handle both foreign and domestic. Mechanics who have expertise in more than one area (for example, with diesel or fuel-injection work) are common at these garages, and many of them carry or can get both new and rebuilt parts. Taking your car to an independent is not always possible, because in many localities garages are extremely busy, have more work than they can handle, and will often act as though they are doing you a great kindness to work on your car. If you live in such an area, the best course of action is to find a good repair shop, establish a relationship with the owner, and stick with the shop as long as the work and the prices are good.

Whether or not you are in this situation, it is best to shop first. The following sections' tips should help.

Finding the Right Shop

Once you've decided what type of repair shop you want, you need assurance that the one you pick offers competent work at reasonable prices. The best way to do that is with legwork. Ask for recommendations, interview shop operators by telephone, and make at least one visit to the shop.

Recommendations

Word of mouth is invaluable in this field. Try to get a referral from a satisfied customer, someone who's had good or consistent success with a particular shop or mechanic.

In the unlikely event you can find no one who can tell you about experiences using the shop you're considering, ask your local Better Business Bureau or government Consumer Affairs Office. Both can tell you if any complaints have been received against the shop you're considering and what those complaints were about.

If you're a member of the American Automobile Association (AAA), call there for a referral as well, but be aware that the garage it refers you to will probably be one the AAA has "approved" or is in some way associated with. You'll have no guarantee of getting the best price available, but at least you'll have the AAA to complain to if trouble develops.

Visit and Ask Questions

If yours isn't an emergency or rush job, it makes sense to visit the shop first, look around, and ask the owner or head mechanic some questions.

Take time to notice what the shop looks like. First impressions are important. A messy garage may mean sloppy work, though there isn't always a correlation. The garage should be clean and well-organized, and the people running it should treat you professionally. Some questions to ask:

What Type of Training Do the Mechanics Have? Ask if mechanics have been certified by the National Institute for Automotive Service Excellence (NIASE), a national training institute that has a voluntary certification program of testing mechanics' competence to perform specific work. A mechanic can be certified in as many as eight categories: engine performance, engine, automatic transmission or transaxle, manual drive-train and axles, suspension, and steering, brakes, electrical systems, and heating and air-conditioning. If mechanics are wearing an ASE patch on their uniforms, it doesn't mean they've been certified in all eight areas. Find out which ones they have been certified in.

Experience also counts. Ask how long the employees have been working as mechanics.

Can You Get a Written Estimate? Most states have laws that require the repair shop to give you a written estimate. Even where it's not required, it's common practice. A responsive mechanic will give you a copy of the estimate before you leave the shop. If you decide to have the shop do the work, the estimate will become your *repair order*—the contract to do the job at the stated price.

The estimate should list the prices of the parts needed and the expected labor charge for installing those parts. Charging more than the estimate without getting your prior approval is illegal in many states. To learn what, if any, amount above the estimate can be charged without your advance approval, call your local Consumer Protection Office.

Will the Garage Return Replaced Parts to You? Don't be afraid to ask for your old parts back. It's common practice, so don't worry that the mechanic will be offended. The best way to make sure the work is done is to mark your parts *before* they're replaced. You can do this with a regular marker or chalk.

Will the Shop Guarantee Its Parts and Labor? Shops are not legally obliged to guarantee their work, but some garages do, usually for a specified number of months or miles. It's up to you to find out what's covered.

To benefit from most "parts" warranties, you need to keep good records and to know what's needed to activate the warranty. For instance, if you get a new set of tires but neglect to note your car's mileage at the time they're put on or the installation date on the repair order, the warranty may not be worth the paper it's written on.

Make sure important information—dates, mileage, and type of repair—is fully reflected on the repair order.

Diagnosing the Problem

When you leave your car to be repaired, never make a blanket statement like "Do whatever needs to be done." Don't try to diagnose the car's problems yourself, but make sure the mechanic pays attention to what you say is wrong. This can save time and money.

If problems are too difficult to describe, a good mechanic will suggest using diagnostic equipment or taking the car on a test drive. Both will allow the mechanic to hear, see, or feel problems that you had trouble explaining, and will give the mechanic a place from which to start further diagnosis. However, because this takes time out of the mechanic's schedule, expect an additional charge.

Before Authorizing Work

It's important to know how shops bill for their time, whether they give estimates on repair work, and whether you're being given the best possible price for the repair.

Understand Billing Practices

Most shops have set fees for labor based on a "book estimate" of how long certain repairs should take. That means if the mechanic does the repair in two hours but the book says it should take four, you'll be charged for four hours. The reverse, of course, is also true.

The "book" that repair shops refer to when making these estimates is actually one of two repair manuals, *Motor's* and *Chilton's*. Both say their estimates are based on "ideal conditions."

Consumer groups have been up in arms for years about flat-rate charges. They argue that the practice is unfair because customers pay more for work than they would if paying by the hour. They also contend flat rates encourage mechanics to rush through repairs, since they are paid based on the number of cars repaired, not the true number of hours worked.

Written Estimates

Most states have laws that require garages to keep your final price to within a specified range of the original estimate, usually 10% to 15%. The only way they can legally charge more than that is with your prior approval. Find out what the law requires in your area by contacting your local Office of Consumer Affairs.

The written estimate is the repair order filled out. Most mechanics, however, will be too busy to write up a repair order on the spot and will instead want to call you later in the day with specific cost estimates. After you hear what the charges are going to be from the mechanic, your okay over the telephone can be given, or, if convenient, you can drop by to sign the full repair order.

It's important to take a copy of the repair order with you even if it lists only your name, address, phone number, and information about what you think is wrong with the car. If your hunches about what's wrong with the car are right but were not addressed, you'll have written proof that the problem still exists even after the shop worked on the car.

Second Opinions

If you find the estimate too high—because of labor or expensive parts or you just don't trust the mechanic's diagnosis—don't authorize the work, because you may want to get a second or third opinion.

Say the radiator on your 1977 car is leaking. You're told a used radiator, for $95 installed, will eliminate the problem. That's when a second opinion can save you plenty: a can of sealant may also solve the problem, and for about $10. If you don't plan to keep the car much longer, the less expensive route might make the most sense.

If you need a second opinion, think about taking your car into an independent diagnostic center not affiliated in any way with the repair shop you're considering using.

Checking Repairs

Before paying, you should understand all the charges on the bill you're given. If you don't, ask the mechanic to go over the bill with you.

Make sure you understand exactly what was done and check the bill to make sure the total is less than the allowed increase over the estimate you approved. If you had parts replaced, ask to see them—both the ones removed and the ones installed. In general, ask to see any work that was done on your car whenever possible.

If you've been charged more than you believe is fair, try to have the bill adjusted immediately. This could save you considerable trouble later, and chances are good the mechanic won't want to risk tying up the total payment for a few dollars.

Pay the bill by credit card. If repairs are done incompetently, fraudulently, unnecessarily, or without your permission, you can legally refuse to pay your credit card bill. A second option is to pay by check. You'll be able to stop payment if trouble arises. This puts the garage in the position of having to sue you to collect instead of forcing you to sue the garage for reimbursement.

If you paid by credit card, the Fair Credit Billing Act (FCBA), a federal law, allows you to withhold payment for "defective merchandise and services." Conditions apply: You must prove you tried to settle the problem first; the repair cost must exceed $50; and the repair shop must be within 100 miles of your current residence or within your home state. That means if you receive poor service out of state, you cannot withhold your credit card payment.

Be sure you *write* a letter to the credit card company explaining the problem and what you want refunded. The FCBA can be triggered only with written proof. Remember to send a copy of your letter to the repair shop as well. Finally, until the problem is resolved, the credit card company cannot charge you interest on the amount in dispute.

For more information about your credit rights, write to the Federal Trade Commission, Credit Practices Division, Washington, DC 20580.

Another, but less desirable, option is to pay the entire bill and then file a small claims court action for reimbursement of the amount in dispute. This procedure is covered in the next chapter.

CHAPTER

13

SOLVING PROBLEMS

You investigate and visit several repair shops, ask all the right questions, get written estimates, authorize specific work, review bills, get parts returned, and still drive away hearing the same noise from under the hood.

If this happens, you have several options, including specialized auto arbitration if it's a new car, before taking your case to court. This chapter outlines those options. It should be read in conjunction with the material in Chapter 4.

As soon as you detect a problem, go straight back to the shop. When you return to a shop to complain about work that was done for you, you're known in the auto-repair industry as a "comeback." Most shops treat comebacks well. They have a vested interest in turning you into a satisfied customer, not someone who will bad-mouth the company.

If appealing to their good business sense doesn't work, however, you still have other, more formal options.

Consumer Agencies

Register a complaint in writing with your local Better Business Bureau or Office of Consumer Affairs. Both agencies deal with auto-repair complaints all the time. If the Consumer Affairs Office is a branch of your local or county government, it may already be familiar with the shop in question. A staff person will contact the owner, investigate the complaint, and attempt to mediate on your behalf. If that doesn't resolve the problem, explore the dispute resolution options in Chapter 4.

If you're a new-car owner with repair problems and your state has a lemon law, you probably can use an auto arbitration program.

Auto Arbitration

Lemon laws, in effect in 45 states and the District of Columbia, require manufacturers to make their cars conform to their warranty within a prescribed time or replace the vehicle entirely. How long manufacturers can take to do these repairs varies from state to state. Typically, they are allowed three or four repair attempts on the same major defect, or a total of 30 days (either business days or calendar days, depending on the state) to service the car within the first 12,000 miles or 12 months.

Lemon laws also encourage manufacturers to establish or participate in arbitration programs to resolve customer complaints when repair attempts fail and the warranty expires.

Home Lawyer Tip

Home Lawyer has more information on lemon laws. Just select Personal Law Topics from the Adviser submenu, point to "Ch. 9—You and Your Automobile," and press [enter]. Then point to "*Lemon Laws" and press enter.

Most manufacturers comply either by: paying an agency, like the Better Business Bureau or American Arbitration Association, to operate such a program; hire an independent group to do it; or run the program themselves. Several states run car-related arbitration programs out of their Consumer Protection Agencies.

What disputes can be arbitrated, who does it, and whether or not you have to go through arbitration before heading to court depends on your state's lemon law. Each state requires something different. The best way to find out what the requirements are is to ask your state's Consumer Protection Agency or the Better Business Bureau.

The following describes some of the better-known automotive arbitration programs.

AUTO LINE

AUTO LINE is a national program established by the Council of Better Business Bureaus to settle disputes between consumers and certain automobile manufacturers who have agreed to arbitrate complaints when mediation fails. General Motors, American Motors, and a dozen foreign car manufacturers have all contracted with the BBB to offer arbitration to their new-car owners. An agreement to refer disputes to AUTO LINE is usually included in the manufacturer's new-car warranty.

In BBB arbitration, when a complaint is filed, a staff person is assigned to negotiate a solution between you and the manufacturer. This may all happen by telephone or in writing. If negotiation fails and the dispute goes to arbitration, each side is allowed to present its case in person, in writing, or by telephone. Most choose an in-person hearing.

Before the hearing, each side is given background information on five arbitrators and asked to rank them in order of preference. The arbitrator with the highest total rank from both sides is selected to hear the case. If there's a tie, the case is heard by a panel of the top three arbitrators selected.

You may bring expert witnesses (for example, a mechanic who inspected the faulty repair) but must notify the other side in advance if you plan to do so. The arbitrator's decision will be binding only on the manufacturer, unless you also agree to be bound. The BBB reports it settled 64.8% of the 28,100 complaints it handled in 1987.

AUTOCAP

AUTOCAP is an acronym for Automotive Consumer Action Panel. It was established by the National Automobile Dealers Association to resolve disputes informally between new-car and -truck dealers and their customers. As of 1989, 198 dealers participated in these programs and helped finance and run them. AUTOCAP programs are *not* offered in 22 states, and are offered only at the regional level in Florida, New York, Ohio, and Oklahoma.

When you file a dispute with AUTOCAP, it is sent to the dealer, who is given a chance to settle directly with you. If any agreements are made during this time, the dealer is obligated to notify AUTO-CAP.

If informal negotiations don't work, AUTOCAP's staff mediates. If that fails, the dispute is submitted in writing to an AUTOCAP panel for review. After a prescribed time, the panel notifies both sides in writing of its decision, but that decision is only advisory; neither side is required to abide by it.

Ford and Chrysler

Both car manufacturers operate their own arbitration programs. In the Ford program, a panel of five (three public members and two dealers) reviews written submissions before issuing a decision. The decision is binding on Ford Motor Company and its dealers, but not on the car buyer.

Chrysler also uses a panel of five: a certified NIASE mechanic, a member of the public, a dealer, a consumer advocate, and a Chrysler representative. The dealer and Chrysler representative are not allowed to vote. Decisions are binding only on the dealer or corporation, not on the buyer unless otherwise agreed to. One catch: Chrysler arbitrates disputes only over its warranty.

Consumer Protection Agencies

Some consumer advocates have voiced skepticism about arbitration programs run by car dealers and manufacturers. Even though the arbitration decisions of these programs are binding only on the car companies, and although panelists with any connection to the auto industry can only offer opinions, statistics show that the decisions still favor car dealers more often than car buyers. The belief is that the panelists who are associated with the industry have a strong influence over the others because they know more about both cars and the arbitration process. This is particularly troubling if consumers are forced to participate in these company-run programs before they can take their case to court.

Eight states—Connecticut, Florida, Massachusetts, Montana, New York, Texas, Vermont, Washington—and the District of Columbia have government panels that hear consumer complaints about cars and car repairs. Three states (California, Delaware, and Ohio) have agencies that regulate the arbitration programs run by manufacturers. If you live in one of these states, all you need to do is file a complaint against the manufacturer with the state's Consumer Protection Agency. It in turn will notify the manufacturer that it is required to participate in arbitration and must report to a hearing within a specified time, typically 15 days.

Court

If direct negotiation and arbitration or private dispute-resolution programs don't work, you can take your case to court. As noted, the automotive industry's arbitration programs are binding only on the car manufacturer or dealer, not you, so taking your claim to them first doesn't change your right to sue—unless, of course, you agree to be bound by the arbitration. If you decide to sue, consider small claims court before municipal or district court (see Chapter 4).

In a civil suit over auto repairs, the burden is on you to prove that the repairs were made in a deceptive or negligent way. If you were quoted an estimate in writing and the final bill exceeds it by much more than the allowed margin, proving deception shouldn't be too hard. However, proving that the mechanic did shoddy work or was negligent may well require testimony by an expert who has inspected the repairs and can testify that the mechanic's work was fraudulent or incompetent. Expect additional time commitments and expenses in lining up such expert testimony, plus the court's fees and, if you decide to be represented, your lawyer's fee.

Resources

For a regional office in your area that offers an automotive arbitration program, contact:

Automotive Consumer Action Program (AUTOCAP)
National Automobile Dealers Association
8400 Westpark Dr.
McLean, VA 22102
(703) 821-7000

BBB AUTO LINE
Council of Better Business Bureaus
1515 Wilson Blvd.
Arlington, VA 22209
(703) 276-0100

Chrysler Customer Arbitration Board
P.O. Box 1718
Detroit, MI 48288
(800) 992-1997

Ford Customer Appeals Board
P.O. Box 1805
Dearborn, MI 48121
(313) 337-6950

Check your local library or bookstore for the following auto-repair guides.

Mr. Badwrench: How You Can Survive the $20 Billion-a-Year Auto-Repair Ripoff. Arthur P. Glickman. Seaview/Wideview Books, 1633 Broadway, New York, NY 10019. 1981 (out of print). 447 pages.

The Armchair Mechanic. Jack Gillis and Tom Kelly. Harper & Row, 10 E. 53rd St., New York, NY 10022. 1988. 176 pages. $8.95.

The Complete Consumer Car Guide. Mike Spaniola. McGraw-Hill Book Co., 1221 Ave. of the Americas, New York, NY 10020. 1987. 249 pages. $9.95.

The Last Chance Garage: A System-by-System Guide to Understanding How Your Car Runs, Why It Occasionally Doesn't, and What You Can Do About It. Brad Sears. Harper & Row, 10 E. 53rd St., New York, NY 10022. 1984 (out of print). 148 pages.

The Shell Auto Care Guide: Tips on Everything You Need to Know as a Car Owner and Driver. Ross R. Olney. Simon and Schuster, 1230 Sixth Ave., New York, NY 10020. 1986 (out of print). 286 pages.

For free brochures that explain how to get hassle-free auto repairs, contact the following:

Communicate with Your Mechanic and Save. Automotive Information Council, P.O. Box 273, Southfield, MI 48037.

Tips on Car Repair. Better Business Bureau, 1515 Wilson Blvd., Arlington, VA 22209.

CHAPTER

14

CONTRACT LANGUAGE

When getting your car repaired, your written estimate and the "repair order" are one and the same. The repair order is so important that many states have laws that excuse you from paying for services if you have not signed one. When you sign it, it authorizes the repair shop to make the repairs or adjustments listed on the order. The following is a typical auto repair contract.

Repair Order

Customer's Name:_____

Customer's Address:_____

Telephone Numbers: *(day)*_____ *(night)*_____

Vehicle: *(make)*_____ *(year)*_____ *(lic. no.)*_____

Odometer:_____

Customer's description of malfunction: *(explain symptoms)*

_____

_____

Repair dealer's diagnosis of these malfunctions: *(mechanic's explanation of the problem)*_____

_____

Promised Completion Date:_____

Service Required: *(mechanic's description)*_____

_____

Parts Description: *(mechanic's list of necessary parts)*_____

_____

Estimate: Time _____   Parts _____   Labor _____

                _____   _____   _____

                _____   _____   _____

                _____   _____   _____

(Mechanic will enter the hours spent, the prices of parts used, and the labor costs involved.)

Parts total: _____

Labor total: _____

Estimate charge: _____

Storage charge: _____

Total repair charge: _____

Tax: _____

TOTAL ESTIMATE: _____

I hereby authorize and agree to pay for all repairs described in the estimate column: _____

Customer's Signature: _____

Date: _____

I want ___ do not want ___ any replaced parts returned to me.

Oral Authorization of Repairs

Notice to Customer—Estimate:

YOU HAVE THE RIGHT TO RECEIVE A WRITTEN ESTIMATE WHICH IS SIGNED BY YOU AND THE DEALER *BEFORE REPAIR SERVICES ARE AUTHORIZED AND BEGUN.*

If, for technical reasons, we are unable to give you a written estimate at the time we are accepting your vehicle for repair, we would not be permitted to proceed with repairs unless you waive your right to a written estimate.

Therefore, if you wish to waive this right, you may do so by signing the waiver below.

"I hereby waive my right to a written estimate prior to authorizing repairs, but substitute oral communications of the same."

Signed: ___*(your signature)*___   Date _____

Notice to Customer:

You will be assessed an estimate charge if you elect not to proceed with repairs after you receive the estimate. If customer orally authorizes repair based on oral communication of the estimate, or modification of estimate costs, reflect oral consent here:

Communication by _____

Authorized by _____

Time _____ Date _____

Service Dealer: Name of Company _____

Date_____

The typical repair order is a preprinted form that comes with three or four carbon copies. The shop gives you a copy, keeps a copy, and sends one to your credit card company if that is the way you are paying.

Make sure the mechanic fills out the repair order completely and accurately to reflect your agreement.

All the following information should be included:

Name and Address: Your full name and current address.

Year, Make, Model, and Tag Number of the car being repaired.

Day and Night Telephone Numbers: It's important to leave a number where you can be reached. The mechanic may need to reach you, for example, to tell you the estimate on repairs or to get your approval before doing additional but necessary work. If a mechanic can't reach you during the day, chances are the car will not be repaired because the mechanic will not want to risk not getting paid for the extra work.

Mileage and Date: Noting the current mileage and date at the time of repair may be important if you later have to rely on the terms of the warranty. You may not receive compensation under the warranty if you have no record of what the mileage was when the parts were installed.

It's also a good idea to keep a record of the dates and mileage at which certain repairs and checkups are done. That will serve as a "proof of maintenance" record if you ever try to sell your car.

Specific Work to Be Done: Make sure the mechanic identifies in writing on the repair order the "symptoms" of the problem as well as the specific work that will be done. That way, if the symptoms persist (e.g., rattling under the hood) after the repair, you'll have proof the car wasn't repaired properly.

Parts and Labor: Estimates for both parts and labor should be included. They're generally listed in separate columns, side by side. If the mechanic is unable to make estimates when you leave the car, make sure the repair order reflects that no work on the car will begin until you have approved an oral estimate by the mechanic.

Exploratory or Estimate Charges: If part of your car has to be disassembled before an estimate can be given, make sure the mechanic writes down the amount you'll have to pay for that work.

Mechanic's Name: Get the name of the person who will work on your car so you know whom to talk to should you have any questions or should problems occur later.

PART V

LEGAL SERVICES PLANS

CHAPTER
15

"PREPAID" LAWYERS

Lynne runs a small boutique in Boston. From time to time, she needs legal advice about handling employees, dealing with customers, and running the store. Her lawyer is always available to help, but at $125 an hour, Lynne is sometimes reluctant to call him.

Janet recently received a mailing that urged her to join a prepaid legal services plan. For less than $15 a month, it offers her unlimited access to lawyers and certain legal documents for free. While it sounds like a good deal, she wonders if, as a homemaker with three kids, she really needs something like this.

At his new job, Mark receives dental, health, and legal insurance benefits. He expected health insurance, but was surprised to discover that he could also participate in a legal services plan at no cost.

Today, 45 million people participate in legal services plans like those referred to above. Most participate through their unions, associations, or employers. Of those participating, 90% are covered under *group* legal services plans, those usually offered through the workplace and not made available to the public. The remaining 10% belong to *individual* or *private* plans offered directly to the public through direct mail, telemarketing, and door-to-door sales. Ordinarily, anyone can join an individual plan. The exceptions are plans sold solely to the members of a specific credit card company or credit union. Because these individual plans involve payment of an annual or monthly fee *before* legal services can be rendered, they are called *prepaid.*

Prepaid legal plans offer members limited services for a flat yearly or monthly fee. Besides giving ready access to lawyers at lower-than-normal rates for basic legal advice, they eliminate the time clients have to spend "shopping" for a lawyer. Under most plans, lawyers have been preselected for them.

Like health maintenance organizations (HMOs), prepaid legal plans rely on the economy of spreading the risk among a large group of people with the expectation that only a few will take advantage of the benefits. They also mirror HMOs in their emphasis on "preventive law."

In general, legal services plans are beneficial because they allow groups of people to pool their purchasing power to get legal services free or at reduced prices. However, not everyone needs to belong to a plan. Some people go through life without ever needing to contact a lawyer. Others find only an infrequent need for a lawyer's help. Evaluate your legal needs carefully before joining a plan, and then, if you want to join, shop carefully for the plan that best meets those needs. How successful legal services plans will be is still speculative, because they are relatively new.

This chapter explains how the plans operate, the different types available, and their relative advantages and disadvantages. It focuses on plans offered to individuals, but the description of typical bene-fits should also be helpful to members of group plans.

Individual Versus Group Plans

Individual plans usually have a higher per-member operating cost than do group plans because they don't have the economic advan-tage of drawing on a large pool of available participants.

In group plans, the sponsor (employer, union, or association) may pay all or part of the membership fees. In individual plans, each member is responsible for the entire annual or monthly fee.

A group plan may or may not be *prepaid*. If no advance fee is required of the group or its members, it is "free." The largest "free" group legal plan, called Union Privilege Legal Services, is offered by the AFL-CIO. It is subscribed to by 49 of its labor unions, with over 10 million members.

In an individual, prepaid legal services plan, an annual or monthly fee is paid in advance in exchange for advice from a lawyer and other, specified routine legal help. The fee, normally referred to as the membership or enrollment fee, is paid either by the sponsoring group or by individual members. If the sponsoring group pays the fee, its members are considered *automatically* enrolled. If members pay, membership begins only after the fee is paid.

Whether it's a group or private plan, a *plan administrator* is responsible for promoting the plan, handling its finances, enrolling members, and paying the fees owed to participating lawyers.

Government Regulation

At least 25 states have specific legislation that governs the way these plans can operate. Some states regulate plans as insurance, while others have statutes that give special jurisdiction to the insurance commissioner but treat the plans as special entities.

To find out how a particular plan is regulated in your state, contact the state insurance commissioner, listed in the telephone book under your state government offices, or the National Resource Center for Consumers of Legal Services, whose address and phone number are on page 153.

What Plans Offer

Because members can consult lawyers without charge, they tend to go to them early, to use them as advisers, and to seek their opinions on subjects not normally referred to lawyers. The adage "An ounce of prevention is worth a pound of cure" is applied on the theory that early information can prevent the need for expensive intervention down the line.

The type, size, coverage, and cost of these plans vary widely. The coverage can also change depending on the state you live in. For instance, Prepaid Legal Services, Inc., operates several different plans; the one available in California is different from the one in Oklahoma.

Most plans, group or individual, offer help in selecting a lawyer, unlimited legal counseling, telephone and letter follow-ups, will-drafting, document review, and reduced rates for legal matters that go beyond what's offered for the annual membership fee. Some offer litigation services.

Help in Selecting Lawyers

Under most plans, the administrator decides which lawyer will be assigned to your legal matter. A few plans allow you to select your own lawyer or to select from a panel of lawyers. The advantage of getting a single lawyer or group of lawyers to pick from is that you don't have to spend time "shopping." The disadvantage is that you lose control and freedom to choose whom you'll work with.

We suggest that when you evaluate plans, you ask if you will be allowed to switch lawyers if the one you work with turns out to be unsatisfactory. Find out how difficult this is to do. Is the plan receptive to such requests, or will you be forced to wait a long time because you want a different lawyer?

Ask also if you can get advance information about the plan's participating lawyers. Typically, such advance information is given only to members who ask for it. Try to find out how long the plan lawyers have been in practice, what areas of law they practice, and whether they carry malpractice insurance. (HALT research shows that plan lawyers have generally been in practice at least five years and are required by plan administrators to carry malpractice insurance.)

Unlimited Telephone Counseling

Most plans offer unlimited telephone consultation. In other words, you can pick up the telephone during normal working hours and get a lawyer at the other end without worrying about the cost. Typically, the number of calls you can make is unlimited, as long as each call is about a new matter. There's also no limit on the amount of time you spend talking. However, you cannot keep calling back about the same problem. Members use this service to get quick advice about such things as resolving a problem with a neighbor, business, or service professional or dealing with traffic violations, simple estate-planning questions, or housing or rental agreements.

With some plans, you do not always get to speak to the same lawyer and therefore have to establish a new relationship, explain who you are and what the problem is, and evaluate again the competence of the person you're speaking to.

If you like the idea of developing a continuing working relationship with one lawyer, ask if that can be accommodated by the plan you're considering.

Office Visits

Under most plans, you also have the option of an in-person visit for any new legal problems. Each office consultation usually has a time limit of one hour or less, however.

If you want to meet with the lawyer more than once on the same legal matter, you will be charged at the plan's hourly rate. That can be from $50 to $100 an hour. Incurring additional expenses this way can be avoided, however, if you can resolve legal matters over the telephone or by asking the lawyer to make a call or write a letter on your behalf.

Follow-ups

Follow-up correspondence, by either telephone or letter, is included under most plans. Some plans allow their lawyers to handle an unlimited number of calls or free letters on your behalf, but others limit such follow-up work. For example, a lawyer may be able to make only one call *or* write one letter on your behalf per problem, per year of membership. If you think you require a lot of lawyer intervention (for example, to deal with ongoing business or unruly-neighbor problems), you'll want a plan that doesn't restrict the amount of "follow-up" help a lawyer can give you.

Documents

For your membership fee, most plans also draft a simple will and review legal documents like rental agreements, incorporation papers, and repair contracts. A few plans go beyond this, adding documents such as deeds or powers of attorney.

Even simple legal documents like wills can cost as much as $200 in some parts of the country. A legal services plan will draw up a will and provide other benefits for less than that. Be careful, however, when shopping for a plan. Find out what's meant by a "simple will" and whether it will take care of your full estate-planning needs. For example, can a "simple will" include drawing up a minor's trust? How many beneficiaries can be named? Does the plan charge extra if you need to make changes down the line? Some plans include changes *(codicils)* at no extra charge. Will the plan charge extra for your spouse's will?

Does the plan limit the number and length of legal documents you can submit for free review each year? Most plans don't limit the number, but do limit how many pages each document can have—usually fewer than 10 pages. Some plans also refuse to review documents that don't have your name on them. In sum, if drafting documents is a major concern, you would do well to consider an appropriate plan.

Reduced Rates

Plans may also offer guaranteed prices on more complex legal matters, like complex estate planning, real estate transactions, adoptions, and divorces. This can be a savings, but it can also be a money drain in disguise. Check prices with lawyers outside the plan to make sure you're getting the best deal and the most suitable lawyer for your task. You might also consider handling some of your legal matters on your own to keep legal costs down. For example, a plan may offer "name changes for $155," which sounds reasonable, but only until you learn you can easily change your name on your own by going down to the courthouse and filing a piece of paper—for a nominal filing fee.

Litigation Services

Don't expect legal services plans to handle any litigation for free. Most do not provide free lawyer representation in court, and of those that do, most exclude criminal cases, services for which a percentage fee is generally charged (such as personal-injury suits), and appeals. Prepaid Legal Services, Inc., for example, provides lawyer representation for members when they are being sued, but not for members who file lawsuits against someone else.

Most plans do, however, provide free advice about litigation and will appoint a litigation lawyer to represent you at reduced hourly rates. Make sure any appointed lawyer is qualified to handle your case. You may find a more qualified and competitively priced lawyer off the plan.

Other Considerations

Ask where the plan is available and whether you can still get coverage if you move or travel out of state. Will the plan accommodate your needs if you live in Ohio but get into trouble with an auto repair shop or traffic court in Michigan?

By making access easier and less expensive, plans encourage people who have legal questions or problems to consult lawyers more often, but you should be careful of becoming too dependent on lawyers. Instead of meeting the plans' objective of lowering legal expenses, such dependency could end up increasing your legal costs.

Types of Plans

Legal services plans vary considerably but divide into two basic categories—access and comprehensive plans.

Access Plans

These concentrate on giving members easy access to lawyers for routine legal services. They are typically offered to individuals, and provide free and often unlimited telephone consultations with lawyers, a review of legal documents up to six or seven pages long, and preparation of a simple will. For more complex legal matters, members are referred to a panel of participating lawyers who agree to perform legal services at discounted prices.

Comprehensive Plans

As their name implies, these cover every legal need you have. They are offered only to groups, *not* to individual members of the public. Typically, an employer sponsors a comprehensive plan as a benefit to employees, who participate for free.

Comprehensive plans give the same benefits as access plans and then some. For example, at no additional cost to the employee, lawyers draft any legal document and provide legal representation in or out of court. The plans even reimburse their members for legal expenses or fees they incur (for example, defending against traffic citations).

Open and Closed Panels

All plans also can be distinguished by how they deliver legal services to their members—through one of two arrangements: *closed panels* or *open panels*. Premiums in open-panel systems are generally higher than in closed-panel systems for a simple reason: Open panels give you more choices among lawyers.

Most plans operate closed panels, whereby an agreement is

reached with a limited number of lawyers to provide legal assistance to all plan members. In general, for a set price the plan manager either hires a group of lawyers to work for plan members or contracts with a law firm to do all the work. Closed plans generally offer you a greater variety of legal services *and* lower premiums.

One disadvantage of the closed-panel system is that members have little or no voice in choosing which lawyers do their legal work. Some closed plans assign you to a specific lawyer, others allow you to choose one from a limited list. Because legal advice is only as good as the lawyer giving it, it's important to find out if you can dismiss an unsatisfactory lawyer and select or be appointed to another.

Open-panel plans allow you to choose your lawyer from a list. Under this system, each lawyer is paid only for the work performed. The lawyer agrees to a schedule of fixed fees for the services offered. Each lawyer is paid by the plan as the specific work is done, much as doctors are paid by health insurance companies. In open-panel systems, while you have greater freedom of choice, lawyers are not guaranteed a certain amount of legal business from the plan and therefore have little incentive to charge below their normal rates.

Shopping for a Plan

1. If you already have a lawyer who is frequently available and charges reasonable prices, there is probably little reason to join a plan.

2. If you have a legal problem that needs immediate attention, spend your time and energy looking for appropriate help, not shopping for a plan. Even though you may find a plan that assigns you to a lawyer immediately, you're leaving it to chance that you'll be referred to the best lawyer for the problem at hand. It makes more sense to shop for a legal services plan when you have time and aren't influenced by specific, pressing concerns.

3. Send for information on all available plans. The National Resource Center for Consumers of Legal Services can send you a list of the major ones and their addresses. Simply send a stamped, self-addressed envelope to the address on page 152.

4. Don't be pressured by aggressive sales language in direct mail solicitation into signing anything before you're ready. These plans need many members to successfully continue offering low membership rates. Your money will be accepted when you're ready to give it.

5. Learn all you can about the history and operations of the organization that's running the program to be sure it's reputable. Plan representatives should be willing to answer such questions as:
   - How long has the program been in operation? (New plans have yet to demonstrate a track record or develop a full array of smoothly operating services.)
   - How many lawyers participate in the plan? Has the number increased or decreased during the past year? (A growing plan is healthier and more likely to meet your future needs.)
   - Are panels open or closed?
   - Can you switch lawyers if you're unhappy with the one appointed to you?
   - How big is the plan? How many people have enrolled?
   - Does it include a grievance or complaint system?
   - Does it allow you to evaluate services annually and drop your membership if you're unsatisfied?
   - What happens if the plan goes out of business? Do you get a refund?
   - What references can they furnish?

CHAPTER
16

SOLVING PROBLEMS

If you have a problem with a legal services plan lawyer, your options are the same as when you have a problem with any lawyer, plus one: You can also turn to plan administrators for help.

Unfortunately, many of the usual places you can turn to for help with consumer problems, such as government-run Consumer Affairs Offices and private Better Business Bureaus, do not handle complaints against lawyers.*

As soon as you become aware of a potential lawyer-client problem, contact your lawyer to discuss it and make sure it's not simply a breakdown in communication. Sometimes problems can be resolved quickly with a telephone call and follow-up letter. Communicate concerns in writing to develop a written record of your attempts to resolve problems.

---

*A full discussion of handling problems with your lawyer can be found in HALT's *Using a Lawyer* by Kay Ostberg, Random House, 1990. Most of the information in the remainder of this chapter is derived from that book and is presented here only as a brief overview.

If your plan lawyer refuses to communicate with you or refuses to try to resolve the problem responsibly, complain to the plan sponsor. If an "800" hot line is available, call there. Ask a company representative to serve as an intermediary between you and the lawyer. The company can't compel the lawyer to act a certain way or to refund your money, but it does have the power to remove the lawyer from its list of approved attorneys. While that may not help you directly, the threat of being booted may be incentive enough for a lawyer to shape up. Whether or not the lawyer is removed, if you chose wisely, your plan probably will let you pick a new lawyer to continue your case.

If direct negotiation with the lawyer and working through the plan administrator don't solve your problem, you have four options:

Client Security Trust Funds

In every state except Maine and New Mexico, the state bar association has a special fund to reimburse money stolen from clients by their lawyers. Whether or not you can collect from the fund is up to the bar association, however. You have no legal *right* to collect from the fund or to challenge it if your claim is rejected. Also, most programs limit the amount they will refund (usually $15,000 to $25,000), regardless of how much was stolen. To find out how to file a claim with your state program and what its limitations are, contact the state bar association.

Fee Arbitration

If you have a dispute over your lawyer's fee, you may be able to take it to a fee-arbitration program, also run by the bar. Unfortunately, arbitration is not always available, and in most states lawyers unwilling to arbitrate can't be required to. In any case, these programs are of limited value because most of the arbitrators are lawyers and because they aren't allowed to consider malpractice issues in deciding whether or not to reduce a lawyer's fee. To find out more about fee arbitration, contact your state bar.

Attorney Discipline

Every state has a lawyer-discipline agency, many of them run by the state bar. You can ask your state's discipline committee to repri-mand, suspend from practice, or disbar your lawyer. You can't receive compensation through this process, however, even if mis-conduct is proven.

Lawyer-discipline systems are slow, secret, and lenient. Of the approximately 70,000 complaints filed each year, fewer than 2% result in suspension or disbarment. Nevertheless, people should file complaints because this is the only forum that has authority to remove unethical or incompetent lawyers from practice. Each com-plaint helps establish the pattern necessary to convince an agency to take action.

Suing for Malpractice

As always, suing should be your final recourse because of the time and expense involved. If you do win a malpractice suit, you can be awarded money and, sometimes, attorney fees. However, legal mal-practice cases are extremely difficult and expensive: You must prove that your lawyer did not use the skill, care, and diligence ordinarily used by lawyers *and* that, as a result of this negligence, you lost money. To prove your lawyer failed to use appropriate care, you must hire an expert witness willing to testify to that. To prove the lawyer's misconduct caused you to lose money, in some instances you must retry the original case you thought the lawyer should have won. This is called the "trial within a trial," and can make your case very expensive indeed.

Finally, it can often be hard to find a lawyer willing to represent you in suing another lawyer for malpractice. Lawyers estimate that if your claim is not worth more than $10,000, it is not economical to sue. Many lawyers won't even take cases unless the potential "win" is at least $50,000. Don't go it alone, however. Taking on your adversary on your adversary's turf, the courtroom, is not easy. If you are considering a malpractice suit, consult HALT's *Directory of Lawyers Who Sue Lawyers,* which contains a state-by-state list of lawyers willing to sue for legal malpractice, plus tips on how to assess the merits of your malpractice case.

Resource

For more information on legal services plans, contact:

The National Resource Center for Consumers of Legal Services
1444 Eye St. NW, 8th Floor
Washington, DC 20005
(202) 842-3503

CHAPTER

17

CONTRACT LANGUAGE

The "contract" to join an individual legal services plan is a simple form that briefly describes the agreement and refers you to a brochure for more details about the terms and benefits of membership. The form simply requires your signature and, if you're paying by credit card, the number.

The information you need to know about the plan is covered *not* in the agreement form but in the brochure. Most such brochures are written in plain language with a lot of sales talk. These promotional brochures list both the free benefits you get by joining the plan and the benefits that are available at reduced rates.

The following section describes one typical plan, Montgomery Ward Enterprises Legal Services Plan, mailed to Montgomery Ward credit card holders. An identical plan, Legal Services Plan of America, also marketed by Montgomery Ward, is offered by major credit card companies and banks to their subscribers.

This plan is representative of an "access" legal services plan. Clarification of the benefits is based both on this contract and on the company's related materials. One final note: if at any time you want to drop your subscription, all you need to do is write a letter to that effect to the plan's administrator.

Montgomery Ward Enterprises is Proud to Offer . . .

A new, much needed approach to legal services protection which can immediately benefit you and your family.

Join this plan and you and your immediate family will be covered for much of the personal and family legal work you would normally expect to require.

For a monthly fee of only $6.75, you and your family will immediately retain the professional services of a firm of attorneys located near your home or office. The plan attorneys are qualified, in private practice and are licensed by your state.

2,380 lawyers from 680 law firms participate in this plan. To be eligible, they must have been in practice at least three years. According to a plan representative, its lawyers have practiced an average of 13.5 years. However, keep in mind that whether they're qualified to handle your case has more to do with their experience at handling similar problems than the fact they're licensed. All practicing lawyers have to be licensed by the state.

This language also states that you and your immediate family are covered. "Immediate family" includes your spouse and dependents.

Coverage commences the moment you are enrolled in the Montgomery Ward Enterprises Legal Services Plan.

IMPORTANT: This enrollment period is limited. Your Enrollment Certificate *must* be received on or before the deadline indicated in order to be eligible. No exceptions will be permitted.

This is an example of a high-pressure sales pitch. *Ignore it.* If you don't respond "in time," you will probably receive another solicitation later, with a different deadline, or you can call or send in your membership information at any time.

The Comprehensive Montgomery Ward Enterprises Legal Services Plan provides much of the legal services normally required.

As a member of the Montgomery Ward Enterprises Legal Services Plan, you will be banding together with thousands of others who will enjoy the benefits of comprehensive legal services.

In effect, joining the Montgomery Ward Enterprises Legal Services Plan puts a group of experienced, professional attorneys on retainer for you and your family. All you pay is the modest monthly fee of just $6.75.

The Plan has two parts:
A) Prepaid Benefits *(services covered by your membership fee)*
B) Bonus Benefits *(services not covered but offered at reduced prices)*

The information on the following pages details your benefits and addresses a number of important questions you may have.

Please read this material *now.* Remember, this enrollment period is limited. Your Enrollment Certificate *must* be returned on or before the deadline indicated in order to be eligible. No exceptions will be permitted.

Exceptions are the rule here. If they weren't, the plan would go out of business in short order. This sales letter from Montgomery Ward appears with a number of different "deadlines," depending when it was mailed. These aren't true deadlines; they are simply "Buy now!" exhortations.

Prepaid Benefits

1) *Unlimited Consultation and Advice by Phone or Mail*

As soon as we enroll you in the Montgomery Ward Enterprises Legal Services Plan, your plan attorneys will immediately be at your service for consultation and advice during normal business hours concerning any personal or family legal problem you might have. You'll never again have to hesitate about seeking advice from your plan attorneys because you're concerned about cost. Simply call the plan attorneys at the phone number on your membership card and they will be ready to help you.

This states that you can call and get a lawyer as soon as the company processes your check or gets your credit card number and sends you a membership card. On that card is the telephone number

of the law firm that has been preselected for you. The plan administrator will pick a lawyer from the firm that's nearest you. Each time
you call or write, you will get that same law firm. (Other plans use
a lawyer "hot line" to take calls. Their members do not speak to the
same lawyer twice, except by chance.)

The Montgomery Ward plan also includes an "800" number to
call if you want an administrator to assign you a different lawyer.
Under this plan, you are not given information on a variety of
lawyers and then allowed to pick the one you want, but you may
later ask to switch if you're not happy with the lawyer picked for
you.

Your lawyer is responsible for answering all your personal or
family legal problems. While most plans provide such free consultation on any legal matter, including criminal matters or litigation
problems, you will have to pay extra if you need in-court representation. The lawyers in most plans accept such additional legal work
at reduced hourly rates.

The number of times you can call or write your lawyer is unlimited in this plan, as is how long your telephone call can last. However, you must call during "normal" business hours. Ask what's
normal for *your* lawyer. It may be 9:00 A.M. to 5:00 P.M., or 7:00
A.M. to 3:00 P.M. Under this plan, anyone in your immediate family
can call, even your fifteen-year-old.

2) *Unlimited Legal Letters and Phone Calls on Your Behalf*

It could be quite costly, without the Montgomery Ward Enterprises
Legal Services Plan, to have an attorney handle legal matters because you
would normally be charged hourly rates for your attorney's time. Under the
plan, your plan attorneys will make telephone calls and write letters which
you both agree are necessary, at no additional charge to you.

Under this plan, your appointed lawyer will handle all the telephone calls and letters you need to resolve your legal problem. The
number of such letters and phone calls that can be made for you is
unlimited in most states.

To comply with state regulations, however, Arkansas, Indiana, Nebraska, and Virginia residents must pay $5 for each letter or phone call a plan lawyer handles for them, and New York residents are limited to three letters or phone calls a year, no more than two of which can be related to the same matter. Other plans, such as Prepaid Legal Services, allow only one letter or call per problem per year.

The Montgomery Ward plan also requires that your lawyer agree that the letters and calls you want are really necessary to resolve your problem. If you disagree, the plan administrator may be able to help you and the attorney resolve the disagreement. If not, see Chapter 16, Solving Problems.

It isn't as bad as it may seem, however, because the lawyer has an incentive to keep you satisfied. Because the lawyer can be required to handle an unlimited number of calls and letters for you, it's in the lawyer's interest to resolve the problem as quickly as possible. Also, the lawyer hopes you will develop a good working relationship so you will return for more help on matters that aren't covered by the plan.

3) *A Simple Personal Will for You and Your Immediate Family*

As soon as you receive your membership card for the plan, you can request the preparation of a simple will for you or any member of your immediate family. Don't worry about cost, you're totally covered. What's more, if at any time it is necessary to have your will updated, your plan attorneys will attend to it at no additional charge. This is just one example of the many benefits you receive as a member of the Montgomery Ward Enterprises Legal Services Plan.

This is typical of most plans. It says you and anyone in your immediate family can get a simple will executed. (In New York, members and spouses are each entitled to one free will and annual updates. Arkansas, Nebraska, and Virginia residents are charged $15 for this service.)

As defined by the plan, a simple will "distributes the property generally and does not involve any trusts, complex tax considerations or guardianships for minor children." It's important to find out in advance how "simple" a will must be to qualify. Be sure the will you get takes care of your needs. If you want more complex estate planning (e.g., creating a trust for your children or leaving the dining-room set to your daughter and the Oriental rugs to your son), the "simple will" is not for you. It is only for people who want to leave their property to one person or divide it equally among a number of people. If you need something more complex, you can get it, but at additional cost.

4) Document Review

Many legal problems are the result of parties entering into undesirable or unfair agreements. You may avoid a potential costly legal dispute by having an attorney examine an agreement before you sign it. Yet, all too often, many citizens fail to do so (and suffer as a consequence) because they are fearful of the expense. You need not fret about such costs. Your plan attorneys will review any legal document as long as six pages—leases, real estate papers, installment and rental contracts, promissory notes, bills of sale, powers of attorney, affidavits, and a variety of other legal documents. Cost? You're covered! (If the document is longer than six pages, it will be reviewed at the guaranteed rate of no more than $50 an hour.)

This plan allows for an unlimited number of legal documents to be reviewed by your plan lawyer during your membership, as long as each document is no longer than six pages. Most plans offer a document review option and place similar restrictions on it.

Under this plan, you do not need to be named in the document to have it reviewed. For example, you could present a rental agreement for review before signing it. Some plans do require your name to be on any document you ask to have reviewed.

5) Warranty Problems

Your plan attorneys will assist you on your warranty problems. They'll write letters and make phone calls on your behalf. And if you have to go to court on the matter, they can be there to represent you for no more than $50 an hour.

Both service and product warranties are covered by this plan. For example, you are promised free advice or help if you're having a problem with the way a contractor renovated your kitchen or the way a vacuum cleaner operates before its warranty expires.

6) *Initial Face-to-Face Consultation on Any New Legal Problem*

When you are confronted by a new legal problem that can't be handled by telephone or letters, you may consult with your plan attorneys on a face-to-face basis. You are completely covered on a prepaid basis for any and all such initial personal consultations.

This entitles you to one visit to your lawyer's office for each new problem. If you must discuss the same legal problem in person more than once, it will cost you $50 an hour. That rate is a good price in most areas of the country and a great price in larger metropolitan areas. However, your plan lawyer will discuss the matter over the telephone as often as you want, within reason, at no extra charge.

Some plans allow unlimited office visits, while others don't allow even one.

7) *Advice on Small Claims Court*

If you go to small claims court to settle a grievance, your plan attorneys will give you advice on how to prepare and present your case and how to complete necessary forms.

This is true of all plans. The type of help you get on any legal matter depends on the lawyer giving it, however. Some lawyers get a lot of requests for information about small claims court and have prepared written materials on the process for their clients. Others give clients a brief "walk-through," and still others offer to help fill out the necessary court papers and discuss presentation styles.

Your lawyer will not go to court with you unless, again, you are willing to pay extra. At $50 an hour, travel, waiting, and court time can add up. Get whatever information you can in advance and then handle this kind of claim on your own. In any event, many small claims courts will not allow you to have a lawyer in court with you.

8) *Advice on Government Programs*

Your plan attorneys will assist you in locating the appropriate government agency to handle your Social Security, Medicare, veteran's benefits or other matters. Then they'll advise you on how the agency operates, where to go and what benefits you may be entitled to receive.

Some lawyers will put you in touch with the right people and give you information that can make collecting benefits a lot less trying. Others may be less acquainted with procedures. Expect the lawyer to charge extra if you ask to have the benefits collected for you.

9) *$1,000 Emergency Bail Bond Service*

Should you or any member of your immediate family ever need bail in a hurry, you need only call the 24-hour toll-free Bail Bond Hot Line phone number and a bail bond of up to $1,000 will be posted as soon as possible.

Depending on the state you live in, a $1,000 bail bond may cover only misdemeanors, traffic offenses, and some minor felonies. For example, many judges set bond at $1,000 in shoplifting and speeding cases. For more serious offenses, some judges demand $10,000 bail. Bond companies collect a 10 percent cash deposit for posting your bond.

Before taking advantage of this provision, ask how long you have to reimburse the bond and whether you'll be charged interest. Under this plan, you are not charged interest and you have at least thirty days to repay. Bail bond services are not included under the plans offered by either Hyatt or Prepaid Services.

Bonus Benefits

In addition to your prepaid benefits, the Montgomery Ward Enterprises Legal Services Plan gives you bonus benefits—which provide you with guaranteed maximum fees for six major legal matters, guaranteed rates on contingent fee matters and guaranteed maximum rates on all matters.

Guaranteed Maximum Fees for Six Legal Matters

Service	Maximum Fees for Plan Members
Uncontested Adoption*	$185.00*
Name Change	$155.00
Non-Commercial Real Estate Closing	$175.00
Will with Minor's Trust	$170.00
Non-Support of Spouse or Children	$240.00
Uncontested Divorce**	$210.00**

*Does not include termination of parental rights.
**Subject to a limit of net marital assets of $70,000, no children under the age of 18, the defendant spouse is not represented by an attorney and all issues are agreed to without negotiation by the plan attorney.

While the prices for these "simple" legal matters are relatively low compared to those of private lawyers in most places, be aware that many of these matters can be taken care of *without a lawyer* for even less.

Two quick examples are name changes and uncontested adoptions. To legally change your name in most states, all you need do is file a "name change" form with the appropriate court, then personally notify people and businesses you think should know about your new name. The cost of filing is usually $100 or less. Many uncontested adoptions also never involve a lawyer. Instead, an adoption agency tells the adopting parents what they need to know, including how to prepare for a hearing.

Still, if you don't feel comfortable handling legal matters on your own, these prices are at least better than average. According to a 1988 study by the National Resource Center for Consumers of Legal Services, the national average for real estate closings is $436, for uncontested divorces is $506, and for simple wills is $83.

Maximum Rates for Contingency Fee Cases

This is an important benefit. Contingency fee cases occur when you are suing someone for damages such as in personal injury and collection cases. The attorney agrees to being paid a contingency fee, a percentage of any financial recovery, rather than an hourly rate. It is important that you have control of this fee, as it directly impacts the net amount of any settlement or award you may actually receive.

Attorney contingency fees can go as high as 45%. (In some cases, the fees have been even higher!) You won't have any such worries. Your plan attorney's percentage is *guaranteed* not to exceed 29% of the recovery if settled before trial, 36% if settled or recovered during or after trial, or 40% if settled or awarded after an appellate brief is prepared. And it may, in fact, be even lower. In matters in which state statutes set the contingent attorney fee, the attorney fee charged will be 10% less than the statutory rate or the attorney's usual fee, whichever is less. For example, in Michigan, personal injury contingency fee rates are limited to 33.3%. There, if an attorney typically charges 33.3%, you would receive the plan rate of 29.9%—a 10% reduction.

This is *not* much of a discount. Contingency fees, almost always used in personal-injury cases, normally run about 30%, not 45%. If you hire a lawyer under this type of arrangement, shop around and see if you can get one to agree to a lower percentage. You may be able to bargain an outside lawyer down from 29%, since you already know you're guaranteed that rate by the plan's offer of 10% off the lawyer's usual rate.

Under standard contingency fee arrangements, if you win, the lawyer gets a percentage of the "take"; if you lose, the lawyer gets expenses but nothing else. The theory is that the lawyer should collect a large slice of the winnings in exchange for the risk of getting nothing; but be assured that any lawyer interested in taking your case is fairly confident of winning. In fact, the more lawyers you find interested in your case, the better your chances of bargaining down the percentage fee.

Guaranteed Rates on Hourly Charges!

On any matter not covered elsewhere, you will pay no more than $50 per hour. For instance, after your initial prepaid personal consultation, your plan attorneys will provide you with further personal consultation or represent you in court for no more than $50 per hour on matters where no maximum fee is involved.

This low hourly rate is much lower than many attorneys would charge the general public. Attorneys' hourly rates vary by years of experience, geographic location and other factors. However, one recently published survey reports the median rate that attorneys charge nationally for family law and general personal matters is $75 an hour—yet you pay no more than $50 an hour when you use Plan Attorneys.

Plus, remember that your initial personal consultation with your plan attorneys concerning any of these legal problems is already part of your prepaid benefits.

According to the 1988 study by the National Resource Center for Consumers of Legal Services, the average hourly rate for lawyers is between $85 and $90. That makes the $50 hourly rate charged by this plan pretty good, especially when you consider that lawyers in large metropolitan areas charge as high as $150 or $200 an hour. Again, however, before hiring a plan lawyer, explore other options for getting routine legal work done, and shop for a lawyer who has the experience to handle the matter at hand. For instance, a legal clinic may be able to help for less money or you may be able to do the work on your own with a do-it-yourself publication.

PART VI

RENTING A HOME

CHAPTER
18

RENTALS

Mary and Nancy have lived in their apartment three years and don't plan to move. Their landlord tells them he needs the apartment for his mother, who is being discharged from a nursing home in two weeks, and they will have to move.

Tim has rented his apartment five years and has kept it clean. He gives the landlord the required notice and moves out, but weeks later, he receives a check for only half of his original security deposit. The landlord says he kept the remainder to paint the apartment.

Jim rents from Jennifer, who lives downstairs. To save money, Jennifer stopped using an exterminator service, and Jim's apartment has become infested with mice. After unsuccessful attempts to get satisfaction from Jennifer, he calls the local housing authority to report the housing code violation and refuses to pay further rent until the mice are exterminated. A week later, Jennifer notifies Jim that he has to move.

In all these cases, the renters have rights they may not be aware of. This chapter explains such rights and what role the rental agreement plays in defining them.

For many, the first major contract we sign is when we rent a first house or apartment. Though most of us don't read our leases carefully beyond checking the amount of monthly rent and the length of the lease, it is only by understanding our rights and obligations that we can feel safe and comfortable in our home.

In recent decades, contract laws and court decisions have significantly changed the rights and responsibilities of landlords and tenants. As a result, the lease has evolved into what is basically a consumer contract, under which the landlord is obliged to maintain the property in a safe, sanitary, and habitable condition.

Pro-tenant laws have proliferated in most large urban areas, where the large number of renters constitutes a natural lobbying group. Some tenants' groups are so well organized they operate telephone "hot lines" that offer free advice. In small towns, however, landlord-tenant laws are less likely to be as pro-tenant, and consumer information is less likely to be generally available.

Types of Agreements

Every rental arrangement is governed by a contract. You will have either an oral agreement or a written agreement, called a *lease*.

Oral Agreements

Without putting it in writing, you and the landlord may verbally agree on the unit to be occupied, the date you will move in, the amount of rent you'll pay, and how often you'll pay it. Although such an oral lease is legal if the term is less than the limit specified in your state's laws (usually one year), *don't* rely on it unless you insist on flexibility and all the risk that entails.

An oral lease will allow you to move out on fairly short notice (typically a month), but you'll have no written record of any promises the landlord made—for instance, to make repairs or to allow you to move in by a specific date. Also, an unwritten lease allows the landlord some flexibility, too: for instance, to be rid of you or to raise the rent on fairly short notice. It's best to avoid oral rental agreements.

Leases

Leases are written rental agreements that cover a fixed time, typically a year. However, they can cover an indefinite or shorter time. The terms, such as the rent you pay, can't be changed while the lease is in effect. This means that a lease offers less flexibility but more security than an oral rental agreement, for both the tenant and the landlord.

Basic Rental Concepts

(This section should be read in conjunction with the explanations of standard lease terms in Chapter 20 and with the next chapter, Solving Problems.)

Housing Discrimination

Federal law forbids landlords to refuse to rent to anyone because of race, color, religion, national origin, or sex. The laws of most states and of some local governments prohibit discrimination on other grounds, such as marital status, sexual orientation, age, physical disability, political affiliation, or the presence of children.

Landlords may not refuse to rent on those grounds, nor may they discriminate in other ways, such as raising the rent for such people. Some landlords are exempt from these laws, however. For example, federal laws don't apply to buildings in which the landlord resides that have fewer than five units.

Landlords also can have valid reasons for refusing to rent. For instance, they may refuse a prospective renter because of a history of nonpayment of rent, or refuse to overcrowd a two-bedroom apartment with a family of seven. It sometimes can be difficult to tell whether a landlord is properly refusing to rent or shielding illegal discrimination behind a valid reason for refusal.

Evictions

All states have laws that govern when a tenant can be asked to leave the rental property, the reasons a landlord can evict, and the notices the landlord has to give before eviction. Typical reasons for allowing evictions include the tenant failing to pay rent or violating the lease by using the residence to operate a business or by housing too many people. Even when such a violation is invoked, however, landlords must follow strict guidelines set out in statutes and court decisions.

In most states, landlords must give notice at least 30 days before an eviction hearing is held. In just about every state, the landlord has to prove in court that the tenant received written notice of the hearing within the prescribed time limits.

If your landlord asks the court to evict you for nonpayment of rent, the court may allow you to "cure" this breach by paying the amount you owe. It is always worth attending the eviction hearing because the court may try to help you reach a compromise short of eviction. If the court does order your eviction, you usually are given a short time before you must leave. If you aren't out by that deadline, a state official will physically remove your belongings from the residence and lock you out. Sometimes a landlord can require you to move out even if you have not violated the lease. Many states, for instance, allow a landlord to ask a tenant to leave if extensive renovations are planned, or if the landlord or a family member plans to use the property as a principal residence. Thus, in the example at the beginning of this chapter, Mary and Nancy's landlord can legally ask them to leave so his mother can move into the apartment. The landlord must still give advance notice, however.

Utilities

Some landlords attempt to force tenants to move out by shutting off utilities. This is illegal. If complaining about it doesn't resolve the problem, you can get a court to order the utilities turned back on. In some states, the landlord can be fined under criminal laws, and in every state the tenant has the right to sue for damages. Also, any tenant forced to move out because the landlord shuts off the utilities does not owe rent for the remaining term of the lease.

Housing Codes

Housing codes set minimum standards of health and safety in rental housing in many states, and virtually every city has such a code, because without it, the city would not be eligible for federal urban renewal funds. If conditions in your rental unit do not seem to satisfy code requirements, try to get your landlord to agree in writing to fix them by a specific date. (See page 180 for information on code requirements in your area and how to enforce them.)

An *implied warranty of habitability* applies to rental agreements in many places. This means that, whether or not it is written into the lease, the landlord must keep rental property habitable. Some local housing codes define habitability; in other places, habitability standards are set out in state law, and in still others, court cases have defined habitability. Call your local housing agency and ask about code requirements in your area.

Before moving into a rental home, walk through it with the landlord and list all minor problems you can find (such as small cracks) so both you and the landlord know what you will and will not be responsible for when you move out. Some landlords will already have a list of items for you to check; add to that list if it is not complete.

In our opening example of Jim, Jennifer, and the mice, in most states Jim would be well within his rights to withhold rent, and Jennifer would have illegally retaliated by attempting to evict him. (Allowing mice to proliferate violates most, if not all, housing codes.) In some states, tenants may legally withhold their rent until housing code violations are corrected. After the violations are corrected, the tenant must pay the rent, but the amount owed may be reduced by a housing or landlord-tenant court, depending on the nature or seriousness of the violation. It is usually illegal to retaliate against a tenant for reporting a housing code violation.

Rent Control

Many localities have rent control laws, especially cities where affordable housing is scarce; these laws vary greatly. The "controls" on how much your rent can be increased may allow the landlord a specified percentage return on the value of the property, restrict annual increases to a specific percentage, or even restrict increases based on each tenant's ability to pay.

Also, rent control laws don't usually apply to all rental units in an area. For instance, they may apply only to landlords who own four or more rental units. Some laws exempt luxury rental housing, while others exempt owner-occupied buildings, new buildings, or single-family dwellings.

Deposits

Landlords may impose special advance fees or deposits as a condition of renting.

A security deposit is the most common. This is money the landlord holds as security against property damage, unpaid rent, and sometimes cleaning costs. Almost all states have laws that govern some aspect of the security deposit: the maximum that can be charged (usually two months' rent), conditions for returning it, the time within which it must be returned, and interest that must be paid on it for the period the landlord held it. Some local laws add other requirements.

In the example at the beginning of this chapter, Tim's landlord illegally withheld part of the security deposit. Security deposits cannot be used to pay for repairing normal wear and tear on the rental unit, such as repainting after five years. They can be used to cover unpaid rent, however, so if you break your lease by moving out early, rest assured your landlord will use your deposit to cover at least part of any rent lost because of your move. (See Renewing Your Lease, below.)

In some places, landlords charge special cleaning deposits to ensure that the premises are left as clean as they were when the tenant moved in. However, cleaning fees—nonrefundable charges used for cleaning and minor repairs—are not legal in some states. If your landlord attempts to charge such a nonrefundable fee, ask your local rental authority or housing agency if it's legal.

Some landlords require that you pay the *last* month's rent before you move in so that there is no difficulty collecting it when you move out. Be sure you and the landlord spell out, in writing, what these various advance costs are, and whether they are returnable. If you have any doubts, check state and local housing agencies to be sure the landlord is complying with them.

Subleasing and Assigning

Prohibitions on *subleasing* are usually legal. When subleasing is allowed, it's usually subject to the landlord's written approval of the subtenant. Ideally, such a provision in your original lease should state that the landlord can't *unreasonably* withhold approval. Some states' courts read this into leases even when it's not explicitly stated. Although subleasing can be convenient for tenants who, say, leave town for a few months, the tenant remains ultimately responsible to the landlord for the rent, the condition of the property, and the like.

Assigning the lease is not the same as subleasing. It means that someone else replaces you as the tenant in the original lease and you can *both* be held responsible for fulfilling the lease obligations. A lease that allows you to assign usually requires the landlord's consent. If you are the one to whom the lease is being assigned, be sure to get the assignment in writing.

Liability for Damage

The landlord's lease may include language disclaiming responsibility for any property damage or personal injury that results from the landlord's negligence in maintaining the property. In many areas, such a provision is illegal. Again, check with your housing agency.

Waivers

The landlord may include language that waives your right to notice, or the right to a jury trial in disputes over the lease. Most such waivers are illegal. If the landlord tries to take advantage of such a waiver, a court will refuse to enforce it and will void the clause though the rest of the lease will remain valid.

Right to Privacy

Not all states' laws specify when the landlord has a right to enter the rental property, but if a lease says the landlord may enter at any time and for any reason, you may have waived your right to privacy. More typically, leases specify the conditions and times landlords may enter. For instance, in some states landlords must give 24 hours' notice before entering to make repairs and may come in only between 9:00 A.M. and 5:00 P.M. Check with your housing agency for laws regarding your landlord's right to enter. If they don't provide guidelines, make sure it's covered in your lease.

Late Charges

Landlords may charge a *reasonable* fee for late rent payments. In some areas, this amount is limited by law. A *fixed* late charge might range from $5 to $35, depending on the amount of rent, and can be even higher for luxury apartments. An *incremental* late charge might start at $5 for the first day after the grace period and increase $2 every day after that, to a maximum of $25 or $35.

An unreasonable late charge is one that's out of proportion to the rent—for example, $50 for a $250 apartment. If your lease doesn't give you a grace period before the late charge applies—typically, three to five days—it's reasonable to ask for one, but recognize that the landlord may not be required by law to offer it.

Renewing Your Lease

Most leases renew themselves automatically. If yours is silent on the length of the renewal, it will renew itself for the length of the original term (typically, a year). However, the landlord does have the right to raise the rent at each lease's expiration.

If your lease explicitly requires that you return the property to the landlord when the lease expires, except in a few pro-tenant jurisdictions, you will have no right to renewal and will have to negotiate a new lease.

If your lease says nothing about renewal, state laws apply. Some states require you to return the property at the end of the lease term, other states have laws that automatically renew the lease month-to-month. If you want to move at the end of the lease and your lease has an automatic-renewal provision, you must notify the landlord a specified number of days in advance, typically 30. If you give notice, then change your mind and don't leave by the time you promised, you may be charged double rent as a penalty while you *hold over.*

If you decide to move before the lease expires, you may have to pay rent for the remaining life of the lease. If you have an oral agreement or are renting month-to-month, you're only obligated to give the landlord appropriate written notice (usually 30 days), and you aren't responsible for rent beyond that period. If you have a longer-term lease, the landlord must try to rent the property to someone else for the remaining lease period. This is the landlord's obligation to *mitigate damages,* explained in Chapter 2.

It's in your best interest to give written notice as far in advance of your intended moving date as you can, to give the landlord as much time as possible to rent the property to someone else, sparing you at least part of the rent due for the period after you leave. If the property is rented again, you will still have to pay any lost rent, however—either for the time the property was vacant or for any difference between the amount you were paying and any lesser amount the new tenant pays. If you leave before the end of your lease, the landlord will keep your security deposit to cover what you owe.

CHAPTER

19

SOLVING PROBLEMS

Landlord-tenant relations are heavily regulated—by federal, state, county, and city governments. If you have a landlord-tenant problem or anticipate having one, both public and private groups can help advise you on your rights.

Try to settle your dispute through direct negotiation with your landlord, then take your complaint to a rental-housing agency operated by state, county, or city government. They hold hearings on complaints that allege violations of rent-control laws, housing codes, the implied warranty of habitability, and sometimes discrimination. Hearing examiners usually can decide cases and award damages. (Some laws call for triple damages on proven overcharges.) Appeals usually go to a higher administrative body, and from there to court. Complainants may be required to exhaust these administrative remedies before going to court.

If you believe you have been discriminated against in a housing matter, contact your regional office of the Department of Housing and Urban Development (HUD). Addresses are listed in Appendix IV. For information on state or local housing discrimination laws, check with state fair housing offices and civil rights commissions. Both HUD and most state agencies have administrative procedures for filing discrimination complaints and enforcing the laws when violations are found.

Another way to fight discrimination is to sue your landlord in court, but this makes sense only when you have clear evidence of discrimination and can prove your damages were high. Otherwise, it may not be worth the legal fees and other expenses.

If you believe a rent increase violated rent control laws, find out if your local government has a rent control board. This office can tell you if the laws apply to your landlord and your rental unit, and if they are being applied correctly. Areas with rent control almost always have an administrative procedure for resolving disputes about rent adjustments.

If all or part of your security deposit is withheld unfairly, ask the landlord for a written statement explaining why. If that doesn't work, call your local rental housing agency to learn the procedure for filing a complaint. In some localities, the agency will not handle this type of complaint, in which case you will have to take your case to small claims court, or, if the claim is more than the court's limit, to higher court. That, unfortunately, will mean higher costs, greater delays, and added complexity.

If your rental home has health or safety violations, notify your landlord in writing that you want them corrected. If nothing happens, notify the housing agency and include a copy of your letter to the landlord. Ask the agency to send an inspector to look at the property. The landlord can be fined for violations and, in some states, you can withhold rent until they are corrected.

In some states, tenants can even use the code violations to defend themselves against lawsuits for nonpayment of rent. If a court or rental housing agency rules that such a defense is valid, it can reduce the amount of rent the tenant owes.

Resources

Books

Although many of the following books are written for landlords, the discussions and information can be useful to tenants in learning and enforcing their rights.

The Rights of Tenants. Richard E. Blumberg and James Grow. Avon Books, 105 Madison Ave., New York, NY 10016. (212) 481-5600. 1978 (out of print). 192 pages. $2.50.

A somewhat outdated source on tenants' legal rights. The book was written in association with the American Civil Liberties Union.

The Landlord's Law Book: Evictions. David Brown. Nolo Press, 950 Parker St., Berkeley, CA 94710. (415) 549-1976. 1986. 170 pages. $19.95.

A comprehensive manual on how to handle each step of an eviction and how to represent yourself in court.

The Landlord's Law Book: Rights and Responsibilities. David Brown and Ralph Warner. Nolo Press, 950 Parker St., Berkeley, CA 94710. (415) 549-1976. 1987. 175 pages. $24.95.

A comprehensive legal guide for landlords with sections on discrimination, insurance, tenants' privacy, leases, security deposits, rent control, liability, and rent withholding.

Landlord and Tenant Law. David S. Hill. West Publishing Co., P.O. Box 64526, St. Paul, MN 55164. (612) 228-2500. 1986. 311 pages. $10.95.

A compact format and reliable guide to the law for both students and lawyers. Uses legalese.

Landlords and Tenants: Your Guide to the Law. Scott Slonim. American Bar Association Press, 750 N. Lakeshore Dr., Chicago, IL 60611. (312) 988-5555. 1982. 48 pages. $3.

A short guide through landlord-tenant laws, giving a general understanding of the law. Useful glossary.

Organizations and Agencies

The U.S. Department of Housing and Urban Development (HUD).

This is the federal agency responsible for administering federal programs related to the nation's housing. HUD is divided into two sections: the Office of Fair Housing and Equal Opportunity and the Office of Neighborhoods, Voluntary Associations and Consumer Protection. The Office of Fair Housing is chiefly concerned with housing problems of lower-income and minority groups. The Office of Neighborhoods protects consumer interests in all housing and community-development activities. For information on available publications and services, contact the regional office near you. These are listed in Appendix IV.

National Housing Institute, 439 Main St., Orange, NJ 07050. (201) 678-3110.

This organization supports nationwide tenants' groups and is a resource for information on tenants' rights.

Legal Services Corporation (LSC), 400 Virginia Ave. SW, Washington, DC 20024. (202) 863-1820.

The LSC represents people who meet income guidelines in eviction cases and other landlord-tenant disputes. Call the national office, ask at your courthouse for a local referral, or check the government listings in your telephone directory.

The Tenants' Resource Center, 855 Grove St., Lansing, MI 48823. (517) 337-9795.

This is a Michigan-based organization whose pamphlets are valuable elsewhere, especially those on *Maintenance, Eviction,* and *Security Deposits.*

The National Housing Law Project, 122 C St. NW, Suite 220, Washington, DC 20001. (202) 783-5140.

This group, funded by LSC, is mainly a lawyer-training organization. It offers tenants a number of informational books and brochures. Write for a list.

CHAPTER
20

CONTRACT LANGUAGE

Most landlords use standard leases and "boilerplate" language usually weighted heavily in favor of the landlord. Some provisions may not even comply with laws that govern the landlord-tenant relationship.

Don't be afraid to bring to the landlord's attention any provisions that are illegal, or to modify them or strike them from the lease altogether. If you do sign a lease that has an illegal clause, that clause is void. A court will not enforce it, though the remainder of the lease will remain in effect.

Following is a standard lease for an unfurnished apartment. The traditional boilerplate language is followed by a plain-language translation and, where needed, an explanation and suggested alternative language to replace provisions unfair to tenants. The provisions included here are typical, though there are many variations. Your ability to negotiate the terms of your lease depends on your leverage with the landlord, but don't hesitate to try. In any case, *be sure to read your lease carefully* and to understand everything before signing it. (For purposes of this example, we assume you are the person renting the apartment.)

Made this _____ day of ___*(month)*___ A.D. one thousand nine hundred and __*(year)*__ , by and between ___*(landlord's name)*___ of ___*(city, state)*___ , party of the first part, and ___*(your name)*___ of ___*(city, state)*___ , party of the second part.

Witnesseth, that the said party of the first part does let and demise unto the said party of the second part the following described premises: ___*(address, including apartment #, city, state)*___ for the term of ___*(number of months or years)*___ commencing on the _____ day of ___*(month, year)*___ to the _____ day of ___*(month, year)*___ for the sum of ___*(amount of rent per year)*___ dollars per annum, payable in monthly installments of ___*(amount of rent per month)*___ dollars, in advance and without demand, at ___*(address where rent is to be paid)*___ , the first payment to be made on the _____ day of ___*(month, year)*___ , and a like sum on the same day of each and every month thereafter.

Home Lawyer Tip

Home Lawyer will draft a Residential Lease. To draft a Residential Lease, select Residential Lease from the Document submenu. Point to "New", and then answer the questions that Home Lawyer asks.

You may wish to edit this lease to reflect the advice in this book. To edit the agreement, you must have first set up the word processor under System Setup. After you have specified your word processing program under System Setup, select Shell to WP from the Edit submenu. When you exit your word processor, you will automatically return to the Home Lawyer Main Menu.

This identifies the landlord and tenant, the property to be rented, the rental fee, where and when the rent must be paid, and the term of the contract. "Party of the first part" simply refers to the landlord, and "party of the second part" to you, the tenant.

Some leases include an "escalator clause" that allows the landlord to increase your rent to pass on any increased operating expenses. This one doesn't.

The word *demise* means "rent" or "lease." With the words *without demand,* the contract waives the landlord's obligation to notify you every month that your rent is due. This is standard.

Usually, once the term of the lease (one year, for instance) is up, you can move out or sign a new lease. The landlord can raise the rent at this time, within any limits set by rent-control laws, and both the landlord and you can renegotiate any terms of the lease.

> 1. This lease agreement is conditioned upon the party of the first part being able to secure possession of said premises from existing tenant, if any, by the commencement datehereof, and if party of the first part is unable to deliver possession of said premises to party of the second part by the commencement date hereof for any reason, such right of possession by party of the second part shall be postponed until such time when said premises shall be put in suitable physical condition for occupancy, or until such time when party of the first part is able to legally deliver possession, without any liability on the part of the party of the first part to the party of the second part for such postponement.

Bad news for tenants: This means that if the apartment isn't ready to move into, you have no recourse for getting your money back or canceling the lease. "Delivering possession" means turning over the premises, handing over the keys to the apartment. In some places, this clause is illegal. Here's some suggested alternative language:

> 1. If landlord is unable to deliver possession to tenant for any reason not within the landlord's control, tenant shall have the option of a) terminating this lease and recovering all money paid to landlord under this lease or b) having rent abated until possession can be given.
>
> *   *   *
>
> 2. It is covenanted and agreed that the party of the second part has deposited with the party of the first part the sum of *(amount of monthly rent)* dollars, $ *(rent in numbers)* to be held by the party of the first part as security for the faithful performance of and compliance with all the terms, covenants and conditions of this lease. If the party of the second part fails to comply with each of said terms, covenants and conditions, the security shall belong to the party of the first part as part payment for the disbursements, attorneys' fees, costs and expenses that the party of the first part may undergo for the purpose of regaining possession of the premises and preparing same for renting; and no portion of said security deposit shall be used by the party of the second part for any payment of any rent due.

This requires you to pay the landlord a security deposit of one month's rent on signing the lease. In convoluted language, it states that if you break any conditions of this agreement, the landlord can withhold the security deposit to pay for legal or other expenses incurred in evicting you and renting the apartment to someone else. You are not allowed to use the security deposit for paying your rent for any month, including the last month of the lease.

Almost all states have laws that govern this security deposit, usually limiting the amount that can be charged, the time within which it must be returned, and the interest that must be returned with it.

Although the amount charged here is within the limit allowed by all jurisdictions (one month's rent), this is a bad clause for you because it allows the landlord to keep the entire deposit, even if your breach doesn't cost the landlord much money. Also, it doesn't specify any terms for returning the deposit to you. Although landlords may try to include language like this, most will agree to something a bit fairer. Here's an alternative plain-language provision:

> 2. On signing this agreement, tenant shall pay landlord *(amount spelled out)* *($ amount in numbers)*, as security. Such deposit, plus ___% interest per year, shall be returned to tenant within two weeks after the term has expired and tenants have vacated the premises. If all or part of the deposit is withheld, landlord must provide a written statement explaining why. Landlord may withhold only that part of the deposit necessary to: a) cover any unpaid rent; b) repair, at reasonable cost, any damage to the premises beyond normal wear and tear; or c) clean premises not left in the same condition as when tenant moved in. On tenant's request, landlord shall provide receipts for repairs paid for from the security deposit. Tenant shall not use the security deposit toward the payment of rent.

> *   *   *

> 3. It is further covenanted and agreed by party of the second part that time is of the essence with regard to the payment of rent when due, and that a late payment charge of *(amount spelled out)* dollars *($ amount in numbers)* shall be paid for any check returned or received after the ___ day of the month.

This sets a late charge for rent that is not paid within a specified number of days of the due date. If a rent check is returned from the bank, it is considered late and a late fee is charged. As mentioned previously, many places have laws that limit late fees you can be charged or require a certain number of "grace" days before a landlord can charge this fee. Make sure the lease is in line with local laws.

4. It is covenanted and agreed that the said party of the second part, upon paying aforesaid rent and performing the covenants and conditions of this lease, shall and may peaceably and quietly have, hold and enjoy the demised premises for the term aforesaid.

This says you'll be entitled to the "quiet enjoyment" of the rental property. This is the most basic provision of your lease—it establishes your temporary possession of the rental property and your right to live there undisturbed. If this is not in your lease, most courts consider it an implied term by law.

5. It is further covenanted and agreed that the said party of the second part will not carry on any business therein nor use said premises for disorderly or unlawful purpose, nor in any noisy, boisterous or other manner offensive to any other occupant of the building; nor shall the party of the second part keep animals or birds of any description in said premises without the written consent of the party of the first part.

This is standard. It requires you to use the rental property only as a private residence and for no other purpose without the landlord's written consent in advance. The rest of the paragraph restricts you from using the property for any disruptive or illegal purpose, from keeping pets and from disturbing the peace and quiet of other tenants in the building by excessive noise or other activity. If the landlord agrees that you can keep a pet, cross out the last clause of the paragraph and be sure it is initialed by both the landlord and you.

For your protection, also add:

5A. Landlord agrees to prevent other tenants and other persons in the building or common areas from similarly disturbing tenant's peace and quiet.

6. It is further covenanted and agreed that the said party of the second part will pay the said rent as above stated, and all bills for gas and electricity used

on the premises, making the necessary deposits at the respective offices to secure same, and that he/she will pay all water rents for said premises during his/her tenancy thereof.

This holds you responsible for paying all gas, electricity, and water charges. Some landlords charge a set fee for one or more utilities. You should know in advance exactly what utilities you will have to pay in addition to your rent. Cross out and initial those charges for which you are not responsible.

7. It is further covenanted and agreed that the party of the second part will conform to the rules and regulations made or hereafter made by the party of the first part for the management of the building, its corridors, porches, lobbies, drives, grounds and other appurtenances, and for the delivery of goods, merchandise and other things by tradespeople and other persons.

This requires that you agree to comply with the landlord's rules and regulations regarding management of the building, the grounds, and deliveries to the building. Check to see if you can get a copy of any rules and regulations before you move in.

8. It is further covenanted and agreed that the said party of the second part will keep said premises, including the building, fixtures, plumbing and appurtenances thereof, in substantial condition and in good repair, clean, and in good working order and proper sanitary condition, all of which premises are now in such condition and repair; and that all repairs rendered necessary by the negligence of the party of the second part shall be paid for by him/her; and the said party of the second part will surrender the same at the expiration of said tenancy in good order, ordinary wear and tear and damage by the elements or public enemy excepted.

If you sign a lease that includes such language, you're acknowledging that the property, including the fixtures and plumbing, is clean and in good working condition. You're also agreeing to keep them that way, except for ordinary wear and tear. If you or people you allow into your apartment damage anything in it, you will be responsible for paying for repairs. That's why it's important to inspect the property first to make sure it is, in fact, in good condition. If it isn't, ask the landlord to fix any problems or note on the lease any existing damage before you move in. Otherwise you may wind up paying for it when you leave.

> 9. It is further covenanted and agreed that the said party of the second part will not make any alterations or additions to the structure, equipment or fixtures of said premises without written consent of the party of the first part first had and obtained.

Almost every lease contains this provision. It prevents you from making any alterations or additions without the landlord's prior written consent. If you do make changes without permission, the landlord may have the right to evict you and certainly will be able to charge for restoring the property to its original state, regardless of whether you believe you improved the property by your alterations.

> 10. It is further covenanted and agreed that the said party of the second part will permit the party of the first part free access at any time to the premises hereby leased for the purpose of examining or exhibiting the same, or in the event of an emergency or fire or other property damage, or to make any repairs or alterations of such premises which said party of the first part considers necessary or desirable.

Beware: this allows the landlord to enter your apartment at *any time*. You should insist instead that visits by the landlord occur only between 9:00 A.M. and 5:00 P.M. (or suitable hours of your choosing) after 24 or 48 hours' notice, except in cases of serious emergency, such as fire.

> 11. It is further covenanted and agreed that all personal property in said premises shall be and remain at the sole risk of party of the second part, and party of the first part shall not be liable for any damage to, or loss of, such property arising from any acts of negligence of any other persons or from any other cause whatsoever, nor shall the party of the first part be liable for any injury to the party of the second part or other persons in or about the premises.

This may very well be illegal, at least in some situations. It exempts the landlord from responsibility for any loss or damage to your property or any personal injury to you or people you invite to the property, *regardless of who is at fault.* Such provisions have been ruled illegal when the landlord has the duty to maintain the property in a safe and sanitary condition and the damage or injury is the landlord's fault. Here's some suggested alternative language:

11. Tenant agrees to be liable for damage to tenant's personal property due to tenant's own negligence or that of others on the premises with tenant's permission. Tenant agrees to be liable for personal injury received on the premises by tenant or others on the premises with tenant's permission, due to their own negligence. Landlord shall maintain the building and grounds in a safe and sanitary condition, and comply with all state and local laws concerning the condition of dwelling units. Landlord shall take reasonable measures to maintain security on the premises, building and grounds to protect the tenant and those on the premises with tenant's permission from burglary, robbery and other crimes. Tenant agrees to make use of such security measures as a reasonable person would.

12. It is further covenanted and agreed that the said party of the second part will not sublet said premises or any portion thereof or assign this lease in whole or in part without the consent in writing of said party of the first part.

This restricts you from subletting the apartment or assigning your lease before it expires. Ask the landlord to add the sentence:

12A. The landlord shall not unreasonably withhold consent.

13. It is further covenanted and agreed that if the said party of the second part shall fail to pay the said rent in advance as aforesaid, although there shall have been no legal or formal demand for the same, or shall neglect to pay the electricity or gas bills at the time and on the day when the same shall fall due and be payable as hereinbefore mentioned, or shall sublet or assign the said premises, or carry on any business therein without the written consent as aforesaid, or shall use the same for any disorderly or unlawful purpose, or break any of the aforesaid covenants, then, and in any of said events, this lease, and all things herein contained, shall cease, and the party of the first part, his/her heirs and assigns, shall be entitled to the possession of said leased premises, and to re-enter the same without demand, and may forthwith proceed to recover possession of said premises under and by virtue of the provisions of the law relating to proceedings in cases between party of the first part and party of the second part, any notice to quit or of intention to exercise said option, or to re-enter the premises being hereby waived by the party of the second part and assigns.

Watch out for this clause! While at first it might appear to simply repeat most of the earlier clauses of the lease to define what will constitute a breach by you, the end of the clause is the real kicker. It defines the landlord's rights if you break the lease. Here, the landlord would have the immediate right to enter the apartment without notice and to institute legal proceedings to evict you. It also waives your right to receive notice that the rent is overdue or that the apartment must be vacated.

As discussed previously, the waivers in this lease are illegal in many states. It is usually illegal to require you to waive your right to receive notice of eviction proceedings. A landlord may also include language by which you waive other rights, such as the right to a jury trial in disputes over the lease. If the waiver is illegal, the clause will not be enforced by a court if the landlord ever tries to take advantage of it.

However, it's best to be prudent and strike through such language. If it isn't crossed out, a court may hold you to it if it decides you knowingly and voluntarily signed the lease and all its provisions.

We suggest splitting this paragraph into two, because the legal remedies available to landlords when a tenant hasn't paid the rent may be different from those used when a tenant breaks other conditions of the lease. Here's our suggested alternate language:

13. If tenant fails to comply with a provision of this lease, other than to pay rent, landlord shall notify tenant of such breach and allow tenant reasonable time to correct the problem. If tenant does not do so, landlord may terminate this agreement as provided by law.

13A. If tenant is unable to pay rent when due and notifies landlord on or before that date of an inability to do so, landlord and tenant shall make reasonable efforts to work out a procedure for tenant to pay rent as soon as possible. If they are unable to do so, landlord may serve notice to pay rent or vacate, as provided by law.

14. It is further covenanted and agreed that no waiver of one breach of any covenant herein shall be construed to be a waiver of the covenant itself, or of subsequent breach thereof or of this agreement; and if any breach occurs and afterwards is adjusted, this lease shall continue in full force as if no breach had occurred.

This complicated language is best explained by example. Say you sublet the apartment without the landlord's consent and the landlord, upon discovering this, decides it's okay for the subtenant to stay (in other words, *waives* your *breach*). The landlord's waiver does not mean you may again sublet without the landlord's consent, nor does it mean the landlord waives your other obligations under the lease.

> 15. It is further covenanted and agreed that, should party of the second part continue in possession after the end of the term herein, with permission of the party of the first part, any such holding over shall be construed as a tenancy from month-to-month at the same monthly rental as hereinabove provided as the monthly installment and such tenancy shall be subject to all the terms, conditions, covenants and agreements of this lease, except that nothing in this paragraph shall preclude party of the first part from increasing the rent at any time after the expiration of the term of this lease.

> 16. It is further covenanted and agreed that the party of the second part shall provide at least thirty (30) days' written notice to party of the first part of his/her intention to either renew, extend or terminate this lease upon its expiration, or upon the expiration of any renewal or extension thereof, although party of the first part shall be under no obligation to renew or extend this lease beyond its stated term.

These are renewal provisions. This lease has a *holding over* provision that automatically renews the lease month-to-month at the end of the first term. Here, the renewal is also subject to the landlord's agreement that you stay. Finally, it allows the landlord to raise your rent anytime after the original lease term expires. The second provision simply says you must give the landlord 30 days' written notice before moving out.

> 17. It is further covenanted and agreed that the party of the second part shall pay and discharge all costs, expenses and attorneys' fees which shall be incurred and expended by the party of the first part in enforcing the covenants and agreements of this lease, whether by the institution of litigation or in the taking of advice of counsel, or otherwise.

This makes you responsible for paying all legal expenses the landlord incurs in enforcing the conditions of the lease, including litigation and seeking a lawyer's advice. It is obviously one-sided. In some areas it is illegal to require you to pay your landlord's legal fees. We suggest that either you each pay your own legal fees or use this alternative language:

17. If either party initiates a legal proceeding to enforce any provision of this lease, the successful party shall collect reasonable attorneys' fees and costs from the other.

In testimony whereof, the said parties have hereunto signed their names and affixed their seals, this _____ day of __*(month, year)*__ .

__*(landlord's signature)*__ for __*(Company, if any) (date)*__(seal)

__*(tenant's signature)*__   __*(date)*__ (seal)

Witnessed by:

__*(witness's name)*__

__*(signature)*__ _____ (seal)

The lease is not binding until it is signed. Seals and witnesses are not necessary, however. The lease will be valid without them.

PART VII

LESSER CONTRACTS

CHAPTER

21

RELEASES

Eric slips and falls in front of an apartment building and sprains his ankle. The owner of the building agrees to pay his medical expenses if Eric signs an agreement not to sue.

Ira is injured in a train collision. The company's lawyer visits him in the hospital and asks him to sign a paper giving up his right to sue in exchange for $5,000.

Releases like these are among the most common do-it-yourself contracts people sign. Because they are brief and straightforward, it isn't difficult to write your own and make them legally binding without a lawyer's help.

In a *release,* one person agrees to pay another to surrender a legal claim. Usually, releases are used to settle small claims, such as those for minor damages from "fender bender" auto accidents. For example, after the other driver admits fault for the "fender bender," in exchange for a small sum of money you may agree not to report the accident to your insurance company and not to sue. If you write down the agreement and sign it, you have created a contract called a release: One side "releases" or gives up an otherwise valid claim.

As explained in Chapter 1, all contracts, including releases, must involve consideration. This means the person who signs the release must receive something in exchange for giving up a legal right or claim. If you sign a release surrendering your right to sue your friend for a back injury you received at her house but get nothing in return from her, the release is void. You have made no exchange to support the contract. If related back problems arise later, you are legally free to sue for damages.

Although money is a common consideration for a release, it's not the only kind. For example, if your cousin seeds your lawn for $400 and the grass fails to grow, she may ask you to drop all legal claims in exchange for redoing the lawn work until the grass grows. If you agree, that's a legal release.

In general, a release is valid if both sides understand the terms and sign voluntarily. If one side later challenges the release, the court will not void the release unless it finds convincing evidence of duress, coercion, or "unconscionability" (see Chapter 1).

General and Specific

Both the releases in our examples were *specific,* based on a particular incident and affecting the outcome of only one incident. Your situation may require a *general* release, however. You may, for example, give up all claims against a relative's estate or against a doctor for medical malpractice in exchange for a sum of money. General releases usually include language like: "For $5,000, I give up any and all legal claims I might have against you, up to and including the date this release is signed."

Read Carefully

Signing away your right to sue can have significant consequences. It's important that you fully understand the value of the claim you are giving up. If you are signing a release that says you won't sue for damages from an injury, be certain you know the full extent of your injuries. Consider getting a medical opinion or two before you sign the release.

Fully assess both the potential gains and costs of settling a claim with a release. Remember, going to court means you'll probably have to pay lawyers' fees, and it may be a long time before the case is decided and you can collect. Further, you'll risk losing the case. On the other hand, when you surrender a claim in exchange for a quick and certain resolution, the amount you'll get will almost surely be less that what you might get in court, if you win.

The following is a hypothetical general release written in legalese, followed by its translation.

Release

I, *(releasor)* , for and in consideration of the sum of _____ in hand paid by *(releasee)*, have remised, released, and forever discharged by these presents for my heirs, executors and administrators remise, release and forever discharge his/her heirs, executors and administrators of and from any and all matter of action and actions, cause and causes of action, suits, debts, dues, sums of money, accounts, reckonings, bonds, bills, specialties, covenants, contracts, controversies, agreements, premises, variances, trespasses, damages, judgments, extents, executions, claims and demand whatsoever, in law or in equity against which I ever had, now have, or which my heirs, executors or administrators hereafter can, shall, or may have, for, upon or by reason of any matter, cause or thing whatsoever, from the beginning of the world to the day of the date of these presents.

_____   _____
Releasor's Signature   *Date*

_____   _____
Releasee's Signature   *Date*

In Witness Whereof, I, _____ have hereunto set hand and seal the ___ day of _____ one thousand nine hundred and ___ .

Sealed and delivered in the presence of:

(notary's signature)
Notary Public

Translation.   This is a general release in language that is both repetitive and unnecessarily complex. It says that for a sum of money, you, the *releasor,* forever give up any right to sue the *releasee* for any legal claims that are based on any event that occurred before the agreement is signed. It also says that your heirs can't sue the releasee or the releasee's heirs.

This agreement also includes the unnecessary notarization (see Chapter 1). Witnesses are not necessary; they do not affect the validity of the contract, although if you foresee a possible challenge to the contract, consider having witnesses sign. Both releasor and releasee, of course, must sign and date the contract.

The only difference between this general release and a specific release is that, instead of including the words "giving up any and all claims up to and until this date," a specific release would state: "giving up any and all claims" that arise from the specific incident, for instance "a car accident at Penn and First Streets in Middleburg" on a certain date.

Here's a release written in plain language:

Plain Language Release

This Release, dated _____, is given:
By the releasor(s) *(your name and address)*, referred to as "I", to the Releasee(s) *(name and address)*, referred to as "You."

If more than one person signs this Release, "I" shall mean each person who signs this Release as a releasor.

1. **Release:** I release and give up any and all claims and rights which I may have against you, including those of which I am not aware.

2. **Consideration:** I, the releasor, have received good and adequate consideration for this release in the form of *(what is exchanged for the release)*.

3. **Who is Bound:** I am bound by this Release. Anyone who succeeds to my rights and responsibilities, such as my heirs or the executor of my estate, is also bound. This Release is made for your benefit and all who succeed to your rights and responsibilities, such as your heirs or the executor of your estate.

Releasor's Signature	*Date*
Releasee's Signature	*Date*

In community property states, spouses' signatures are also required if any joint property is affected.

CHAPTER
22

POWERS OF ATTORNEY

Sally is terminally ill and concerned about who will make health decisions should she become mentally unable to. She wants to put her sister in charge and put it in writing.

A *power of attorney* is a contract that permits another person to act on your behalf. It must be in writing. People generally use a power of attorney to allow someone else to handle one or more of their business transactions—paying bills, withdrawing money from a bank, selling or buying a house, even making investments. For example, you might authorize someone (called your *agent* or *attorney in fact*) to sell your car while you are on vacation.

Conventional Powers of Attorney

Limited Power of Attorney

To designate someone to act on your behalf for one or more specific business transactions, use a *limited* or *conventional* power of attorney.

Unlimited Power of Attorney

You can also use a power of attorney to authorize someone to handle all your business decisions. This is done by a *general* or *unlimited* power of attorney. These come in handy any time you're away from home, in the military, temporarily relocated overseas for your job, or away on vacation, but people use them to grant authority even while they stay in the area. An unlimited power of attorney gives the person you choose the power to make all necessary financial and other business decisions.

Durable Power of Attorney

A *durable power of attorney* authorizes someone to make medical and/or financial decisions for you if you become physically or mentally unable to make them. For example, if you're ill, you might give a durable power of attorney to a family member or friend who would sign checks, pay bills, and take charge of your financial affairs. A durable power of attorney can be limited or unlimited.

A durable power of attorney remains effective *when you become incapacitated,* and removes the need for a court to step in and appoint a *guardian* or *conservator* because you have already made that assignment. You can write one that becomes effective *only* when you become incapacitated.

Consumer Tips

Find a Trustworthy Agent. Because a power of attorney transfers considerable responsibility and power over your affairs, caution is advised. Only give your power of attorney to someone whose honesty and business judgment you fully trust.

Use a Limited Power of Attorney If Possible. It's best to transfer the least amount of responsibility and power over your financial or medical affairs to another. You can do this best with a limited power of attorney. If you are creating a general or durable power of attorney, be particularly careful whom you entrust with this responsibility.

Powers of Attorney Can be Canceled at Any Time. It's important to know that you can cancel the power of attorney at any time, with one exception: if it is a durable power of attorney and the court considers you incapacitated. To revoke a power of attorney, simply prepare a second document that states you are revoking it. This is true even if you do not have a clause about revocation in the original power of attorney.

Home Lawyer Tip

Home Lawyer will draft a Revocation of Power of Attorney. This document is used to revoke a previously executed power of attorney. To draft a Revocation of Power of Attorney, select Power of Attorney from the Document submenu, and then select Revocation of POA. Point to "New," and then answer the questions that Home Lawyer asks.

Set an Expiration Date. It's a good idea to include a date on which the power of attorney will expire, whether the contract is general or limited. Even if you're leaving town to care for an ailing parent and don't know how long you'll be gone, choose a date. If the power of attorney is needed after the expiration date, you can always execute another one. This date protects you from the power of attorney being misused after it has been revoked.

Check for Required Forms. The Internal Revenue Service (IRS), banks, and other institutions sometimes have specific power-of-attorney forms they want you to use. In some cases, they may refuse to acknowledge a power of attorney not completed on their form. Make sure you complete the correct form for the uses you anticipate.

You Don't Need a Notary Public. You don't need to get your power of attorney notarized, although notarizing it doesn't make the agreement any less valid.

Notify People and Institutions When You Give or Revoke Your Power of Attorney. Be sure you give a copy of your power of attorney to anyone who'll be affected. For instance, if you're giving someone a power of attorney to withdraw money and write checks on your bank account, send the bank a copy. Later, if you revoke the power of attorney, send the bank a copy of the revocation as well.

Following are a limited power of attorney and a plain-language durable power of attorney:

Limited Power of Attorney

I, _____ hereby appoint _____, my true and lawful attorney for me and authorize her/him in my name to demand payment of claims to become due for _____ located at _____, and to give releases of discharges for the same, also to perform and execute those things which she/he deems necessary for the carrying on of said business.

_____   _____
Signature   *Date*

Translation. This power of attorney is "limited" because it appoints someone only to handle the transactions of a specific business, named in the document. For example, under this power of attorney the agent can pay employees' salaries and buy whatever the business requires, but not withdraw money from a personal banking account or handle any matters not related to the named business.

Durable Power of Attorney for
Health Care and Financial/Asset Management

1. Creation of Durable Power of Attorney
To all those concerned or involved with my finances/assets and/or health care, including my family, relatives, friends and my physicians, health care providers, community care facilities and any other person who may have an interest or duty in my medical care or treatment: I, _____, being of sound mind, intentionally and voluntarily intend to create by this document a durable power of attorney for my health care and the management of my finances and assets, by appointing as the person designated as my attorney in fact to make health care decisions for me and manage my finances and assets for me in the event I become incapacitated and am unable to make health care decisions or manage my finances and assets myself. This power of attorney shall not be affected by my subsequent incapacity.

Home Lawyer Tip

Home Lawyer will draft a General Power of Attorney. This document allows one individual (the attorney-in-fact) broad and wide-ranging powers regarding the personal affairs and property of the principal. To draft a General Power of Attorney, select Power of Attorney from the Document submenu, and then select General POA. Point to "New," and then answer the questions that Home Lawyer asks.

Home Lawyer will also draft a Medical/Special Power of Attorney. This document allows one individual (the attorney-in-fact) specific powers regarding the personal affairs and property of the principal. It may be used in place of the limited power of attorney described above to authorize medical care and treatment for the minor children of the principal; to authorize the sale of transfer of real estate on the principal's behalf; or to provide for the sale of items of the principal's personal property. To draft a Medical/Special Power of Attorney, select Power of Attorney from the Document submenu, and then select Medical/Special POA. Point to "New," and then answer the questions that Home Lawyer asks.

You may wish to edit your powers of attorney to reflect the advice in this book. To edit the agreement, you must have first set up the word processor under System Setup. After you have specified your word processing program under System Setup, select Shell to WP from the Edit submenu. When you exit your word processor, you will automatically return to the Home Lawyer Main Menu.

This paragraph establishes that you, the writer, declare that you are of sound mind and voluntarily create this durable power of attorney. It transfers authority for health-care decisions and financial and asset management, but becomes effective only if you become incapacitated and unable to make health-care and financial decisions for yourself.

2. Designation of Attorney in Fact

The person designated to be my attorney in fact for health care and financial/asset management in the event I become incapacitated is _____ of _____. If _____ for any reason shall fail to serve or ceases to serve as my attorney in fact, _____ of _____ shall be my attorney in fact for health care and financial/asset management.

This paragraph names the agent or attorney in fact and, if that person cannot act as the agent, also names a replacement or second choice.

3. Effective on Incapacity

This durable power of attorney shall become effective in the event I become incapacitated and am unable to make health care decisions for myself and/or manage my own finances/assets, in which case it shall become effective as of the date of the written statement by a physician, as provided in Paragraph 4.

This document becomes effective only upon the writer's incapacity and inability to make health-care decisions and decisions about managing finances and assets. It becomes effective on the date a doctor issues a written statement of incapacity, as provided in the two next paragraphs.

4. Determination of Incapacity

(A) The determination that I have become incapacitated and am unable to make health care decisions for myself and/or am unable to manage my finances/assets shall be made in writing by a licensed physician. If possible, the physician shall be _____ of _____.

(B) In the event that a licensed physician has made a written determination that I have become incapacitated and am not able to make health care decisions for myself and/or am unable to manage my finances/assets, that written statement shall be attached to the original document of this power of attorney.

This section provides that a licensed doctor must make the determination of incapacity, and that the determination must be put in writing. The author of this power of attorney also names the doctor who is to make the determination, if possible, and requires that the written statement of incapacity be attached to the original power of attorney.

5. Authority for My Attorney in Fact over Health Care Decisions

(A) Authority in General

My attorney in fact shall have all lawful authority permissible to make health care decisions for me, including the authority to consent or withdraw consent or refuse consent to any care, treatment, service or procedure to maintain, diagnose or treat my physical or mental condition, EXCEPT:

Here the writer should enter any desired limitations or directions for the attorney in fact, such as:

(A.1) No life support systems shall be used to artificially prolong my life if I have an incurable disease.

*   *   *

(B) Authority for Inspection and Disclosure of Information Relating to My Physical or Mental Health

Subject to any limitations in this document, my attorney in fact has the power and authority to do all of the following:

(1) Request, review, and receive any information, verbal or written, regarding my physical or mental health, including, but not limited to, medical and hospital records.

(2) Execute on my behalf any releases or other document that may be required in order to obtain this information.

(3) Consent to the disclosure of this information.

(C) Authority to Sign Documents, Waivers and Releases

When necessary to implement the health care decisions that my attorney in fact is authorized by this document to make, my attorney in fact has the power and authority to execute on my behalf all of the following:

(1) Documents titled or purporting to be a "Refusal To Permit Treatment" and "Leaving Hospital Against Medical Advice."

(2) Any necessary waiver or release from liability required by a hospital or physician.

This defines the agent's authority over health-care decisions. In this example, the scope is wide and includes consenting to or refusing any treatment or medication. This is the place to make exceptions or prohibitions, however. Here, for example, you might state that you do not want to use artificial life support systems; your agent would then be forbidden to order such treatment for you.

The agent is also given access to all information and records on your physical and mental health. To carry out health care decisions, the agent has your authority to execute on your behalf any necessary waivers or releases and documents, such as a "Refusal To Permit Treatment."

6. Authority of My Attorney in Fact to Manage My Finances/Assets
(A) Except as specified in Section 6(B), I grant my attorney in fact full power and authority over all my property, real and personal, and authorize him/her to do and perform all and every act which I as an owner of said property could do or perform, and I hereby ratify and confirm all that my attorney in fact shall do or cause to be done under this durable power of attorney.
(B) My attorney in fact has no authority to give any of my property to himself/herself.

This defines the attorney in fact's authority over your finances and assets. It gives unlimited power over all real and personal property, with only one restriction: The attorney in fact may not make your property his or her own. This sensible restriction makes clear that the agent is not free to manipulate finances for personal benefit.

7. Reliance by Third Parties
The powers conferred on my attorney in fact by this durable power of attorney and my attorney in fact's signature or act under the authority granted in this durable power of attorney may be accepted by any third person or organization as fully authorized by me and with the same force and effect as if I were personally present, competent and acting on my own behalf.

No person or organization who relies on this durable power of attorney or any representation my attorney in fact makes regarding his or her authority, including but not limited to:
(1) The fact that this durable power of attorney has not been revoked;
(2) That I, *(your name)* was competent to execute this power of attorney;
(3) The authority of my attorney in fact under this durable power of attorney;
shall incur any liability to me, my estate, heirs, successors or assigns because of such reliance on this durable power of attorney or on any such representation by my attorney in fact.

All third parties are notified by this language that the agent alone has full authority to act on your behalf. A third party will never be held liable for any action the third party takes because he or she relied on the validity of the document.

8. Duration
I intend that this Durable Power of Attorney remain effective until my death, or until revoked by me in writing.
Executed this _____ day of _____ at _____.

*(your name)*_____
Principal

*(witness's name)*_____ *(witness's name)*_____
Witness   Witness

This durable power of attorney will remain in effect until the author revokes it or dies. It's best to have it signed by at least two witnesses, although the exact number needed varies according to state law. The attorney in fact need not sign a power of attorney for it to be valid.

CHAPTER

23

PROMISSORY NOTES

Your brother Bill agrees to sell you his stereo for $300. You agree to pay him your next paycheck. You decide you want the agreement in writing so he doesn't change his mind and sell it to his girlfriend.

Promissory notes like this one are usually loans between family members or friends. These loans are not regulated, like bank or lending-institution loans. In fact, the only laws that apply to promissory notes are usury laws: They restrict the interest the lender can charge. Promissory notes can be used for secured loans, but they are most often used for those that are unsecured.

You might use a promissory note when you loan your daughter money to make a down payment on a new car. It would include the amount of the loan, the repayment date and any interest owed, as well as your signatures. A promissory note might set up the installment payment plan to buy a stereo from someone who advertised in your local newspapers.

Promissory notes can be written so that the amount borrowed is payable in a *lump sum* or in smaller *installments*. The method of payment you choose depends on your circumstances. If you're the lender, you may want the right to transfer the note to a third person who will be able to collect the debt for you if you move, become incapacitated, or die.

To sell or transfer a promissory note simply by signing it over, like a check, it must be *negotiable.* That means it must include:

- The names and addresses of both the lender and borrower

- Language making the debt payable to the lender

- A specific sum to be paid and the interest rate, if any

- The address to which payments must be made

- The date and city where the note is signed

- The signature of the borrower

Promissory notes may also be assigned. See Chapter 24 for advice on drawing up an assignment contract.

Two negotiable, unsecured, plain-language promissory notes follow. The first is an agreement for a lump-sum repayment, the second for repayment in installments.

NEGOTIABLE PROMISSORY NOTE FOR A LUMP SUM

$_____

Ninety days after today's date, or on the ____ day of _____, or on demand, I promise (or we jointly promise) to pay _____ or bearer, _____ with ____ % interest, for value received.

_____   _____
Borrower's Signature   *Witness*

PROMISSORY NOTE FOR INSTALLMENT PAYMENTS

$_____

On or before _____ for value received, I promise to pay _____ the sum of _____ dollars, with ____ % interest.

I agree to make monthly payments on the ____ day of each month for ____ months in the amount of _____ with the first payment due _____.

_____   _____
Borrower's Signature   *Witness*

Home Lawyer Tip

Home Lawyer will draft a Promissory Note. This document will obligate one party (the Maker) to pay money to another (the Payee). To draft a Promissory Note, select Credit and Collections from the Document submenu, then select Promissory Note. Point to "New," and then answer the questions that Home Lawyer asks.

Home Lawyer will also draft a Demand for Money Owed. To draft a Demand for Money Owed, select Credit and Collections from the Document submenu, then select Demand for Money Owed. Point to "New," and then answer the questions that Home Lawyer asks.

CHAPTER

24

ASSIGNMENTS

Kevin's brother Richard owes him $500 that is reflected in the promissory note they signed a year ago. Kevin lives 3,000 miles away in New York, and all his attempts to collect have been ignored by Richard. Their sister, Lisa, is going to visit Richard. Kevin decides to assign the note to Lisa for $400. Lisa will collect and earn $100 profit.

You use an *assignment* to transfer to someone else a debt that's owed to you. For example, suppose you've sold your car and received a promissory note for $300 a month, but you want the money paid directly to your parents. You *assign* your promissory note to them. This means you've given your parents your *interest* in the money from the car sale. You no longer can personally collect the debt.

An assignment is exchanged for consideration—something of value. You might assign someone your promissory note in exchange for money. Say, for example, you hold a $1,000 promissory note payable in a year and you suddenly find you need money immediately. Your friend agrees to give you $900 now in exchange for the note. The friend makes a $100 profit, and you get $900 without having to wait the year.

You can assign virtually any definable interest you own. In addition to debts owed to you, you can assign your wages, your *accounts receivable*, your rights under a contract, even an expected inheritance. Although you cannot assign your right to sue (a court would rule that the person you assigned it to would have no legal right to sue because that person was not the one with a claim), you may assign your rights under a lawsuit already in progress.

Three sample assignment contracts follow. The first is a standard form in legalese, the second is a plain-language assignment of a promissory note, and the third is a plain-language assignment of a contract. You may choose to have the contract witnessed and notarized. Although the contract is no less valid if it is not witnessed, it may be easier to withstand a challenge if you have someone who can testify it was signed by both parties.

ASSIGNMENT OF A PARTICULAR ACCOUNT

_____ of _____, herein referred to as assignor, in consideration for _____, receipt whereof is hereby acknowledged, assigns to _____ of _____, his/her executors, administrators, and assigns, herein referred to as assignee, to his/her or their own proper use and benefit, all assignor's right, title, and interest in and to any and all sum or sums of money now due or to become due on the attached, or sales, services, loans, or whatever transaction may be the basis of the account. Assignor gives to assignee, his/her executors, administrators, and assigns, the full power and authority, for assignee's own use and benefit, but at assignee's own cost, to ask, demand, collect, receive, compound, and give acquittance for the same, or any part thereof, and in assignor's name or otherwise, to prosecute and withdraw any suits or proceedings at law or in equity therefore.

_____   _____
Signature   *Dated*

You, as the *assignor*, give the account entirely to the *assignee*. The heirs (the people who will inherit at death) of both of you are also bound by this agreement. Every right or claim, including money and services owed, is given to the assignee.

If any lawsuits are transferred with the assignment, the assignee owns the suit and can continue it or not, as he or she wishes.

PLAIN-LANGUAGE ASSIGNMENT OF A PROMISSORY NOTE

For _____ received, I, _____, of _____, assign to _____, of _____, all of my rights to the promissory note dated _____, payable to my order on demand in the face amount of _____ and executed by _____.

In witness whereof, I have executed this assignment at _____.

_____
Signature

With this assignment, you have transferred to the assignee all rights to a promissory note that's owed to you by another person. The promissory note is identified by the amount, the date, and the people who signed it.

GENERAL ASSIGNMENT OF A CONTRACT

In consideration of _____ , I, _____, assign and transfer to _____ all rights and interest that I have or would have in the attached contract, called *(name of contract)* between *(the other party to the contract being assigned)* and me, subject to all its conditions and terms, and in so doing release and quit claim to all rights that I have or would have to receive property under that contract.

_____   _____
Name   *Signature*

_____   _____
Name   *Signature*

_____
Date

In this assignment, you, as the assignor, have transferred to someone else, your assignee, all your rights under a contract. Both of you sign the agreement. The contract that's being assigned is attached to this assignment and is also identified by naming it and the other party who signed the contract with you. You also state that you give up all your rights and claims under the contract and that the assignee accepts all those rights and claims.

BOOK
2

REAL ESTATE

INTRODUCTION

If you can afford it, you can buy a house, co-op or condominium* simply by sitting back and hiring professionals to make all the arrangements for you. You can find a professional for each step of the way and never do more than look at the houses they find for you, make your choice, then sign the papers they thrust in front of you. In fact, that is exactly the extent to which most people participate in the purchase of their home—they sign where and when they are told, relying blindly on the professionals.

We have prepared this book because we believe there is a better way to manage the purchase of a home. This is probably one of the most expensive purchases you will ever make. You will be served best if as much of the mystery as possible is removed from the process and if you play an active role in the decision making.

This book is intended for prospective home buyers who want to

---

*Throughout this manual, the terms "house," "home" and "unit" are used interchangeably. All denote the same thing for the purposes of the buyer—the residence being bought, whether it be a condo, a co-op, a single-family house or a town house.

work with real estate professionals in an informed way. It introduces the professionals involved in the selling and buying of homes, describes the role of each and tells you whose interests correspond to yours and whose are opposed. The more informed you are, the better you can participate in the discussions that go on among brokers, appraisers, lenders and all the others involved.

Although this book is written from a home buyer's point of view, those selling their homes will also find it useful. From whichever side you approach the process, the players and their roles in the process remain the same. It pays to be as well informed about them as possible.

How to Use This Book

To get the greatest benefit from this book, especially if you are buying your first home, read the full text first and look for other resources as well. Then refer back to the book at each stage of the process and follow the specific suggestions for where you are in the process.

A Word About Terms

Insider knowledge of the real estate profession is communicated through many industry "terms of art," shorthand language that, like all legalese, can be needlessly complex. In many cases, the terms can be replaced with common words without loss of meaning. This book tries to use both the common, plain-language terms and the terms of art you will need to understand. When a term of art is used, it is in italics and explained in plain language. Still other terms are defined in the glossary (Appendix III). The more familiar you become with these industry terms and their meaning, the more confidently you will participate in the negotiations and make the necessary decisions.

CHAPTER

I

SOME GROUND RULES

Real estate consists of land and buildings. This includes everything that is naturally a part of the land, such as minerals, and everything that is more or less permanently attached to the land, such as swimming pools and fences.

Residential real estate comes in three basic forms. Single-family homes are what most people think of when they think of home buying. Condominiums and cooperatives are two alternative forms of homeownership. They are discussed in Chapter 2. All other designations—town house, apartment, unit, duplex—are merely names for one of the three kinds of homeownership.

To acquire real estate, people exchange money or something else of value. To represent and act as a record of the exchange, people draft a *contract.* Once real property is exchanged, the seller *(grantor)* gives the buyer *(grantee)* a *deed,* which is the statement filed as the record of ownership.

The Deed

The formal representation of ownership you receive when you purchase real estate is the *deed*. It is a written instrument that states who you are, what you own and from whom you received it. It includes a specific description of the property involved and a statement that the named seller is transferring his or her interest in the land to the named buyer. It is filed as a public record, available for anyone to see.

Forms of Property Ownership

Whether you have a right to all or only a part of the real estate you own depends on how the deal was structured, what portion you were granted in the exchange and whether you own it alone or in partnership with someone else.

Property ownership can be in any of several different forms. The most common—and most complete—interest you can own in real estate is called the *fee simple,* or absolute ownership. When you own a fee simple interest, you own the real estate itself, everything below it (*mineral rights*) and everything above it (*air rights*). In most states, unless the document of the transfer of real estate specifies otherwise, it is assumed that the ownership being transferred is a fee simple.

Less common forms of ownership or interest in real estate include *fee tail* and *life estate*. These forms involve less than total and absolute ownership and control. The terms are derived from property law of centuries ago but are still used today in some states. More likely than not, unless you inherit land or are involved in an unusual transfer, you will be purchasing or selling a fee simple and will not need to concern yourself with these other terms. However, if you do come across them, read a textbook on property law and study their meaning carefully before you act. They are defined in the glossary (Appendix XII).

You can own fee simple property alone or with someone else. If you do share ownership with one or more persons, it can be structured in any of several different ways. The way you choose will have important resale and inheritance implications.

Tenancy in Common

When two or more people share ownership of real estate, they are said to have a *tenancy in common*. Each co-owner owns a designated percentage of the property and can do as he or she pleases with it. The co-owners can sell their portions separately or leave their portions in their wills to whomever they wish. When a co-owner dies, that co-owner's interest in the property passes to the co-owner's heir, who becomes a co-owner with the surviving original owner or owners.

Joint Tenancy

Joint tenancy is also ownership of a piece of property by two or more people. However, in a joint tenancy, the co-owners can be thought of as one person. Both of them own the full 100% of the real estate. No single owner can choose to sell or dispose of any or all of the property without the agreement of the other(s). Also, the property cannot be left in a will. When a co-owner dies, the remaining co-owners assume control of the property on their own, removing any requirement of probate.

Tenancy by the Entirety

Only married couples can own property under a *tenancy by the entirety*. As in a joint tenancy, each spouse has a "right of survivorship" that enables either of them to assume total ownership when the other dies. Again, one major benefit of this form of ownership is that, when one spouse dies, the transfer of ownership is usually not subject to probate.

Community Property

Community property is recognized by the property laws of eight states: Arizona, California, Idaho, Louisiana, Nevada, New Mexico, Texas and Washington. In these states, all property owned by a married couple is considered community property. This includes all property acquired during marriage that was not a gift or inheritance to one spouse or specifically kept separate. The earnings of both spouses and any property derived from those earnings are both considered community property. In some states, income earned by separate property (e.g., rental housing owned by one spouse) is also community property.

In the eight community property states, each spouse owns half interest in all the marriage's community property. Unlike joint ownership, community property does not include any rights of survivorship. When one spouse dies, the survivor owns only his or her share of the community property (in most cases, half of all the earnings and property acquired by both spouses during the marriage).

The share owned by the spouse who has died can be transferred by his or her will, or by the state if there is no will. The deceased spouse's share of the community property usually must be probated, although this varies from state to state. Also, half of the community property owned by the spouse who died will be included in calculating estate or inheritance taxes.

Commercial Property

In real estate transactions that involve commercial property held for income or tax shelter purposes, many people choose other, more complex title-holding devices: corporations, partnerships, land trusts and real estate investment trusts (called REITs). Free information regarding these can be obtained from the trust department of most local banks or savings and loans. Because they are beyond the scope of the average home buyer's interests, they are not discussed in this book.

Local Custom

Even though the sale and purchase of real estate is a highly regulated field, much about the process depends on local custom that has evolved over the years among area professionals. Don't be surprised to hear things like "the buyer usually handles that" or "the buyer and seller usually split that fee." Many of these customs have to do with closing costs, but some have to do with which side is responsible for performing or arranging for a certain task, such as an inspection, to be performed. If you have a buyer's broker, look to him or her for advice. If not, you may have to rely on the seller's broker to tell you what local custom dictates or ask friends and neighbors who have bought homes in the area.

CHAPTER

2

CONDOS AND CO-OPS

Two forms of homeownership have become increasingly popular—condominiums and cooperatives. Both represent strategies for pooling home-purchasing power. They evolved in response to changing life-styles and shifting conditions in the real estate marketplace.

Ever since condominiums became popular, they have represented a growing portion of the nation's "housing starts." (Housing starts are government calculations of the number of new houses that enter the real estate market each month.) Like cooperatives, "condos" are attractive because they often enable you to own property without having to care for a yard or tend to other outdoor maintenance. They also afford potential savings on utilities.

The way you buy a condominium or cooperative differs significantly from the way you buy a traditional family house. If you are shopping for either a condominium or cooperative, you may want to supplement this book with additional materials that are specific to the subject. This book can be used for the purchase of condos and co-ops, and it points out differences between these and standard detached homes. You will also want to shop for a broker who specializes in these markets.

Condominiums

The term *condominium,* or condo, describes a kind of ownership, not a kind of building. It is a form of ownership in which the owners of more than one home share the ownership, use and responsibility for certain common facilities. The individual owners control their own homes, or *units,* and pay a fee to have the common areas maintained. The common areas may include hallways, lobbies, parking lots and garages, recreational facilities and all of the other parts of the development not defined as a unit, including the roof.

The purchaser of a condominium unit receives a deed that gives *exclusive* ownership of the particular unit and *partial* interest in the common elements associated with the business or community in which the unit is located.

Each unit owner is automatically a member of the condominium association, the organization that operates the community as a business enterprise and insures compliance with the association's bylaws. The association elects a board of directors to run the condominium and to collect fees from the unit owners to maintain the common areas and to pay insurance and other expenses, such as utilities, that aren't paid individually.

The condominium fee may vary from building to building and from unit to unit, depending on the size and value of the unit and how the board of directors decides to structure the fees. The size of this fee should be considered before buying a unit, because it is paid in addition to the mortgage a buyer must pay. Be aware, too, that condominium fees have been known to rise steeply after the purchase. Study the terms of condo membership carefully or you may find yourself with a mortgage you planned on and provided for but a condo fee that far exceeds your expectations or ability to pay.

Condo living is available in a variety of styles: communities of single-family houses, attached town houses, apartment units in either high-rise or low-rise buildings, and garden apartments. There are condo communities for the elderly and for "singles." There are parking garage condos and commercial condos. Residential condo units can be mixed in the same building with commercial condo units. In fact, just about any combination you can imagine is now possible.

Large, planned communities have been established throughout the country, with neighborhood condo projects bound with other forms of ownership under a master "umbrella" community association. Unit owners may find themselves members of two associations, one formed primarily to maintain the exteriors of their buildings and the other formed to maintain parks and recreational centers common to several projects. The costs of all such factors need to be weighed in determining what you can afford.

Condominium Financing

In many ways, financing the purchase of a condo is similar to financing a single-family home. However, some differences are worth noting. Condo advertisements for newly built or newly converted units that offer "low-rate mortgages" are common. They frequently offer below-market rates as incentives to get you to buy. This usually means the seller or developer and a lender have struck a deal in which the seller agrees to subsidize low-cost loans by paying a few percentage points. This is called a *buy-down*. It can be a good deal, but be sure to read the fine print.

If you are considering a buy-down, ask specific questions. For example, the average buy-down lasts from one to five years. After that period, the seller ends the subsidy and the interest rate returns to the market level. Be sure to ask whether the loan continues in effect after the buy-down expires or whether you will have to find another loan.

You should also ask about the terms of any continued financing you may be locked into. Will it be a fixed rate? An adjustable rate? A rate that is a few points above market? (These rates are defined in Chapter 9.)

Cooperatives

There are some important differences between condominiums and cooperatives, or co-ops. The main distinction is that you actually purchase real estate when you buy a condominium; you obtain a deed and must pay your own property taxes. When you buy a co-op, you are buying not the property, but stock in a corporation that owns the property. Your stock represents your ownership interest in the unit and gives you voting rights.

You will pay a monthly amount that consists of essentially three payments. The first is the loan payment against what you borrowed to buy the unit from the seller. The second part is the portion of the co-op's overriding mortgage that you as a buyer assume. The third is the monthly maintenance or "carrying" charge for upkeep, insurance, taxes and some utilities.

The corporation issues you a lease that gives you the right to occupy your unit and use the common areas. You must come up with the purchase price, usually from a bank loan, but the monthly loan payments you make to the co-op are not really payments on a mortgage; instead, you are paying off a personal loan to the corporation. You also pay no real estate taxes directly; the corporation pays these, but in figuring your income taxes, you can deduct that part of your co-op or residence fee that is used to pay property taxes.

Your co-op fee may seem a lot like rent, but it is actually nothing at all like it. When you pay rent, you buy a service: the right to live on someone else's property. Once you use the service, you can't get your money back. When you pay your co-op fee, however, you are paying for services: maintenance of the property, repairs, utilities, and so on. Also, as you pay off the purchase price of your unit, it may seem like rent, but it's more like a mortgage: you are investing in ownership and accumulating the salable value of what you own—your equity in the corporation's stock. Afterwards you have something you can sell, with the hope of getting some or all of your investment back—or more.

Co-ops are popular in certain areas of the country and virtually unheard of in others. Because what you are really buying into is a corporation and not a piece of real estate, many of the government protections and regulations that apply to ownership of real property do not apply. This allows the co-op's board to be more selective in its choice of whom it permits to live on the property. You will have to be approved by the board of directors that governs the co-op. This process can be pro forma, involving only disclosure of your financial stability as proof that you can afford to live there, or it can involve a personal profile, references of past residences and a personal interview.

This selection process is as important to you as it is to the co-op board. You will want to learn as much about the building, the association management and other owners as you can. The section of this book on "Questions to Ask" (page 14) offers a few tips on choosing a particular co-op to live in.

Cooperative Financing

The difference between the legal structures of cooperatives and condominiums has important consequences. For one thing, it's often harder to borrow money for a co-op than for a condo, mostly because the co-op buyer receives a corporate stock certificate instead of a deed. The buyer therefore doesn't have the same physical collateral to offer the lender as insurance that the loan will be paid on time.

Because co-op buyers have no deed to offer as collateral, their loans are usually considered more as personal loans than home mortgages. In such cases, lenders are more likely to examine a borrower's credit record closely and require a higher down payment than they might for a loan backed up by the deed to the property being bought.

Also, because payment of taxes, some utilities and other assessments on the property will be out of your control, lenders may want to get a more detailed analysis of your current and expected income and debts—your ability to pay back the loan. This will add to the paperwork and time it takes to approve your mortgage application.

Finally, cooperative associations are themselves financed by an overriding, or "blanket," mortgage for the whole co-op. When you buy into a co-op, you tie yourself directly to the other owners: you incur a share of their overall debt. To the lender you ask for a loan, this will mean evaluating much more than your own financial profile. The bank will also want to look at the co-op's financial profile. This is the reason lenders are sometimes reluctant to make mortgages for co-ops and the reason many co-op boards are very selective about whom to accept as a buyer. A co-op with a reputation for having only the most qualified and reliable owners will have an easier time getting financing for its own needs.

Lenders have responded to all this with "share financing," especially in areas where co-ops are prevalent. This allows you to obtain a mortgage for the cost of your co-op based on the overriding mortgage of the entire co-op. You are really getting what would otherwise be known as a second mortgage, one based on the equity in an existing mortgage.

When co-ops first entered the market, the real estate industry found it hard to adapt. Things are somewhat better now, especially in areas where co-ops are popular. One major adjustment was made by the secondary mortgage market, which purchases loans from mortgage companies, banks and other lenders. Some of the large companies that "buy" loans to sell to secondary lenders (for instance, "Fannie Mae"), now purchase co-op loans, making more lenders less reluctant to make these loans to co-op buyers. But it may still take some looking.

Again, if you are thinking of buying a co-op, remember to look closely not only at the co-op loan rate, but also at the monthly maintenance fees. You have no accurate way of predicting how high or how fast these fees will rise, but if you examine past trends in the development, you may get an idea of what to expect.

Questions To Ask

Buying a condominium or co-op ties your fate to the actions of others—your fellow members of the condo association or fellow stockholders of the co-op corporation. Before buying, you will want to know as much as possible about the way the association or corporation is run and how its decisions are made. You especially need to know whether you will be free to sell and get out if you become displeased and whether you'll be charged a penalty for doing so.

Read the articles of incorporation and bylaws of the co-op corporation. You will be given a copy to read and often will be asked to sign a statement certifying that you have read them. If you're not automatically given these documents, insist on seeing them. Many standard contracts and state laws require disclosure of these documents as well as past and future budgets. They also require a "contingency" that is not released until you've certified that you've had a chance to read them. Finally, you should receive a letter certifying whether the unit's assessments are paid in full.

Read the governing papers of the association. How is the board of directors elected? How long do directors serve? What does it take to remove them from office? Are you bound by every decision they make? On what matters do non–board members get to vote? How much say will you have over who gets the contracts for things like fuel and maintenance work? All of these questions should be answered fully *before you buy.*

You should also get a financial picture of the corporation: budgets, minutes of meetings, planned future expenses, lists of special assessments, copies or descriptions of outstanding mortgages or loans, engineers' reports from past or projected repairs or renovations. Talk to the co-op or condo treasurer.

Finally, it is a good idea to learn what you can about the aspirations and tendencies of the condo or co-op board. You will want to know whether its members are thrifty or extravagant and will want to get a sense of how they have been spending (or not spending) the association's money. The last thing you want is to move into a co-op or condo where the board decides to redecorate the lobby each time a new president is elected. You can get a sense of this by looking at previous as well as current budgets and by talking to real estate agents who are familiar with the property, the other owners and the current officers.

Here are some things to pay particular attention to:

- What are the fees? All of them? How often are assessments made?

- How large a down payment is required? This is especially important and restrictive in co-ops, not only for you; it also bears on whether you'll have trouble finding a buyer when you want to sell.

- How large a reserve does the association maintain? Are there plans to increase or deplete it dramatically?

- Are there limits on what you can do to your unit in terms of remodeling? Painting? Air-conditioning? Shrubbery? Satellite dishes? Room additions? Appliances?

- Does the association have any "rights of first refusal"? Do you have to sell your unit to the association if it matches any offer made by another buyer? (This could mean trouble finding a buyer, who may not want to go through the trouble of tendering an offer only to have the association buy the unit instead.

- What are the limits on your ability to rent out your unit? On whom you can sell to? On whether you can have house guests?

- Is the property restricted to owner-occupied units? Many buildings stipulate that only owners are allowed to live there. Others let owners rent their property but only for a limited time or permit only a certain number of units to be rented. Some association boards believe residentowners tend to take better care of the property than owners who buy units to use as rental property. If residence is not restricted to owners, you can use the property as an investment or source of rental income.

- Are there limits on pets, children, whether you can marry (in the case of "singles" condos)?

Condo and co-op buyers are usually given estimates of the expenses of owning the unit, including all fees and estimates of utilities. Remember, these are subject to change. Indeed, it is wise to assume they will increase, especially in the case of new developments or newly converted units.

When a developer or seller misrepresents the actual costs of operating a condo unit, it is called "low-balling." Victims of this tactic have successfully sued developers in several cases.

Introductory Offers

In some developments the condominium fee is waived for an introductory period or kept artificially low to attract buyers.

It's wise always to be wary of introductory incentives, especially the most attractive ones. They often look better than they are. Low introductory fees can climb rapidly once the designated period is over, and there is little you can do to prevent it. One reason is that many of the expenses paid out of the fees—utility bills, for example—are out of the control of the condo association. The best you can do is look for a condo that has a reputation for being frugal (but not too frugal to let important maintenance tasks slip by) when it comes to assessments against the unit owners.

Condo/Co-op Conversions

Many people find themselves in the position of having to decide whether to buy a home without ever wanting one and without being prepared. This is because the building or development where they are renting is undergoing a "conversion" to a condo or co-op. Many states have laws that govern when rental property can be converted by a developer or owner.

Generally, the laws were passed either to preserve low-income rental housing in the community or to give existing tenants the "right of first refusal" to purchase their unit or, sometimes, another unit in the building at a below-market price. If you find yourself in this position, look closely at the offer you're being given, learn your rights under your state's law and pay careful attention not to miss the deadlines for action or notices on your part. After the initial offer and your acceptance, most of the transaction will proceed much like the sale of any other condo or co-op. Tenants usually, at this point, form an association to investigate the offer, the conditions and their mutual interests.

All tenants will receive a notice of the owner's intention to convert and an offer to buy a unit at a below-market price. This offer is known as a "red herring." The laws typically work so that if a certain percentage of residents accept the offer to buy or "convert," then the building can go co-op. In some states those who don't accept will be forced to move, but a provision in many laws protects residents by giving them the right to remain in the building as renters if the building goes co-op and they do not want to buy.

Before you accept a purchase-price offer, compare yours with other tenants' and get a statement in writing about any restrictions on your right to sell within a certain period of time.

Condo/Co-op Warranties

If you're buying a newly constructed condo or co-op, you will need to know about your protection under warranties. Warranties are legally enforceable assurances about the quality or condition of a property or its appliances and systems. They can be in the form of a contract between two parties or an across-the-board pledge. They can be imposed by states or by the federal government. Warranties under one federal law, the Magnuson-Moss Warranty Act, apply to such things as appliances and furnaces in new homes, and a clause in your contract will reflect this.

The same warranties that are available to purchasers of single-family houses (see Chapter 7) are available to purchasers of condos and co-ops. These include direct warranties by the builder as well as guarantees by contractors or manufacturers of components and appliances. These latter warranties are rarely revealed until the title is obtained, however. At the least you should make sure the purchase contract provides for delivery of all warranties at the closing (see Chapter 14). Also, be sure to purchase insurance if you want to make sure you're covered if something not covered by a warranty breaks down during the first year of ownership.

Specifically ask for certain warranties that are frequently omitted from the purchase contract or through failure to deliver separate written guarantees. These include warranties for kitchen cabinets, bathroom vanities, flooring, air-conditioning ducts, wrought ironwork, roofing, siding, concrete work other than foundations, electrical systems and painting. While reputable builders usually insist that the subcontractors they hire provide them with effective warranties covering defects in materials or installation, the terms and application of those obligations are rarely expressed in the buyer's contract or even worded in favor of the buyer.

Be sure also to look for warranties that cover things outside your own dwelling unit. Correcting defects in parking lot pavement, elevators or swimming pool installations will have to be paid for by you and the other unit owners unless you have warranties.

A Special Note

If you plan to use a lawyer* or other professional in buying a condo or co-op, start early. Purchasing a unit requires reviews of the contract, all warranties and the condominium association or corporation papers. No one can be expected to digest and evaluate all these documents at the last moment. If you want help, get it early to avoid last-minute delays or surprises.

*See *Using A Lawyer* by Kay Ostberg in association with HALT, Random House, 1990.

CHAPTER

3

PROFESSIONALS

The real estate industry supports a wide variety of professionals who, for a fee, provide just as wide a variety of services. They include brokers and agents, mortgage bankers, developers, investors, financial planners, appraisers, escrow agents and, of course, lawyers. You may never need any of them or you may need them all, but you will be better off if you understand what they offer—and where their interests lie. Only then will you be able to participate confidently in decision making.

Even if you decide to proceed on your own or work only with one or two professionals, you should be familiar with the roles they all play—because the seller may have hired them.

Sellers' Real Estate Brokers and Agents

Brokers are professionals who find prospective buyers for a seller's home. *Agents* usually work for brokers. Both must pass a test to be licensed. Both work for the seller, not the buyer. Realtors are real estate brokers who belong to the National Association of Realtors—a trade association of 800,000 real estate professionals.

Some people acquire a real estate license but work only as part-time agents or brokers to supplement income from their full-time careers; others do it full time. Be aware that some part-timers may be far less knowledgeable or connected to the local market or available than their full-time counterparts.

People who want to sell their homes contract brokers to advertise and secure ready, willing and qualified buyers. This is called *listing* the home with a broker. The listing can be either "exclusive," meaning the seller is restricted from looking elsewhere for a buyer for a specified period, or open and unrestricted. Some sellers include a "reserve" clause in their contract with the broker, giving them the right to find a buyer on their own. If they do find a buyer without the broker's help, they do not have to pay the broker anything. If you know that a seller can avoid paying a commission to a broker, either because of a reserve clause or because the home is "for sale by owner," you may be able to negotiate a lower price.

Multiple Listing Service

Many brokers work through a *multiple listing service* operated by local real estate associations. This is a computer bank of homes that are on the market. It describes their characteristics, price and other features. Most brokers have access to these listings, and a seller who uses a broker often includes in the contract that the home will be listed with the "multiples," as it is called in the trade. This method gives the seller a much broader pool of potential buyers and usually means the home will sell faster (see Chapter 5).

Commissions

If the broker finds a buyer and the deal goes through, he or she collects a percentage of the purchase price, called a *commission*, from the seller. As a buyer, you can go to a broker, be shown every home on the market, and pay nothing for the service. Be aware, however, that if you buy a house this way, the broker's commission is probably already included in the price you're paying. In effect, the seller doesn't pay the broker, you do.

The broker who signs the contract with the seller is called the "listing" broker or agent. If this broker finds a buyer, he or she is paid the full commission the seller negotiated and contracted for, usually 4% to 7% of the purchase price.

If another broker produces a buyer either by using the multiples or by bringing a buyer to an "open house," the listing broker still gets a commission but has to split it with the broker who produced the buyer. This person is sometimes called the "secondary" broker. Mostly because of the multiples, splitting commissions has become widespread.

Broker Loyalty

One caution: although brokers can provide a valuable service to prospective home buyers by saving them the irritation of having to search on their own, it is not the broker's job to guarantee that you get the best price or that the property has no problems or defects. That's your job or a responsibility you can hire others to handle.

Many people think that because a broker escorts them to homes and gives them information about a seller that sounds like advice or inside knowledge, the broker is working for them. This is a grave mistake. Even though they may call themselves "your" broker, they are not working for you but for the seller. This distinction gets even more blurred in buyers' minds when two brokers are involved—a quite common occurrence.

In the eyes of the law, brokers are responsible only for representations they themselves make. Of course, happy customers make for a better reputation and the broker does have an incentive for getting you to buy the home: it's called the commission. Thus, if a broker has an interest in satisfying you, it's a publicity and marketing decision, not an enforceable legal duty. Although your interests may correspond to those of the broker to some extent, don't assume they do in all aspects of the deal. The bottom line is that the loyalties of both the listing and the secondary broker run to the seller, not the buyer.

Buyer's Agents

A positive trend for home buyers is the recent rise in the popularity of *buyer's agents*. A buyer's agent is paid an hourly or flat fee determined before you begin shopping for a home. Because the fee is known beforehand and is not based on the price of the property, the agent has no incentive to push you toward a more expensive property. Some buyer's agents, however, may encourage you to have them split the commission with the seller's broker. In other words, the more you pay, the higher the fee. As you can imagine, such an arrangement is not to your advantage.

The U.S. Department of Housing and Urban Development (HUD) encourages home buyers to explore a buyer's agent arrangement because of its potential for improving the quality and integrity of services. One of the advantages is that you have an all-purpose consultant—if you shop around and hire a good one. A buyer's agent can go with you on house-hunting trips, review or even negotiate your contract, tour the home with you to look for defects, examine the management and financial records of the condo or co-op association, help with financing and be at your side for the closing.

And, unlike a seller's agent, there's no confusion about which side the loyalty runs to. A buyer's agent is on *your* side.

Don't be surprised if agents don't know what you are talking about when you ask them to be your buyer's agent. In many parts of the country, most agents have not picked up on this trend. Whatever you do, shop around, be clear that you are looking for a *buyer's* agent and get the best price.

Appraisers

Before buying a house, you will want one or more people to judge its value so you can know whether the asking price is fair. Professionals who do this for a living are called *appraisers*. Any prospective buyer can have an appraisal done at any time. When you hire a professional appraiser to give you an objective valuation of the property, you can be reasonably sure the person is not on anyone's "side" and has no common interest either with you or the seller. The professional is merely selling a service.

Sometimes two appraisals are done for the same home sale because some lenders, banks for example, require a separate appraisal before approving a loan. It's a good idea to check first with your prospective lender to make sure the appraisal company you choose is acceptable. Many people have only one appraisal done—the lender's. The choice is yours and you can save money following that route, but if you're at all suspicious of collusion, have an independent appraisal done by someone of *your* choosing.

Lenders

Banks, savings and loans, insurance companies, union pension funds, credit unions, and other lending institutions can all provide you with the money to buy a home (see Chapter 10). At this point you need to know only that, unlike appraisers, lenders have a direct interest in the deal you strike and the quality of the property you buy. If, in the future, you fail to make your loan payments (*default*), the lender will take your home (*foreclose*) and sell it to regain the lost money. That's why the lender wants to make sure you are buying a home that can be resold for at least as much as the amount of the loan you're asking.

Although lenders do have an interest in the value of the property, don't expect them to be your allies. For all practical purposes, lenders don't really care if you pay an inflated price for a house. They care only that, if you default, they can make up their losses.

Escrow Agents

An *escrow agent* arranges all the paperwork, documents and payments involved in a house closing. Sometimes the escrow agent is a real estate broker, agent or lawyer, sometimes an uninvolved professional. The term escrow refers to the depositing of money or documents with a neutral party who has a duty to hold them until certain conditions are met. Where an escrow agent performs the closing tasks, that agent is responsible for holding all of the documents until all promises are fulfilled, at which time the money is released and the necessary papers filed.

Lawyers

More than any of the other professionals, lawyers are the ones you hire to look after your interests each step of the way. They have a duty to watch over your interests, but be cautious: what they do for you depends on the terms of your agreement.

You can hire an experienced real estate lawyer for any or all of the following services: to draft or review your purchase contract; to negotiate with the seller or the seller's agent; to check that the appraisals are not unrealistically high or low; to conduct the title search; and to attend the closing with you (see Chapter 13). At the least, many buyers rely on lawyers to do the *title search,* a check to be sure that there are no conflicting claims or problems with the ownership of your property (see Chapter 12).

However, even in the present complex real estate market, more and more people are routinely buying homes without the help of lawyers, especially people who are buying their first home, those with no existing home to sell and those considering a home that is under the "conforming mortgage" limit. This is a limit, set by the large companies in the secondary mortgage market, that ranges around $170,000–$180,000 (see under "Secondary Mortgage Market" in Chapter 10).

The trend toward buying a home without a lawyer is occurring despite charges by state and local bars that nonlawyer agents who draw up real estate contracts are guilty of the unauthorized practice of law. As more and more agents defy such threats and perform functions traditionally reserved for lawyers, both buyers and sellers save money.

Clearer laws, plain-language requirements and more efficient government agencies and processes will enable still more people to purchase their homes without the additional expense of hiring legal counsel. While we wait for the government to act on these reforms, however, buyers who do proceed on their own are cautioned to utilize every resource that is available and to be well-informed shoppers.

Many people hire an all-purpose real estate law firm to do all their paperwork and make sure the transaction complies with the law. This is especially true when people sell their home without a broker and need a neutral party to act on their behalf.

Large real estate companies also may offer this service through a local law firm, and they will undoubtedly let you know about this when you sign the contract. Using such services can save you some money, because the fee is decided in advance and split by the parties. One caution, however: make sure the company is acting as a neutral "closing" agent and not working for either side in the sale.

Who Costs What?

Sellers' brokers and agents are paid on commission. They receive a percentage of the price of the home when they provide a ready, willing and qualified buyer. The rate usually ranges from 4% to 7%. If two brokers are involved—a listing broker and a secondary broker—they split the commission, usually down the middle. (They, not you, will negotiate their percentage.)

Keep in mind that brokers and agents who work for real estate firms routinely turn half their commission over to the company to cover overhead, including office space, telephone, and advertising. This doesn't affect your price, but it's important to know that often only half the commission goes to the broker. If a deal has two brokers and one of them works for a company, that broker can end up with only a quarter of the total commission.

Buyer's agents can be paid an hourly, flat or percentage fee, depending on the deal you negotiate. Shop around to get the best price and be aware of the possible conflict of interest that can arise from a commission arrangement (page 242).

Appraisers are paid by the buyer, either a flat fee or a commission based on the property's selling price.

Lenders are paid by charging "points," a percent of the loan, and other fees. These will be disclosed to you in advance (see Chapter 9).

Escrow (or closing) agents' fees are usually split between the buyer and seller. If the escrow agent is one of the parties working for the buyer or seller, many of the closing costs—for example, document preparation—will be paid, usually in a flat fee, to that agent.

Lawyers usually charge a flat fee for a specified range of services, including the title search, contract review, overseeing some of the inspections, doing a final walk-through inspection of the property to check its condition, preparing some or all of the documents and attending the closing. Their fees range from $200 to $1,000. Be sure to get a written lawyer-client contract that spells out what services* are included and at what cost to you.

*See *Using a Lawyer* by Kay Ostberg in association with HALT, Random House, 1990.

CHAPTER
4

BENEFITS AND COSTS

Before you begin shopping, weigh the benefits and burdens of homeownership in light of your goals, life-style and financial and other commitments. This will give you an idea of your home-buying potential. You may or may not want to ask the help of one or more professionals—a financial planner or real estate counselor—but read the rest of this chapter first. It may convince you that you can do all or most of the evaluation yourself.

The Benefits

Building Equity

Homeownership is part of the American dream, an investment for the future. Regardless of how reasonable your rent, paying it does nothing to help your financial future. It is money spent and gone. Even though interest rates may be high, many people are attracted to the idea of having a home in which to build *equity*. Equity is that part of the home's value that is yours, the part you would keep if you sold the home and then paid off what was left of your mortgage. The idea is that with each mortgage payment, your equity in the property increases as it does with increases in the market value.

A major question for many people who want to buy a home is whether they should do it now and settle for less than their dream house or wait until they are better established financially and can get the real thing. Caution never hurts, but the idea behind equity is that money paid into a mortgage, less interest, will almost always be recovered upon sale of the home even though the full mortgage hasn't been paid off. (In fact, few people, unless they live in the same house for twenty or thirty years, pay off an entire mortgage without first selling the home.) Thus, buying a small "starter house" now could well be a springboard to buying a better one later. Under present tax regulations, you don't have to pay income taxes on the profit you make selling your present home if you reinvest it in another home within two years.

One warning: under certain circumstances homeownership may be a dream that can make you poor. Many people scrimp and save to make a down payment on a house, then tie themselves to a mortgage they can barely afford. As a result, they have no spare money for the things they once enjoyed—movies, vacations, sports, dinners out. Be careful to compare your desire to own a home with the risk of being "house poor."

Tax Breaks

Having a mortgage to pay can be a particular advantage if you need or want to shelter some of your income from taxes. At present, all the interest you pay on the mortgage can be deducted, dollar for dollar, from your income when calculating your income taxes. This is an especially big and early bonus to those whose mortgages are structured so that most of the first few years' payments are interest (see Chapter 9).

Building Credit

Maintaining a mortgage also builds your credit capability. Although you tie up a lot of cash in a home purchase, you will be allowed to borrow money based on the amount of the loan you've paid off. As a result, each year that you make all the payments on time, new credit doors will open if you need them.

Inheritance

As a homeowner, you can pass most types of ownership on to your heirs. Also, by selecting carefully from among the forms of ownership discussed in Chapter 1, you can set up the ownership so that it avoids probate.

What Can You Afford?

The most important element of buying a home is how much you can afford. Lenders will ultimately make the decision for you by deciding whether to give you a mortgage. Without a mortgage, few people can afford a home. While lenders do consider whether you seem reliable, most of their decision is based on cold calculations of your assets and income.

Each lender has a different formula, and even within one company, how this decision is made can vary depending on the type of loan you're applying for and the size of your down payment. A good rule of thumb is that you will not be approved for a loan if the monthly payments, including taxes and fees, exceed 25% to 30% of your income. There are exceptions, but this is a good yardstick to keep in mind.

Secondary Loan Market

Most mortgage loans are "sold" immediately after the closing to large companies in what is known as the secondary or conforming loan market (Fannie Mae and Freddie Mac are two institutions that buy loans from lenders for sale to the large investors on the secondary market). Virtually all lenders use the guidelines issued by these companies to determine whether to give you a mortgage. A conforming loan is one under an amount that has been about $187,000 and that conforms to the following standards:

- That no more than 28% of your monthly income is used for your mortgage (25% if your down payment is less than 10% of the cost of the home)

- That no more than 36% of your income is used to pay regular debts (33% if your down payment is less than 10% of the cost of the home)

- If you apply for an FHA mortgage, you have more flexibility: 29% of your income can service the loan and 41% of your income can be used for other debts

Analyze your financial potential rationally, the way a lender will, so you won't be found financially unqualified *after* you have begun negotiating for the home you want. Calculating what you can afford is the first and most important step. How well you do it determines how well your investment will turn out.

Many home buyers rely on the lender to put their financial picture together for them. This can lead to problems down the road—even outright disaster—because too many lenders may not know or care whether you are committing yourself to spending more than you can comfortably afford. After all, their interest is in getting *their* money's worth, not yours. The two goals aren't necessarily the same.

Try very hard to weigh and consider *all* your expenses, including hidden ones. A lender will ask about fixed monthly expenses, bills, tuition, car payments, even transportation expenses, but you will have to include and determine for yourself the "style of life" expenses that will cut into what you have left after these essentials. These include recreation, hobbies, movie and theater tickets, dining out and travel. Unless you factor these in, you will end up with a skewed idea of what your budget can absorb.

Start Early

It's worth saying again that the search for a loan is at least as important as the search for a home. Because of this, you should start the search *at the same time* you begin to look for your dream house. Talk to people who have done it before. Talk to banks, friends, relatives, colleagues at work. Build a list of possible sources of loans, what seems to be the going interest rate, lengths of loans and any other facts you think pertinent.

The "Up-Front" Costs

Try to arrive at a good estimate of the total cost of buying a home. Be sure to count fees for professional services, inspections, adjustments, closing costs, homeowner's insurance, property taxes, utilities and maintenance. In many instances, what these fees are will depend on the price range of the home you're considering, but they can be estimated ahead of time. (Chapters 7–14 will help you make these estimates.)

In addition, you may also need cash for furniture, appliances and other household items. Be sure to include them in your list because they can add up to a significant outlay.

The Down Payment

The largest single item you'll have to pay is probably the down payment, the amount of cash the lender wants "up front" against the purchase price *before* a loan is made. This sum reduces the amount of the loan. For example, if the home costs $100,000, the lender will likely require a minimum down payment of $20,000, leaving a mortgage balance of $80,000 to be paid over time. Depending on market conditions, the size of the minimum down payment usually varies from 10% to 25% of the purchase price.

Alternatively, it can be as low as 5% for housing in the lower price range that qualifies for an FHA loan, and no down payment is required for veterans receiving VA loans (see Chapter 10).

When interest rates are low and stable, it makes sense to put as little cash "down" as possible and to borrow the rest. That way, if interest rates go up during the life of your loan, you'll be in a good position paying the low rate. With higher and more volatile interest rates, it is wise to borrow as little as possible. Nevertheless, such decisions depend on your personal financial situation. If, for example, tax savings are very important to you, you may want a large loan so as to use the interest payments to reduce your income tax.

Your Net Worth

After you add up all the cash outlays you can expect to make before moving into your new home, it's time to calculate your net worth. This is particularly useful in determining how much cash you can afford to put down on a home. Your net worth is arrived at by totaling all your assets and subtracting your debts. You will need this information before making any important decisions, so it's best to get it out of the way early. Besides, your lender is going to require it anyway.

Your calculations tell you how much money you have available for your down payment and other up-front expenses. Remember, you may have to use some of this money for other moving-in expenses, too, so be cautious. Subtract from your net worth all of your estimated fees, expenses and moving costs.

Now evaluate how much cash reserve your particular family needs. A college fund? Vacation money? A reserve for uncovered medical expenses? Money for orthodonture? For a computer course? Calculate such possibilities for your own situation. Then ask yourself: How much money do I need in the bank to keep me from feeling I am off to the poorhouse?

Subtract these estimates from your net worth and you will know what down payment you can actually handle. Use the following worksheet to get started:

NET WORTH WORKSHEET
as of_____
(date)

ASSETS

Bank account balance(s) (checking, savings) _____

Stocks _____

Bonds _____

Insurance (cash value) _____

Certificate(s) of deposit _____

Accounts receivable (cash-in value owed to you) _____

Real estate (appraised value) _____

Automobile(s), boats, planes (resale value) _____

Personal property (antiques, jewelry, furs, silver, china) _____

Annuity(ies) (surrender value) _____

Other assets _____

TOTAL ASSETS _____

LIABILITIES

Debts to banks and other lenders (nonmortgage and auto loans) _____

Real estate mortgage(s) (balance due) _____

Outstanding credit card account bills _____

Unpaid income taxes _____

Auto and other vehicle loan(s) (balance due) _____

Personal debts _____

Other debts _____

TOTAL LIABILITIES _____

TOTAL ASSETS (from above) _____

LESS TOTAL LIABILITIES _____

LESS "RESERVE" _____

NET WORTH _____

Monthly Income

After calculating the down payment you can afford, the next step is to determine how much you can afford to pay each month on your mortgage. Unless you're applying for a government-backed loan, the lender will usually trust your estimate of your cost of living. To figure your monthly income and expenses, list all sources of income: salaries, interest, stock dividends, trust payments, pensions, rental income, royalties, alimony, child support, and so on. Then list all expenses: food, clothing, recreation, transportation, charities, installment payments, credit card bills, dues, entertainment, and so on. If you calculate well, you will have determined how much you have available for monthly mortgage payments.

A word of caution: lenders will be particularly sensitive to large monthly payments you are already making and will use them to reduce their estimate of the monthly payment they will approve for you. For example, if you are paying $200 a month on your car, some lenders will reduce their estimate of what additional loans you can handle by twice that amount or more. To be attractive to lenders and realistic with yourself, it's a good idea to rid yourself of as many monthly payments as you can and plan to keep new commitments low.

Your total monthly payments for housing—including mortgage, taxes, insurance, utilities, maintenance and repairs—should not be more than 25% to 30% of your monthly income. Of course, this figure is subject to your specific circumstances and your lender's requirements.

Before making this calculation, check whether your mortgage estimate includes taxes on the property. Many people "escrow" their taxes, which means the mortgage company adds this to the monthly payments and pays the taxes to the government for the homeowner at the appropriate time. Make sure you don't forget these taxes or double-count them.

How To Figure Monthly Mortgage Costs

To estimate how much you can afford each month, you need some fancy mathematics. It is not simply a matter of taking the total mortgage, calculating the interest and dividing by the number of payments. This is because loans are "amortized," meaning that each year's declining balance and the interest on the balance are added up and then divided by the number of payments.

You can find an amortization table for mortgages in some real estate books, in guidebooks for realtors and in some accounting books. The tables provide the interest rate and the number of years of the mortgage. They then use a "multiplier" you use with the number of thousands of dollars in your mortgage. Some pocket calculators have the table already programmed. Or you can ask your loan officer to calculate the figure for you.

Your Credit Rating

All this calculating may be in vain if there is a credit "skeleton in your closet." You can be sure that if it's there, your lender will find it. It's one of the things lenders do best.

Check your credit report *before* beginning the search for financing. You can get the information from your local credit reporting agency for a small fee. However, because the efficiency of reporting systems varies greatly, it's wise to ask a few major lending institutions in your community where they go for residential loan credit reviews.

If you have had problems with one or more creditors in the past, try to reach an understanding with them. If you feel you have been treated unfairly, write a well-documented letter supporting your position and file it with your local credit bureau *before* you apply for a mortgage.

Lenders are especially concerned about prior bankruptcy judgments, court collection judgments, garnishment of wages, attachment of assets and defaults on prior loans. These are what make "red flags" go up; 99% of the time, any such problems in your past will spell automatic denial of your mortgage application. A few late or missed payments on loans, overdue credit card balances and even a bill being sent to a collection agency may not spell automatic denial, but needless to say, they can't help.

Sometimes, however, such matters are not even reported or listed on a credit reference service's report. For example, action against you by a collection agency may not be reported to the credit bureau or to the lender requesting the report unless a lawsuit is filed against you and you lose. To make sure what will and what will not cause a problem, get a copy of your credit report before the lender does, then be prepared either to make good on your debts or explain them convincingly.

CHAPTER
5

HOUSE HUNTING

Now that you have determined what kind of down payment and monthly loan payments you can afford, you can begin looking seriously for a home. The way to ensure that you find the best is to plan carefully, follow your plan and exhaust all options.

Begin by drawing a clear picture of the kind of home you're looking for. Make a list of the characteristics of places you have liked and disliked. Then rank these characteristics as "musts," "options" and "dreams."

For instance, a "must" may be two bathrooms if you have a large family, or off-street parking if you're moving to the center of a city. An "option" may be a fireplace, a terrace or a kitchen pantry. A "dream" may be a greenhouse, skylights, a health club or a roof deck. After making your list, think about where you will compromise.

Be Extravagant In the world of real estate, just about everything is negotiable. For you this means that, in the beginning, nothing should be ruled out. Even the highest-priced house in the wealthiest neighborhood may be within your reach—for example, if it needs work, or if the owner needs to sell quickly. Now is the time to let yourself be a little extravagant.

Get Started Early The more time you have, the better. If you start your search well before making a commitment to move out of your current home, you have the luxury of being free to take your time. If you can do this, you won't have to live with the uncertainty of not knowing whether you bought the right house or apartment.

Plan Your Search If you have defined your housing requirements accurately and fully, you are in a position to make the best use of real estate guidebooks and homebuying seminars and avoid hit-and-miss hunting techniques. Attending one or more community classes on home buying can be particularly helpful, considering how the process varies from one place to another. Check the bibliography (Appendix IV) for other resources.

What Are You Looking For?

You need to make decisions on where you want to live and what kind of property you want. Consider the kind of neighborhood—city, suburban or rural—and the proximity to services and amenities like schools, shopping, places of worship and transportation. Next think about such questions as the number of bedrooms, bathrooms and closets, yard space, terrace, separate dining areas and so on. (Many such considerations are listed in the discussion of inspections in Chapter 7.) Make your decisions now based on the ideal—your "dream" house—then weigh them against what is realistic after you start seeing what's available in your price range. Here are some questions to ask when you're looking for the right neighborhood:

- Do you want a detached home, a town house or an apartment?

- Are you interested only in new homes? Do you want to live in a development that has recreational facilities?

- What kind of neighborhood are you looking for? Quiet? With shops, restaurants and atmosphere?

- Do you have children or plan to have them soon? Do you need a home near a playground or away from dangerous traffic? Will you need a place to walk the dog?

- What is the crime rate?

- How far are the school, bus or subway line, grocery store, dry cleaner, hardware store and place of worship?

- How is the parking?

- How good are city services? Will you pay extra for trash collection?

- Are the real estate values likely to rise or decline?

It's also a good idea to ask your prospective neighbors what they think about the neighborhood, development or building. Ask about the rate of commercial development, whether house break-ins are common, the level of police activity, how far you are from a thoroughfare for emergency vehicles. Ask these questions of people who have no direct interest in having you move there. A seller's broker can answer some questions, but be sure to check with neighbors, shopkeepers and even the local police. Brokers want to make the sale and will paint the best picture possible. You want a more critical analysis.

Once you know what kind of neighborhood you're looking for and have narrowed your search to a specific community, you're ready to find a home for sale.

Check Classified Ads The want ads provide a survey of the entire community, a cross-section of the day-to-day offerings in the residential market, an idea of prices, and a sense of what various neighborhoods are like. The ads are often divided into separate sections for detached houses, condominiums and co-ops. Saturdays and Sundays are the best days to look for ads, although they do run on other days and some papers make a point of advertising homes for sale on Friday to get ahead of the competition.

Checking the real estate ads daily for a few weeks will give you an idea of how quickly properties are sold, the prices being asked and which the dominant real estate companies are.

Classified ads take some skill to decipher. If you're having trouble, you can find out what all the abbreviations mean by calling the classified ad section of the newspaper or consulting a real estate agent. Be aware that these ads are intended to lure you into calling, so it is important to read them carefully. Don't get your hopes up until you see the property being advertised or at least talk to the seller or the seller's agent.

In any case, you'll have to telephone to get information that isn't in the ads. Before calling sellers and agents, be sure to compile a written list of important questions based on your listed "musts," "options" and "dreams."

Attend Open Houses To narrow down your list of what's important, list what you like and don't like in your current home, even if it's rented. Then go to "open houses" and get a feel for the market. These are hours during which anyone, with or without a broker, can tour a property that is on the market. In many parts of the country, when sellers contract with a real estate broker, they arrange for a certain number of open houses.

Where they are used, open houses are advertised in the newspaper, usually for the weekends. They are indicated by real estate company signs out front of the property and, sometimes, a block or so away, directing passersby. If your search is limited to a relatively small area, you can probably just stroll around looking for such signs. Especially in the high selling seasons of spring, summer and early fall, it's not unusual to find one or two residences for sale on any city block. If you're looking in a suburban or rural area, you will want to check the classified ads first, then narrow your driving time by getting directions to the homes you want to see.

During each open house, ask questions that will help you understand the home-buying process and differentiate among your musts, options and dreams. Some questions you might ask are:

- Do you have a fact sheet on the property? This will give you the basic information, including square footage, age of appliances and systems (plumbing and electrical), and type of ownership (condo, co-op or single family).

- How long has the property been on the market?
- How many square feet are there?
- Have major renovations been done recently?
- What kind of floor is under the carpeting?
- What is the neighborhood like?

You want to encourage give-and-take with the broker or seller to increase your sophistication and knowledge about what is and what isn't going to be acceptable and realistic when you make an offer to purchase.

After enough open-house visits, you'll be able to tell the difference between real wood floors and imitation, between ceramic tile and imitations. You'll know whether you want a kitchen large enough for dining or a separate dining area, whether you want or need a bathroom with a window. You'll look knowledgeably at closets and other storage space, finished basements, signs of water damage. You'll consider security systems, storm windows and screens, heating systems and air-conditioning. You can gain such awareness from open-house tours.

Ask Real Estate Companies It's almost impossible to do a thorough search for a home without dealing with a broker. This is where most homeowners go when they want to sell their houses. Real estate companies offer them a place to list their homes so that a large pool of prospective buyers will hear about them. The seller signs a contract that gives the company the right to try to sell the property. The company "shows" the house and makes a sales pitch to prospective buyers. For this service, the company receives a commission—a designated, agreed-upon percentage of the sale price of the house when it is sold.

In the course of trying to make the sale, brokers can help the home buyer too. They will give information about available houses and neighborhoods, take your list of requirements and match it to houses on the market and take you to see one, two or ten houses that fit your price range and other requirements. In addition, many real estate companies publish booklets that can tell you about the local market, available financing and closing costs.

But brokers are running against the clock. If they fail to produce a ready, willing and qualified buyer within the time specified in their contract with the seller, they can lose the contract and will have wasted the time spent showing the home and talking to prospective buyers. The pressure is on them to sell the home to you, so expect all brokers to put pressure on you to get you to buy.

To find a broker to show you homes, talk to people who have done it before. Consider brokers you ran into at open houses, especially those who seemed most helpful. Look for competence and a style you like—polite, aggressive, knowledgeable about the market, well connected. Especially look for brokers who can help with connections to other aspects of home buying—financing, inspections, appraisals and title searches.

If you plan to use a real estate company, choose carefully. Select companies and agents that best suit your needs. For example, some offer discount services to their sellers, charging a flat fee instead of the usual percentage. These discount services began in the late 1980s, and the companies that offer them have prospered. They can offer these reduced costs because they allow homeowners to "show" the home themselves and help with other tasks. In return for the flat fee, the discounts provide the usual services—placing the home on the multiple listing service, providing "for sale" signs, helping with financing, etc. A discounter will charge as little as $1,000 to $1,500 to help sell a home worth less than $100,000. From the buyer's point of view, this can be beneficial if the seller is willing to pass the savings along to sell the home faster.

Some brokers are local, with deep roots in the community, others are nationwide, with listings from all over the country. Big is not necessarily better. In some cases, it may be the small, community-based broker who works best for you. Such brokers may know the area better and be able to give more in the way of a personal service than the high-volume, high-turnover companies.

The Multiple Listing Service

The *multiple listing service* (MLS) is a computerized network of homes for sale in a region. Most brokers have access to this data base. This means that in most parts of the country the MLS can put you in touch with a very large percentage of the properties on the market.

A "listing" broker puts the property on the multiple listing. This broker is under contract with the seller to sell the property in exchange for a commission. The broker who is showing homes to you, the buyer, can punch your requirements into the MLS and come up with a list of prospects. You and the broker then go to the homes you select. If you decide to make an offer, you do so through the broker who showed you the home. If the sale goes through, the broker who accompanied you splits the commission with the listing broker.

If the listing firm shows you a home it has the contract for, it in turn gets the full commission. For this reason, brokers may try to steer you first to homes they are listing to avoid splitting a commission. Nevertheless, splitting commissions has become so common that this will probably not be a problem.

If you feel you're being directed only to properties the broker has listed, consider switching. Such steering can limit your choices drastically. Be clear with brokers who show you around that you want a full showing of many homes, including those on the MLS.

You and the Seller's Agent

Your relationship with an agent who represents home sellers is not one of employer to employee. It is a nocontract, informal understanding between two parties, the relationship of a customer and a salesperson in a department store. The agent hopes to sell you a property at the highest price. You hope the agent can produce a property you want and can afford.

Despite laws that bind agents to serve sellers, it is common for them to try to lead buyers into believing they are looking out for the buyer's interests, too. Agents want both sides to be happy with the deals that are struck, but they are interested primarily in getting the highest commission possible. The higher the sales price, the higher that commission will be.

Agent Disclosures Some states have passed laws requiring agents to disclose to you their relationship or "fiduciary duty" to the seller when they first start showing you homes. Members of the National Association of Realtors are also required under association rules to make such a disclosure.

One Agent or Two? Many people question whether they are cheating one seller's agent if they also ask for help from another agent. As we've noted, agents work for the seller to produce a buyer; you have no contract or obligation to them that prevents you from working with another. In some places, local custom allows you to ask as many agents for help as you'd like, while in other places, that practice is unheard of. When you're *selling* a house, it may sometimes be to your advantage to work with an agent on an exclusive basis.

Learn what you can about the local custom from friends and other home buyers. Don't ask the brokers. They have no incentive to tell you you can also get help from their competition, even if it's true. If you do work with a second or third agent, let each one know so they don't duplicate work.

If you also plan to look for homes on your own, tell the broker who is showing you around. You especially will want to do this if you plan to look for homes that are "for sale by owner." In these cases, having an agent escort you may actually hurt your chances: the seller will not want to accept your offer because doing so may require paying the agent a commission. Avoiding such a commission is why they decided to sell the property on their own in the first place.

Here are some tips when shopping for an agent:

Start on Your Own Whether or not you plan to use real estate agents in your house hunt, it's always a good idea to shop on your own first. That way you will come to the agent with some awareness of local market conditions and what you might reasonably expect to find.

Classified ads will list houses that individual owners are selling on their own. Visit some of these, price them and educate yourself on their advantages and problems. These ads will also tell you which the major real estate companies in your area are and which seem to be listing the most homes that fit your needs. Other sources of such information include friends and relatives, people at work, neighborhood residents, supermarket bulletin boards and community organizations.

Protect Yourself It's advisable to visit several realty companies to see what properties are available in your price range. Let the agents know you understand the nature of the agency relationship and the agent's obligation to serve the seller.

Be Discreet Even though you have to give the agent some idea of your price range and your requirements, preserve your bargaining power by being discreet about what you divulge. The agent will try to gain your trust by seeming to reveal the seller's position, but be aware that the seller will hear about any weaknesses you reveal to the agent—including a need to act quickly or any overeagerness you've shown. An agent will probably ask to do a financial worksheet on you, both to be able to make offers to prospective sellers and to know the range of prices you can afford. There is no harm in doing this.

Don't Feel Pressured If an agent tells you another buyer is looking at the house today or is deciding today whether to buy the house, don't feel you have to make a quick decision. Balance your desire to buy the best home available against your need to act quickly.

Get It in Writing The law prevents agents and sellers from intentionally misrepresenting the properties they are advertising. This does not prohibit a certain amount of exaggeration, however. It's always best to have important representations about the property stated in the contract, particularly when the agent has to rely on information supplied by the seller.

A final note about the agent's commission. By law, agents' commissions are negotiable. In practice, however, they are almost always 4% to 7%. If more than one agent is involved in the purchase of your home, they will split the commission. In theory, sellers pay these commissions, but in reality, buyers pay them because the commission is included in the sale price.

One warning merits repeating here, because you must always bear it in mind: seller's agents and brokers can help you—but they don't work for you. Your interests and theirs seldom coincide.

You and the Buyer's Agent

If you want an agent to work for you, hire one. Although buyer's agents have been arranging commercial property sales for a long time, home buyers traditionally have had no representation in the real estate marketplace. Only recently have such agents become popular among residential buyers. Hiring your own agent to help you find a house and negotiate a deal is often a good idea, especially because buyer's agents can show and bargain for almost any house listed in the community, even those for sale by owners. They cannot, however, show you properties listed for sale by their own real estate companies because that would involve them in a conflict of interest prohibited by law.

Shopping for an Agent

Any licensed real estate agent can represent home buyers. Some agencies specialize in representing buyers instead of sellers. Most of these are located in medium-sized and large cities.

Look for someone with whom you can establish a good relationship, because you might be working together for weeks or months. Important professional qualities to consider are experience, intelligence, integrity, resourcefulness and intuition. Knowledge of the industry, houses and the community are particularly important. Again, the one- or two-office brokerage may well prove to be the best bet; it can offer you personal service and spend more time answering your questions and looking after your needs. Such personal attention can go a long way toward eliminating the anxiety of home buyers caught in the complexities of the real estate marketplace.

The first thing an experienced agent will do is ask questions to find out whether you are qualified to buy the type of house you're looking for. At this point you should also be evaluating the agent. Ask if the agent has a strong background. Talk to others about the agent's record. Find out about the agent's technical know-how, perhaps by talking to a former client. Ask about expertise with contracts, negotiating ability, record of cooperation with other brokers and influence with moneylenders.

The Buyer's Agent Contract

When you hire a buyer's agent, you enter a contract for services. With a fee "up front" or an hourly fee, you pay the agent to find you a house and negotiate a deal for you. You should reasonably expect agents to save you both time and money. If they can't tell you how they'll do this, you may want to look elsewhere. Here are some questions to ask when negotiating your service contract:

- How will the fee be calculated?

- Is there a minimum charge?

- How long will the contract be in force?

- What happens if you find a house on your own?

- How will disputes be resolved?

Most buyer's agents will offer to work for a flat fee. Few will work on commission and, as we've discussed before, if you find one who does, stay away, as this arrangement gives the agent an incentive to sell you a home at the highest possible price. This creates a conflict you will want to avoid.

"For Sale by Owner"

Some owners choose to sell their houses on their own, without a broker. At first glance, this looks like an automatic saving for the buyer in every case, because no commission has to be paid. But be sure to examine carefully any "discount" and to keep in mind that an owner unwilling to pay a commission to a broker may be just as unwilling to pass savings on to you.

Always remember the overriding truth about buying and selling anything: sellers charge what the market will bear. Although an owner can offer a house for a few thousand dollars less than what the asking price would be if a broker's commission had to be paid, there may be little incentive to pass the savings on to the buyer; many owners prefer to keep it for themselves.

Use this as a bargaining chip when you're the buyer. Suggest to the seller that he or she is already saving a substantial amount by not having to pay a broker's commission and ask for a price reduction that at least splits this amount between you. Find out what the prevailing commission percentage is in your area and reduce the seller's asking price by half of that percentage. You'll probably strike a deal.

Preparing To Buy

If you plan to sell your current residence first, it may be best to start advertising it for sale before beginning your search, but make sure you have already done your homework and can begin home hunting immediately. Be sure not to commit yourself to purchasing a new home until the old one is sold. On the other hand, give yourself enough time, and try to sell to a buyer who is willing to wait until you find your new home.

If you find a new home first, you'll be more likely to sell your current one quickly and perhaps too cheaply. Also, unless you can afford to own two homes, you may find yourself in a weak position—offering to buy the home only if you sell yours first—an offer sellers may be reluctant to accept.

The danger of being without a place to live can be avoided by delaying the closing on your existing residence. You can also rent, but until you buy your new home, you'll be sacrificing your income tax deduction of mortgage interest and you will incur the expense of moving, of committing to a lease, and possibly of storage charges.

CHAPTER
6

LEGAL LIMITS

In your search for a home to buy, you should consider the physical aspects of the property such as garage and storage space and whether the roof is sound. These will be covered in the next chapter. This chapter is concerned with the legal inspection—those rules that could seriously restrict your freedom to use the property you buy in any way you want.

The state, county, city or neighborhood can all legally restrict your right to use your property. Unless you ask the right questions now, you may be in for surprises later.

Easements and Shared Use

Separate elements of what you own, such as the underground mineral rights, can be sold or leased without giving up ownership of the land surface. You can also allow another person limited use of your real estate by granting an *easement*—an interest in real estate that lasts forever, unless otherwise specified, and that allows a specific limited use of a parcel of land.

Easements are granted for a wide range of activities. The most common easements are for streets or public utility lines. Another common easement is for the use of a common driveway to reach the backyards of neighboring houses.

Ask the seller or agent if there are any *formal* easements on the property. If there are, they will show up in the title search (see Chapter 13), but it's better to know about them now and decide beforehand whether you want to buy into the limitations they'll impose on your use of the property. Ask also if any *informal* easements or agreements exist. Sometimes, for example, there is an agreement to allow a neighbor to come onto the property to cut overhanging branches. Sometimes, by custom, neighbors use a path that cuts through the property. Although these informal understandings between neighbors are not always enforceable in court, your awareness of them can make for better relations after you move in.

Existing uses of another's property can be enforced in three ways. The first is through an easement that has developed over time and is all but permanent, such as the use of half of the driveway (a "party driveway") you share with your neighbor.

The second is through "adverse possession," what most of us think of as "squatter's rights." This is a legal doctrine that permits a squatter to hold ownership rights over someone else's piece of property if the squatter meets certain legal requirements set down in your state's case law. Typically, these requirements include open and uncontested use of the property with no attempt to hide for a designated number of years. If the owner makes no protest during that time, the property can be declared owned by the squatter.

The third is through the "party wall" doctrine. A party wall is the shared wall between two properties. Each owner has an equal shared interest in the wall. Each can do as he or she pleases with his or her side of the wall. Most attached city residences have party walls.

Zoning

Zoning laws classify property by the way in which it can be used. They restrict what is otherwise an owner's complete freedom to use property. One of the first things you need to do is match what you want to do against the property's zoning classification. For example, making holiday ornaments for sale at your home or taking in children of working parents during the day may be illegal in a residential-only area.

Some common classifications are "residential only," "single-family dwellings only," "commercial only" and "mixed use." You have no assurance that the present classification won't be changed, but, as a property owner, you'll be warned about it if a change is being contemplated. You will at least have a chance to speak your mind about it at any public hearing or by writing letters to the zoning authority. Zoning changes are often hotly contested, especially in residential areas where rezoning requests are to allow commercial development.

Variances

Even more hotly contested are *variance* requests. These are individual owners' requests to allow special exceptions to zoning restrictions. An example would be a request by someone in a residential-only zone to be allowed to open a dentist's office. Sometimes when such requests are made, a sign is placed in front of the property and a notice is mailed to all owners within a specified distance advising them of a public hearing on the matter. Hotly contested variance requests can tear a neighborhood apart. Check to see if any are pending before you buy.

Zoning is important not only for what you want to do with your property, but also for what your neighbors want to do with theirs. If high-rise apartments are permitted in the neighborhood and you don't want to live next to one, think hard about that choice. Agents, the local recorder of deeds and the city or county zoning office can all tell you how the neighborhood you're interested in is zoned.

Restrictive Covenants

Restrictive covenants are similar to zoning restrictions but are much more specific to each parcel of land. These restrictions are as enforceable as zoning laws.

Such covenants go beyond general zoning restrictions to require that residents perform certain tasks such as mowing their lawns every two weeks, or refrain from doing certain things considered harmful to the community. Some communities ban backyard satellite dishes. Others ban cars in favor of horse-drawn vehicles.

These kinds of covenants are typical in many communities, ranging from large sprawling suburban developments that restrict the type of landscaping to co-op apartments that prohibit installation of fireplaces or hot tubs.

If you are thinking of buying into a condominium or co-op, try to talk to current residents and ask what covenants are in place, whether they are enforced and whether the association's governing board ever acts on requests by members or groups of members to change them. The bylaws of the association should spell out what it takes to amend these rules.

Restrictive covenants can be found in your deed, in the bylaws that govern the association that runs the co-op or condominium, and in resolutions that have been passed by the association. Ask for a compilation of earlier association resolutions, which is not usually provided when you are given the bylaws and other governing documents. Also, look at the minutes from recent board meetings to see what issues the association has been dealing with.

For single-family, detached housing, you will want to contact any local neighborhood association and talk to neighbors. If you don't ask about something, you may not become aware of a restriction on how you can use your new property until you violate it. You may also not know that certain amenities—a pool, for example—are unprotected by any written agreement and may be taken away.

In the past, restrictive covenants were widely used to prevent owners from selling their houses to members of minority groups.

Now all such discriminatory covenants are illegal and should be reported to the nearest office of the U.S. Department of Housing and Urban Development (see Appendix II).

Development Patterns

If you are on or near the dividing line between two zoned areas, you will want to know what is permitted in the area next to you. If a huge factory is across an open field from you, it's safe to assume that if the company expands, the open field is likely to become a megawatt electricity generator or a parking lot. Survey the neighborhood. Ask neighbors, agents and merchants about past development trends and known or expected developments in the future. Is the area fairly stable or in transition? Has any developer announced a major project in the vicinity? Is the local government planning to close a school, build a new prison, open a new subway route? As always, a little homework now can save headaches and surprises later.

Red Tape Requirements

What you can and can't do with your house depends a lot on your local, county and state governments. Cities and counties often require permits and inspections for everything from building a sun deck to installing electrical appliances. There are rules about parking cars on the street at night, barking dogs, burning leaves, shoveling snow, trash pickup and size and location of mailboxes. Many rules are for safety—prohibition of portable kerosene heaters, for example. Others can seem to be nuisances you would prefer to avoid.

Although some regulations may seem trivial, all of them can be enforced by fines. The best way to learn what they are in your area is from the state, county and local offices of licensing, regulatory affairs and public works. Also check with any property owners' associations, tax districts, club management and other organizations by whose rules you will be governed should you purchase a particular property. Also ask your prospective neighbors what you have to do for permission to add an extension to your house, build a patio or install central air-conditioning.

Consumer Protection

By now you may feel you're being thrown to the wolves. You've been warned that the broker may sound friendly but has interests that are contrary to your own. You've been warned that the seller's first objective is collecting a high price. And you've been warned about a host of rules, restrictions and red tape. It's all true, and you do have to be careful, but here comes the good part: it's not a jungle out there. Laws have been adopted to protect real estate buyers from certain unethical practices, and the number of such laws increases each year. There are also business standards that are enforced by professional associations.

A Code of Ethics

The National Association of Realtors has adopted a code of conduct for realtors. You can get a copy by writing to the association at 430 North Michigan Ave., Chicago, IL 60611. The code applies only to brokers and agents who are members of the association, however. Violation of the code does not necessarily lead to legal action, but it could result in disciplinary action after a proceeding. All violations should be reported to the association. Among other things, the code provides for:

Fairness Realtors must protect and promote the interests of clients. In doing this, they are obligated to treat fairly all parties to the transaction, including the buyer.

Misrepresentation Realtors must not exaggerate, misrepresent or hide pertinent facts.

Investigation Realtors must discover all adverse facts a reasonably competent investigation would disclose. Agents are not, however, required to conduct their own inspections of the houses they sell and disclose to prospective buyers all defects they find.

Full Disclosure If a realtor receives compensation from more than one party to a transaction, all parties must be informed of it. They also must disclose to buyers that they work for the seller.

Conflict of Interest Realtors are forbidden to provide professional services involving a property in which they have a present or contemplated interest unless full disclosure is made.

Written Notification All financial obligations and commitments regarding real estate must be in writing that expresses the exact agreement of the parties.

Unauthorized Practice of Law The code forbids realtors from engaging in the unauthorized practice of law (UPL). Realtors are obligated instead to recommend that legal counsel be obtained. This limitation is also included in bar association rules and is discussed in Chapter 8.

Court Protection

Breach of Contract Because the purchase of a home is a contract, as a buyer you can sue the seller if you find intentional misrepresentations that caused a breach of that contract. You'll probably also be able to sue the seller's broker if he or she participated in any deceit—lying about the kind of tile in the kitchen, providing a false set of co-op or condo bylaws that omits certain provisions, misrepresenting the age of appliances, and so on. Any breach of the contract that is substantial can be the basis for a lawsuit.

Condominium Development Problems In some areas a significant history of fraud and misrepresentation has been developing in the sale of new condominiums. Unscrupulous developers and sales representatives have lured buyers into deals with sophisticated sales pitches and then sold them defective units or failed to make proper disclosures.

States have responded with laws that require certain written disclosures up front and give consumers redress for violations. To find out more about special protection for condominium purchasers in your state and what you should expect, call your state office of consumer protection and ask for the office that handles condominium sales.

Court battles over these issues are both common and messy. They also cover a wide array of abuses. Sometimes the developer has fled the state or declared bankruptcy and gone out of business. Other developers have signed contracts to sell units but with no deadline for the sale and then delayed completing construction until the buyer backed out, kept the buyer's deposit and sold the unit to another buyer at an inflation-increased price. Lawsuits over condo construction defects are also common.

Your best bet is to check up on the developer and talk to other owners, especially in areas where many condominium developments are being built. Remember that fraud flourishes and hides best where business is booming.

Although your right to file a lawsuit is secure, doing so is difficult and expensive. If you believe you are the victim of developer fraud, try to band with others similarly situated and hire legal counsel to work for all of you. Combining resources can make your lawsuit less a drain on your budget and emotions.

Discrimination Under the federal fair housing laws, it is illegal to discriminate because of race, sex, color or national origin. The realtors' code of ethics requires the same. Some local and state laws have even stricter standards. For instance, in the District of Columbia it is illegal to discriminate in housing based on any of sixteen different characteristics, including age, marital status and political affiliation.

Certain cities have their own laws: for instance, New York forbids discrimination on the basis of sexual orientation or the presence of children. You can find out on which bases discrimination is forbidden by calling your state or local office of human rights. They may also have pamphlets or other consumer information on this subject.

Discrimination is sometimes hard to detect. Examples of how it is practiced include:

- You're told the home is sold when it is not.

- You're told there are competing offers.

- You are asked to leave your telephone number, and if the first three digits can be traced to a minority residential area, no one calls you back.

- You're told the seller has decided not to sell or has raised the price.

- The broker says there's nothing available in your price range and refuses to show you the listing of homes for sale.

- No one is available to show you the home, you can't get an appointment or the agent cancels an appointment without explanation.

- You're told the house isn't what you want, is too expensive or isn't desirable.

If you think you've been the victim of discrimination, you have several options. You can file a civil lawsuit, complain to the area office of human rights or to the office that handles discrimination complaints, contact the U.S. Department of Housing and Urban Development (see Appendix II) or contact the National Association of Realtors. Your remedies will vary depending on how you proceed.

A civil lawsuit can result in your receiving damages. A complaint to the National Association of Realtors will not. Depending on your state's human rights law, you may be able to receive damages from the administrative agency if you prove discrimination. All of these options, however, are time-consuming, and inconvenient and can be expensive. Many of the state and local offices of human rights have caseworkers who will work with you to file a charge. In addition, depending on the type of discrimination, there are national and state organizations that may be able to help, such as Legal Counsel for the Elderly, the National Association for the Advancement of Colored People and the National Organization for Women. Even though they can't enter the case directly, groups such as these should be able to provide information and referrals.

Reforming the Profession

As you have seen, you do have recourse if you think you have been unfairly treated as a buyer of real estate. Nevertheless, it is important that you be cautious. You are making a major investment of money that will probably require a major change in your family life. Protect yourself by going to reputable brokers, by getting written assurances along the way, by consulting the professional watchdog organizations and government agencies and reading as much consumer information as you can find. Bear in mind that although not everyone is "out to get you," you are, in the end, your own best advocate.

CHAPTER

7

INSPECTIONS

After you've found one or two homes you're interested in, it's time to learn what they're worth. This chapter tells you some of the things to look for as well as how to protect yourself against current and future problems.

The Showing

Usually several inspections are made. First is a showing by the owner or broker. As mentioned earlier, this can be an open house for all comers or an individual showing with just you and a broker. If the home is for sale by its owner, the owner will probably show you around. No matter how it's done, the primary purpose is the sales pitch—an orchestrated attempt to get you to see all the positive things being offered.

At this early stage in the house-buying process, you need not be too concerned about detailed structural characteristics. That comes later. For now, listen to the sales pitch and ask yourself how many of your requirements—your musts, options and dreams—will be satisfied by this home. Is there central air-conditioning? Is the home heated by gas, oil or electricity? How high are the winter fuel bills? What is the neighborhood's zoning classification? Is street parking restricted? What school services the neighborhood? What is the general appearance of the other homes in the area?

Feel free to open doors and go places the agent isn't showing you. People who are having their house shown should have prepared for it. They should expect you to snoop around. If they don't want you to, be suspicious.

Try not to leave the house until you have a good idea of whether you want to follow up on it. You'll have a chance later to do a more thorough inspection. Now is the time to decide whether the house is a definite "no" or a definite prospect.

The Detailed Inspection

Sometime before closing, you need a detailed inspection of the home. You should also have the property *appraised* to make sure the asking price is in the right range. Many buyers skip these important steps because the lender, usually a bank, will also inspect, appraise and survey the property. The lender's inspection and appraisal, however, don't protect *you,* because the law doesn't require them to be comprehensive.

Several good guides and manuals are available that itemize what you should look for when you inspect the house (see the bibliography, Appendix IV). They will alert you to where and how to look, and in some cases how to interpret what you find.

If you're buying a home that is more than ten years old and expect to live in it for several years, you should consider hiring a professional inspector or at least consulting with someone whose judgment you trust, who has inspected homes in the past and knows what to look for. If, however, you decide to make your own inspection, consult the checklist in Appendix I as well as books in the bibliography.

Professional Inspectors A professional inspector can be an architect, engineer, carpenter, contractor or building consultant, but avoid using someone who might benefit from work you expect to contract for later. Companies that do this work are called building or home inspection services. Listings can be found in your telephone book, or you can get referrals from the broker or from friends who have used services in the past. Be cautious about proceeding blindly without references: anyone who wants to do so can advertise as an inspector. Ask for recommendations and check qualifications and professional affiliations. Members of the American Society of Home Inspectors, for example, must pass a comprehensive entrance examination, agree to participate in continuing education classes and either complete 1,000 paid house inspections or meet additional education requirements and complete 400 paid inspections.

The inspection will usually take one to two hours. If you are buying an older home or one that is being bought "as is," the inspection may take as long as five or six hours. Standard charges range from $100 to $300, almost always paid by the buyer. Many inspectors encourage buyers to go through the home with them. You should do this and take notes. Many of the inspection services routinely include in their price a written report and a binder that describes the home's systems. But you should also ask for a written report on major structural elements:

- The capacity of the heating and cooling systems in relation to the size of the house

- The age of the systems and their normal life expectancy

- The condition and adequacy of the electrical wiring and plumbing

- Notes on appliances and water heater

- Repairs and additions that may be needed soon

- The condition of the basement, crawl spaces and attic, with attention to moisture, ventilation, insulation and construction

- The condition of the roof, gutters, downspouts, drainage, siding, caulking and paint, and the extent of impending structural repairs

You need not bother too much with an inspection for termites. Most home purchase contracts require the seller to order and pay for that.

Inspections for Radon, Asbestos, Lead and Chemicals These are services that you may want to inquire about, especially if the locale has a history of this or the property is near a chemical plant. These inspections usually cost $40 to $200 and sometimes take additional time. For instance, a test for radon, a carcinogen, can be done in two days but may also involve a test that takes thirty days.

Before signing for these additional inspections, ask the companies you're considering hiring whether they have done homes in the area and whether they have found traces of any of the agents mentioned above. You can also call your state's environmental protection office and see if your community has any history of these problems. If both of these inquiries produces a "no" answer, you probably do not need to incur the extra expense.

Many buyers include an "inspection contingency" clause in their contract. This gives them the right to withdraw from the contract if the inspection reveals defects (page 286).

After the inspection you will have a specified number of days to negotiate with the seller about whatever was revealed that you want fixed before you remove the "inspection contingency." A limit of three to seven days is typical. Many buyers total what they think making the repairs will cost and present this figure to the seller. Often, part of the inspection includes estimates of repair costs. A seller who does not want to make the repairs may simply reduce the asking price by that amount if it's reasonable.

Homeowners Warranty (HOW)

If the house you want to buy is less than ten years old, it may be covered by a Homeowners Warranty (HOW), a warranty from a private insurance company that gives new houses ten years of protection against faulty construction. The warranty is backed by insurance and remains with the house if it is sold within the first ten years. Subsequent purchasers within ten years of building are covered. The policy transfers automatically.

If a builder refuses to correct mistakes, insurance covers the repairs. A built-in dispute-settling process determines the outcome when the buyer and builder disagree. This allows you to avoid costly, long, difficult litigation if problems arise.

The builder pays a fee for the HOW policy that is usually passed along to the buyer as part of the selling price. A buyer of a $100,000 house, for example, can expect that $200 to $500 of that price is for the HOW coverage.

During the first year, HOW builders guarantee their new houses are free of defective work and materials, major structural defects, and flaws in the electrical, plumbing, heating, cooling, ventilation and mechanical systems. They guarantee the same items during the second year of the policy, but don't guarantee the work and materials. In the remaining eight years of HOW protection, the house is insured only against major structural defects.

Ask about HOW protection if you are buying a home less than ten years old. Many builders selling new homes use the HOW as a promotional device, so expect a strong sales pitch and to be told that the builder is paying for it for you. If you are the second or subsequent buyer, ask about the HOW and get a copy. More likely than not, if a policy exists, you will be given a copy.

Other New-Home Warranties

Some builders choose not to purchase HOW coverage, and some offer warranty programs of their own. It is expected that during the next few years, more builders will decide to offer their own warranty programs and other national and local programs will begin competing with HOW.

In evaluating a warranty, check first with your state insurance commissioner's office. Ask whether that office has any information on the company offering the coverage. A history of complaints against the company should serve as a warning. Also make sure the policy requires arbitration of disputes because without it the policy is a good-faith promise rather than a true warranty.

Used-Home Warranties

If you're thinking of buying a used home, be sure to have a careful inspection. You can purchase insurance that protects you from defects not revealed during an inspection. Usually, the cost is about one-tenth of one percent of the home's purchase price and carries a low deductible, typically a few hundred dollars. Policies are offered for one year and are not available after that without a new buyer and new inspection.

A warranty service or insurance doesn't tell you whether a house is well built, and it won't tell you if the house is underwired or if the plumbing is badly corroded. All that is assured by the typical warranty is that specified mechanical equipment will remain operating for a year after you buy the house.

The buyer usually buys the warranty and is responsible for paying a deductible if anything goes wrong during the warranty period. And remember, the warranty is not in any sense an assurance that the equipment is in good condition. In fact, rarely do any of the major companies that offer warranty services inspect the properties they cover.

If you want to purchase this policy, call companies in your area and ask if they require an inspection and which inspection services are acceptable to them. Use one of those companies.

When To Inspect

Don't spend money and time on an inspection and appraisal unless you're prepared to buy the property if everything checks out. If you are prepared to buy, then by all means inspect the property. The information you get could help significantly during price negotiations.

When you make an offer to buy a house, do it in writing and

include a statement that gives you enough time to have the property inspected and an "out" if the property doesn't pass muster. Normally you won't be given much time because sellers and brokers are reluctant to take the property off the market for long. Also, they worry that a buyer with second thoughts can use the inspection report to get out of the deal.

Chapter 8 discusses purchase contracts that protect your interests. At this point you need know only that unless your preliminary contract makes the sale contingent on a satisfactory inspection of the house, you will *not* be protected. Inspections should satisfy you and you should release the contingency only when they do.

If you're buying a new property, many state laws protect you and you can purchase HOW coverage. Just to be sure, add a clause to your contract requiring the builder to comply with all state, local and county regulations.

The Appraisal

Though your lender will do an appraisal after you apply for a loan, you may want one for yourself now. Before you hire a professional appraiser, you should understand what determines the true value of a house. A house is not valued for its carpeting or wallpaper, the owner's furnishings or appliances, fancy lighting or bathroom fixtures, paint colors, equipment you don't want or need, or the sentiments of the present owner.

True value is determined by the amount of land and landscaping; the size and number of rooms and bathrooms; the size of the kitchen and its storage space; the size and condition of the basement, attic and screened-in porches; the quality of construction; whether electrical, plumbing, heating and cooling systems are new or in good repair; energy-saving features such as storm windows, insulation and heat pumps; new roof, gutters and siding; and the convenience and value of the location.

Ask the agent selling the house to show you a recent market analysis of the property, but recognize that it may be unrealistically favorable to the seller. Try to determine whether the person who did the analysis was a trained, objective specialist. If you're satisfied that the house is priced fairly and in line with what similar properties have sold for recently, you probably can safely dispense with an independent appraisal. However, if you discover something unusual, by all means have your own appraisal done. Warning signals to watch for include property that has been on the market a long time, property that has an expensive new addition, and property that is much less developed than its neighbors.

For your appraisal, you can hire a disinterested real estate broker or a professional appraiser. Remember that the institution that loans you the money to buy your house will want an appraisal too, so if you can get the lender to approve of your appraiser, it could eliminate the need for and cost of a second appraisal.

These professional appraiser organizations require training and an internship:

- The American Institute of Real Estate Appraisers, 430 N. Michigan Ave, Chicago, IL 60611

- The Society of Real Estate Appraisers, 645 N. Michigan Ave., Chicago, IL 60611

It is important to hire an appraiser who knows the community. Look for a company that has good local ties and connections.

Appraisals vary, so before you hire an appraiser explain exactly why you want an appraisal and ask what it will cost. Depending where you live, you can pay anywhere from $150 to $350. The appraisal should include a list of *limiting conditions,* those aspects of a house that reduce its value: for example, an old roof or a cracked foundation. It should also include pictures of the house and street, a map locating the site and, possibly, a floor plan.

The Lender's Role

Your lender is sure to inspect and appraise the home before making you a loan. The inspection and appraisal determine only whether the lender will be able to sell the property and get back the amount invested if you fail to make your payments. Beyond that, the lender's interest goes only far enough to assure that the house is structurally sound enough that you won't go bankrupt repairing it and have to default on the loan. You will want your own inspection to be so comprehensive that it reveals all defects that will need repair, not only the major ones.

Let the Buyer Beware

The overriding motto for property buyers used to be "let the buyer beware." Now more than half of the states have enacted laws that impose on builders an "implied warranty of fitness or quality" in work and materials. The enactment of such laws in so many states reflects a growing tendency by government to protect home buyers from defects in home building. However, most states that have such implied warranties protect only first-time buyers, not resale purchasers. Few states give resale purchasers the same protection they give first-time buyers. To find out whether your state has a law creating an implied warranty of fitness or quality, look in your state code under the section on property or real estate or call your state department of housing.

The rule to follow is still simple: whatever you're buying, the more warranties you can get in writing, the better. The next chapter covers some warranties you should consider putting in your purchase contract.

CHAPTER
8

THE CONTRACT

Once you have found the home you want, it's time to negotiate a contract with the owner. This contract will control everything about the property transfer, including the financing, so by now you should also be well along in your search for a loan. (Chapter 9 discusses financing in detail.)

Getting a purchase contract signed and in force involves five steps:

- *The offer to buy.* The first step is your written offer to purchase. It includes the price you are willing to pay and any other conditions you want to impose and is backed by a deposit of a check, called *earnest money.* Many people make the initial offer in writing, using a prewritten contract form; then, when the deal goes through, the same piece of paper serves as the final contract.

- *The counteroffer.* The seller now accepts your price or makes a counteroffer, also in writing. When many offers and counteroffers are made, the parties may put only the final, agreed-upon price and other conditions on the contract form, or write the terms into a separate agreement.

- *The binder agreement (or tentative contract).* When you and the seller agree on the price, you both sign an "agreement to agree," known as the *binder* or preliminary contract. It formalizes the acceptance of a price and the promise to continue negotiating.

- *Purchase negotiation.* All the terms of the purchase—date, type of financing, inspections, condition of the title and property and all other details—now have to be negotiated in good faith.

- *The final contract.* The final step is the signing of the final purchase contract. This contract is what your negotiating produces. It lists every aspect and term of the deal. Contracts for the sale of real estate must be in writing to be enforceable.

The Offer

To get the ball rolling, you, as the buyer, make an offer. All serious offers should be in writing and signed by you or your agent. You should make your offer through the seller's broker, if the seller has one. In fact, if an agent or broker is involved, you may not meet the seller until the closing. Include a time limit for a response, but don't allow too long—a few days, perhaps three to four in a competitive market—should be enough. The more time you allow the seller to scout for other offers, the more likely it is that yours will be topped.

State in your written offer that you are prepared to back it up with cash—called earnest money. This is money you are ready to hand over as soon as your offer is accepted. Its purpose is to demonstrate your seriousness. It is not the down payment. Even on a very large, expensive house, $1,000–$5,000 is quite routine. Whether your earnest money is refundable if the deal falls through is a matter for negotiation. You may want to state in your initial offer that your earnest money is to be refunded if you can't strike a deal.

The Counteroffer

The seller either accepts your price and preliminary terms or makes a counterproposal. That counteroffer may be to accept your price but leave all other matters to negotiation. Alternatively, the seller might ask a higher price but agree to your other conditions, such as refunding your deposit if the deal falls through. You can agree to disagree and go shopping for another home to buy, you can make another offer or you can agree to the seller's terms. To go forward with negotiations, sooner or later you'll have to agree at least to a price. When you do, it's time to sign the binder agreement.

The Binder Agreement or Tentative Contract

The binder is your agreement to agree, but despite its name, it is not fully binding. It simply demonstrates your desire to go forward and discuss the details of the contract. It does, however, bind both sides to a price and forbids the seller from signing a contract with someone else. The seller may, however, continue to accept "backup" contracts in the event your negotiations fall through. You are now into full scale negotiation. Again, the terms you negotiate are usually preprinted directly on a standard-form contract; provisions you or the seller want that are not already printed on the form can be added in an addendum or rider.

Negotiating the Purchase

Once the binder is signed by both sides and the earnest money is handed over, the seller must negotiate in good faith. This doesn't mean you, the buyer, can't walk away from the deal. It means that if you do walk away from it, you may lose your earnest money unless provisions were made in advance about its refund. This is true on both sides. If negotiations reach stalemate, you can both walk away from the deal. If the seller is the one who refuses to negotiate further, you can and should demand a refund of your earnest money.

Although most agents and sellers use standard-form real estate contracts, there's room for negotiation on every provision, especially if you are persistent, informed and reasonable. Some of the terms to watch for and insist upon in your contract are discussed later in this chapter, but every property is unique. In addition to the items discussed here, you should also develop your own conditions for going through with the deal. You will have to include these in your initial offer.

Contingencies

Buyers typically put four standard "contingencies" in their contracts that are recognized throughout the industry. It's important to note that any contingency will weaken your position relative to a competing buyer's offer that has fewer strings attached, but these four are the most common and you should consider them:

- Making your offer contingent on an inspection of the premises that is suitable to you

- Making your offer contingent on your reading the condominium or co-op bylaws and budgets

- Making your offer contingent on the sale of your existing residence

- Making your offer contingent on obtaining financing

Needless to say, the last two can be a problem to the seller who will have no control over them. In many instances the seller will not want to take the chance that you won't be able to sell your home or get financing. One way to reduce the seller's concern over such contingencies is by putting a deadline on each or demonstrating that there will be no problem, such as by showing you already have offers to buy your existing residence or agreeing to get a "preapproval" letter from a loan officer. You usually can get a loan preapproval with one interview; although it doesn't bind the lender, it is recognized as assurance that you will get financing if all your information is confirmed.

The Price

Think long and hard about the price you will offer. Many people rely on suggestions from those in real estate and in other guides and offer 85% to 90% of the asking price. This is no hard and fast formula, however, and you should consider a number of things before settling on an offer. For instance, consider:

- How long has the property been on the market?

- How many condo or co-op units in the same building or houses on the same street are for sale and competing with this one?

- What is the market like? In broker's lingo, is it "soft"? Are interest rates so high that people aren't buying? Are you entering the holiday season, when sales are really slow? A slow market means you may not have a lot of competition. A fast market has lots of buyers competing with each other and could mean your offer should be *higher* than the asking price.

- How badly do you want the place? Many people make low offers and then learn that if they had offered $1,000 more they would have succeeded. Weigh your desire for the home against your desire to get a good deal.

- What else can you offer the seller to sweeten the deal or to make you more attractive and less risky than the next buyer? Are you offering a large down payment, thereby reducing the risk you'll be turned down for a loan? Can you offer to pay a large chunk of the closing costs up front?

- Does the seller have to unload the home, for example because a divorce is in progress or the seller is under pressure to close the deal on another home?

In your negotiations with the seller or the agent, keep everything businesslike and avoid showing any emotion about your interest or enthusiasm for the property. Good agents will play on these emotions. Likewise, the more you can find out about the property and seller's situation, the better you will be at making offers and setting terms. If you want to talk directly to the seller, insist on it. Brokers frown on this practice, but it is done. The broker needs you to make the sale and has an interest in pleasing you. Remember that the more time a particular broker "invests" in you, the more he or she stands to lose if the deal falls through.

Finally, be forceful but not stubborn. Depending on the market and the availability of other potential buyers, the seller may bend, but you also run the risk of breaking the deal. Try to get an indication from the broker of how far you can push the seller. All the information you collected about the seller and property will be helpful in determining how to negotiate.

Negotiating the purchase of real estate is one area in which reading general materials can be especially helpful. Check the bibliography (Appendix IV) for sources.

The Final Contract

The final purchase contract contains an exchange of promises. The seller promises to deliver to you a good and marketable title along with the deed, and you promise to pay a specified sum in cash. The contract binds both the buyer and seller to go through with the deal on mutually agreed-upon terms. It can also give the buyer time to arrange a mortgage, to make sure there are no defects in the seller's title to the property and to arrange title insurance.

A final real estate contract is generally assumed to be all-inclusive. Everything of importance should be written into it. Your contract should include the purchase price, down payment, a description of the property and a list of other items being sold with the house. It should specify how the ownership is to be transferred to you, the method of payment, the financing arrangement, the amount of the deposit, the conditions under which you or the seller can void the contract, any defects in the property or title, the settlement date and how financing will be arranged.

Some people ask a lawyer to review their contract. By all means, if it has provisions you don't understand, ask someone, possibly a lawyer, to interpret it. However, you probably don't need to pay a lawyer to look after your interests, especially if you are already represented by a "buyer's broker" or have been through the process before. (See page 299 if you decide to use a lawyer.)

The following paragraphs describe the most important protections you need to negotiate and write into your contract.

Getting Back Your Deposit When you put down a deposit (earnest money), you assure the seller that you plan to go through with the deal. Make sure, however, that your purchase depends on whatever developments might force you to cancel the deal—the contingencies—and build in the obligation to return your money if these points cannot be resolved.

Nonfixtures Anything that isn't more or less attached to the land is not automatically included in the property transfer. Those things that are permanently attached to the house—a fireplace, for instance—are deemed fixtures and are transferred automatically with the sale. If you want possession of anything that is in the house but may not be a fixture, write it into the contract. Ask about anything you're unsure of. For instance, bookcases, cabinets, wall units that look built in, chandeliers, above-ground swimming pools, picnic and outdoor furniture, built-in barbecue grills, and stoves, refrigerators and other appliances. A good time to get all this nailed down is during the inspection. Then write it into the contract.

Settlement Costs In the negotiation of the contract, certain of the closing costs can be assigned to the parties. Others are often determined by local custom and aren't put into the contract. You can save money by figuring the closing costs ahead of time and including them in the contract as part of the purchase price. That way they will be covered by your loan. Chapter 13 discusses the closing in greater detail and includes a comprehensive list of common closing costs.

Contingencies Write all your contingencies into the contract: inspection, financing, sale of your existing residence, review of the condo or co-op association bylaws.

Warranties If you have agreed to accept the property with any defects, have them listed specifically. Include any warranties that "run" with the property such as the HOW purchased by the builder for any homes less than ten years old, as well as other builder warranties. Also, if other warranties are available from recent renovations or repairs, it's a good idea to include them.

Closing Date Require the seller to pay you rent if the home isn't vacated and available to you by the agreed-upon date. This is called a *rent-back* clause.

Standard-Form Contracts

In almost all cases, you will be offered a standard real estate contract, a "complete" document with blank spaces for provisions such as a description of the property and other matters unique to a specific property. Matters you want included should be discussed *before* signing, not conceded merely because they were not contained in the standard form.

Because everything in a real estate contract is open to negotiation, every contract is unique. The standard "fill-in-the-blanks" form real estate professionals use should be modified to fit your purchase. You will have to add important provisions, delete others, modify still others.

It's important enough to repeat: *nothing about a real estate deal is enforceable unless it is in writing and in the contract.* Any changes you make to the standard form must be initialed by both you and the seller. Even when standard forms have no room to add words, you are free to insist that provisions be crossed out and that additional provisions be included on a separate page as a rider or addendum.

The standard contract used in various forms all over the country is by no means a plain-language document. When you are handed one, take the time to read it carefully, line by line, and *make sure you understand every clause.* Don't be rushed. Words like "warrants," "guarantees" and "marketable" all have specific meanings. (Most of the terms you're likely to see are included in the glossary, Appendix III.) Custom in your area can also affect how certain language in the contract is interpreted. A plain-language contract is preferable and you certainly should ask for one, but don't feel you have failed if you're told to accept the standard contract or look elsewhere. Our society is still far from the day when laws require that all contracts be written in language that can be understood without specialized training or education.

You can get a sample standard-form contract from a broker. If you familiarize yourself with it beforehand, you are less likely to be intimidated or deceived when your seller's agent hands you a contract.

Take Your Time

Don't be rushed into signing anything you are unsure about. Ask questions, voice doubts, read materials, inspect again. Talk to professionals. Talk to others who have bought houses recently. Educate yourself by reading as much as you can and ask intelligent questions. Doing your homework is always the best way to become a confident and informed buyer.

Lawyers' Help

Because the contract you're offered probably will not be written in plain English, it's prudent to hire a professional to review the terms and make sure they protect your rights. You might be able to find an agent to do this for you. If not—and many agents won't do it for fear of prosecution for unauthorized practice of law (UPL)— your other option is to hire a lawyer. An experienced real estate lawyer should be available for such work at an hourly fee or a flat fee. Prices will vary in different parts of the country, so make a few phone calls to get an idea of what local real estate lawyers charge.

Decide also what role you want the lawyer to fill. You and the seller may want to share a lawyer who will act only as the neutral closing agent and prepare all the papers. If so, you will split the cost and the lawyer will not represent either of you. On the other hand, you can hire a lawyer to protect your rights by reviewing and interpreting the contract, suggesting language, setting up the title searches, preparing the deed and attending the closing with you.

A lawyer won't protect you against every risk, however. You must recognize the distinction between the practical risks every buyer takes and the legal risks a lawyer can explain and help you avoid.

For example, it is up to *you* to make sure the property you're buying is solid land and not a landfill dump that has been landscaped; that it is not in a flood plain; and that the price is right. Once you have advised your lawyer of the practical problems you've discovered, it is up to the lawyer to draft the legal protections to cover them. This doesn't mean your lawyer can't point out practical as well as legal risks, but if he or she does so, you are getting more than legal service. Following are some legal services you can expect from a lawyer's preparation or review of your contract:

Consequences of Breach of Contract Often a buyer and seller agree upon the performance required of each side but fail to discuss or agree on what happens if one party fails to meet the obligations of the contract. It's always better to plan for all contingencies and decide ahead of time how problems will be handled.

Omissions Unless you have considerable experience in this area or have done your homework well, you probably won't know whether your contract covers all the necessary points.

Future Effects Some provisions of a purchase contract may have far-reaching effects, especially when variables like zoning regulations are involved.

Validity The most important service a lawyer can provide is to assure that the contract is a legally enforceable, binding agreement. This often can depend on including special key phrases unique to the real estate industry.

Negotiation The difference between negotiating a deal yourself and having an attorney, agent or someone else do it for you is the time the latter allows you to reflect on proposals *before* making a legal commitment to them. When you speak for yourself, you are legally binding yourself unless you state explicitly that you are not. When your agent or attorney negotiates, he or she can allow time to consult with you before responding to the seller. This lets you consider all aspects of an offer without having to make on-the-spot decisions.

Also, if the seller fails to live up to the contract, a negotiator can explore remedies for you better than you can yourself, because friction is less likely when a third, uninvolved person discusses such matters. A negotiator, whether an attorney or not, is paid by you to protect your interest, as a result, a seller is unlikely to question your representative's motives.

Agents and UPL

Remember that if you can find one, you can hire an agent to negotiate for you and advise you about contract provisions. In many places, it is even customary for agents to draw up the contract using standard forms.

Such activity, however, can be restricted by rules that prohibit the unauthorized practice of law (UPL). In many places, nonlawyer brokers and agents cannot write contracts or provide legal advice without running afoul of such laws and facing the risk of prosecution by state bar associations. This has little or nothing to do with the brokers' or agents' abilities. Experienced brokers and agents can describe and advise you about standard real estate contract clauses easily as well as lawyers can, and usually describe them in understandable language. Rather, it is a question of being allowed to compete with lawyers, who provide such routine services for a living.

The problem isn't really yours. It is the broker's or agent's and the organized bar's. You need only be aware of it. If you find experienced brokers or agents willing to provide such services, by all means feel free to use them. You may be able to save a considerable amount of money.

CHAPTER

9

THE MORTGAGE

Few people can afford to buy a home without borrowing some of the money. A working knowledge of mortgages, lenders and how interest rates work is not only helpful, it's essential if you are to avoid being "taken." The uninformed enter the world of financing at their own peril.

Your search for financing should have begun when you decided to start shopping for a home to buy. Given the size and diversity of the modern loan market, you'll need plenty of time to explore the choices of loans and lending institutions available to you.

What Is a Mortgage?

When most people speak of home mortgages, they generally are referring to the types of loans that are available to home buyers. A mortgage is *not* a loan. It is the formal document that you, the home buyer, sign pledging your property as security that you will pay off the loan you made to buy it.

In the western United States and in a few areas in the east, a slightly different formal pledge is used. It is called a *deed of trust.* Its only distinguishing characteristic is that it makes it easier for the lender to *foreclose*—the process by which you lose your home if you fail to make your payments on the loan. Otherwise, "mortgage" and "deed of trust" mean the same thing.

Mortgage Costs

The costs of getting a mortgage loan vary, but you can plan on paying some or most of the following:

Points or Discount Points The lender charges a fee, called *points,* for making the loan. Each point is equal to 1% of the loan amount. It is paid at the closing by the buyer, by the seller, or by both, depending on local custom and, more importantly, on the terms of the contract you negotiated.

The points are prepaid interest to the lender to increase the amount of money the lender takes in initially and to cover the lender's costs of making the loan. The points are interest you would otherwise have to pay later; instead you pay it now, up front. The commitment fee, origination fee (see below) and other service charges may all be included under the umbrella of points, depending on how the lender structures them and local custom.

Loans are offered by lenders for a combination of interest and "up-front" points. Usually you can get a lower interest rate by paying extra points. For example, you may be able to choose a loan at 10% interest plus 4 points, one at 10.5% interest plus 3 points or one at 11% interest plus 2 points. If you have enough cash to pay the higher points at the closing, you can save some interest in later mortgage payments.

If you can get the seller to pay at least some of the points, you'll be even better off, because your seller will be providing some of the up-front cash that lets you choose the lowest-interest-rate loan. Splitting the points between buyer and seller is the custom in some places, so it's worth trying. Ask the seller to pay half the points up to two; this will give you the option of choosing a low-interest loan that requires as much as four points and still only pay two points yourself.

Loan Origination Fee You'll pay this fee for the administrative cost of processing your application for a loan. It usually is a small amount (1%) of the total you're asking for. It is paid at the closing. On a loan of $100,000, the typical origination fee would be $1,000. It may be included as points.

Commitment Fee This fee is also paid to the lender. As soon as you decide to accept the lender's financing, it is paid to assure that you will go through with the deal. It usually amounts to 1% of the loan amount. Again, it may be included as part of the points.

Down Payment This is paid at the closing. It can range from 5% to 20% of the purchase price, but few loans are made for less than 10%. However, a loan can usually be obtained with as small a down payment as 5% under some special government programs. (There are even programs requiring nothing down.) Some states offer guaranteed low-interest loans to first-time home buyers with low down payments. Typically, these are granted according to strict financial-need guidelines. New York, New Jersey, Connecticut and Wisconsin have sponsored such programs. Ask about their availability of any lender that offers home mortgages in your area.

Interest This is the most important cost you have to consider. Lenders charge interest for the use of their money. This is their primary source of income and your biggest expense. Incurring a loan of $90,000, payable over thirty years at 11% fixed interest, will mean you pay $857.09 every month. If you don't prepay any part of it, you will have paid $308,553.40 by the time you are finished paying off the loan.

Banks set their rates based on the *discount* rate charged to them by the Federal Reserve Board and the *prime* rate. The prime rate is the rate banks charge their "best" customers—usually major corporations. Your rate will be a little higher. Because rates fluctuate and are rarely predictable, lenders offer *adjustable-* or *variable-rate* mortgages, which permit the rate to change during the course of your mortgage.

The Ever-Changing Marketplace

The most difficult part about home buying is finding the right lender and negotiating the right loan. Many good sources of financing information are available. You should look at more than one or two. You will find some recommendations in the bibliography, Appendix IV.

In recent years, the risk caused by fluctuating interest rates has been shifted from lenders to borrowers. Under certain circumstances it may be harder to find loans with fixed interest rates, so that ownership of real estate is no longer a protection against high interest rates and therefore against inflation. When you have an adjustable- or variable-rate mortgage, you can expect to pay higher interest on your loan when inflation drives interest rates up. The net result to you is a higher mortgage payment: your home is costing you more.

When interest rates stabilize, lenders do show signs of going back to fixed interest rates. Nevertheless, fixed-rate loans do not dominate the home market the way they once did. They cannot be counted upon.

Many adjustable- or variable-rate loans offer low initial interest rates, fewer fees in advance and a better payment schedule. In addition, fixed-rate loans now come in terms of fifteen or thirty years. In general, home buyers have more choice and are able to find more finely tuned responses to their borrowing needs in the marketplace.

As a shopper, you will want to consider what lending format is best for you. In particular, you want to consider:

Fixed or Fluctuating? A fixed rate assures that you'll know what you'll pay regardless what happens to the economy and interest rates. If rates are low, shop for a low-interest fixed rate. If rates are high, consider a fluctuating rate with the knowledge that it will probably go down sometime during the life of the loan and you won't be locked into a high fixed rate.

Also, be wary of low initial interest rates that are sometimes offered to get you to accept a variable-rate loan as an incentive. For instance, you're probably better off with a fixed rate of 10% instead of a loan with a fluctuating rate that starts at 7% for the first two years. If, however, the variable-rate loan can go up by only one percentage point each year and you plan to move in five years, you'll probably pay less interest over that five-year span with the variable-rate loan.

The Rate of Interest and Points Every additional percentage point you're charged will add thousands of dollars to your total payment, so even if you've decided on a fixed rate, shop for the lowest one possible. Compare lenders and combinations of interest rates and points to get the best deal. A good place to start is the weekly real estate section in many regional and national newspapers. Many list the going rates for lenders in the area.

Term Like interest rates, every extra year of your loan's life adds thousands to what you'll eventually pay. If you can afford the monthly payments, consider a fifteen- or twenty-year mortgage instead of the more common thirty-year term.

Prepayment Make sure you're allowed to prepay your mortgage. Most lenders permit this, and because few people stay in the same home for the full life of the loan, you'll want to be sure you have this option.

Refinancing All loans can be refinanced except those that forbid prepayment. Some loans have refinancing built in, with no requirement that you pay closing costs again. For instance, some variable-rate mortgages allow you to convert to a fixed-rate mortgage for a small fee at designated times. Find out about these options. They're especially helpful if you are forced to take a variable-rate loan because interest rates are high and you don't want to lock into a high fixed rate.

Traditional Mortgages

A conventional loan is an indebtedness or mortgage made between a lending institution and a borrower, without participation by a third party such as the VA or FHA (see Chapter 10).

Most conventional loans are paid off in equal monthly payments spread over fifteen, twenty, twenty-five or thirty years. The interest rate stays the same for the life of the loan, and the amount you pay each month also remains constant. When interest rates rise, a low fixed-rate mortgage is better for the borrower, but the lender finds it costly because the money loaned to you at a low rate could be earning higher interest. When interest rates go down, the borrower is better off with a flexible rate that takes advantage of the decline. The trouble is that no one can accurately predict future interest rate shifts. Borrowing money is always a gamble.

The advantage of conventional mortgages is that they usually involve relatively little red tape and can be processed quickly. A loan can be approved in as little as two to four days. (Look for lenders who advertise "speedy approval" if you're under a tight schedule.)

Until recently, the traditional fixed-rate mortgage was routine in home purchases, and they still make up a significant portion of all mortgages. The difficulty is that their rates are generally higher than the low initial rates of variable loans. But the certainty of knowing that the rate will never change is very attractive for many people. Rates do vary, however, so careful comparison shopping among lenders, their rates and other charges is advisable.

Private Mortgage Insurance (PMI)

One way to finance your loan with a low down payment is to purchase private mortgage insurance from your lender. Most lenders require such insurance to protect them against the risk of loans with less than a 20% down payment. Companies that offer PMI insure loans only at the market interest rate (see Chapter 10 for FHA and VA loan programs).

PMIs are simple. You pay the insurance company an annual premium to cover the lender's security requirement. The obligation normally runs out after seven years. If you're contemplating shopping for a government-backed loan, compare the cost of using PMI instead to obtain a loan with a low down payment.

Graduated-Payment Mortgages

Some loans have a fixed rate of interest but obligate you to gradually increasing monthly payments. The early payments on the loan are lower even than the amount of interest that is due. Later payments are based on an increasing loan balance and are therefore larger. In effect, the longer you pay, the more you owe—for a while. Normally, payments rise for five to ten years, by which time they exceed the interest due on the loan, then level off as you begin paying off the loan itself.

Because payments are lower in the early years, graduated-payment mortgages may make sense to young buyers whose incomes may be relatively low now but who expect their earnings to increase steadily in the future. Remember the cost of this arrangement, however: the amount you don't pay in the early years serves to increase your total indebtedness. If you sell after only a few years, you could end up owing more than you borrowed in the first place. This is called *negative amortization.*

Tax Implications Negative amortization makes graduated mortgages undesirable for those who plan to sell their homes within a few years. It also means your equity takes longer to build because you are paying only interest at first (and not even all of that). On the plus side, you'll get a large tax deduction on the interest you're paying. For most people, however, that isn't quite the bonus it may seem. For those with low incomes now, this interest deduction is not the benefit it would be to people in a higher income bracket. It will be a great disadvantage later, when they are earning more and could benefit from the deduction. When that time comes, they will be paying mostly the principal and only a declining amount of interest, the only payments that are tax deductible.

Adjustable-Rate Mortgages (ARMs)

The *adjustable-rate mortgage* (ARM) or *variable-rate mortgage* is a long-term mortgage with no fixed interest rate. At predesignated times, the lender adjusts the interest according to general market conditions, usually using a specific *index.* Some of the most commonly used are the U.S. Treasury Bill rate, the rate set by the Office of Thrift Supervision—the agency that regulates S&Ls—and the national average of mortgage interest rates.

Different kinds of adjustable-rate loans are available, and your choices will vary from one lender to another, so shop carefully. Also, when you shop for an adjustable-rate loan, it's best to describe the type you're looking for instead of trying to name it.

Always remember that lenders offer adjustable-rate loans to protect themselves—not you. They want to be able to increase the interest rate if and when general interest rates go up. They offer a number of features to entice you into paying these changing rates, so be careful to weigh all the advantages and risks when you compare one ARM with another or with a fixed-rate mortgage. The two most important things to find out are: what protection you will have against unpredictably high payments, and how the adjustments are handled.

A change in the interest rate, whether upward or downward, is generally reflected in the monthly payments you have to make. There may or may not be limits (*caps*) on how much the interest rate or the payments can be changed at any one time. Look for them and try to get them included in your mortgage.

Alternatively, the repayment schedule can be tailored to your needs. In other words, you can agree to make constant payments and let the balance of what you owe be adjusted up or down as rates change. If the rate is adjusted down over the long term, you'll repay the loan in less time. If it is adjusted upward, repayment will take longer.

One advantage of the ARM is that you usually can negotiate a below-market interest rate for a short period of time. For example, some lenders may offer loans for as low as 7% interest for the first year at a time when fixed rates are 10%. At the end of the introductory period, the loan's rate is adjusted to the current market rate, using one or a combination of the indices.

Because the initial rate may be low, an ARM is particularly attractive to the young, first-time home buyer who can't qualify for a fixed-rate mortgage. However, before committing yourself to an ARM, ask for some essential information:

Is There a Cap? Does the adjustable-rate mortgage limit the rate of interest you'll have to pay? Does it limit the total potential monthly payment you'll have to pay? If interest rates climb again, you don't want to be caught having to make monthly payments higher than you bargained for.

What Kind of Cap? Lenders offer different kinds of caps. One is a *periodic* cap that limits how much the interest rate may change at any one time. For instance, it can require that even if the index increases 2% in one year, your rate can go up by only 1% in that year. Alternatively, an *aggregate* cap limits how much the rate can increase over the entire life of the loan. For example, even if the index goes up 10% in five years, your cap can limit your rate increase to 5% under an aggregate cap. Also watch for downward caps, which protect the lender's profits in times of declining rates. These work against you in that you will not get the entire benefit of falling rates.

You can also get a cap on payments, limiting the additional amount—to say, $500—that you'll have to pay in any given year, regardless what happens to interest rates. A cautionary note: even though your actual monthly payment increases only a little, if the interest rate rises significantly, the amount of your payment that is set against the interest rather than the principal increases and your equity payment shrinks. What could occur under a payment cap plan in a rising-interest economy is the same negative amortization danger that can result from a graduated-payment mortgage, discussed earlier: your monthly payment may be used entirely to pay interest. If it is not enough to cover the interest due, your indebtedness grows with each payment period.

Are There Prepayment Penalties? Some lenders charge a penalty to make up for some of the interest they lose when a borrower pays more than is required in a monthly payment. Most ARMs don't carry these prepayment penalties, but check to be sure.

You can get comprehensive information about ARMs from lenders. Ask for a free copy of the booklet *Consumer Guide to Adjustable Rate Mortgages* published by the Federal National Mortgage Association (Fannie Mae).

Rollover Mortgages A rollover mortgage is another version of flexible or adjustable-rate mortgages. With the rollover, the interest rate remains constant for a specified number of years, with the understanding that it will then be renegotiated. Make sure you understand early what the renegotiation will be based upon and when it will occur. Sometimes it will be renegotiated using some economic indicator, such as the treasury bill or prime rate; other times no indicator is used.

The rollover can be renegotiated to a lower rate, but in virtually every case the lender is in the driver's seat. This is because your only recourse as a borrower is to pay this loan off by getting a new one. If you go to a new lender to pay off the first, you may be almost forced to agree to the lender's terms. Before choosing a rollover, think about other options, especially variable-rate mortgages, which offer all the same advantages and few of the drawbacks.

Balloon Mortgages

Some people say a good rule of thumb for when to agree to so-called *balloon mortgages* (or balloon formats of other mortgages) is "never, never, never under any circumstances." This is a little extreme, but it does reveal an important truth about this form of loan. It is extremely risky.

Under a balloon mortgage, your payments remain constant for a specified number of years, then end in a single, final "balloon" payment of the entire outstanding debt. In most cases, the balloon payment comes quickly, perhaps in three to five years. For those without a great amount of cash on hand, this final payment can be disastrous. People who may benefit from a balloon mortgage are probably using the house to shelter income and plan to sell it before the mortgage is paid.

Because it comes so soon after the loan is made, the final balloon payment can often amount to 70% to 80% of the original loan. Most people don't have that sort of money on hand. In response to this, some lenders offer automatic refinancing at the end of the balloon mortgage, but beware: you aren't guaranteed an interest rate and may end up having to choose between making a $50,000 cash payment and refinancing the loan at sky-high interest rates.

The Ever-Changing Market

Recent years have brought many and fast-paced changes to home buying in America, particularly in the ways the purchases are financed: who loans the money, how much the loans cost, how they are repaid.

Interest on the loan you make to buy your home often costs more than the home itself. The affordable loan can still be found, but it is likely to be quite different from what used to be the conventionally financed arrangement.

In the past, once you found the home you wanted and could afford, financing it was routine. Today locating a suitable loan and getting approval for it can be arduous. Lenders have responded to the changing market by adjusting their business practices to protect themselves. As a result, even when you get a loan, it is unlikely to resemble the fixed-interest, fixed-payment loan package of yesterday.

After skyrocketing to more than 20% in the 1970s, interest rates returned to a relatively stable level, but there is no telling what tomorrow will bring. Inflation has also been less than the double-digit rates of the 1970s, but here too even the experts can't predict what will happen in the years ahead. One thing you can be sure of, however: lenders will respond to whatever market conditions exist by structuring loans in terms they find most favorable to themselves.

Be diligent in your search for the right plan and shop for your mortgage as carefully as you shop for the home itself. Many plans that seem affordable at first glance may be unrealistic.

Because finding the money to buy a home is often harder than finding a home to buy, you should be working on both at the same time. Neither effort should be made independently of the other. The two are dealt with in separate chapters, but that does not mean they are unrelated. From the time you decide to buy a home until you close the deal, you should continue to think about both.

CHAPTER

10

MONEYLENDERS

Most home buyers turn to conventional lending institutions like banks and savings and loan associations, but you should be aware that other sources of obtaining financing are also available. These include the federal government and the seller.

Different lenders and different loan formats make different demands on borrowers. Conventional lenders who make fixed-rate loans require down payments that are higher than other loan formats require. Government-assisted loans, such as FHA and VA, have little or no down payment requirements. Community savings and loan associations (S&Ls) often require a *note of personal liability* in addition to posting your home as collateral. This means that if you fail to make your payments and the S&L sells your home to get its money back, you've agreed to make your other assets available to make up any loss that the sale of your home doesn't cover. The S&L also can transfer your note to a collection agency (or to anyone else, for that matter), which then takes over collecting from you.

Some lenders require that your loan be *nonassumable*. An assumable loan is one that can be transferred to a buyer when a house is sold. Its major benefit is that if it carries a low interest rate, that rate can be passed along to the new borrower even if prevailing interest rates at that time are higher. If you can arrange a loan with a low interest rate, having the ability to transfer your loan will make you an attractive seller later on.

Secondary Mortgage Market Many people have heard the nicknames Fannie Mae, Freddie Mac and Ginnie Mae. These are large lenders, some private, some government-operated, that buy loans from local and even regional lenders and sell them to investors on the secondary market. Without the ability to transfer loans to larger institutions, smaller lenders would soon run out of money to loan to other customers.

All this means for you, the borrower, is that your lender will expect your loan application to meet the requirements set by the "secondary" market. As noted earlier, for loans to be purchased by these secondary lenders, they must conform to industry rules on how much of your income you can devote to the mortgage and how much debt you can have (see Chapter 4).

Secondary market lenders vary, and if your lender tells you your situation won't be acceptable to its secondary lender, a different institution with a different secondary lender may have less restrictive rules. As always, shop around.

Conventional Lenders

Savings and Loan Associations The single largest source of private residential financing in the country is savings and loan associations. S&Ls offer several advantages. They are usually rooted in the community, they are generally relatively small operations that emphasize personal contact, and they can make a more knowledgeable appraisal of the property and neighborhood than can other lenders. S&L mortgages tend to have longer terms than others. They almost always require a note of personal liability, but they tend to go less "by the book" in their judgment of you as a credit risk then other lenders do.

They also have disadvantages, however. Their loans often cost more in fees and points, carry prepayment penalty charges and usually can't be transferred from you to a future buyer of your home at the same or similar interest rate—that is, they are nonassumable.

For those buying their first family home, S&Ls present an attractive option because they are interested in building goodwill and long-term customers in the community. This doesn't mean they'll accept wild credit risks, but it does give the first-time buyer a fighting chance to establish creditworthiness.

In 1989 the savings and loan industry underwent major challenges and changes. In response to frequent S&L failures usually caused by mismanagement and fraud, the U.S. Congress changed the way the institutions are regulated and managed. Formerly S&Ls were regulated by the Federal Home Loan Bank Board and insured by the Federal Savings and Loan Insurance Corporation. The 1989 law eliminated both these agencies and turned S&L regulation over to the Office of Thrift Supervision in the Department of the Treasury. Insurance was assumed by the Federal Deposit Insurance Corporation, which insures banks. Also, new regulations were enacted to restrict lending practices and the level of assets a lender needs to make loans.

Commercial Banks The lending area of most commercial banks, even those that are locally based, extends farther than that of the typical S&L. The cost of making the loan may be lower than at an S&L, and because banks want your other banking business, they may be more lenient about such things as prepayment penalties.

The disadvantages are that commercial banks will probably charge slightly higher interest, they are unlikely to loan you as much money as an S&L and they favor shorter-term loans.

Credit Unions These institutions are a good source of financing if you are a member and have little credit history outside of the credit union. Credit unions favor government-assisted loans and longer terms. Not all credit unions make mortgages, however, and those that do often don't have sufficient funds for financing large amounts of real estate.

Mortgage Companies These companies "place" mortgages. They sometimes advertise low rates, speedy approval and flexible terms:

fifteen-year loans, for example, or loans that can be paid in twenty-four annual payments. Often mortgage companies immediately sell your loan to a large bank or other investor on the secondary market. So if you like dealing with a local bank officer, you'd do better to look for lenders that keep their loans in the community.

There are also mortgage servicing companies that handle all the paperwork involved after the home is bought. These companies are often hired whether or not a loan is sold. They will provide the coupon books, send the statements of your taxable interest and even pay your taxes and mortgage insurance premiums.

Mortgage Brokers and Bankers

Mortgage brokers match people with money, any money. They are not affiliated with any particular institution but may specialize in certain kinds of investments. Mortgage bankers, on the other hand work for "funds," large pools of moneylenders with large cash reserves.

Both know the market and can plug you in. Mortgage brokers and bankers can be especially helpful for borrowers on the edge of qualifying for conforming loans, those who have credit problems and those in a hurry.

Profits from these transactions come from commissions or, in some cases, from collecting payments and otherwise servicing loans. For this, they get a fraction of 1% of the outstanding balance owed.

Following are some of the sources of money that can only be accessed through mortgage brokers and bankers. Although you are more likely to use one of the sources we've already covered, it may be useful to consider mortgage bankers and brokers if it is hard to get a more customary mortgage.

Insurance Companies If the property you are buying is considered a "good investment" but is priced beyond what most lenders are willing to lend for it, you might be able to get financing from an insurance company. Insurance companies prefer to invest in large commercial development mortgages, often through mortgage brokers, so you'll have to sell them on the soundness of investment in your purchase. Your personal charm, local residence and other factors that might play a part in dealing with local banks and S&Ls will count for nothing in dealing with insurance companies. The only thing that counts is the wisdom of the investment. If you succeed in selling that, however, you may be able to save significantly on points, fees and interest.

*Real Estate Investment Trusts (**REITs**)* These special mortgage trust companies lend money on unusual deals and tend to be more flexible with loan features and gimmicks. They are a particularly good source of home construction financing and short-term loans. As with insurance companies, however, personal contact will have little influence.

Pension Funds and Endowments These groups, which have substantial capital to invest, usually buy mortgage "packages" from a mortgage broker. If you learn of one that offers terms that appeal to you—for instance, through a pension plan you belong to—by all means inquire.

Private Money

The unlikeliest source of all for financing a home is a private loan from a friend or family member. Not many individuals have the money it takes to finance a home purchase. Even when a person does have such money available, far more secure and profitable investments are available.

Nevertheless, a private loan can be a last resort. If you can't obtain financing elsewhere, ask a mortgage broker or real estate broker about private financing possibilities. Recognize, however, that such private money is much more likely as a source for your down payment or for the additional money you may need to make up the difference between the sales price and what an institutional lender is willing to loan you.

Many people borrow or are given money by family members for the down payment, then look to traditional sources of financing for the remainder. If you are given the money, you will be asked to submit a "gift letter" that certifies you will not have to pay the money back. If you are loaned the money, the lender will want to know this and will calculate it into your monthly debts when deciding whether you qualify for a loan.

Cosigners

First time home buyers or those with little credit history may be asked to have a family member, friend or employer cosign the mortgage. This means that if you fail to make your mortgage payments, your cosigner may be asked to pay. Such an arrangement should be used only as a last resort.

Typically, newly married couples buying their first home are often asked to have a parent cosign a note and offer their own property as additional security. Don't be pressured into this sort of financial bondage unless you have no other way of getting a loan and your cosigners understand fully that they can be called upon to make good on the loan if you fail to make your payments.

Government-Backed Loans

Government-backed loans, usually supported by the Federal Housing Administration (FHA) or the Veterans Administration (VA), are in a special class called *assisted mortgages*. Unlike private lending institutions, government agencies have no claim on the future increased value of the property and provide help as a matter of public policy to encourage citizens to become homeowners.

The loans are not made by the government agencies themselves. Rather, the agencies give lenders assurances that they will be paid if you are unable to meet your payments. This is done by requiring you to buy insurance. If you default, the lender is covered for at least some of the loss.

For many people, homeownership is an unreachable dream without VA or FHA help. They simply cannot afford the down payment required for commercial loans. Information about how to apply is available at lending institutions and from the government agency offices themselves.

FHA Loans

The main attraction of an FHA loan is the low down payment and reduced initial costs of making the loan. Major disadvantages are bureaucratic delays and paperwork that make many lenders reluctant to deal with them.

The FHA has a wide variety of loan programs. For full information, check with local FHA-approved savings and loan associations, commercial banks, mortgage bankers and mortgage brokers. These are the distinguishing features:

- Loans are fully assumable at their original interest rates and terms.

- The down payment is 5% or less, compared with a 10% to 20% requirement for most conventional loans.

- The FHA limits the loan amount it will back. The limit is based on the cost of housing in your area. The largest FHA loan amount is $124,875 in the highest-cost-of-living areas. Your lender will know the limit for your area.

- An FHA-approved appraisal of the value of the home is required. If the appraisal shows the property is worth less than the loan amount requested, you are not allowed to use a second mortgage to make up the difference.

- FHA loans may be prepaid without a penalty charge.

Until 1983 the government fixed interest rates for FHA loans. Since then it has allowed the rate to fluctuate with market conditions. As a result, the programs are now more attractive to lenders who, in the past, had been forced to charge the seller the lost interest percentage points in order to make a profit.

Lenders were forbidden to charge these points to the borrower. This often meant that sellers paid them instead and simply added the cost to the sale price of the house. The law now allows lenders to charge points directly to borrowers instead. Unfortunately from the buyer's point of view, FHA loans are usually accompanied by such a high number of points (four or five is not uncommon) that the up-front charges can offset the other advantages of FHA loans.

An insurance premium payment ranging from 1% to 4% of the loan also is required up front.

VA Loans

Loans backed by the Veterans Administration (VA), also known as GI loans, are available to all current members of the armed services and veterans who have served on active duty. Others can only get VA loans if they have a qualified veteran cosign.

The VA requires no down payment, but some lenders refuse to make any loan, government-guaranteed or not, without one. Also, some home buyers themselves choose to make a down payment to lower their monthly payments.

VA loans are available for just about any loan that is within the conforming loan level. They are like FHA loans in two important respects: they can be assumed by future buyers of the property at their original rates and terms, and they can be prepaid without penalty.

VA loans require a fee (approximately 1% of the loan) to be paid to the lender. The rates fluctuate with the market and, like the FHA loan program, points can be paid by the borrower.

Borrowers can apply for FHA and VA loans through regular lenders, who will have the forms you need and will know the loan limit, the going interest rate, the cost of necessary insurance, points and the length of time it will take for the application to be processed.

Seller Financing

Home buying can also be financed by home sellers. In fact, second mortgages and other forms of seller financing accounted for more than half of all mortgages in 1980, when high inflation and high interest rates were making it difficult to find assumable fixed-rate loans. Lenders insisted on writing "due on sale" clauses into mortgage contracts to prevent subsequent buyers from assuming the mortgages at the old—and lower—interest rates. The availability of adjustable-rate mortgages has made such seller-financing arrangements less desirable, but they are still worth exploring.

If you are thinking about asking for seller financing, check with the seller's broker. In some markets, where interest rates are high and people aren't buying homes, the broker may even suggest this as a way of making a sale. You may find yourself with a seller willing to set up any of a variety of financing arrangements—assumption of the earlier loan, a wraparound or a second mortgage. If you decide or are asked to go this route, be sure to read some of the mortgage books listed in the bibliography, Appendix IV.

Assuming the Old Mortgage

If the property you're buying is already mortgaged, the seller is probably planning to pay off the mortgage as soon as you pay the purchase price. An alternative is to keep that mortgage alive by assuming the obligation to make the payments on it yourself. The major advantage is that you will maintain the interest rate that was set when the mortgage was first created—presuming it was lower than what you can get now.

Lenders who handle FHA and VA loans usually allow you to assume the seller's mortgage at the original interest rate. Those who offer adjustable-rate mortgages will do the same, but you should recognize that the interest will change periodically with market conditions anyway. Most conventional loans, however, have "due on sale" clauses that make the balance of the old mortgage due when the house is resold. This prevents direct assumption, but it doesn't prevent you from bargaining with the lender. You can ask for new terms on the old mortgage that net you a better deal than you would find elsewhere on an entirely new mortgage. For one thing, the original lender is likely to be favorably inclined because the value of the property involved is already known.

If the lender is willing to transfer the old mortgage to you with its original low interest rate, it will probably involve an extra charge. Whether this represents a net saving to you compared to taking out a new loan depends on the size of the charge and on how many years you will be paying the mortgage at the lower interest rate. Make sure you do your arithmetic before agreeing.

Because an assumable mortgage is usually attractive to buyers, it's also attractive to sellers—which you will be one day if you decide to sell your home. When you get your mortgage, whether it's a new one or an assumed one, always try to reserve the right to permit others to assume your mortgage if and when you decide to move on.

Wraparound Mortgages

One of the most common ways a seller can serve as your lender is to continue making payments on the old mortgage and to "lend" you the purchase price at a higher interest rate. This is known as a wraparound mortgage.

A wraparound might be made by a commercial lender or the seller. The idea is to take advantage of a low interest rate on an existing mortgage to reduce the amount of "new money" needed to complete the transaction.

For example, suppose the house you want to buy is priced at $100,000. The seller holds an 8% mortgage and still owes $50,000 on it. You give the seller $20,000 as a down payment and the seller keeps the existing mortgage in place and "lends" you the $80,000 you need at 10% interest, two percentage points below the market rate of 12%. The advantage to the seller is that you will make regular payments as if you had borrowed $80,000. Out of that, the seller makes the old mortgage payment at the original 8% rate and pockets the difference between what you pay and what is owed on the original mortgage.

Alternatively, a commercial lender could "buy" the original mortgage by giving the seller the $80,000 outright, then do the same thing—collect 10% from you and pay the original lender 8%.

The advantage of a wraparound mortgage to the buyer is that both the interest rate and the monthly payments may be less than they would be with a new mortgage. A potential disadvantage is that you may have no assurance the original loan will be paid unless those payments are handled by a commercial lender or some other third party such as an escrow agent. If the payments are supposed to be made by the seller and he or she fails to do so, you could find the original mortgage foreclosed and your ownership in jeopardy.

A further caution about wraparounds: the seller isn't subject to all the federal oversight, reporting regulations and recommended practices commercial lenders are. Recognize that you're gambling that you or your attorney can write a mortgage contract with the seller that will give you all the safeguards and remedies you expect from any lender, especially regarding late payments and foreclosure.

Second Mortgages

Another way sellers can help finance your purchase is by holding a *second mortgage,* also called a *second trust,* on the property. In effect, the seller loans you the part of the purchase price you couldn't find financing for and holds a mortgage for it. That mortgage is subject to the foreclosure rights of the holder of the first mortgage. In other words, if you don't pay your mortgage bills, the lender who holds the first mortgage is the one who has the right to take the property from you. Second mortgages are particularly well suited to buyers who have only a small amount of cash available for a down payment but have an assured monthly income high enough to handle payments on both mortgages.

Conclusion

This discussion of lenders and loans has described the more common types. If none of them meets your needs, consult the bibliography (Appendix X) for additional sources of such information.

CHAPTER

II

GETTING YOUR LOAN

You are now ready to apply for a loan. The following list covers the information you'll need for the loan application:

- Your annual wages and those of others in your household

- A description of other private income, such as from stocks, bonds, partnerships or royalties

- A written explanation of any large cash gifts you receive regularly

- Identification number and balance of each savings and checking account

- Account number and current balance of each credit card

- Account number of each certificate of deposit (CD), money market fund and security account and the value of those accounts as of a recent date

- A list of all outstanding installment debts and the amount and number of payments due on each loan

- If you already have a mortgage, the name of the mortgage holder, account number, monthly payment, original loan size, current balance and number of payments still due

- If you are the beneficiary of any trust, estate, IRA or Keogh plan, the cash value involved

- A written description of any lawsuit you are involved in and outstanding legal judgments for or against you

- A statement of your net worth—list the present market value of major holdings, such as your current home less marketing costs and outstanding mortgages, the resale value of your car, stocks and bonds, the cash surrender value of insurance policies, and all other assets, list also your major debts, such as mortgages, automobile loans and credit card balances, then subtract what you owe from what you own; this is your net worth (see the worksheet on page 253)

If you're prepared with this information when you apply for a loan, it will both speed the process and impress the lender with your seriousness.

Remember, the lender will also get a credit report on you to see how you have handled past debts. You should check the report yourself first (see page 255).

Shopping for a Lender

First determine which lenders in your area make loans of the size and type you want. For example, if you want an FHA or VA loan, find out which S&Ls and banks are willing to make them. This can be done by telephone or by talking in person with a loan officer where you bank.

Many regional newspapers have a weekend real estate section that lists the going rates for mortgages at the area's largest lenders. Consult this and then get on the telephone for the exact figures.

If you've been a regular customer of a bank or S&L, check there first. If your banker is willing to give you the type of loan you need at a price you can afford, your search may be short, but it's always wise to check with at least a few other lenders to compare prices. If your banker doesn't offer what you want, try the other sources of conventional and government-insured loans in your community. Determine the best loan for your needs and visit the appropriate lending institutions described in Chapter 10.

If you're still unsuccessful, try the institution where your employer, best friend, credit union co-members or church members bank. They may be willing to put in a good word for you. With such a recommendation, a bank or S&L may be a little more accommodating.

Many good lender-borrower matches are thwarted because people are so happy to find someone willing to "give" them the money they need that they jump at the first offer and look no further. Remember, whether or not you think you have a solid financial footing or an excellent piece of property, there is no reason to accept anything other than the best possible loan agreement. In the long run the loan agreement you buy can be far more important—and expensive—than the house itself. You can find the best agreement only by shopping diligently for it.

Be patient, careful and businesslike. Differences in the term and interest rate you agree to can have a dramatic effect on the total price you'll have to pay to borrow the money. A no-penalty prepayment option or an assumption option can mean literally thousands of dollars to you later on. Never jump at a loan just because it's available. If it's there today, it will still be there tomorrow. If it isn't, be suspicious. You even have a good chance of duplicating or improving on the offer at another institution down the street, so prepare to shop around. This is one case in which you hold more cards than you might think. Lenders want to make safe loans, true, but without borrowers they would make no loans at all—and earn no profits.

Using Professionals

Finding a lender may seem overwhelming, and it definitely requires some self-education. If you feel you need help, an array of professionals is prepared to offer it to you. Some you'll have to pay. Others you won't, at least not directly. They'll help you sort through the forms you need, assemble the numbers and come up with a workable plan. Many people who may find it hard to get financing and first-time home buyers will find these services helpful. You may especially want to consider the following two because they offer free help to borrowers:

Mortgage Broker Instead of doing an exhaustive do-it-yourself search of the financial marketplace for the best loan, you can ask a mortgage broker to help you, especially if you've tried on your own without any success. The lender pays the mortgage broker a flat fee or a percentage of the loan it "places." They are paid to know the answers to all the routine questions: Where is money available? Which lenders are making what kinds of loan? What is the range of interest rates available? Is a bargain rate available on the size, type and term you're looking for? Which lenders' property or credit analysis will tend to favor your particular circumstance?

An experienced broker not only keeps up with changes in the local market but maintains working relationships with loan officers and other lending professionals. If you have proceeded on your own and have had no luck, don't give up before consulting a broker.

Clearinghouses Thanks to modern technology, a one-stop method of mortgage shopping is also now available to home buyers—computer mortgage clearinghouses. These are relatively new institutions, but they are growing in popularity. At present there are only a few nationwide companies, but others operate regionally or locally. They are able to offer many times the number of loans and many more variations than other lenders can.

The information required and the information produced by the computer system depend on the company, but in general the clearinghouses work much the same way computerized dating services do—matching lenders and borrowers. The participating lenders in the area list their mortgage formats with the computer clearinghouse, including the amount they'll loan, their terms and their requirements. Information about your income, debts and cash on hand is fed into the computer. Based on this information, the maximum fixed-rate and adjustable-rate loans you qualify for are

calculated and converted into the maximum price and down payment the computer thinks you can handle. Some systems offer you
several alternatives and show you what would be available if your
income or cash on hand were a little higher.

After the figures are produced, the computer prints out those
mortgages it knows about that meet the requirements. In most cases
these services are just a starting point and you still have to apply and
be approved for a loan. However, in other systems, you choose the
loan you want and your information is sent to the lender for
approval. Some companies' computers are even programmed to
print out the specific application for the loan you choose. Mean-
while, once the computer has made its initial evaluation the lender
makes a provisional commitment to loan you a specified amount at
a specified rate, contingent on an appraisal of the property and a
check of your credit.

A major benefit to the system is that the borrower doesn't pay to
use it, the lending institutions do. Your expenses are only those you
would pay otherwise—the closing costs. Some clearinghouses even
offer personal loan advice, and some can tell you the potential future
costs of loans under different economic conditions.

The disadvantage is that most of the data banks do not include
community savings and loan association mortgages. You will have
to shop for those on your own. Also, any personal contacts that can
be helpful in terms of moving a loan application along later down
the road will not be useful here.

To use one of these services, ask the broker showing you around
or your own broker if you have one. If you want just to call for
general information, any real estate broker, mortgage banker or
broker or lending institution can tell you which clearinghouses are
available in your area. Some are accessible only to members of the
profession or, in the case of the clearinghouse run by the National
Association of Realtors, accessible only to its members.

The Loan Application

Sooner or later you'll have to take that step through the door of a lending institution. Whether it's a bank, credit union, S&L or insurance company, once inside, you will be directed to a mortgage loan officer. It is that officer's job to receive all requests, to separate the serious, qualified shoppers from the browsers and the clearly unqualified, and to process the loan application. (In some instances, if you have chosen a mortgage company and not a bank, you may meet with an officer at his or her home, your home or the office of a local real estate broker.)

The two of you will work together to fill out your loan application. When it's completed, the loan officer will submit it and a personal recommendation to a review board at the institution. The officer's recommendation is often crucial, unless the lending institution has strict rules about formal criteria for making loans.

Lenders consider both you and the property you're buying in their attempt to evaluate the risk you're asking them to take. The amount they rely on and how they analyze the various factors may, however, be open to negotiation. Your loan officer may be willing to share insights into your strengths and weaknesses with the review board, based on past performance, so don't be reluctant to ask.

Be aware that loan officers are not obliged to tell you all the standards and methods of analysis they use to evaluate you and your property, but they will often give you "ballpark" figures, or a profile of their "average borrower." If you don't come up to this standard, ask how flexible the loan officer thinks the board is.

The negotiation between you and the loan officer is just that—a bargaining session. The key is to find out how your application is perceived, then to discover if the perception of you as a loan applicant varies from one lender to another. It probably will.

Shopping for the best loan, or even negotiating better terms, isn't difficult once you understand what the loan officer is looking for in a borrower. By anticipating demands, you can satisfy them in a way that appears most favorable to your position. At that point the loan officer should be willing to listen to your loan preferences.

Some of the things to ask a loan officer about:

Amount Financed This is the total amount of your loan. Make sure it is going to cover the cost of your home minus the amount of your down payment.

Annual Percentage Rate This is the rate of interest you will pay. If your rate is fluctuating, find that out as well as the indicator that is used.

Finance Charge This is the total amount of money you will pay in interest. When you combine this amount with the amount financed, you get the "total of payments," the amount you will pay if you keep your mortgage for its full life. The amount financed, annual percentage rate, finance charge and total of payments are costs of loans lenders are required to disclose to you on the *truth in lending disclosure statement,* which will be given to you immediately after you apply for your loan (page 353).

Prepaid Charges and Deposit These are all one-time charges made by the lender before or at settlement. These items, discussed in Chapter 12, often include application, commitment, and loan origination fees; discount points; fees for assumptions, periodic inspections, or FHA contractors; prepaid interest or insurance payments; and fees for preparing papers, such as the schedule of your payments.

Payment Amounts and Dates Unless you have a variable-rate loan or one that involves unequal or balloon payments, you should receive a simple schedule of how much you have to pay, how often, for how long and on what dates. Each payment amount will include a combination of the principal and the interest. In addition, unless you choose otherwise, many lenders will want you to have your property taxes and insurance "escrowed," meaning that you pay an additional amount with each monthly payment that the lender uses to pay your property taxes and premiums.

Late and Prepayment Charges The first is charged if you are late on a monthly payment, the second if you pay off the loan before its life is up. Ask how they are computed and when they must be paid. For the late charge, see if there is a five-, ten- or fifteen-day grace period. Most mortgages have these.

Paying off thirty years' worth of a loan early may not seem likely now, but you could win a lottery or receive an inheritance and want to pay it off ahead of time. In fact, the vast majority of people pay off their mortgages early because few people stay in one home for thirty years. Prepayment penalties can mean a substantial cost to you, so shop around to get a mortgage that has none or one in which the prepayment penalty lasts only for the first few years of the mortgage.

Lien Type and Extent You will want a clear statement about the sort of lien that will be placed on your property. If you default, under what terms can you redeem (get back) your property? What will the charges be?

Cancellation and Acceleration Policy This is related to payment amounts and dates. All loans are *callable* (the entire unpaid balance becomes due immediately) under certain conditions. Under what conditions your lender has the right to call your loan is crucial. When you miss two payments? Three? If you are late three times?

Assumability Policy Can you transfer your mortgage to another borrower when you sell your home?

Other Costs These costs usually include fees for the title search and insurance; charges for preparation of deeds, settlement statements and other documents; payments into a special account to cover taxes, insurance and utilities; fees for notary and credit reports; and any other inspection or application fees.

Locking In Often you will not have to accept a specific rate of interest and points when you fill out the application. You will be permitted to "float" your loan. This means that after you apply, you will be allowed to call the lender each day and get the latest rates the lender is offering. (They change daily.) When you're ready, you choose the rate, locking it in, and get a statement confirming the rate. The lender will have a requirement as to how long after you lock in you must close or lose that rate. Make sure you choose your rate within a comfortable amount of time from closing.

CHAPTER

12

THE TITLE

When you buy a home, you are buying the seller's *title*—the right to possess, use, control and dispose of the property. The written legal evidence that the ownership rights have been transferred to you is a properly executed and recorded *deed*.

The Deed The *deed* is a written document that, if properly drawn up and delivered, transfers title to real property from one owner to another. Different types of deeds convey different types of rights. Try to get the seller to agree in the purchase contract to give you a "warranty deed" and "good and marketable title." This means your title is "clear" and can be safely transferred to another. Getting a deed with this language, along with your title insurance and a survey, will protect your title against another's claim.

Sellers sometimes offer a *quitclaim deed*, also called a *contract of deed*. Be wary. Such a deed offers little protection to the holder. All you get with a quitclaim deed is the interest in the property that the seller owns, which may be no interest at all. Because the quitclaim contains no title warranties, you have no protection from title defects, such as improperly drawn boundaries or *mechanics' liens*—

claims filed by contractors who were not paid for work they did on the property. Quitclaim deeds are often used for transfers between family members. Otherwise avoid them.

Decide ahead of time the form of ownership by which you want to take title. The consequences of tenancy in common, tenancy by the entirety and other forms of ownership were discussed in Chapter 1. State your preference in your contract of purchase so it can be transferred to the deed.

Assuring Title

Getting and keeping title to your property is a three-step process: searching the title; buying title insurance; and buying extra coverage, called *endorsements.*

All your searching for the right home and the right financing will be in vain if the property you find doesn't have "good and marketable title." Unfortunately, this is the one area in which you probably can do little on your own to ensure that it does.

The real estate industry's system of deed registration, or the *chain of title,* can be searched to determine if your title is good, but this *title search* is such an archaic, complicated process, it cannot be done by the uninitiated, no matter how well prepared. The current system was created in fifteenth-century England under Henry VIII. It should be replaced with computerized record keeping similar to what is now used for automobile ownership records. Indeed, the sale and purchase of real property should be no more complicated than the sale and purchase of a car. The day of such simplification remains far in the future, however.

Title Searches

Despite the shortcomings, you have a way of assuring you are getting a good title. This involves a search of the records. For this you have to pay a separate charge from the title insurance policy premium. The price of this search varies widely, and can cost anywhere from $300 to $800.

Before the title insurance is issued, a title report is prepared, based on a search of the public records. The report, called a *certificate of title,* describes the property and identifies the owner, title defects, liens and encumbrances of record, including any judgments against the land. The company normally insures the title only after examining it for defects. If problems are discovered, the company can still insure the title, but it will require that certain conditions be met or make the insurance subject to specified exceptions.

Your best bet is to have the title company that is issuing the insurance also do the search. In some cases, however, the company that issues the insurance may accept one of the two options described below, review them and then insure the title. This is especially helpful if the attorney you hire to do your closing includes a title search in the fee. Don't be surprised, however, if title companies insure only titles they themselves search. Whatever you do, do not rely solely on one of the searches below. Get insurance.

Abstract and Lawyer's Opinion The title assurance you get can be in the form of an *abstract* supported by an attorney's formal opinion or letter. An abstract is an historical summary of everything that affects ownership of the property and is available from the title company currently insuring the title. It includes not only the chain of owners of the property but also all recorded easements, mortgages, wills, tax liens, judgments, pending lawsuits, marriages and anything else that affects the title. When you buy the property, you can hire and pay an attorney to examine the abstract and give you a formal written opinion as to the validity of the title—including who the owner of record is and the lawyer's judgment of whether anyone else has any right to or interest in the property. This official opinion is known as the certificate of title. It too is to be paid for *in addition to* the cost of the title insurance. Typically, it can cost as little as $200 but can be higher depending on the number of past transactions that have to be described. Before you incur this expense, make sure your title company will issue insurance based on such a certificate. Many will not.

Attorney's Record Search You (or the title company) can hire an attorney for a flat fee (typically $150–$400) simply to search public records and issue a certificate of title. This can be risky because, unless you buy title insurance, the only thing that protects you is the lawyer's malpractice insurance: if something goes wrong with your title, you can sue the lawyer's insurance company for damages—small consolation to those who have lost their "dream house." Again, ask the title insurance companies you're looking into if they will accept another lawyer's search.

Title Insurance

As noted above, the title company will most likely search the records and issue an insurance policy. This doesn't mean no one can ever claim ownership of your home, nor does it mean if someone does, you'll be assured you'll get to keep the home. What it does mean is that if at any time while you own your home someone else has a claim on it that should have been revealed in the title search, you will be reimbursed for your loss. The insurance pays if a conflict is later discovered that should have been found in the research into all of the previous owners of the property.

Your broker or agent, if you have one, will work closely with the title company. The company can issue either of two kinds of policies—a lender's policy, which covers only the lender until the mortgage is paid off, or an owner's policy, which covers you as long as you own your home.

Even though title insurance companies are regulated, the insurance rates vary enough to make it worthwhile to shop around. A one-time premium payment has to be made at the closing. The costs will vary depending on the value of the home you're buying. A good rule of thumb is $4 or $5 for every $1,000 of the purchase price. Special endorsements, discussed below, cost extra.

When you ask about title insurance companies and the fees they charge, also ask exactly what is covered in each case. Some routinely include the cost of handling the closing, the title search, title report and insurance protection.

If you're getting a new mortgage, the lender will probably make you buy a lender's title insurance policy, both to protect the lender's claim (*lien*) on the property and to make the mortgage an attractive enough investment to sell to mortgage bankers in the secondary mortgage market. Be aware, however, that the lender's policy doesn't protect *you*. To protect yourself you must buy an owner's policy and pay extra for it, or buy in an area where sellers customarily provide title insurance for buyers. If you do have to get both your own and your lender's title insurance, it's usually cheaper to buy them from one company and at the same time.

In general, title insurance policies have two parts. Schedule A includes a description of the property, your name, the seller's name and the amount of the insurance. Schedule B is more important. It lists what is excepted from the coverage. It can specify that the following conditions are not covered: unrecorded leases, mechanics' liens, unrecorded easements, utility company easements and rights-of-way and most other encumbrances and liens.

Schedule B and other policy exceptions may include:

- *Zoning.* They do not protect against the effects of zoning changes.

- *Eminent domain.* They do not accept responsibility if the government takes your property through its power to seize it for a public purpose, provided you are paid a reasonable price.

- *Claims.* They do not protect against defects, liens, encumbrances and other claims that are discovered after buying the property.

- *Errors.* The insurer may omit coverage for errors in the title search. This is especially likely when an outside lawyer does the search.

- *Inflation.* The insurer covers you only up to the amount of the property's existing value at the time of purchase. You will have to ask for and pay for additional coverage for increases in the property's value—a worthwhile expense.

If any of these exceptions holds, your title will be unmarketable and you could lose your home. The way to get around this is to purchase endorsements from your title company that negate these exceptions to coverage. It is usual to do this.

Endorsements

Almost all title insurance policies follow a standard format. Take time to read yours. If possible, have someone knowledgeable go over the details with you before closing. Pay close attention to what your policy covers and what it doesn't.

If you want coverage for something that is excepted in Schedule B, you can get an *endorsement* or *affirmative insurance* to delete that exception, but you will have to pay extra for this and meet requirements set by the insurer. The requirements will depend on which of the exceptions is being deleted. You may have to provide affidavits about possession, surveys, easements, liens or special assessments. Getting around exceptions by using endorsements is usually a matter for negotiation, so if you want them, ask for them in your preliminary discussions with the insurer.

You should get endorsements that remove exceptions for faulty boundaries and property lines, zoning and restrictive covenant changes, eminent domain, errors in the title search, mechanics' and other liens and inflation, plus a catchall Schedule B endorsement.

Other Title Company Services

When you hire a title company, you often get not only insurance but a number of other services. Don't be surprised to hear "The title company usually takes care of that." Title companies are hired to prepare and register the deed and do all of the paperwork necessary to effect the transfer, including filing and paying taxes and submitting materials to the lender. They also insure the title after closing. There may be additional services. Be sure to ask and shop around for the best deal.

Reissue Policy One way to save money and still receive full protection is to ask where the seller has title insurance and whether you can assume it at a reissue rate. In many cases a reissue can be obtained at a lower rate, sometimes even from a company other than the original insurer.

CHAPTER

13

CLOSING THE DEAL

When you have struck a deal with a seller and found your financing, it's time to pay for the property and receive the deed. There is no standard name for this step. Depending on where you live, it may be called the *closing, title closing, settlement,* or *escrow.*

Settlements and Escrow

Often the closing takes place at a meeting of all those involved. When that happens, the process is commonly called a *settlement.* If no meeting occurs, it's more often known as *escrow* and is handled by an *escrow agent.* In such cases, the buyer and seller usually sign an agreement to deposit certain funds and documents with an escrow company, which acts as agent for both sides. When all the papers and funds are in, the escrow is *closed* and the agent records the documents and makes the appropriate payments.

Settlement, however, involves much more than the formal acts of *passing the papers.* All the details, loose ends and additional services required to conclude the deal must be tended to. This is when the full cost of buying a home becomes clear—not just the purchase price or the cost of the loan to buy it, but the actual costs of the process of buying as well. Be warned: these closing costs can add up to 8% of the purchase price of the home. As the buyer, you can expect to pay 3% to 6% of this sum.

Before the Closing

Between the day you sign the contract and the day you take title, you need to attend to other details besides your mortgage, title search and title insurance arrangements.

If you feel the seller may not honor part of the contract after the closing, don't count on litigation as a practical solution to your problem. Insist instead that the seller leave a deposit in a special account for several months to protect the terms of the contract. Should the seller fail to live up to the contract, the deposit will be turned over to you.

For example, if the seller has agreed to cart away debris from the basement but has been unable to schedule the hauling service, you should ask that an amount equal to the cost of doing so be put away to ensure it happens. The other alternative is to ask that your purchase price be reduced by the amount you will have to spend, then hire the hauling service yourself.

If a survey was not done by your lender, have the property surveyed if you have any doubt about its boundaries. Check with the clerk's office at your county courthouse to be sure no outstanding liens or lawsuits are pending against the seller that might result in the property being seized or attached. In many areas these tasks are handled by the title insurance company in the course of doing the title search. Ask your title searcher if they were included.

The Final Inspection

This is commonly known as a "walk-through" and should be done with a suspicious eye toward all of the verbal and written promises made about the property, including all fixtures and appliances. This also may be the first time you get to see the home with little or no furniture in it because the seller may have started moving or at least packing to move. Look around and make sure no surprises were hidden behind furniture. Check again for defects and last-minute removal of fixtures you expected to remain with the property. This is not the time for a professional inspection or checking the condition of specific things, such as appliances. That should have all been done during earlier inspection visits.

If you're buying a newly built home, get a certificate of completion of construction from the local government's building or health departments. Also make sure all utilities have been turned on. Finally, review, or have someone review for you, the plans and building specifications to make sure the construction is in full compliance.

Closing Costs

The key to a successful settlement is to get estimates of your charges as early as possible. You should have received rough estimates when you first started shopping for a loan, but once your purchase offer is accepted, you should have more detailed estimates from both the sales agent and the lenders to whom you applied for a loan.

Your lender will have given you a "good faith estimate of closing costs" soon after you applied for the loan. You also have the right to receive, at least one day before closing, a settlement statement on a HUD-approved form that lists all the closing costs. These may change a little because of last-minute messenger charges or other miscellaneous fees, but it should be pretty accurate when you receive it. HUD's *Special Information Booklet* contains very detailed explanations about many of these potential closing costs.

The Special Information Booklet To assist home buyers and to protect them, the U.S. Department of Housing and Urban Development has published the *Special Information Booklet*. It is a clear, straightforward message to consumers about the specific rights and remedies they have in their dealings with the professionals of the real estate industry. It also contains an excellent reproduction of a settlement statement, with each cost explained. Get it and use it as a reference when you receive your settlement statement. It will explain much of what you need to know about each charge.

Law requires that all lending institutions give a copy of the *Special Information Booklet* to anyone who applies for a home loan. Lenders may put their own cover on the booklet, but they may not alter its text. Also, the cover must by law include the words "settlement costs," for example: "HUD's Guide to Settlement Costs" or "Your Guide to Settlement Costs."

You need not wait until you apply for a loan to get a copy. The *Special Information Booklet* is included as part of a HUD publication entitled *Real Estate Settlement Procedures Act,* a sixty-four-page guide to buying a home. A copy can be purchased by calling or writing your regional office of HUD (see Appendix II) or by writing to the Consumer Information Center, P.O. Box 100, Pueblo, CO 81009.

Your settlement costs are influenced by, among other things, what county you live in, how you financed your purchase and what your lender required before making you the loan. Local custom influences whether the buyer or the seller pays any particular charge. This is why it is important that your purchase contract state explicitly who pays what. In some areas the buyer pays for title insurance because the buyer's lender requires the protection. In others the seller absorbs that charge as a selling cost. Sometimes the buyer pays the *recordation tax,* sometimes the seller does. The same is true of points.

The largest part of your settlement costs will be the lender's fees for your loan. These fees—the points—were discussed in Chapter 9. If the down payment and loan don't cover the entire cost of the property plus the buyer's share of expenses listed below, you must be prepared to make up the difference. Additional charges you may be asked to pay are included here. If you don't understand them or feel they are not applicable to your situation, discuss the matter thoroughly with the lender before proceeding.

Of the following potential closing costs, many go to the lender and some go to the seller, while others are paid to the title company, inspection company, and so forth. Some will apply to your purchase, others won't. Most fees paid to the lender are paid by the buyer, but again, this is negotiable and will turn on local custom. Some of these fees will be deductible from your income taxes. Consult with an accountant.

Charges Paid to the Lender

Points, Origination Fee, Commitment Fee Prepaid interest. They increase the lender's initial intake to cover the administrative costs of making the loan.

Appraisal Fee Payment for the lender's appraisal.

Credit Report Fee Reimburses the lender for getting a copy of your credit history.

Inspection and Survey Fees Reimburses the lender for these services.

Title Insurance The premium that protects the lender. It may be paid directly to the title insurance company.

Interest Interest for every day between closing and the date the first mortgage payment is due.

Attorneys' Fees Payment to lender's lawyer to review all the papers.

Down Payment Paid now, this sum goes to the seller.

Assumption Fee If you're assuming the seller's loan or doing any kind of seller financing, the lender will have fees that must be paid.

Mortgage Insurance If required, or if you chose to buy it, you usually are required to pay two or three months' premiums up front at the closing. The money goes into an escrow account the lender uses to pay the premium when it's due.

Property Taxes Whether you escrow your taxes with the lender or not, you will be asked to deposit with the lender enough money to cover two or three months' property taxes.

Hazard Insurance This is required by the lender to cover the cost of one year's insurance against loss from fire or natural disaster. After that, most people buy homeowner's insurance. Check what your hazard insurance covers so you don't duplicate the coverage during the first year you own the home.

Taxes

Transfer or Recordation Taxes This state fee is paid, usually to the title company, whenever property is transferred. Local custom dictates who pays and the exact name will vary in each state.

Recording Fee This fee for filing the deed is also paid to the title company for handling this task.

Other Fees

Inspection Fee If you hired a professional inspector you have not already paid, the fee may be included here.

Survey Fee If you had your own survey done, it may be included here.

Title Insurance and Search The insurance premium will be paid here to the title company. If you hired a title company that included the search in its overall price, it may be a single charge for both the work and insurance. If you hired a separate lawyer to do the search or abstract, you may have to make two separate payments.

Assessments These are charges you might owe the seller if you are moving in the middle of the month. For instance, it includes any part of the month's condo or co-op assessment or utility bills that the seller paid through the end of the month but that you will get use of. Prepaid taxes will be similarly apportioned.

Termite, Flood Inspections Each state and county has its own regulations about what is required. Hazard insurance will cover some things, but the inspections here are additional. For example, in flood-prone areas an inspection will certainly be required. These charges may be the responsibility of the seller, buyer or the title company, depending on local custom.

Brokers' Commissions The seller's broker and any buyer's broker fee must be paid.

Attorneys' Fees If you or the seller hired an attorney to review documents, that may be paid for at this time, or you may be billed later.

Closing or Escrow Fee If you and the seller split the costs of the paperwork through an escrow or closing agent, this fee will be divided between you.

Miscellaneous Fees Document preparation, notary fees and messenger fees will all be separated out. Local custom dictates who pays, but don't be surprised if it all ends up in the buyer's column at closing. Still, who pays these fees is negotiable.

Know the Players

If yours is going to be a traditional closing, expect a large gathering. In addition to yourself, those present may include the seller, the seller's lawyer, your lawyer, agents, the lender, the title insurance representative and the closing agent. Understand the role of each before the meeting so that during the meeting you can focus your attention on the procedures.

Settlement Agent Someone will be on hand to orchestrate the give-and-take of money and papers. This normally is an employee of the title company. As noted earlier, title companies do a lot more than insure titles; among other things, they also perform closings. Expect to see a title company representative at the closing armed with all the papers. He or she may be sitting at the head of the table and running the show.

Title Insurance Representative The sole purpose of this individual may be to present the title insurance policy to the owner, lender and buyer and ensure that all of the descriptions and figures are correct. Or this person could coordinate the closing and play the role of the closing agent. It depends on how he or she was hired.

Lawyers and Agents The lawyer's role is to protect and advise the client, whether the seller, buyer or both, on the charges the client pays and the documents the client signs. If you have hired a buyer's agent, he or she should be able to represent you without an attorney. You can represent yourself, but if you choose to do so, prepare well. You'll be in a room full of professionals who know precisely what they're doing. Also, before deciding to go it alone, it's best to inquire about local custom: if self-representation in your area violates long-standing custom, you may want to reconsider.

At the Closing

In many parts of the country, the procedures at closing have become less of a personal exchange in recent years. Often buyer and seller don't even meet. The buyer simply receives the signed deed and a statement of closing costs by mail from the lender or title company. However, whatever the outward changes, the legal considerations and significance of the documents involved have not changed. What follows is a general description of the exchanges that take place at settlement, whether in person or by mail.

The lender, title company representative or broker hands over the mortgage papers for you or your agent or attorney to examine. If they are in order and contain no surprises, you sign them. Check all addresses and numbers closely.

You then get a check for the amount of the loan. If the mortgage is guaranteed by the VA or FHA, you also get VA or FHA loan forms to sign.

The title company produces the title insurance policies that protect the lender, and you if you purchased it, against defects in the title. These are checked against the description of the property in the deed and against the survey, if one was made.

If the home you are buying is new, the builder may be present and give you a certificate of occupancy, a document issued by the local government. It states that the house was built in accordance with local regulations and with the plans submitted for approval before construction. (Some cities or counties require certificates of occupancy for all homes, old and new.) The builder also hands you whatever written guarantees of materials and work were specified in the purchase contract. Examine these papers to be sure they accurately reflect what you expected.

The seller or the seller's lawyer hands over the deed for examination by you, the lender and the title company representative. It should already be in your name. The written description of the property in the deed should be carefully compared with what is in your purchase contract, with any surveys that were done by you or by the title company, and with descriptions in earlier deeds to the same property examined by the title company in its search. This is your last chance to make sure you're getting exactly the property you expect to own and under exactly the terms you negotiated. This is not the time for surprise revelations.

When you are satisfied the deed is properly drawn, the seller signs the deed and hands it to you. Endorse the lender's check over to the seller and give the seller your check for any balance you still owe on the purchase price. This sum is usually the down payment plus fees.

The escrow agent, title company representative or seller's lawyer and you or your lawyer will have calculated how much each side owes toward divided expenses, such as real estate taxes and fire insurance. The settlement papers will have two columns of figures, one for the seller, one for the buyer, listing all the closing costs with totals at the bottom. From these totals the final payments will be determined. One person, usually whoever is orchestrating the closing, will have a bank account for depositing and writing checks. At this time the checks are written, signed and handed to the appropriate party.

The seller or broker will already have your deposit, and you can use that to offset any money you owe. The seller's broker will make out the correct check, returning your deposit with interest. If you need additional money, you can probably pay from your regular checking account. Bring your checkbook, but check the day before with the escrow agent or the seller's broker to make sure a certified check is not required.

You or the representative of the title company must see to it that the deed and mortgage are recorded with the proper authority as soon as possible after the closing. After the closing you'll be sent a summary of the transaction, called the closing statement.

Closing Problems Among people's greatest nightmares is an argument arising over some unexpected closing cost that causes the deal to fall through. Your best insurance against this is to go over carefully the estimates of closing costs you receive the day before. Read them over on your own or with your representative. Call the seller, the seller's broker or the closing agent if you have questions. Try to leave nothing to be decided at the closing except who pays for the doughnuts and coffee.

That concludes the purchase: you now officially own your new home.

CHAPTER
14

CONSUMER RIGHTS IN LENDING

Consumer awareness and pressure have brought about a broad range of regulatory mechanisms to restrict corrupt, illegal and deceitful activity in the housing marketplace. These include the Real Estate Settlement Procedures Act (RESPA), the Truth-in-Lending Act, the Unfair Trade Practices Act, certain Office of Thrift Supervision regulations governing savings and loan associations and the Home Mortgage Disclosure Act.

RESPA

The Real Estate Settlement Procedures Act (RESPA) requires that almost all private-home purchases that involve financing must include a series of disclosures that protect you from paying high fees for poor service. Following are the major provisions:

Special Information Booklet When you apply for a loan, the lender must give you a copy of the *Special Information Booklet,* published by the U.S. Department of Housing and Urban Development (HUD). Read this booklet carefully, cover to cover, as soon as you get it. Better yet, get a head start by getting a copy from a HUD regional office or by writing to the Consumer Information Center, Box 100, Pueblo, CO 81009. The booklet explains in detail all your rights with respect to lending and closing practices. It also provides work sheets, forms and detailed information about all possible closing costs.

"Good Faith" Estimate The lender is also required to give you a good faith estimate of the closing costs you'll have to pay at settlement. This should be based on the size of your mortgage and the specific services the lender's system requires you to pay for. The lender has to get this information to you within three days of receiving your loan application.

Referrals The lender is allowed to suggest, or even require, that you buy particular services from specific vendors, but in some cases, unless you are allowed to choose from at least two sources for any given service, the lender must formally disclose to you information about the recommended vendor. You must be told the full name, address and telephone number; the fee charged for particular services; and whether or not the lender has a business relationship with that provider. Unfortunately, the requirement applies only to title services, legal work and the use of a particular person to conduct the closing.

RESPA also outlaws kickbacks or unearned fees for referrals. One way lenders get around this protection, however, is for the recommended service provider to maintain large interest-free accounts at the bank or S&L that is referring clients. The "fee" earned by the bank is the interest it doesn't have to pay on the account. Always ask if a recommended provider maintains an interest-free account with the lending institution that is handling your financing. If you uncover an illegal arrangement between a lender and any service provider you're told you have to use, you can sue for three times the size of the fee you're charged. Report any violations you suspect to your HUD regional office (see Appendix II).

Advance Settlement Statement The day before closing you have the right to see an advance copy of the Uniform Settlement Statement, the government form used to record the costs of all settlements under RESPA. This statement must be used regardless of who conducts the closing. It is designed to conform with the analysis of lender costs and practices in the *Special Information Booklet*. The advance disclosure and your day-before preview are intended to eliminate the surprises and dismay home buyers used to encounter at settlement. The statement is an estimate of all closing costs, and as described in Chapter 13, it sets out all the costs in two columns.

Truth in Lending

The U.S. government has enforced truth-in-lending laws since passage of the Consumer Credit Protection Act of 1968. When applied to RESPA transactions, the law requires those who make loans as a business to give borrowers crucial information in a standard format that allows them to compare offers. The lender is required to give you this statement free of charge.

Home Mortgage Disclosure Act

The Federal Reserve Board is responsible for investigating *redlining* practices under the Home Mortgage Disclosure Act. Redlining is the discriminatory refusal to make loans in neighborhoods populated by minority groups. Its name derives from the practice many lenders once had of outlining in red on a map those neighborhoods they felt were too risky to do business in. If you have reason to believe that redlining has occurred, contact the nearest Federal Reserve Board office, listed in your telephone directory under "U.S. Government."

If you are dealing with a savings and loan, the Office of Thrift Supervision has ruled that under the Disclosure Act, you must be given full information on all charges related to required legal services valued at $100 or more, including who will perform the services and whether they will benefit you or only the lender.

In recent years, the Federal Trade Commission (FTC) has been investigating the residential real estate industry. Send any complaints you have to the FTC, listed in your telephone directory under "U.S. Government," if:

- You are not getting full disclosure of important information

- You are having to contend with what you consider unfair or deceptive forms or practices

- You suspect collusion among the various professionals with whom you have to deal

- You believe your rights have been violated in any way

Fair Housing Laws

Fair housing laws protect all citizens against residential housing discrimination of any sort. You are guaranteed the right to buy, rent, deal or negotiate and receive the same terms and conditions as anyone else. You must be told when housing is available for inspection, rental or purchase, and no lender or service provider may conduct any real estate negotiation that in any way violates your civil rights. The law prohibits all practices that discriminate among customers and potential customers because of race, color, creed, religion or national origin.

CONCLUSION

As with all large investments, the process of buying a home should not be entered into without careful preparation. Study this book carefully, use experts as it seems necessary. As you enter the housing market, review and bear in mind the following general considerations.

Prepare carefully, and know the role of each professional you deal with. Careful preparation is necessary, especially in arranging your financing and in contract negotiations. The complexity of the transactions involved in a home purchase makes it inevitable that you will have to deal with professionals at just about every stage—real estate brokers, lawyers, bankers, closing agents, inspectors, appraisers, title insurers and others. To save money and make sure your investment is a sound and safe one, you must understand the role of each of these professionals, whether or not you choose to employ them. The more you prepare, the more confidently you will deal with them.

Watch for trends in the mortgage market. This manual discusses the recent and continuing revolution in the mortgage market in some detail. The number of options for financing increases each year, and the popularity of any one option rises and falls with changes in the housing market and the greater economy.

One thing is certain: adjustable-rate mortgages are here to stay, regardless of the state of the economy, because interest rates now change more rapidly than they once did. Lenders wish to protect themselves from the fluctuations, both with adjustable rates mixed adjustable/fixed-rate loans, and with stricter credit guidelines.

Nationwide building standards have been abolished. The Federal Housing Administration (FHA) has ended the setting of uniform standards for housing. It will now be up to states, counties and local communities to establish such standards. It is especially important, therefore, that you very carefully inspect or have an expert inspect the home you want to buy for structural failures and other problems.

Reforming the System

Despite its complexity, most of the work involved in title searches and settlement is routinely performed by nonprofessionals. It rarely consists of more than verifying items on a checklist and completing standardized forms. Complications in property transfers rarely arise. Less than 5% of all property transfers develop complications, and those are usually easily resolved. However, studies have revealed that home buyers are often charged for closing work that was, in fact, done several years earlier for a previous buyer.

The complexity of the system is needless. It seldom benefits anyone but the professionals who sell their ability to untangle it. Transferring real property can and should be simple and inexpensive. The use of intermediaries would be less costly—and often unnecessary—if procedures for transferring and recording real estate were simplified. Most countries in the industrialized world long ago instituted a land registration system in which the transfer of real property is as simple and as inexpensive as the transfer of an automobile is in the United States.

Consumers do have one ray of hope, however. It is that computerization of the land title system, recently pioneered by Wisconsin and a few other states will spread to more states.

There is little reason why everyday legal transactions cannot and should not be handled without the help of professionals. This is as true in the real estate marketplace as in other arenas that involve the routine application of law. However, for this to occur, more education of the general public is essential. Laws and regulations must be drafted in plain language, and unnecessarily complex and cumbersome procedures must be simplified.

BOOK
3

SMALL CLAIMS COURT

INTRODUCTION

The small claims court is a court of law that considers only non-criminal matters. It is called "small claims" because it usually settles money disputes involving a few thousand dollars or less.

A small claims court operates according to rules that are far less complicated than the procedures of other trial courts, and for small claims, a growing number of states are doing away with the technical language and legalistic forms normally associated with going to court. Like other courts, small claims courts have a judge and, at rare times, even a jury, and an increasing number also operate arbitration or mediation programs that try to resolve problems before they reach the courtroom. Finally, although rare, small claims cases may even involve lawyers representing one or both sides.

This book will help you answer the following questions:

- Should I go to small claims court with my problem?

- If so, how do I present my case to the court?

- If I'm sued, how do I defend myself in small claims court?

Before answering any of these questions, you must know something about how small claims courts operate. You must also be able to recognize the types of cases that a small claims court will and will not consider. Finally, you must be able to apply the rules of your state's courts to your particular problem.

This basic preparation will help you determine if your case meets the "entry requirements" of the small claims court in your state. If it does, you must then decide if going to a small claims court is the best way to resolve your problem. You may find that you can get a better solution outside the court. What kinds of situations are handled in small claims court? Here are a few examples:

- A dry cleaner ruins a jacket and refuses to pay for it.

- A landlord will not return a security deposit.

- A dog owner won't compensate a neighbor for the damage caused by a dog bite.

- An appliance store won't repair or replace a dishwasher that repeatedly breaks down.

- A building contractor fails to seal a roof properly.

- A motorist dents someone's fender and doesn't have insurance to cover the damage.

- A retailer, repair person or professional cannot collect on an overdue bill.

Small claims courts allow consumers to resolve small but important money disputes quickly and inexpensively. When small claims courts are available, consumers are afforded greater access to courtroom resolution without the need for full-fledged litigation. If the number and location of small claims courts were increased as well as the dollar limit allowed, the public would be better served.

A Word about Terms

This book uses common, everyday language. Fortunately, not a great deal of technical language is used in small claims court. Where familiarity with a legal term can be helpful, however, a plain-language definition of the legal word or phrase is also included in this book. Knowing these few legal terms can help you complete forms more easily and deal with clerks and judges more effectively.

Appendix XII is a glossary of legal terms. Many of these terms do not appear in the text but are included because they are used in Appendix VI.

How to Use This Book

This book offers information that you must know to secure your rights in small claims court. Careful use of this book won't guarantee you a victory, but it will prevent you from ruining your chances because of mistakes that could have been avoided.

Read the text for general information and then refer to the appendices at the back for specific information about the rules and resources in your state.

Whether or not you initiate the suit, you should also know about alternatives to lawsuits (Chapters 1 and 2); the legal basis for a suit (Chapter 3); how to file a legal claim (Chapter 4); the rules for *service of process* (Chapter 5); and how to collect your evidence and present it in court (Chapters 8 and 9). If someone is suing you in small claims court, refer to Chapters 6 and 7 for specific methods of defending yourself.

Court Personnel and Lawyers

If, after reading this book, you still have questions about your case or need more information about local procedures, ask the clerk in small claims court for help. These clerks realize that most cases brought into small claims court will be presented by the people involved and not by attorneys.

Although small claims court clerks are usually more willing to offer help than the clerks of other trial courts, they still feel the threat of bar prosecution for giving "unauthorized" legal advice.

Because of this, some may refuse to give you anything more than the most basic information.

If you have questions that cannot be answered by this book or by the small claims court clerk, don't assume you have to hand your case over to a lawyer. You may want to consider hiring a lawyer as a *pro se* coach or consultant to answer your specific legal questions, to review legal documents or to make suggestions. If you do need this kind of help, find a lawyer who will agree to work under such an arrangement and to charge a reasonable hourly rate. [1]

[1] For tips on hiring and using lawyers, we suggest *Using a Lawyer* by Kay Ostberg in association with HALT, Random House, 1990.

CHAPTER

I

BEFORE COURT

Small claims courts offer a relatively quick and inexpensive way to settle disputes. Still, you should be aware that, although pursuing a small claims case does take less time and money than would be required for a formal civil trial, a small claims suit will probably require at least two trips to the courthouse during business hours—once to file the appropriate papers and once for the hearing. And if you encounter postponements or problems with collecting a judgment, you could be forced to make as many as four or five return trips.

Quicker, less expensive and often more effective methods for resolving small claims are also available even *before* you go to court. Not only can these alternatives save you time and trouble, they will also greatly strengthen your case if you are forced to go to court. Judges in small claims courts expect both sides in a dispute to make every reasonable effort to resolve their problem before resorting to court action. If you can demonstrate that you sought peaceful resolution but the other side refused to communicate, cooperate or act in good faith at all points before the hearing, your chances of victory will be greatly increased.

The following suggestions may seem basic, but it is important to follow them carefully. Remember that you are not only complaining—you are also methodically building a case.

The Telephone Call

The first step in seeking a remedy to your problem should be a businesslike telephone call to whoever is responsible for it. Before you begin, have a pen and paper at hand, plus notes about your case—names, dates, the amount of money in dispute, and so on. What you say will depend on the nature of the problem, but the form of the conversation should be as follows:

1. Identify yourself and your address. If you have dealt with the other side previously (for example, if you are calling a company that didn't repair your roof properly), give your name as it might appear on their records: "This is Mrs. Elizabeth Jones of 321 Baker Street."

2. State the reason you are calling. Don't explain it, state it. Don't waste your explanation on a receptionist and don't allow yourself to be sidetracked.

3. Ask to speak to the appropriate person—whoever has the authority to offer an immediate remedy. It's extremely important that you deal with the right person from the beginning. If the problem involves a child, you'll want to speak to the parents. If it's a small business, speak to the owner. If it's a large store or manufacturer, ask to speak to the customer service manager.

4. Identify yourself again and your problem. This time, follow up with the question: "Are you the person responsible for handling this sort of problem?" Get a definite answer before you continue.

5. Ask for the name and title of the person with whom you are speaking. *Write this down.* Ask for the correct spelling of the name. This will assure that you'll have a record of whom you spoke with and that a follow-up letter, if necessary, will go to the right person.

6. Describe the problem. Keep your description as brief as it would be in a short business letter. Refer to your notes so you can be sure you are being accurate.

7. Make a firm demand. State precisely what you expect to be done about your problem. Be polite, but be firm. (Example: "I expect your repairmen to be out here tomorrow to seal this roof properly, or I want all of my money back. Moreover, I expect compensation for the water damage to my carpets and wallpaper.")

8. Get an answer. Don't accept "I'll have to think about it" or "Maybe we can squeeze it in next week" or "See the manufacturer," or mumbo jumbo about "implied warranties." You need a specific promise or a clear refusal to rectify or compensate you for the damage or injury done. Without this, the telephone call has been a waste of time. Don't be rude, but persist until you get a "yes" or "no" answer. ("Then you will send somebody out tomorrow? And you'll pay for any damages not covered by my insurance?")

9. Set a deadline. Agree to a schedule and expect the other side to meet it. When that deadline has passed, it's time to move to the next step.

The First Letter

With any luck, one letter may resolve your problem. If it doesn't, it will help convince the judge that you behaved reasonably at all times and made a sincere effort to resolve the matter before going to court.

The letter should be similar to your telephone call: concise, unemotional and firm. It should be no longer than one page. It should be a succinct record of what happened.

Always use plain English and avoid legal terms or you may say something you didn't mean and end up sounding foolish. Most important, write so the letter and therefore the dispute can be clearly understood by a disinterested third person.

The disinterested third person may turn out to be the company president, a representative of the manufacturer, a Better Business Bureau official, an arbitrator or ultimately a judge. Such persons, particularly judges, will not have the time or inclination to read an eight-page tirade about your woes. They will simply want to know who, what, when, where and how much. Don't worry about boring the person you're writing to by recounting the facts. It's important to remember that your letter may become a "minibrief" for that disinterested third person.

These third persons will also want to know if you have behaved reasonably throughout this difficulty and if your account of the situation can be believed. Their verdict will depend in part on the reasonableness of your demands. It will also depend on the tone and length of your letter. Anyone who cannot get to the point in one page and refrain from name calling and exaggeration will be treated with skepticism if not ignored completely. After a judgment of this sort, your chances of success are greatly reduced.

Your first letter should be straightforward. Again, the content will depend upon the dispute, but your letter probably should include these points:

1. *The right addressee.* Send the letter directly to the person you spoke with on the telephone. If you handled the telephone call properly, he or she should be the person in charge and the one who made a commitment to you.

2. *The date, nature and location of the incident.* To refresh your correspondent's memory and to establish the facts for the future, briefly describe your cause for complaint. Be sure to include the names of all those involved, such as salespersons and repairpersons.

3. *The broken promise.* Here you must establish, morally and legally, that the other side is responsible for your difficulty. If you purchased goods or services, you did so with a reasonable expectation of getting your money's worth. If you gave your landlord a security deposit, you expected to get it back after leaving the apartment in good condition. If your neighbor's dog bit you,

you reasonably expect the owner to accept responsibility for the failure to keep the dog confined.

4. *Your efforts to resolve the problem.* Mention your telephone call and the failure to respond adequately to your complaint. Describe any commitments made on the telephone and say why they failed to satisfy you.

5. *Your demand.* This demand may or may not be the same as the one made over the telephone. If the response to your first demand was insufficient, you may want to draw the line here. Keep your final demand simple and reasonable: for example, ask that your money be refunded, or insist on compensation for the damages you suffered.

6. *A reasonable deadline for compliance with your demand.* In most cases two weeks will be perceived as reasonable.

7. *Don't make threats.* This is not the time to threaten legal action. It will make you seem unreasonable and eager to invite conflict. Moreover, it's poor strategy. One mention of legal action may leave you speaking with the legal department instead of customer services.

A good letter should look like the sample that follows:

> Mrs. Elizabeth Jones
> 321 Baker Street
> Midland, MI 33242
> Tel.: 438-2614
> January 5, 1990

Mr. T. Williams
Hottin Roofers, Inc.
26 Tobacco Road
Midland, MI 33242

Dear Mr. Williams:

On November 20, 1989, I hired your firm to repair the roof of our house at 321 Baker Street. On November 21, two men from Hottin Roofers (a Mr. Bates and another man with a large mustache) arrived and began repairs. They worked for two days. I received a bill for $1,650 and paid it in full on December 7, 1989.

It rained on December 13. The roof leaked at the exact spot where the "repairs" were performed, and there was substantial damage to the carpet and wallpaper below. When I hired your firm to repair the roof, I was promised high-quality repair work. The job performed by your employees clearly fails to meet this standard.

When I called you on December 14, you refused to send someone to seal the roof, and you refused to discuss compensation for the damage caused by the leak. Given the circumstances, I think the only way to settle this matter is for you to refund the $1,650 I paid Hottin Roofers, plus $350 to cover the deductible for my homeowners' insurance policy. I expect a check from Hottin Roofers within 14 days.

Sincerely yours,
Mrs. Elizabeth Jones

cc: Homeowners' Insurance Company

Type your letter. Just as no third person will take the time to read an eight-page letter, few, if any, will bother trying to decipher your handwriting. Also, typed letters look more serious and businesslike.

Make several copies of the letter. You'll need copies for your files, for other interested persons, to include with your second letter, and for the judge or arbitrator. Photocopies are better than carbons.

Send the original of the letter by certified mail, return receipt requested. Besides getting the attention of the person you're writing, this will prevent that person from claiming that he or she never received the letter.

Send copies to all *interested* third persons. At this stage, send copies only to those who are actually involved in the original incident or who have a direct financial or legal interest in the resolution of your dispute. In Mrs. Jones's case, for instance, she should notify her insurer that she has contacted Hottin Roofers about compensation for that portion of the damage not covered by her policy.

When other persons also suffered damages, they should be notified. For example, if you and a friend were bitten by a neighbor's dog, send a copy to the friend. But that's it. Don't overdo the "cc" tactic. Some people "cc" everyone from the White House to their suburban newspapers. Not only is this unnecessary, it often destroys the credibility of the person complaining.

Now wait. If you gave the other side fourteen days to reply, wait the full fourteen days. Don't start calling or sending updated versions of your first letter. You may make yourself appear unsure of the merits of your claim. You may also make it possible for the other side to claim that you changed the demands contained in your original letter.

Start a file. You don't need anything elaborate, but you do need a folder, envelope or box to hold all correspondence, invoices, canceled checks, names of witnesses, estimates of damage and the like.

Home Lawyer Tip

Home Lawyer will draft a Defective Product Complaint Letter. To draft a Defective Product Complaint Letter, select Defective Product Complaint Letter from the Document submenu. Point to "New," and then answer the questions that Home Lawyer asks.

The Second Letter

If you don't get an answer to your first letter, or if the other side makes a counterproposal you think is inadequate, write a second letter. This one should be even briefer and precisely to the point:

Mrs. Elizabeth Jones
321 Baker Street
Midland, MI 33242
Tel.: 438-2614
January 19, 1990

Mr. T. Williams
Hottin Roofers, Inc.
26 Tobacco Road
Midland, MI 33242

Dear Mr. Williams:

Two weeks ago I wrote to you and asked for a refund of the $1,650 I paid Hottin Roofers to fix our roof. I also asked for $350 to compensate for the damage done when your "repair" failed to prevent the roof from leaking. You have not responded to my request. [*Or:* I don't think your offer of $500 is sufficient.]

I still believe a full refund plus the $350 is the only fair and reasonable way to resolve this matter. If you do not make a reasonable settlement offer in the next week, I shall be forced to take further action. Please contact me immediately.

Sincerely yours,
Mrs. Elizabeth Jones

Enc: My letter of 1-5-90
Your reply of 1-11-90 [if any]

cc: Homeowners' Insurance Company
    Better Business Bureau
    XYZ Homebuilders Association

Warn that you may take "further action," not "legal action." For all the reasons mentioned in discussing your first letter, you still don't want to seem too eager to rush into courtroom combat. Plus, it's still important to keep all your options open at this stage. Even if it is possible to take your case directly to small claims court, you may have a better chance of getting what you want through alternative dispute resolution procedures. (Your options—and when you should consider using them—are discussed in the next chapter.)

Be sure to enclose a copy of your first letter and the reply, if you received one. Also include these copies if you "cc" any interested third persons. Again, send the letter by certified mail, return receipt requested, and keep a copy for your files.

If you are dealing with a supplier of goods or services, it may help to send a copy of your second letter and all enclosures to the Better Business Bureau, the Chamber of Commerce or a relevant local trade association. Always attach a note to copies of your letters and explain to these organizations that you will be seeking help if the matter cannot be resolved otherwise.

These organizations probably will not do anything about your problem simply because you've sent a letter. You usually have to file a formal complaint to guarantee assistance. This procedure is discussed in the next chapter. However, it is important to let your opponent know that such organizations are being informed. The merchant may feel safe in ignoring you, but he or she can't ignore the risk of a bad reputation in the business community.

If you bought an appliance from a retailer, send a copy of your letter to the parent company that sold the retail franchise, plus a copy to the manufacturer of the product you bought. A letter to these companies often results in direct action. To get their addresses, consult a business directory at your local library. Start with *Standard & Poor's Register of Corporations, Directors and Executives.* It contains information on more than 50,000 American business firms. If you know the name of the product but don't know the corporate name of the manufacturer, look in the *Thomas Registry,* available at your local library.

CHAPTER

2

ALTERNATIVES

Sometimes you can't take your problem to small claims court. If a dog keeps digging holes in your yard and you want the owner to keep the dog on a leash, small claims courts in most states cannot help you. You could seek money for the damage the dog caused, but in this type of dispute, nuisance and aggravation are more the issue than money. Small claims courts can't settle long-running family or neighborhood disputes, and they can't prevent future problems. In all but rare circumstances, they can award money only for proven damages.

Small claims courts also cannot hear cases in which the amount of money sought exceeds the limit set by state law. You should claim as much as you can justify but never more than the dollar limit allowed (see page 406.) The limit ranges from $1000 to $5,000. More than half of the states have set their small claims court dollar limits between $1,500 and $2,500. In the example used in Chapter 1, Mrs. Jones would not have been able to sue Hottin Roofers for $2,000 in the small claims courts of fourteen states. (Though to get into small claims court, Mrs. Jones could reduce her claim to $1,500 since that is her state's dollar limit.) Check Appendix VI for the dollar limit in the small claims courts in your state.

If your dispute cannot be settled by paying you money or if the amount of money in question exceeds your state's limits, you will be forced to seek alternatives to small claims court. You may also want to try these alternative resolution measures even if your claim is eligible for consideration in small claims court. Sometimes the best strategy is to stay out of court—or to use the court as a last resort.

Most of these alternatives are tailored to particular types of disputes. If your dispute fits within one of these categories, the alternative procedure may well give you the quickest, least expensive and most satisfactory solution. The remainder of this chapter discusses these alternatives and the types of problems they deal with.

Consumer Action Agencies (CAAs)

Consumers often buy goods and services whose value exceeds the dollar limits set by their state's small claims courts. If you buy a major appliance or a car or hire a contractor for home improvements or repairs, it is unlikely that you will be able to take a "full refund" demand to your small claims court.

Even if you can sue, it may be better to take your complaint first to a consumer action agency (CAA). Most small claims courts can offer only cash awards, and you may want something else—such as a replacement, new parts or a prompt repair job. Also, suing a large company can be complicated and time-consuming.

Registering a complaint with a CAA, on the other hand, is simple, and the agency will do most of the work for you. Another advantage is that large companies are more likely to cooperate with a CAA than to respond to the possible threat of a small claims trial.

CAAs are classified by the manner in which they are funded and operated. Some are run by government, some by private consumer groups and some by business and individual groups. Note that all of these will expect you to have made a personal effort to resolve your dispute (for example, by the telephone call and two letters discussed in Chapter 1) before turning to them for help.

Government Consumer Action Agencies

Most states have consumer action agencies at the state, county and city levels. These offices are familiar with local and state laws and will either help you directly or refer you to the proper agency.

Many complaints are handled at the local level. Call your local office and ask that a complaint form be sent to you. Fill it out and return it with copies of supporting documents such as sales slips, other sales documents and whatever correspondence you've had with the merchant. (Most offices will accept a written letter with supporting documents in lieu of their complaint form.)

After your complaint is filed, an investigator will be assigned to your "case." If additional information or an on-site investigation is needed, you will be contacted. When the information is compiled, the investigator will negotiate with the merchant in an attempt to reach a mutually agreeable solution. This may take several exchanges of telephone calls and letters.

Some areas have strong consumer protection laws that empower the CAA to take legal action against merchants if necessary. They can negotiate cease-and-desist agreements, issue subpoenas and civil citations and file lawsuits. Not all consumer protection offices have this kind of clout, however.

If your area has no city or county consumer office, try the state office. Some states have a separate consumer affairs office, while others have it within the governor's office, the attorney general's office or both. Appendix VIII lists the addresses and telephone numbers of state consumer affairs offices.

If your dispute concerns the sale of professional services, state licensing and regulatory boards may be able to help. Doctors, funeral directors, lawyers, electricians and hundreds of other professionals must meet licensing standards set by state agencies. These agencies often handle consumer complaints and can bring disciplinary actions. However, the usefulness of filing such a complaint varies from profession to profession and from state to state. Before spending a lot of time taking a complaint to a licensing board, check with your local private CAA or a consumer affairs reporter at a local television station to see if the effort is worthwhile.

Federal agencies usually have their own consumer affairs office. Most provide general information but only a few (notably the Post Office) investigate individual complaints. For more information on the various federal agencies and the types of matters they will consider, write for a free copy of the *Consumer's Resource Handbook*, Consumer Information Center, Pueblo, CO 81009.

Private Consumer Action Agencies

All states and the District of Columbia have private consumer groups that may operate at the local as well as state level. These are usually staffed by volunteers and can give you information and advice on how to handle your problem. These groups usually don't have the authority to force a resolution, but they can put you on the right track and are an invaluable source of information about local business practices.

To locate private consumer groups in your area, check with your state or local government consumer office or call a local television news department and ask for the consumer affairs reporter. If these sources can't help you, contact national consumers' groups like the Consumer Federation of America or the National Consumers League, or try the Division of Consumer Organizations in the U.S. Office of Consumer Affairs. Their addresses and telephone numbers are listed in Appendix VII.

Media Programs

Some newspapers and many TV stations help consumers with a "hot line" or "action" service. If your efforts (the telephone call and the two follow-up letters) don't get a response, find out if your area has a media-sponsored consumer action program. Media programs of this sort are often successful because the businesses involved act quickly to avoid bad publicity. You can find out if your community has such a media-sponsored program by simply calling your local newspapers and radio and TV stations, and asking if they have a consumer reporter.

Business Consumer Action Agencies

Both local business communities and national industry groups also sponsor consumer action programs. Like media programs, these tend to get quick results because the offender wants to avoid getting a bad reputation with colleagues, competition and prospective customers. Filing a complaint with a business CAA is a good first step because if they are unable to resolve your problem, you can still take your case to small claims court. The three most important business CAAs are the Better Business Bureaus (BBBs), Consumer Action Panels (CAPs) and trade associations. Addresses and telephone numbers for the last two are listed in Appendix VII.

Better Business Bureaus

BBBs are nonprofit organizations organized and funded by local and national businesses. Most of the 180 BBBs in the United States offer general consumer information, including records of previous complaints against individual companies.

The national office reported that BBBs received 11.5 million consumer inquiries and complaints in 1988. Home improvements, service firms, and retail sales ranked as the three areas that received the most inquiries "from consumers seeking to check out the reliability of individual companies and various offers before buying."

BBBs accept written complaints against a business and will contact the firm on your behalf. They will help you settle the case until you are satisfied or the company can convince them your claim is unjustified. Some BBBs also offer binding arbitration if all other attempts at resolution fail (see "Arbitration," page 381.)

Consumer Action Panels (CAPs)

As consumer awareness spread during the early 1970s, several industries initiated consumer action panels to handle consumer complaints. Two industries still have such panels: the automobile dealers (AUTOCAP) and the makers of major home appliances (MACAP).

Upon receipt of a complaint, the panel writes a formal letter to the manufacturer or dealer asking for an explanation of the problem and encouraging a resolution that will satisfy the customer.

If the problem is not settled after a fixed period—usually a week to 10 days—it is brought before a review board composed of industry and consumer representatives. The board studies the file and recommends a solution.

While these recommendations are not legally binding, a manufacturer may be prodded into agreement rather than face trade association sanctions. The consumer is free to pursue remedies elsewhere if dissatisfied with the panel's decision or the results. Since it is always in the interest of a business to have a clean record, the panels achieve a high rate of success. In 1988 MACAP resolved to consumers' satisfaction approximately 77.2 percent of the 645 complaints it received.

Trade Associations

Many national trade associations can handle consumer complaints, but not all have consumer action panels. This does not necessarily reduce their effectiveness, however.

Local trade associations have been created in some communities by auto dealers, homebuilders and others. Some of these associations investigate consumers' complaints, but they were formed primarily to protect their members' interests and only a few are truly aggressive about helping consumers. To find out if a relevant trade association exists in your area—and if it's worth approaching them with your problem—contact a local consumer action agency or consumer affairs reporter.

Two notes of caution: whether you're taking your dispute to a

BBB, a consumer action panel or a trade association, remember that each of them has restrictions on the types of cases it can handle and that their effectiveness is reduced when the manufacturer or dealer you are complaining about is not a member of the industry group that sponsors the program.

Arbitration

Resolving disputes through arbitration is often easier and more satisfactory than appearing in court. The technique of arbitration is as old as Solomon, but its use has grown dramatically in recent years. It is now used extensively by businesses in labor contract negotiations. Lately, courts have also moved to make arbitration available for settling minor disputes in both criminal and civil matters.

In arbitration, the two disputing sides appear for a hearing before a neutral third party who listens to arguments, considers the evidence and makes a decision. It is similar in many ways to the small claims court procedure. In practice, however, arbitration is even simpler than small claims procedures. Little paperwork is involved, and formal rules of evidence don't apply. When and where hearings are conducted is often determined by the preferences of the two sides and the arbitrator. This allows quick, easy and informal proceedings, which are particularly helpful when on-site inspection is needed to arrive at the truth.

Arbitration is almost always voluntary: both sides must agree to it and agree beforehand to accept the final decision of the arbitrator. Once arbitration is agreed to, the two sides select an arbitrator, usually an expert on the type of problem at hand. Sometimes a panel of three or more arbitrators is required. The agency sponsoring the arbitration, usually the Better Business Bureau (page 382) or the American Arbitration Association (page 383), will give you a list of arbitrators and an explanation of the rules.

The hearing is informal and conducted in a private, relaxed atmosphere. You'll be able to state your case and ask questions of the other side. The arbitrator may also ask questions and may have arranged for an expert witness to present additional information.

Lawyers are permitted at the hearings in most cases, but this depends entirely upon who is sponsoring the arbitration.

The arbitrator will try to encourage the two sides to come to agreement. If this is not possible, the arbitrator's final decision will be made within a set period of time—usually ten days. The decision is written, binding and enforceable by the courts.

Depending on the rules, you may or may not be able to appeal the arbitrator's decision, so be sure you know the rules before you begin.

Arbitration has several obvious advantages beyond the speed and ease of the process. For example, an arbitrator has more flexibility than a small claims judge; the arbitrator can decide that a service—and not a cash award—is required. Also, both sides may be asked to do certain things to effect the resolution, whereas a judge is limited to deciding which side should be required to make restitution. Further, arbitrators are not subject to the dollar limits that are imposed on small claims court cases.

Several different agencies sponsor arbitration. The following descriptions should help you determine which forum best suits your needs.

Better Business Bureaus

The Better Business Bureau operates the National Consumer Arbitration Program in more than 140 major metropolitan areas. The BBB's arbitration program handles only consumer business disputes. It excludes personal injury and property claims, allegations of fraud and violations of criminal law.

The BBB pays for the cost of its arbitration, and the arbitrators usually are local volunteers—businesspeople, homemakers, educators, lawyers and doctors. You and the other side will be allowed to help choose the arbitrator for your case.

As mentioned before, when you approach the BBB with a complaint, it will first try to settle it by contacting the business and asking that the complaint be resolved. If this fails, the BBB will offer arbitration if it's available in your area.

If the other side agrees to arbitration, the BBB will explain the rules and help you arrange a hearing. This is a simple, inexpensive and highly recommended method of resolving otherwise difficult consumer problems. Contact your local Better Business Bureau to see whether arbitration is available in your area.

American Arbitration Association (AAA)

The American Arbitration Association (AAA) is a nonprofit public service organization dedicated to resolving disputes. It has thirty-three regional offices around the country. For a local address and telephone number, check your telephone directory.

Using the AAA has both advantages and disadvantages. It can handle cases concerning large sums of money without limits. Also, it considers a broad range of problems not handled by the BBB. And, as an independent organization, the AAA may be more flexible in meeting the special needs of your dispute.

The primary disadvantage is the cost—the fees charged by the AAA to arbitrate a case are based on a sliding scale. Cases involving up to $25,000 require a 3 percent administration fee, with a $300 minimum charge. This is paid by the side that initiated the complaint, but apportionment of the costs may be included in the arbitrator's final award. Cases over $25,000, but less than $50,000, require a 2 percent administration fee with a $750 minimum charge. Between $50,000 and $100,000, it's a 1 percent administration fee with a $1,250 minimum charge.

Court-Sponsored Alternative Dispute Resolution (ADR) Programs

Today all courts, especially those with a heavy backlog of cases, promote the use of alternative dispute resolution (ADR) programs. ADR is an umbrella term used to describe a variety of nonadversary, out-of-court techniques for settling disputes. The best-known examples are mediation and arbitration.

If you're lucky, the small claims court in your area sponsors an arbitration or mediation program. Alaska, California, Connecticut, Illinois, Louisiana, Maine, Massachusetts, Michigan, New York, Ohio, Oregon and the District of Columbia each has a small claims court that refers cases to mediation or arbitration (see Appendix VI). Several other states also offer mediation or arbitration programs at higher court levels.

The procedure for getting your case to arbitration varies from state to state. For example, in New York City litigants are asked when they appear in court if they are willing to have an arbitrator hear and decide their case. If they agree, they immediately meet with a volunteer lawyer serving as an arbitrator. In California the arbitration of small claims cases within a given monetary range is voluntary for the person bringing the suit, but if he or she opts for arbitration, it becomes compulsory for the person being sued.

Small claims courts in some areas of Connecticut, New York and Ohio have compulsory arbitration for all disputes within a certain dollar range. In many places, New York City for example, arbitration is faster and simpler than litigating the dispute, but the arbitrator's decision is final: you cannot appeal.

Maine, Massachusetts, the District of Columbia, and some districts in other states offer mediation for small claims (see "Mediation" below). Mediation relies on the two sides involved to reach a mutually agreeable settlement. If mediation results in a written agreement entered into the case file, it is binding and enforceable by a court.

In the District of Columbia small claims are referred directly to mediation through a pilot project called the Multi-Door Dispute Resolution Program that matches people and their problems to the most appropriate dispute resolution mechanism. The program, sponsored by the American Bar Association, is part of a nationwide effort to relieve court congestion by increasing the availability of alternatives. Multi-Door programs have also been established in Boston, Massachusetts, Houston, Texas and Tulsa, Oklahoma.

Mediation

The first mediation programs in the United States were created in the late 1960s and early 1970s. At that time mediation was almost exclusively used at the community level to resolve problems between family members, neighbors and local businesses and their customers. Community-based mediation enjoyed so much success that it caught the attention of courts, legislators and private and governmental agencies, all of which eventually explored the possibility of instituting mediation programs.

Mediation works best among persons who will have an ongoing relationship after the dispute is settled. That's why many small claims disputes are easily mediated. The dry cleaner has a vested interest in keeping customers, neighbors usually must continue to live next to each other and immediate family members, for better or worse, will continue to see each other.

Mediation is voluntary and informal. The parties do not need to submit evidence or bring witnesses. Each side simply tells its version of the story. If they cannot agree on what the main issues or problems are, the mediator meets with each party separately.

Once problems and issues are listed, the mediator uses a variety of communication skills to get the two sides to come to an agreement. The mediator asks questions, discusses areas of compromise, and may even make suggestions; but a good mediator does not impose a decision, as an arbitrator or a judge would. The final decision is made by the parties themselves, not the mediator.

Once agreement is reached, it is put into writing and signed by both sides. Like any contract, the agreement is legally binding and enforceable in court. If you do not like a proposed agreement, you cannot be forced to sign it. If you have questions about the meaning or validity of an agreement, you should ask a legal professional to review it with you *before* you sign it.

Mediation programs are offered at the community level, through some local courts, and by independent private mediators. Court-sponsored mediation was discussed in the previous section. Brief descriptions of community and private mediation follow.

Community-Based Mediation

Dispute resolution centers (also called neighborhood justice centers) were first developed to reduce the burden of courts handling minor civil and criminal disputes. They have done just that and, at the same time, have provided a quick and inexpensive alternative to court. More important, they can often confront and deal with the underlying problem between two parties—not just the official accusation that is the focus of a particular case. Examples of such cases include juvenile vandalism, neighborhood noise disputes and police-community relations.

More than 400 dispute resolution centers currently operate in the United States. There are also many private practitioners who provide services to courts and communities. Each center has its distinct purpose and its own rules of procedure. The major differences among the dispute resolution centers involve: (1) the type of disputes handled; (2) the sponsorship and funding of the project; (3) the method of resolving disputes; and (4) the types of mediators and arbitrators used.

Private Mediation

The growth of private dispute resolution services in recent years can be attributed to the public's dissatisfaction with the expense and delay of traditional litigation.

Private mediation is offered through organizations like EnDispute in Washington, D.C. and Chicago; American Intermediation Services in San Francisco; the Center for Public Resources in New York City; and Dispute Resolution, Inc., in Hartford. Mediation groups like these provide full-time mediators who encourage the other side to participate and also offer extensive follow-up services. Many of these groups mediate disputes involving amounts of money well above small claims court limits.

To learn more about community or private mediation services in your area, you'll need to do some telephoning. Try your city attorney general's office, the small claims court clerk, the mayor's office, local consumer groups or your local bar association. You can also check under "Mediation Services" in the yellow pages or write to the Standing Committee on Dispute Resolution, American Bar Association, 1800 M St. N.W., Washington, DC 20036. The ABA's Standing Committee acts as a clearinghouse of information on alternative dispute resolution and it also publishes a *Dispute Resolution Directory* that describes hundreds of community-based mediation programs.

CHAPTER

3

DO YOU HAVE A CASE?

Of alternative dispute resolution procedures are not available in your area, if they are not applicable to your problem, or if they fail to produce an acceptable settlement, it's time to consider taking your case to small claims court. At this point, you must answer two questions: Is your dispute eligible for small claims court? and Do you have a case?

The first question is relatively easy to answer. Your dispute is eligible if it involves less than the dollar limit set by law for small claims courts in your state and if it does not involve an issue specifically excluded from the court, such as libel or slander. The way to calculate the amount of your claim will be discussed later. For the moment, check Appendix VI of this book to see if there are any obvious reasons why your dispute might be excluded from your state's small claims courts.

The second question—Do you have a case?—is not so easy to answer. You should begin by examining your state's eligibility requirements. Besides restricting the amount of money at issue and the type of cases heard, most states also restrict settlements to cash

389

awards. In other words, whatever loss or damage you have suffered, whatever rights have been violated, you must ask the court for compensation in the form of a specific amount of money. For example, you cannot ask the court to order the defendant to replace your Waterford chandelier with the exact model, but you can ask that you be compensated in cash for the value of the chandelier you lost.

Restricting settlements to cash awards enables judges to process small claims cases more quickly. Faced with hundreds of cases a week, judges naturally seek to reduce problem solving to a simple formula. This formula generally includes four basic questions: *What happened? Who did it? Were they wrong? How much did it cost?*

Remembering this formula will help you determine if your case is the sort that the court, in *any* state, prefers to handle. Cases that involve a landlord who refuses to return a security deposit are easily decided by the formula. The two sides in the dispute are known; the amount in dispute is clear; the landlord will offer reasons for failing to return your money, and, if the judge finds the reasons unacceptable, the amount and form of compensation are obvious: a cash payment of the amount of your deposit.

Dog bites and falls on icy sidewalks also account for many cases on small claims court dockets. However, beyond medical bills and damage to your clothing, it can be difficult to prove that any other damages should be translated into cash. Other elements, such as pain and suffering, inconvenience and annoyance, introduce value judgments that are not welcomed by small claims court clerks and judges. Such factors are included in some cases, however, and will be discussed later. Just remember that small claims judges simply prefer cases that involve specific damages that can be easily documented and resolved by a payment of cash.

The second thing to keep in mind is that, in most states, small claims court is a court of law and not a court of equity. That means a judge cannot give a ruling based solely on what he or she deems is "fair," but must rule based on the law, regardless of how unfair the results may be. In most states that means you can win only if the judge can "apply the law to the facts." For example, if you can provide written evidence that you sold your car "as is," it doesn't matter if it breaks down on the buyer that same week. The judge will have to rule in your favor because you have written proof of a legal and binding contract—whether that seems fair or not.

In small claims courts, the judge will not expect you to know the law. In fact, she or he will probably resent any attempt you make to argue fine points of law. Instead, you will be expected to tell your own story in your own words. When you present your case, deal only with the simple facts about what happened and don't get into probing and legal diagnosis.

If you are aware of the basic questions and issues the judge is trying to resolve, you can and should emphasize the important aspects of your case by bringing appropriate evidence. Knowing the underlying legal structure of your case will help you marshal your factual evidence in a way that will do the most good. For example, if you're a landlord trying to evict a tenant, you should be aware of what the grounds for eviction are—damage to property, disturbing the peace and nonpayment of rent are just a few. Knowing this allows you to come to court prepared with convincing evidence—pictures of or actual damaged property, neighbors who will testify about noise levels or bounced checks that prove rent hasn't been paid in months.

The remainder of this chapter discusses the legal questions you must answer to "prove" your case and the types of verdicts allowed by law. Because small claims court judges have a fair amount of leeway in making decisions, the following discussion cannot be definitive. It can only serve as a guide to help you organize your presentation in court.

Basically you must answer only two questions. The first: Have you suffered a loss that can be documented in court? The second: Is the person you are suing liable (legally responsible) for your loss?

Did You Suffer a Loss?

The emphasis on dollar limits and cash awards points to one of the essential elements you must prove in court: loss of other elements—pain and suffering, for example, can enter a small claims suit only on the coattails of a solid case that documents *monetary* loss.

In six states, judges are not so narrowly restricted. In those states a judge who believes your claim is justified may order a specific act to be performed by the person being sued, if that seems to be the fairest way to resolve the dispute. For example, a judge in one of those six states could order someone to return a one-of-a-kind object if merely paying for it wouldn't be adequate. This will be discussed further, but it's worth noting here that to get into small claims court, *you must assign a dollar value* to your dispute regardless of what outcome you want. As a result, your case will still be limited to the maximum dollar amount the court is allowed to consider.

Is Anyone Liable?

Loss is not the only element you'll have to prove. The other is *liability*—the law's way of establishing blame and determining responsibility. The problem is not as simple as discovering who did or didn't do the act that started the dispute. Rather, you must answer: "Is the defendant liable?" That is, did the person you are suing do something wrong—or fail to do the right thing—and *did that act cause your loss?*

Bear in mind that someone can do something wrong and not directly cause you a loss. For example, your neighbor may have ruined your plans to run errands in the morning because he boxed your car in with his. This doesn't mean you can hold him responsible for a car accident you had while doing your errands in the afternoon. You can't claim that the accident wouldn't have happened if he hadn't boxed you in earlier. Your neighbor's action was not the direct cause of your car accident.

The "wrong" you must demonstrate is what will interest the judge, who will want to answer at least one of these three questions:

- Was the defendant negligent ("wrong" by not acting carefully or responsibly)?

- Did the defendant commit the act intentionally ("wrong" by willfully causing you harm)?

- Did the defendant break a valid contract ("wrong" because of a broken promise)?

If the "wrong" falls into one of these three categories and you can demonstrate that it caused your loss, the defendant is liable and should be required to make restitution. Once the facts are determined, it's as simple as that. But facts can sometimes be difficult to pin down.

Was the Defendant Negligent? Establishing negligence or willful wrongdoing can be more complicated than it might seem. A standard often used is what is called "reasonable care," the degree of precaution that should be expected from anyone under similar circumstances. If you can show that the person you are suing failed to act with reasonable care, in effect you show that that person acted recklessly or negligently and is therefore responsible for the damages the careless action caused.

For example, a driver who is speeding in a residential area and plows into a child's bicycle would undoubtedly be found guilty of "negligent behavior." But negligence may be—and often is—attributed to either or both sides in a small claims suit. Not only defendants, but persons who bring suit have a basic obligation under the law: they must have acted responsibly to reduce the loss.

This means that when you accuse someone else of negligence, the judge may be equally interested in how you behaved. If the person you are suing can prove you also were negligent or failed to act responsibly to reduce your loss, the judge must compare the consequences of your acts and those of your defendant. In the example we've just seen, the driver could claim that his own safety as well as the safety of others was endangered because the bicycle was lying in the middle of the street and he had to hit it to avoid hitting someone or something else.

In the case of Mrs. Jones and Hottin Roofers, Mrs. Jones was responsible for preventing further damage by sealing the roof and mopping up the water as soon as possible. If she let the water stand for days, or suffered further damage when it rained two weeks later, the judge will want to know why she didn't do something to prevent part of the damage.

When both sides are partly responsible, the judge may apply the legal doctrine of comparative negligence or contributory negligence depending what state rules apply. Under "comparative" negligence, the judge assigns each party a percentage of the blame and applies it to the claim. For example, if you sue for $500 and are found responsible for 10 percent of the damage, then the defendant's 90 percent responsibility will entitle you to $450. Most states apply comparative negligence.

"Contributory" negligence is less kind to people who sue: if you are negligent in any way, you cannot recover anything from the party you are suing. In the few states that use contributory negligence, you may be allowed to raise additional defenses to eliminate your own contribution to the damages you suffered. For example, if it can be shown in an auto accident case that even though both parties were at fault, the defendant had the "last clear chance" to prevent the accident from happening, an opportunity the plaintiff didn't have, then the plaintiff's share of negligence could be eliminated.

Say, for example, that Joe Plaintiff drives through an intersection at 8 P.M. without his car's headlights on. Sally Defendant, in a hurry to get home, runs a stop sign and sideswipes the back end of Joe's car as he is making his left turn. Joe will claim that Sally is at fault for running the stop sign. Sally will say she didn't see Joe's car because he didn't have his headlights on and therefore he is partly at fault. Joe could counter with the "last clear chance" doctrine: that he was well into his turn and didn't have time to get out of the way, but that Sally had plenty of time, judging from where she hit his car, to prevent the accident if she had just applied her brakes. In this example, Sally would not succeed in shifting the blame to Joe.

Was the Harm Intentional? Even though your loss is the same through intentional or accidental acts, the amount you can recover will be more if you can prove that the wrong committed against you was intentional. For example, if you can prove that a neighbor drove over your fence and knocked down your tree because he doesn't like the fact that your son is dating his daughter (and not because his steering wheel locked and caused him to swerve into your property) you can ask the judge to award additional "punitive" damages. The total amount you ask for, however, cannot exceed the small claims court dollar limit.

Has a Contract Been Broken? Most small claims cases involve contracts. This might surprise you unless you know that a contract does not have to be written to be binding. You enter into oral contracts all the time (hiring someone to cut your lawn or paint your house, selling personal belongings at a garage sale, renting out your basement as storage space, ordering goods through the mail). For most matters that arise in small claims court, a good working definition of a contract is "any agreement that involves an exchange of promises or a promise exchanged for some act or compensation."

When a contract is in dispute, even if it was never written down, the judge's task is fairly simple. Evidence will be asked about the terms of the contract, how it was created and whether it was actually agreed to and is binding on both sides. If the person you are suing failed to keep a promise and loss or damage resulted, the judge will order that person to compensate you. Say, for example, you offer to sell your stereo to a friend for $800. She accepts by paying $400 now and promising to pay $400 by the end of the month. The end of the month comes and goes without any payment. When you call to ask for the balance she comments that $400 was more than enough for your stereo and slams down the phone. You sue her for breach-of-contract even though you never asked her to sign anything.

Most contract disputes in small claims courts involve breach-of-contract or fraud. In breach-of-contract cases, the person who sues claims that the contract is valid and should be enforced. In fraud cases, the person who sues claims that the contract is *not* valid and should *not* be enforced.

In breach-of-contract cases, you are saying that the person you are suing has failed to fulfill the obligations as agreed to in the contract.

This requires you to prove three things: a valid contract existed, that it was broken and that as a result, you suffered a loss. Proving this follows a fairly straightforward path. The technique for preparing and presenting a convincing case will be discussed in Chapters 8 and 9.

A judge also has the power to rule that a technically legal contract is nevertheless invalid because it is grossly unfair or fraudulent. An example of a legal but unfair contract would be a landlord's rental agreement that charges twice the going rate for rent to a non-English speaking immigrant. Fraud is the misrepresenting or concealing of facts with the intent to deceive and thereby gain advantage over another person. In a suit based on fraud, you will have to prove that an important fact was knowingly concealed or lied about (for example, that the odometer had been rolled back on a car advertised as having "low mileage" or that the papers on a prize-winning Doberman are false). Proving fraud can be difficult, given the limits on time and evidence in small claims court. Because most fraud cases are also subject to criminal prosecution, if you think you have a case that involves a fraudulent contract, check with your city or county district attorney's office before filing suit in small claims court. If the district attorney's staff decides to prosecute, it will collect evidence, and perhaps win a conviction, that will make it easier for you to collect your small claim.

"Fairness" is a less common reason for overturning contracts. In such cases, a judge decides that the circumstances, experience, knowledge and sophistication of the people who entered into the contract were so unequal that the contract, though technically complete, should be canceled. Judges are reluctant to do this, however, both in deference to the legal principle of *caveat emptor* (Latin for "let the buyer beware") and because defendants usually appeal when judges rule that their contract was "unfair."

What Will You "Win"?

What all small claims courts have in common is their ability to settle disputes by ordering payment for proven losses or damages. What varies from state to state is the maximum amount of money the injured person is allowed to claim (see Appendix VI).

As we've seen, however, six states also allow small claims judges to order the defendant to do something other than simply pay you money. These states are said to allow "equitable relief." Their small claims judges are said to have "equity powers." In plain language, "equity" means "fairness." If fairness demands that the only way to compensate you is to require that a specific act be performed for you, the judge with equity powers may so order. For example, you may have sold an antique that you would like to have returned because the other side refuses to pay. In six states, small claims judges have the authority to order the return of your antique.

In another nine states, small claims courts have *limited* equity powers. Judges in these courts are limited in what they can order either side to do. In North Carolina, for example, the judge has no equity powers except to order enforcement of a lien. In Tennessee the judge's power is limited to issuing restraining orders.

In those states whose small claims courts have no equity powers, the judge can only order that you receive the payment you agreed to.

Remember that even where it's allowed, it is the judge's option, not yours, to offer equitable relief. If the judge feels that a cash award is the best way to settle your case, you will have to accept the money. Check Appendix VI to see if your state's small claims courts allow equitable relief.

Judges in states that do not officially offer equitable relief may encourage remedies that look very much like it. If a cash settlement appears to be a poor way to solve your problem, the judge may be willing to suggest solutions "off the record," before deciding on a verdict. He or she may suggest that you and the person you are suing step into the hall to "work things out." If you can't, the judge will have to award a money damage. If you can, you might get money and a promise that the problem won't happen again—for example, reimbursement for geraniums that were destroyed by the neighbor's dog and a promise that the dog will be kept on a leash or behind a fence.

The chances of getting something other than a cash award in small claims court depend partly on your state's laws and partly on the whim of the judge. You shouldn't count on getting noncash relief any more than you should count on getting the full amount of money you're asking for. This is why, if money clearly won't solve your problem, you should seek arbitration or mediation rather than going to small claims court.

To learn if the judge in your local small claims court allows or encourages anything other than cash awards, check with the courthouse clerk. Explain the sort of resolution you'd like to see, and ask if it is possible. Then ask if it's likely. The second question really concerns the judge's preferences in verdicts, and only a clerk—or your own observations in the courtroom—can provide an answer.

CHAPTER

4

FILING SUIT

You now have an idea of what a qualified small claims dispute might be: you have suffered a loss, someone else is liable, and you think you can prove it. The next step is to make sure you file your complaint properly. Since each small claims court has its own administrative process, established through local rules, it's a good idea to ask the court clerk if a brochure is available that describes how the process in your area works. Though the brochure won't be thorough, it will tell you what the local procedure is for filing a suit and may also tell you whether the rules of the court have been revised recently. (For example, the dollar limit may have been raised.)

You can probably get a copy of the brochure by calling the clerk's office and asking that one be mailed to you. The name of the small claims court in your state is listed in Appendix VI of this book, and the telephone number of the nearest courthouse will be in your local telephone directory. If you have to pick up the brochure at the courthouse, bring your documents with you and plan to file your suit while you're there and save yourself a trip.

When you file suit, you will have to pay a filing fee, usually $5 to $10 but sometimes as high as $35. You will also have to fill out a form called the "Plaintiff's Statement" or "Statement of Claim" or some variation of these. The name varies from state to state. Some states also require a second statement, called a "Declaration under Penalty of Perjury," in which you swear that everything you've stated is true. Others simply have you sign the Plaintiff's Statement. Either way, you are responsible for the truth of any statement you make. The forms for Plaintiff's Statements vary among states, but they seek the same basic information: your name, whom you are suing and the amount you are seeking.

Answering these questions properly can be more difficult than it appears. This chapter will help you avoid making technical errors, but if you have any questions that are not answered here or in the court's brochure, ask the court clerk.

Small claims court clerks are generally helpful and will try to answer most questions if they think you've made a serious effort to prepare in advance. In some large metropolitan areas (such as New York City, Chicago and Los Angeles) trained paralegals or legal assistants may be available to help you. If your case is unusual or complicated or involves a large sum of money, you may also want to seek legal help (see Chapter 7).

Before you can complete the Plaintiff's Statement, you'll need enough information to answer the questions that follow. Try to get these answers by telephone or a trip to the library before you spend an afternoon running back and forth to the clerk's office.

Where Should You Sue?

The court's legal term for where you should sue is "venue," the locality in which a case may be tried. This is established mostly for the convenience of the two sides in the dispute and is left to the discretion of the judge.

To decide where to sue, you first need to know how the small claims court system in your state is subdivided. You may be allowed to file suit in more than one small claims district. If so, you'll need to decide which you prefer.

Each small claims court has its own district, with specific geographic boundaries. New York City has several districts, but most small claims districts encompass an entire city, several cities or even an entire county. Only occasionally—as in Louisiana, Montana, Oregon and Pennsylvania—do the rules and dollar limits vary among the districts within a state. If you live in such a state, examine your case and the resolution you're seeking. You may be able to choose a district where one or more of the variations works to your advantage. For example, if your case involves a relatively large amount of money, you may want to sue in the district with the highest possible dollar limit. If your state has no variations, or if they don't matter, choose a district with the proper venue that is most convenient to you.

The questions of choice arises because state requirements usually indicate where you *can* sue rather than where you *must*. Courts often have the power (jurisdiction) to take a case within a wide geographic area. Start by checking Appendix VI of this book to see what your options are. Regardless of which state you live in, you can always sue in the judicial district where the defendant lives or does business at the time you file suit. This rule anticipates the defendant's objection that it is too inconvenient to appear.

The defendant's proper address shouldn't be too difficult to find. Look first in the telephone book, then in city registers or directories, police files and tax records. These records are usually kept in or near the courthouse where you file your Plaintiff's Statement. If you're naming a business in your suit, some states specify that you must give the address of the business headquarters rather than simply the "place of business." If you're suing a large national company that has many offices, you may be forced to file suit somewhere other than where you did business.

The odds are that you won't have to go to great lengths to track down your defendant. In more than thirty states, you can sue where the injury or damage occurred. With a contract dispute, it's where the contract was signed or, in some states, where the act specified by the contract was to be performed. Thus, most retail or service companies—even if they are a franchise operation of a national corporation—will have to face you in a local small claims court. Another option, available in only a few states, is suing in the district where the defendant was living or doing business *when the contract was created.*

Problems you might encounter in trying to serve your defendant with the Plaintiff's Statement may also influence your choice of where to sue. Some states require that the defendant be served in the small claims district in which the suit is filed, so be sure you read Chapter 5 before making a final decision on where to sue.

Whom Should You Sue?

Always sue the person, persons or business that harmed you. If the offenders are married, you must sue both. Whenever you sue more than one person, be sure to name them individually. The Plaintiff's Statement will have space for you to name more than one person. List each name and address separately.

Cars and Motorists You should always check to see if the driver of an auto is its legal owner. If the driver of a vehicle is not its registered owner, in most states you must sue both. The owner's and driver's names should be available from the accident report if one was filed with the police. If not, give the state department of motor vehicles the license number, explain why you need the information and ask for the registered owner's name. If a business owned the vehicle, sue the driver *and* the owner(s) of the business.

Minors If the offender is a minor, you must name a parent or legal guardian as well. In such cases, liability varies from state to state, but often a child's actions must be shown to be "willful misconduct" before a parent will be judged automatically liable. Laws may also limit the damages that can be recovered from minors. For example, in most states minors cannot be held to contracts they have signed. For other matters, the parents probably are liable and you should name them.

Businesses If you're suing a business, you need to determine whether it is owned by an individual, a partnership or a corporation. If the business is not incorporated, find out who owns it and sue "[owner], d.b.a. (doing business as) [name of business]"—for example, John Smith, d.b.a. Smith Roofers. To find the owner's name, check the premises for a business license or try the records at the city or county tax offices. Finding the owner's name is crucial because unincorporated businesses *cannot* be required to pay a judgment. Your state's court rules will specify how complete a name you must use (for example, whether the first and/or second initials are acceptable). The clerk should be able to answer your questions, but if you're having trouble finding the owner's full name, the name he or she generally uses is usually enough, unless it's a nickname.

Partnerships All partners in a business are individually liable for the acts of that business, so you should find and name each partner separately, besides naming the business itself. Failing to name all partners (for example, if some of them live out of state) will not disqualify you, but it will result in fewer people from whom to collect should you win a judgment.

Corporations Corporations are "persons" for the purposes of legal action. Individual officers are usually not liable for the debts of the corporation, so you must concentrate on finding the exact legal name of the corporation. Don't assume that the name on the door of a company is the corporate name. For all you know, "Jake's Cleaners" may be legally incorporated as "International Cleanomatic Corporation, Inc." To determine the right name, try checking the business license office, tax records or the local or state office that supervises corporations, usually the secretary of state.

Every state except California requires you to sue a corporation under its corporate legal name. As a practical matter, however, you shouldn't worry too much about this because you will usually be permitted to amend pleadings (your Plaintiff's Statement) if you get the name wrong.

Public Officials If the offense was committed by a public servant acting in an official capacity, that person is probably shielded by the regulations of the city, county or state agency. If this is the case, you must sue the public body—and deal with entirely different problems. Some states prohibit all small claims suits against government agencies or their employees. If you are allowed to sue, you probably won't be able to get the officials to court until you've filed a claim with the agency and followed all agency procedures established for such disputes. The agency may take what seems to be forever to review your claim, but you must wait until the process is completed before you will be allowed to bring suit in small claims court. And if you finally get to court, don't be too optimistic about your chances of winning. Your opponent will, where it's allowed, probably be represented by an attorney from the government agency, and the judge will be inclined to protect the interests of local or state government.

Who Is Suing?

Many of the same rules about properly identifying defendants also apply to you as the plaintiff. If you are not the only one suing, all plaintiffs' names and addresses must be included on the Plaintiff's Statement. Only one of you needs to sign the statement and Declaration under Penalty of Perjury, if that is required. Owners of businesses must bring suit for themselves and personally sign the declaration. Partnerships generally must sue under their business name, and any of the partners can sign the statement and the declaration. Some states allow unincorporated businesses to send an employee to represent the business in both filing the papers and appearing in court.

Corporations should sue under their own names, with a corporate officer or someone appointed by the officers signing the statement and declaration on the corporation's behalf. Any appointed representative of a corporation should carry a signed statement of authorization. In Illinois, Minnesota, New Mexico and the District of Columbia the corporation's representative must also be an attorney. New York, Pennsylvania and Rhode Island also require corporate representatives to be lawyers unless the corporation is a small business with limited assets. Ohio corporations need to be represented by attorneys unless they do not plan to argue the case or cross-examine witnesses.

Giving small-business owners a forum in which to settle minor disputes was one of the original goals of the small claims court system. Critics now contend that the courts are becoming glorified collection agencies in states where businesses are not barred from suing, or where no limit is placed on how often they may bring suit. Court policies vary regarding business plaintiffs, usually reflecting the court's own philosophy about how it should be used. For example, many states specifically prohibit "assignees" (third parties, usually collection agencies) from bringing suit to collect a bill on behalf of someone else. Also, many states limit the number of times anyone can bring suit within a given year—a further check on the use of the court for frequent debt collections. Check Appendix VI and ask the court clerk about any limitations on business plaintiffs.

In general, the person or business that has had a loss must bring suit. If, for example, the small claims suit is for damages to a car involved in a collision, the registered owner or owners of the car must file the suit. The driver, however, will probably be needed to testify in court.

In some restricted circumstances, rules expressly authorize third parties to bring suit on behalf of those injured. For example, minors are not allowed to sue but may get their claim into court by having a parent or legal guardian appointed as *guardian ad litem* to file suit on their behalf. Further, if a plaintiff is bedridden or severely disabled, judges in most states can appoint a friend or relative of the plaintiff as legal representative to file the small claims suit.

When Should You Sue?

For every type of small claims dispute (personal injury, property damage, contracts, and so on) your state's law specifies a time limit within which you must file suit. These limits (known as "statutes of limitations") are rarely less than one year and usually from one to five years.

If the original incident in your dispute occurred well over a year ago, you should check the statute of limitations in your state. The court clerk might know if your case has passed the deadline. If he or she does not, try a local law library. Your state's laws will be collected in a book called *Annotated Codes, Compiled Statutes* or something similar (the title is included at the head of each state's listing in Appendix VI) and the information you need will probably be indexed under "Limitations of Actions." If you need help, ask the librarian.

If you are nearing the end of the statute of limitations, you may have another problem. The judge will want to know why you waited so long to file your suit. Your best answer is to show that you've been pursuing the complaint all along, reasonably and responsibly, and you were forced to turn to the court only because the statute of limitations was running out.

Remember that if the person you're suing was acting as an employee of a governmental agency, you must file and pursue a claim with that agency before you can file suit in court. Also, the time limit for filing a claim with the agency's grievance system may be very severe—often as short as thirty days—and if you miss that deadline, you may be precluded from suing in court at all. Check with the agency immediately after any incident to learn if you are facing a deadline.

What Should You Claim?

Claim as much as you can justify, but never more than the upper dollar limit allowed by the court. Remember, the judge has the power to award you less than you request but cannot give you more than the court's dollar limit allows. Because judges are allowed to award a percentage of your claim, it usually pays to estimate your damages on the high side when the real value of an item is uncertain. Costs involved in bringing your case to court are a separate matter, and will be discussed later.

The dollar limit in each state is occasionally raised so inflation won't rule out the types of disputes the court was intended to handle. Always check with the clerk about the current dollar limit. If your claim is larger than the current limit and you still want to use the small claims court, you are permitted to reduce your claim to fit within its limit. But if you do so, you are taking an irreversible legal step. Once you file a complaint on a particular matter for a stated sum, you automatically "waive the difference" and cannot claim more later. (See Appendix VI for the limit in your area.)

In many cases, that makes sense because the cost of hiring a lawyer to represent you in formal court would be more than you would win. Say you have a $2,000 claim in a district that allows small claims cases up to only $1,500. Talk to local attorneys about their fees. If you can't find a lawyer who will take your case for $200 or less (including all legal fees and miscellaneous costs) and you believe you could represent yourself successfully in small claims court, you'll probably be better off there. But remember: you should feel confident that you can handle the case yourself and can convince the judge to award you most or all of the $1,500 limit allowed. To decide whether to go into small claims court on your own or into formal court with a lawyer, weigh carefully the strengths of your case and the costs involved. Then consider how you feel about the lawyers you interviewed, the amount they charge and whether you yourself have the time to prepare carefully for small claims court. [1]

There is another way to alter your claim to fit within your state's dollar limits: split it into two or more separate actions. In the case of Mrs. Jones and the roofers in Chapter 1, she could try splitting her $2,000 claim into a $1,500 claim seeking a return of the money paid for the "repairs," and a $500 claim for the water damage to her home.

If you plan to take this route, be sure your claim can be split into logically distinct parts. Issues that might appear separable to you may not be so in the eyes of the law. The small claims clerk may be willing to give you an opinion, but only the judge can decide whether you truly have two distinct claims. If you can build a defensible case for each, the judge will allow them and rule on each claim separately. If not, the judge will reject them and ask you to reduce the total amount to the court's limit, thereby waiving the difference, or take your case to a higher court. Be prepared to make this decision and to accept whatever the judge decides.

Once you're clear about the upper dollar limit, you must still compute your claim according to two primary rules: you are entitled only to damages that you've actually suffered; and you must be able to prove them.

---

[1]Before interviewing or hiring a lawyer, consult *Using a Lawyer*, by Kay Ostberg in association with HALT, Random House, 1990.

Property Damage When you sue for something that has been destroyed, you cannot recover what it cost, only what it was worth. For example, automobiles are valued by looking up advertisements for comparable models, and using the estimates in the "blue book" *(National Auto Dealers' Association Official Used Car Guide)*. If the car is only damaged and you produce repair estimates for less than the official value of the car, you can recover what it will cost to fix it.

However, beware: your car's total worth may be less than it would cost to fix it. In that case, whether or not it looks it to you, your car is a "total loss." You will be able to claim only the car's book value, minus what the car is worth as junk—"salvage value." Unless you can produce repair receipts to show that recent improvements make your car worth more than the standard book value, you'll probably be limited by this general formula.

Proving the value of other property is less formal and sometimes more difficult. Generally, you will have to prove what the item cost originally and to estimate how much of its useful life had been used when the damage occurred. With appliances and nonpersonal items, the court may resort to standard tables of depreciation, but when your wardrobe is marred, ruined or lost, judges are usually more willing to listen to claims about its personal value. Judges realize that damaged clothing must usually be replaced rather than repaired. If the clothing was relatively new, try to claim its original cost. If it was older, you can ask for slightly less than the original price, but expect the judge to reduce it somewhat.

Personal Injury Personal injury cases that involve medical bills generally exceed small claims court limits. Minor injuries, however, are often part of small claims suits. When you calculate injury claims, remember that judges do not like to duplicate insurance benefits. You will be expected to prove all the expense you claim and to verify that none of them were covered by insurance or other benefits programs. These expenses may include transportation to the doctor's office and loss of wages, but you'll have to show that any wage loss caused by your injury wasn't compensated for as sick leave.

You can also claim compensation for the "pain and suffering" caused by your injury. Judges generally will accept this sort of claim only if it is accompanied by medical evidence of injury (such as medical bills or a statement from your doctor), plus a sincere account from you of the discomfort caused. It's always difficult to place a dollar value on misery. The easiest way is to subtract the total expenses you are claiming from the dollar limit allowed in court, then claim the difference for your pain and suffering. For example, in a personal injury case where you claim $2,000 in medical bills not covered by your insurance company and the court's dollar limit is $2,500, you could claim the remaining $500 for pain and suffering.

Contracts Contract cases tend to be easier to determine because the amount in question is usually specified in the contract. If interest payments were mentioned in the contract, you'll have to compute the total interest due and specifically request it in the Plaintiff's Statement as part of your claim. If interest wasn't mentioned, you may want to try to claim it anyway.

Landlord-Tenant Some states have created special penalties for landlords who unjustly fail to return cleaning or security deposits. In California, it is $200 plus the deposit. In Illinois, Michigan, New Jersey, Pennsylvania and several other states, it is double the deposit plus, sometimes, attorneys' fees. In Colorado, Georgia, Hawaii, Maryland, North Dakota, Texas and the District of Columbia it is triple the deposit. Texas is the toughest: it allows a claim of $100 plus three times the deposit, plus attorneys' fees. Since the judge may reduce your claim in court, you should always claim the maximum allowed. If you're a tenant planning to sue a landlord, you should ask the court what, if any, penalties are allowed in your state.

Some states that allow only cash awards also allow judges to issue eviction notices. Others have a separate landlord-tenant court. Still others will consider eviction only when the amount of rent due is less than the court's dollar limit. If your state allows eviction, a landlord may ask for it rather than a cash judgment.

Equitable Relief If you live in a state that allows noncash relief, you must place a dollar value on the cause of the dispute, then request a specific remedy. For example: "The market value of the vase was $500, but since it is irreplaceable I would like to request that it be ordered returned to me." Remember, it is entirely up to the judge to decide whether you receive the money or your specific request.

Other Costs You can collect any costs you had to pay to bring the case to trial, such as filing fees and the costs of legal services. Because you won't know the total amount of "costs" at such an early stage, you can in your original claim state that you are claiming "$———— plus costs." Later, in the courtroom, you can request the actual amount you have spent.

Why Are You Suing?

You will notice that the space in the Plaintiff's Statement where you must state your complaint is minimal—usually no more than two or three lines. You are not pleading your case here, nor should you try to anticipate your opponent's objections. State the central facts only: indicate the type of dispute and perhaps the basic reason the defendant is to blame. For example: "Hottin Roofers failed to adequately repair the roof of my house and, as a result, substantial water damage occurred."

When Is the Hearing?

When you've completed the Plaintiff's Statement, set a date for the court hearing. In some states it is required that the hearing be held within a certain number of days from the date of filing. Others are less specific, but you can usually count on getting a hearing within four weeks.

The clerk will suggest a court date. You should accept it only if it seems convenient and gives you enough time to serve the defendant properly (see page 413). Give yourself at least a couple of weeks to make sure that the defendant is properly served with notice of your suit. If your case depends on the word of a witness, be sure to pick a day when you know your witness can appear. If it suits you better, ask the clerk if evening or Saturday sessions are available.

Recognize, too, that a court hearing set for 9 A.M. may not reach the judge until 3 P.M. Always get a good idea of how long the hearing *could* take before committing yourself to a particular day. It is an unfortunate fact that most small claims courts don't set an order for hearing cases until the morning of the appointed day.

You must be there for the roll call, even if it means waiting several hours to appear before a judge. Ask the clerk what hours the court is in session. If it's 9:00 to 5:00, plan to be there all day. If it's 9:00 to 12:00, you should be free by lunchtime.

If you have trouble serving notice on your opponent, you can call the clerk and ask that the hearing date be postponed. If you've served your opponent and then either side cannot make the hearing because of a scheduling conflict, you can have the date changed either with a letter to the clerk signed by both sides asking for a new date, or with a formal letter to the judge from either side explaining why a later date is necessary. In either letter, be sure to indicate clearly your case number (which will have been stamped on the Plaintiff's Statement by the clerk). Always send a copy of your letter to the judge and to your opponent.

What Else Is Needed?

If you have specific questions about filing your claim, don't hesitate to ask the clerk. One of the clerk's primary duties is to make sure all filings are technically complete. Determine what your state requires and ask the clerk to look over your Plaintiff's Statement to see that it is correct. Some courts require certain documents as evidence (copies of contracts, bills, receipts, and so on), that must be submitted with the filing. The clerk will tell you what you need. Just be sure to bring *copies* of all relevant documents. Always keep the originals in your file.

The clerk will also ask you how you intend to serve the papers that notify the defendant you are suing. The various methods of "serving papers" are discussed in the following chapters.

CHAPTER

5

SERVING NOTICE

Once you've completed the Plaintiff's Statement and paid the filing fee, you must see that copies of the statement and other documents are properly delivered to the person you're suing. That person has a right to be informed fully of the claims, and to be given enough time to prepare a defense. The process of delivering the Plaintiff's Statement and other materials is called "serving the papers."

Each state has a specific sequence of procedures you must follow to serve your papers properly. The burden is on you to follow your state's rules exactly. If you do this, the court accepts that the other side has been notified and summoned to appear in defense. If the defendant then fails to appear in court in spite of the notice, you automatically win your case.

This victory is called a *default judgment*. The judge may ask you to state your case briefly to make sure the defendant was liable and that you haven't claimed too much, but you can be reasonably sure of being awarded most of your claim by default. In 1978 researchers John C. Ruhnka and Steven Weller published a valuable and unique two-year study that examined 7,218 cases from 15 small claims courts across the U.S.[1]

Ruhnka and Weller found that 44 percent of the cases ended in default. Because you stand a chance of winning your case by default, it's imperative that you do not ruin it because of improper service.

Some general rules about serving papers apply almost everywhere:

- You must serve the defendant a specified number of days before the trial, not counting the day of service or the day of trial.

- All defendants must be served individually, *even if they are married to each other.*

- You can serve someone who is in active military service, but no default judgment will be entered if that person fails to appear.

- In most states, although you can name a corporation as a defendant, you are required to serve one of its officers; some states, however, do allow you to serve an employee at the place of business.

- Out-of-state corporations may be required to have an in-state "registered agent" whom you can serve. If so, the office of the secretary of state in your state keeps these names and addresses on file. A registered agent is a person authorized to act on the company's behalf.

Methods of Service

You can serve your papers in several different ways: by mail, in person and by "substituted service." States' rules vary about which method is preferred. Ask the court clerk about the preferred order of service in your jurisdiction.

It is almost always acceptable to have a law officer serve your papers, although they are permitted to do so only within their jurisdiction and generally charge a fee. The charge for service by a sheriff or marshal ranges from $2 to $15. A professional process

[1] *Small Claims Courts: A National Examination,* published by the National Center for State Courts, 1978.

server can also be hired for about $20. Some states even permit service by a court-approved "disinterested adult"—anyone of legal age who is not a party to the suit.

In most states, mailing the papers by registered or certified mail and getting a return receipt signed by the person you're suing will prove you served the papers and when. Some states require that this method be tried first. Generally, the clerk does the mailing and you pay postage and handling costs when you file your suit. Some states require that the papers be served within the small claims district where you file your suit. This can cause you a problem if you and the defendant live and work in different districts. In this situation, you are virtually forced to file suit in the defendant's small claims district, not yours—the one instance in which you might be forced to file suit where it is inconvenient for you.

What Can Go Wrong?

States that allow or require certified or registered mail will want a signed receipt by the defendant as proof of service. Because the court clerk handles this in most states, you'll have to call the clerk's office to find out if the signed receipt has arrived. The problem with service by mail is that some mail carriers will let anyone at the correct address sign for the letter. It is *not* a valid service if the defendant does not sign or, in some states, if he or she personally refuses to accept the letter. When you call the clerk to ask if the delivery has been recorded, always ask if the defendant's name is the one signed on the receipt.

If service by registered or certified mail fails, you must go on to the next step, probably in-person service. This means the Plaintiff's Statement and other documents must be handed personally to the defendant, but not by you. You can't personally serve the defendant, but if your state permits personal service by a disinterested adult, you can save the process server's fee by asking a friend or relative to do it for you. Usually, the server need only be an adult resident of the state. You can hire a law officer or professional process server, of course, but this will increase the cost of bringing your case to trial, an expense that might not be reimbursed if you lose the case, if the judge decides against awarding costs or if you have a problem with collecting your award.

For personal service, you'll need a packet of forms from the court known as a "Declaration and Order." The server signs part of this (the "Proof of Service" form) and returns it to the court. This verifies that service was accomplished. If the defendant later claims that the papers were never served, the court will ask the server who signed the form to testify whether the service was performed or not.

If you are concerned about an evasive or abusive defendant or dangerous neighborhoods, law officers or professional servers should be used. Law officers' fees usually are less expensive and most people are intimidated enough by the authority of a sheriff or marshal to accept the papers. If the person you're suing refuses to accept the forms, the server, whether a law officer or disinterested adult, should simply state what the papers are—a notice of a lawsuit in small claims court—and leave them there. For most courts, testimony from the server that papers were delivered is enough.

Beyond these general rules, each state's requirements for proper service are different. Some of these procedures are relaxed or otherwise changed, when you are suing a business. You can get a basic idea of what your state requires by checking Appendix VI, but the final word must come from the clerk of the court in which you file suit. Don't hesitate to ask for advice about the preferred or required methods of service.

CHAPTER
6

IF YOU'RE SUED

If you are being sued (the defendant), you will prepare for trial in almost the same way as the person suing you. The only significant difference is that you will not have to file a Plaintiff's Statement. To seek alternative resolution procedures, to collect evidence, to prepare for trial and so on, simply use this book as a plaintiff would.

If you know how a plaintiff goes about proving loss and liability, it will not be too difficult to make basic decisions about your defense. Essentially, you must weigh the merits of the case against you and decide between defending yourself and paying the claim.

Filing an Answer

In some states, if you intend to defend yourself, you must file a "responsive pleading" (generally called an "Answer") to the Plaintiff's Statement *before* the trial. This simple form requires you to state whether you intend to contest the claim and if so, to state the basis of your objection to it. You may deny liability completely or merely object to the size of the plaintiff's claim. The majority of states do not require you to file anything—all you need to do is show up on the day of your trial.

While one state, South Carolina, allows an oral response, it encourages defendants to submit written responses. If you insist on giving an oral one, it must be given directly to the judge. The important thing is to give your Answer, whether oral or written, to the appropriate person (clerk or judge) within the required number of days before trial. (Be sure to ask if weekends or holidays are counted.) If you fail to meet this deadline, you may be subject to an automatic default.

If you must answer in writing, always call the clerk to make sure your Answer was received on time. Be sure to ask if evidence supporting your defense, such as bills and receipts, must also be filed before the hearing. If you've missed the deadline for filing an Answer because of late or improper service, or because of extenuating circumstances, ask the clerk about filing a "Motion to Vacate Judgment" (see Chapter 9).

Defending Yourself

You can construct a solid defense for yourself in one of three ways: by arguing that the amount of money being claimed is greatly exaggerated; by denying you're the one to blame for the loss; or by denying you're to blame and filing a counterclaim against the person suing you.

Challenging the Amount When you contest only the size of the plaintiff's claim, you will be admitting at least partial responsibility. You will argue either that you are not entirely responsible for the total damage, or that the damage was not as great as the plaintiff claims. You may try to argue both points.

Denying full responsibility means you'll have to prove the plaintiff was partly responsible for the damage. In the example of Mrs. Jones and the roofers, this might mean proving that she allowed the water to sit for days, compounding the damage. Denying an inflated dollar claim, on the other hand, means proving that the plaintiff's evidence of loss is either insufficient or incorrect. In either case, collect and present your counterevidence exactly as you would if you were the one suing.

Denying Liability You may be able to deny all liability. If you are in no way responsible for any loss suffered by the plaintiff, collect the evidence required to prove it. (The way both plaintiffs and defendants collect and present evidence is discussed in Chapter 8.)

"Technical" defenses can also be used against liability. For example, the statute of limitations may have expired. If the case involves the sale of a product or service, state or federal consumer protection statutes might protect you completely. You may, however, need legal advice to unearth such defense strategies (see Chapter 7).

If you were not served notice of the suit in the required way, as described in Chapter 3, that fact alone is not a valid defense. At best, it is a good reason to ask for a continuance or Motion to Vacate Judgment (see Chapter 9). Even if you know that the service of the Plaintiff's Statement was technically invalid, do not fail to show up at the trial. If you are not there, you will probably lose by default.

Counterclaims You may want both to deny you're at fault and to file a counterclaim for damages you suffered because of the original incident. If, for example, you are being sued because you failed to pay for the rental of an automobile tow bar, you may want to countersue, claiming that the bar was so poorly made it damaged the car you towed with it. This is one of those cases in which the other side beat you to court even though you had better grounds to sue. Many unscrupulous people believe that the best defense is a good offense. Don't be taken in: you have the right to sue even while you are being sued.

Remember that filing a counterclaim is just like filing an independent suit: you must establish loss and liability. In the tow bar example, proving that the equipment rented was worthless exempts you only from fulfilling the rental contract: you won't have to pay the rental fee. To have a valid counterclaim, you must also prove you suffered a further loss—the damage to your car—because of the defective equipment.

To file a counterclaim, prepare a "Claim of Defendant." In some states you must do this before the trial on the original suit. Completing this form is exactly like filing a Plaintiff's Statement, and, like the plaintiff, you must pay a fee. In a few states you may wait and counterclaim at the trial, but this has little "surprise" value because the person suing you will probably request and be given a continuance to collect further evidence.

Be careful about counterclaiming in excess of the small claims court's dollar limits. If you do so, in most states it will automatically transfer your case to a higher court. The amount of money involved may be enough that you want to go to formal court and accept the higher costs involved, but this should be avoided if possible. New York, North Carolina, Vermont and Washington do not even allow counterclaims that exceed the court's dollar limits. In other words, in those states, your case will not automatically be transferred; you'll have to file a separate lawsuit in the higher court. For more information on counterclaims, see Appendix VI.

You might also consider a cross-claim. This is a suit brought by you as one defendant against a *codefendant,* asking for full or partial relief if that person was responsible for the damage that led to the suit against you. For example, if your landlord sues you and your roommate for nonpayment of rent, you could file a cross-claim against your roommate to recover money you already paid her to help meet the rent payments.

Other Options

Jury Trials Small claims are almost never decided by a jury, though in a few states the defendant can ask for a jury trial. Usually this means your case is transferred to a higher court, but a few states do offer small claims jury trials. These trials take longer to schedule, and you may have to post a bond or pay a fee to cover the added cost. This almost always makes requesting a small claims jury trial a waste of time and money.

Transfers Some states allow a defendant to ask for a transfer to a higher court without either counterclaiming or requesting a jury. Because a defendant who loses may be forced to pay the plaintiff's court costs, this is an extremely unwise maneuver, especially as court costs are much higher in upper civil courts than in small claims court. For more information on jury trials and transfers, see Appendix VI.

Settling out of Court

If you know you're liable for the loss and the dollar claim is reasonably accurate, the best defense is to cut your losses: offer to settle out of court for an amount less than what the plaintiff is asking.

Plaintiffs usually overestimate their losses because they expect the judge to reduce their claim. If that's the case, try urging the person suing you to settle for less and to save the irritation and time that could be spent collecting evidence and sitting in court.

As discussed in Chapter 9, most plaintiffs settle for about 75 percent of their original claim. Knowing this, defendants usually offer about 50 percent and then negotiate upward to a mutually acceptable figure.

If you and the person suing you can agree on a settlement figure, you may also be able to work out a plan of installment payments. This will reduce your immediate financial burden and help assure the plaintiff of eventually receiving payment. If you can't agree on an amount or a payment schedule before trial, you'll have to decide between arbitration and a court hearing. Chapters 2 and 9 discuss these options.

After the Judgment

If you are sued in small claims court and lose, you have an option not available in other courts: you can ask the judge to order installment payments, allowing you to distribute your payments over a long period of time. This method prevents the person who sued you from garnishing your wages. It also means your personal property won't be seized as long as you meet the payment schedule.

Such installment payments are an alternative in almost every small claims district, but not all judges will order them. Ask the court clerk if your judge allows installment payments. If he or she does not, ask for a continuance or postponement and hope for a more enlightened judge. For more information on installment payments, see Chapter 10.

CHAPTER

7

LEGAL HELP

You must decide if you want to be represented in court by a lawyer. If you did not have trouble completing the Plaintiff's Statement or the Answer, it's highly unlikely you will need a lawyer's services. Private lawyers are not, of course, the only source of legal help, and we will discuss less expensive alternatives.

Before making a decision about using a lawyer, check your state's small claims rules. Some states prohibit the use of lawyers in small claims courts; a few require corporations to be represented by a lawyer; others permit both the plaintiff and the defendant to bring a lawyer to court. The use of a lawyer by both sides in a few of these states will, however, mean that the case is transferred to regular civil court. For your state's rules, see Appendix VI.

Do You Need a Lawyer?

Ruhnka and Weller, whom we discussed earlier, discovered in their 1978 survey that plaintiffs who used lawyers won just as often as those who did not—when going up against defendants without a lawyer. The researchers also found that when plaintiffs hired or consulted a lawyer, judges awarded them less of what they had sued for than they awarded plaintiffs who did not use a lawyer.

It is especially interesting to note that plaintiffs in the lowest educational and income groups received considerably higher awards when they were *not* represented by a lawyer. Ruhnka and Weller suggest that better-educated plaintiffs were able to select better lawyers, but a more likely explanation is that judges, who are normally predisposed to protect plaintiffs, are even more likely to do so when they think the plaintiff is not sophisticated.

The story *appears* to be different for defendants. Defendants *with* lawyers won more often when facing unrepresented plaintiffs than defendants without lawyers. And defendants with lawyers always did better in reducing the claim against them, whether the plaintiff did or did not have a lawyer.

The statistics, however, don't give the whole picture. Ruhnka and Weller note that plaintiffs generally have more time to collect evidence and have more information and help in preparing for trial. If nothing else, plaintiffs can learn a lot from a clerk while preparing their initial Plaintiff's Statement. Most defendants, on the other hand, don't prepare for court and simply show up on the day of the trial. Further, they aren't given the basic information in the court's brochure when they are served with the Plaintiff's Statement. It should not be surprising, then, that defendants with lawyers are better prepared and therefore more likely to win.

Lawyers can be particularly helpful to defendants in consumer cases. The failure of a manufacturer or creditor to observe state or federal consumer protection laws is usually a complete defense against liability for what you might owe that manufacturer or creditor. For example, the Fair Credit Billing Act says that you may stop payment for any poor-quality goods or services purchased with a credit card if you have made a genuine attempt to solve the problem, as discussed in Chapters 1 and 2. To qualify, however, the purchases must have been made within the same state as, or within 100 miles of, the cardholder's billing address.

Ruhnka and Weller also found that most judges they interviewed knew little or nothing about federal regulations such as the Consumer Product Safety Act, Consumer Credit Protection Act, Fair Interest Labeling Act, the Magnuson-Moss Warranty Act, or even state provisions such as the Uniform Consumer Credit Code (UCCC). This should not be surprising as most consumer cases do not involve enough money to be taken to formal court, where judges are more apt to deal with and be informed about new laws.

The Verdict on Lawyers

It's worth noting that plaintiffs and defendants, both winners and losers, who used lawyers were less satisfied with their small claims experience than those who had not. Ruhnka and Weller believe this is "possibly because the additional cost of a lawyer reduced their recovery or added to their loss." It's easy to agree with this assessment.

Here are some guidelines for whether you, as a plaintiff or defendant, should hire an attorney to handle or help you with a small claims suit:

If you are a plaintiff and don't have difficulty understanding this book or filing the Plaintiff's Statement, it is unlikely you will need a lawyer. This is true even if the other side is represented by one. If you have a lawyer in this situation, it could reduce the size of your recovery, push the matter into a higher court and perhaps lose the judge as an ally.

A judge's willingness to help an unrepresented person is perhaps the best argument for appearing without a lawyer in court. Judges recognize that nonlawyers are at a technical disadvantage when facing a lawyer in the courtroom, and most judges try to correct the imbalance. As one judge told Ruhnka and Weller: "When one side is without a lawyer, the natural tendency of a judge is to favor the underdog—and when the judge is acting as lawyer for one side, as well as the judge, you can imagine that the judge's client will not lose too often."

If you are a defendant, legal advice can be important, but having a lawyer in court may be both counterproductive and expensive. What's important is that unrepresented defendants tend to lose, not because they don't have a lawyer, but because they do not have adequate information and are unprepared for court. You don't have to hire a lawyer to seek specific legal advice or to prepare your case. Less expensive and better alternatives are available, as we will see.

Seeking Legal Advice

Even if your small claims court prohibits the use of a lawyer in court, nothing stops you from seeking legal advice beforehand. The particulars of your case may lead to legal questions about such matters as liability, court limitations and consumer protection laws. Still, you needn't pay a lawyer a lot of money to get the answers.

Some small claims courts (in California, Chicago, New York City and Washington, D.C., for example) have law students, advisors or paralegals in the courthouse to answer questions and help you prepare the necessary papers. Also, many law schools operate clinics that help people answer basic legal questions. Ask the court clerk if this sort of help is available in your area.

Next, try a private or governmental consumer action agency if your case involves a purchase of any kind. These agencies have staff lawyers and paralegals knowledgeable about consumer protection and other laws that govern commercial transactions. If you do need a lawyer with whom to discuss your consumer case, the private agencies will probably be able to recommend someone.

Other sources of free legal advice are also available. If you are having a problem with a creditor, for example, talk with the lawyer at your bank. Other questions might be resolved in a brief meeting with a staff lawyer in the company where you work.

If you do need to consult a private attorney, you'll want to keep the cost as low as possible. When you make an appointment, be sure to say you want to seek legal advice, not representation in court. If you have your materials properly prepared, you could be out of the lawyer's office in a half hour—getting all the advice you need for a relatively small sum.[1]

---

[1]For more information on cutting the costs of legal help, see *Using a Lawyer* by Kay Ostberg in association with HALT, Random House, 1990.

CHAPTER
8

PREPARING FOR TRIAL

You must do two things to prepare your case for trial: collect the evidence and plan your presentation. If you are the one who is suing, you can begin even before you leave the clerk's office. If you are being sued, you should probably go to the clerk's office even if you don't have to file an Answer to the Plaintiff's Statement.

Ask the clerk if the small claims court is currently in session and get directions to the courtroom being used. Also ask the clerk if the judge who is presiding will be presiding on the scheduled trial date. This is unlikely. Judges usually preside in small claims courts only for a specified period and then rotate back to higher courts. If the present judge will not cover your case, ask the clerk when the rotation occurs. You may want to return before your trial and watch your judge in action.

In any event, it's wise to visit the courtroom. As you will see, the only significant difference between a typical small claims court and a formal trial court is that usually the courtroom has no witness stand and no jury. The judge sits at a raised bench, a clerk sits at a small table before the bench, and they are faced by a long table or tables for the plaintiff, defendant and witnesses. A railing behind the plaintiff and defendant separates the participants from seats provided for the public.

If a hearing is in progress, take a seat at the back and watch the proceedings. A few minutes of your time will demonstrate the two essential elements of a small claims trial: it is extremely short and the judge is completely in control.

Most small claims trials last no more than twenty minutes. This means you probably will have about five minutes to present your case. If you are disorganized and fail to get essential information to the judge in this amount of time, you may well lose. Judges tend to be sympathetic to plaintiffs. They know you probably wouldn't have gone to the trouble to come to court unless you honestly believed you had been wronged. However, a small claims court is a busy place and dozens of other people will be waiting to have their cases heard. If you can't make your case in a few minutes, the judge will simply have to make a decision based on whatever you have managed to get across.

This brings up the second essential point, the role of the judge. All judges apply the law's standards to the facts *as presented*. They then reach a decision that establishes responsibility and the extent of damage. How they manage to arrive at that decision varies considerably.

Some small claims judges are "active," while others are more passive. The activist judge conducts court like an investigation. Based on the Plaintiff's Statement and supporting materials such as your two letters, the judge will quickly decide what the legal essentials are and begin questioning both sides in an attempt to get to the heart of the matter. Judges who use this approach do so to move the trial along. They do not want to listen to either side ramble on about unessential matters.

Passive judges behave more as they do in higher courts. They sit back, listen to both sides tell their story, then make a decision. If either side wants to ramble and fails to make a case, so be it. The judge sees the judicial role as that of an aloof, impartial arbiter of the facts presented.

Ruhnka and Weller's examination of small claims courts across the country found the number of active and passive judges to be about equal—even within individual districts. You may have to appear before either type, so be prepared for both. Whichever sort of judge you are assigned, the preparation is the same with respect to gathering your evidence. The real difference occurs in the presentation of that evidence. The activist judge will expect you to have it ready when he or she asks for it. The passive judge will expect you to present it to him or her in a coherent order of your own choosing.

Collecting Evidence

Ruhnka and Weller also asked judges what aspect of small claims cases caused them the most trouble. Most said difficulties almost always resulted from unclear recitation of facts and damages. In such cases, neither side offered a "preponderance of evidence."

The preponderance-of-evidence rule is legal jargon that simply means that it's up to the plaintiff to present more evidence to support a claim than the defendant can present to challenge it. In other words, at least 51 percent of the facts must favor the plaintiff for the case to succeed. Judges often compare this rule to a set of balance scales. The plaintiff and defendant each puts all of the available evidence on opposite sides of the scale. If the plaintiff's side is heavier, the plaintiff wins. If the defendant's side is heavier—or if the scale seems level—the defendant wins.

The preponderance-of-evidence rule applies in formal civil courts as well as in small claims courts. Some small claims judges, however, relax the rule somewhat. If the evidence for both sides is roughly equal, they tend to favor the plaintiff. Passive judges are usually more strict about the rules of evidence, but even they tend to sympathize with plaintiffs.

Nevertheless, no judge will decide for a plaintiff if the defendant clearly is supported by most of the evidence. It's up to you to collect and organize every available piece of evidence or risk the consequences.

The evidence you need depends on your case, but whatever the case, certain rules will apply. All you need to know about the rules in small claims court is that small claims judges will rate evidence in the following order of importance:

- Documentary evidence

- Expert testimony

- Witnesses

- Your testimony and opinion

As you can see, your testimony and opening remarks are of less importance than hard documentary evidence. If your presentation amounts to nothing more than telling your story to the judge and the other side shows up with hard evidence or witnesses, be prepared to lose.

Documentary Evidence

Documentary evidence is not hard to collect. It consists of your two earlier letters demanding restitution for your losses plus receipts, canceled checks, police reports, photographs and other physical evidence. If you've followed the instructions in Chapter 1, most of the documents you'll need are already in your file. The two complaint letters are especially important. They demonstrate that you behaved responsibly throughout and, more important, they set the agenda for the trial. They briefly summarize what happened, how much money was involved and why the person you're suing is liable. They will focus attention on these specific points and force the judge to see why your evidence is relevant and conclusive.

The letters do not "prove" the essential points of your case. They only help you determine what other documents are needed. You will need further evidence to establish loss and liability.

Evidence of Loss Before you filed your Plaintiff's Statement you determined the amount you lost. The supporting evidence you'll need includes any document that justifies the amount you're claiming. All relevant repair bills, estimates, receipts, contracts, canceled checks and the like are essential.

If you can bring the damaged item into court (such as a coat damaged by the cleaners), by all means do so. If that is not possible, bring photographs, if they clearly show the amount of damage. A photo of your water-damaged wallpaper, for example, can be very convincing.

Some small claims courts have their own rules of evidence for proving damages. Many, for example, require three independent repair estimates to establish a claim in an auto accident case. Be sure to ask the clerk if any such special requirements apply to your case.

Evidence of Liability Documentary evidence that establishes liability is harder to collect. For example, if you were in an auto accident and a police report was filed, neither that report nor a traffic ticket issued at the scene automatically establishes liability, although both may support your contention.

If a written contract is involved, liability may be a little easier to establish. Be sure to bring a copy of the contract to court with you: it contains the other side's promise to do something. In contract cases, you only have to concentrate on showing how that promise was broken.

Beyond that, proving liability can call for some creative thinking on your part. An expert witness may be the solution. In other situations, look for a visual aid to demonstrate the problem to the judge. Judges often have difficulty reaching a decision because it's difficult to visualize what's in dispute. For instance, you could diagram on posterboard the intersection where the auto accident occurred to show exactly what happened. If your dispute involves the faulty installation of a pneumatic compressor, you'd better find a way to simply and clearly demonstrate what a compressor is and what it is supposed to do. Remember: most judges know little or nothing about electronics or complex machinery, and you will have less than five minutes in which to explain it.

Expert Testimony

Because judges cannot make on-site inspections of damage and often know little about the subject matter in dispute, you may need the help of an expert witness—someone who is qualified to report on the damage or liability and who is not involved with either side. You may want such witnesses to be present or to supply you with an affidavit.

Consider, for example, a dispute involving an appliance store's failure to repair or replace your defective TV set. If you drag the set into court, the judge won't be able to decide anything just by looking at it and the store's technician will probably blame your troubles on your misuse of the set. Who will the judge believe—you or a professional? However much the judge may want to believe you, you'll have to help. The best method is to have an independent technician look at the set and either come to court or sign an affidavit declaring under oath that the flaw is in the set.

For repair or installation problems, it's always wise to secure expert testimony. The problem is both getting it and getting it to court. Service representatives will probably charge you for an estimate, and few will want to spend an afternoon sitting in court.

However, if you have followed the advice in this book, you may have some of this evidence already in hand. If you tried to resolve your problem through a Better Business Bureau, Consumer Action Panel, consumer action agency or trade association, for example, one or more of those agencies probably sent an expert to check your claim. You might be able to use this expert's testimony at no charge. If this hasn't happened yet, these same agencies may provide or recommend an expert who will do this free or for a small fee. Testimony from an expert working with these associations should effectively demolish any technical bluffing from the other side.

Getting an expert to appear in person in court can be troublesome and costly and is usually unnecessary, at least in small claims court. A notarized letter to the court on business stationery describing the problem, its origin and the extent of the damage is probably enough. Always check with the court clerk to make sure that a signed and perhaps notarized letter is acceptable.

It is *always* a good idea for your expert witnesses to list telephone numbers where they can be reached on the day of the trial. Many judges will call from the bench to clear up any objections raised by the other side. If it becomes abundantly clear during the trial that you need your expert in court, ask the judge to postpone the hearing until you can arrange an appearance (see "Continuances" on page 446).

Other Witnesses

At times you may need other witnesses to verify what happened—people who were involved in the events or who merely observed them. The best are those who are neither involved in the dispute nor related to you. Passers-by who witnessed the auto accident or dog attack are ideal. Friends and relatives can also testify on your behalf, but a judge is obliged to recognize that they may be prejudiced in your favor.

Any witness is better than none. This is particularly true in landlord-tenant cases when the landlord withholds a security deposit claiming you damaged the rental property. Without "before and after" photographs or a detailed itemization of conditions when you moved in, it will be your word against the landlord's unless you have witnesses.

If you have friends or relatives who saw the place when you moved in and when you moved out, you should get their testimony. It will be particularly useful if your witness helped you clean the place when moving out. Judges understand that most landlords have an overly narrow definition of what constitutes normal wear and tear. What you need to establish, through a witness or through receipts, is that you made a reasonable effort to maintain the place properly.

It's important that you try to get your nonexpert witnesses to appear personally in court rather than sending a letter or sworn statement. A judge may believe the affidavit of an expert who has professional training and a need to preserve a professional reputation, but nonexpert witnesses' credibility depends largely on their behavior before the judge. If they seem rational and not excessively prejudiced, the judge is more likely to believe them.

If your witness absolutely cannot appear, you will have to settle for an affidavit. Be sure your witness explains in the affidavit why it is impossible to be in court; see that the witness's description of the incident is clear; and get a telephone number where the witness can be reached during the trial, if necessary.

Your Own Testimony

Your own testimony and opinion will be summarized in your first complaint letter. In court, the principal purpose of your testimony is to clarify any questions the judge has.

If you are facing an especially passive judge, your testimony may have to tie all of the evidence together, but your job is only to present the facts, not to establish their truth. Otherwise you'll be caught in a my-word-against-yours trap, and if the other side has evidence to support his or her version of the events, the preponderance of evidence will weigh against you. Present the best, hardest evidence you can find and let it speak for itself. Your job should be only to hand it to the judge and explain its relevance.

In negligence cases, you may be the only witness on your own behalf. In that case, your testimony is the evidence with regard to liability, but proving the amount of your loss will still require other evidence: receipts, canceled checks, bills and the like.

Planning Your Presentation

Your role depends largely upon the sort of judge you're assigned. But whether you have to display your evidence in a logical order before a passive judge or simply wait for an active judge to ask for it, the evidence must still be ordered properly and readily available.

The most important thing is to weed out material that is not essential or relevant to the points you must prove. Prepare a folder or file for presentation to the judge. Include three sections: documents that give a chronological history of the dispute; documents that establish liability; and materials that prove the extent of your loss.

The first section needn't be more than your two letters of complaint and something to verify your attempts to seek out-of-court resolution—through the Better Business Bureau, a consumer action agency or arbitration. The second section should include relevant warranties, repair bills and affidavits from expert witnesses, if any. The third section should contain repair estimates, receipts and the like.

Put these materials in a logical order so the judge can see the history of the dispute at a glance. Don't expect the judge to read any more than the Plaintiff's Statement, perhaps your two letters, and a particular affidavit. Remember the constraints on the judge's time.

If you have any doubts about what may or may not be essential evidence, check with the consumer action agency or similar office you've dealt with before. Such groups have a lot of experience with small claims procedures. Keep your "marginal" evidence in a second file and be prepared to present it only if the judge asks for clarification on some point.

Your first folder's material will serve as your outline for a presentation if you face a passive judge. The verbal description of the incident and your attempts at resolution can be a simple recitation of the facts from your first letter and a description of facts supported by other evidence in the file.

A judge who wants to see other evidence—an expert's letter, for example—will ask for it. The important thing is to let the judge know you have it available. With any luck, even the passive judge will want to see your folder the first time you refer to it. Once you have presented your hard evidence, there's little if anything you should have to add.

If you think you'll be facing a passive judge, you might want to practice your presentation before a friend, neighbor or colleague, not as a form of amateur theatrics but to see if you can tell your story in five minutes or less and make sense of it to someone who knows none of its history. Your listener may have questions that never occurred to you. Those questions may even prompt you to collect further evidence.

Getting Evidence to Court

The evidence you will need for trial should be fairly easy to collect. However, special situations arise when knowing how to subpoena a witness or evidence can be useful. As you read the remainder of this chapter, remember that subpoenas are designed to resolve particular problems. They should never be used indiscriminately.

Subpoena of Witnesses

In most states, you can force a witness to appear in court by having a subpoena issued. Subpoena forms can be obtained from the clerk, and the process of serving the subpoena is like that of serving a Plaintiff's Statement. State rules vary but many require two things: that the witness you are subpoenaing live within a specified distance of the courthouse, and that the witness be entitled to collect a fee on demand when served the subpoena. The typical fee is $30 to $35, plus mileage.

Never force a witness who is unwilling to come and testify in your behalf. A witness who is angry about being dragged into court is unlikely to be very helpful before the judge and may even testify against you. If your witness needs a subpoena in order to take time off from work, arrange the court date in advance and get the witness's approval *before* you get the subpoena.

Make sure the witness's version of what happened is the version you want to have told in court. Nothing is wrong with coaching a witness about what part of the testimony is essential to your case. In fact, it is a good idea to rehearse with the witness to make sure that the testimony given will be favorable to you. Of course, you should never ask a witness to lie on your behalf. The penalty for this, if it should come to the court's attention, could be jail for both of you—you for obstructing justice and your witness for committing perjury. If you and your witness can't agree on what happened, *don't bring the witness to court.*

In some states, you can subpoena a police officer to appear if testimony is needed to supplement a vague police report. This can be expensive, however, because you usually have to pay a deposit equal to a day's wages for the officer and unless the appearance takes significantly less than a full day's time, you probably won't get any of it back. A more sensible alternative is to see if the officer has a "court day" scheduled during the month, then try to have your hearing scheduled for the same day.

In any event, it's seldom worth the expense to subpoena a police officer to appear in court. As with other expert witnesses, an affidavit will usually do. If it becomes clear the officer does need to be in court, the judge will postpone the hearing until a later date.

Subpoenas of Documents

You can subpoena documents just as you can witnesses. It's unusual in small claims court, but at times it may be necessary. For example, you may need copies of invoices, receipts, delivery records, or other documents to establish that a business transaction occurred.

To subpoena documents, ask the clerk for a form called a *subpoena duces tecum*—Latin for "under penalty you shall take it with you." It's much like the form for subpoenaing a witness, except it provides ample space for describing the documents you want. Always be specific about what documents you want brought to court. Give dates, invoice numbers, a description of the goods or services you bought, and so on. If you are not exact, the other side may show up with a 500-page computer printout no judge will take the time to look through.

You must attach to your subpoena a sworn statement explaining why the documents you want are essential in presenting your case. To save time, prepare the statement before you go to the clerk's office and bring extra copies. Sign it (and the copies, if necessary) in front of the clerk.

The clerk will help you complete the subpoena but, as with your

Plaintiff's Statement, you must do some research before you go to the clerk's office. You'll have to know the name and address of whomever is directly in charge of the documents you are seeking. If you get the wrong person, your subpoena may be ignored. The safest bet is to name the person in charge of the correct department, the manager of the bookkeeping department, for example. You can get this person's name simply by calling the company or institution involved.

The person you name in the subpoena must be served personally and, like subpoenaed witnesses, is entitled to a witness fee. That person will then be ordered to appear in court on the day of trial and to present the requested documents to the judge—not to you. If you need to see the documents, ask the judge if you can look them over while other cases are being tried.

Caution: a subpoena of documents, like a subpoena of witnesses, should be used only as a last resort. Never subpoena documents unless you are sure they are critical to your case and then only after all other efforts to get them have failed. A telephone call asking for photocopies may get you what you need. As with police officers and other expert witnesses, it's usually best to let the judge decide whether the original documents are required in court.

Collecting Your Costs

It should be clear by now that subpoenaing expert witnesses, other witnesses and documents can be expensive. If you win, you can ask the judge to add these costs to your damage award. If the judge feels the subpoena was necessary, you'll probably get your money back. If, however, the judge believes you've needlessly wasted a day of a police officer's or anyone else's time, expect to have to pay a bill as high as $100.

That's why it's wise to let the judge decide if it is necessary to subpoena someone. If it becomes clear that an affidavit or a follow-up telephone call won't resolve important questions, the judge's willingness to grant a postponement signals that he or she at least believes a subpoena is necessary. This makes recovering your costs virtually a sure bet—if you win.

CHAPTER

9

BEFORE TRIAL

When you sue in a small claims court, you have a good chance of winning. As Ruhnka and Weller's study showed, almost half of all small claims defendants fail to show up for trial and thus lose by default, and when both sides do appear in court, 72 percent of the plaintiffs win.

If you're the one being sued, don't give up hope if you have good reasons for having the suit dismissed or the claim reduced. It's not difficult to win if you collect and present your evidence coherently.

For either side, the important things are: to know how the small claims system works; to be prepared; and to make the best possible presentation. If you've followed the advice in this book, your appearance in court should be something of an anticlimax. All you have to do at this point is follow a few basic rules.

Your Arrival

The first and most basic rule is get to court on time. If, like most defendants, you haven't been to court before, or if you aren't sure which room the hearing is in, go early. The small claims session may begin with a roll call by the clerk, and if you're late, you may lose by default. Also, the option to appear before an arbitrator or mediator might be offered only at the beginning of the session.

Before the session begins, check the court calendar. This is a list of the cases to be heard that day. It is usually posted on a notice board outside the courtroom. If it is not, try the clerk's office. Sometimes only the clerk in the courtroom has a copy and your best opportunity to hear it is during the initial roll call.

Make sure your case is on the list. If it's not, ask the clerk why.

The next thing is to see if the calendar is divided into "case" and "motion" lists. If your case is on the "case" list, it will be heard during the session. If it's on the "motion" list, it means the other side has asked that the hearing be postponed. If the motion was made the same day as the trial so you couldn't have known of it even if you had called the clerk in advance, it's probably a delaying tactic and you should plan to fight it (see "Continuances," page 446.)

Defaults

If you're the one bringing the suit and the other side (the defendant) fails to show up on the day of the trial, the judge will usually, as a matter of procedure, enter a default judgment against the defendant. That means you win.

On the other hand, if the defendant shows up for trial and you don't, one of several things can happen. The judge will either dismiss the case or decide it on the basis of the defendant's evidence, even though you're not there. If the judge does the latter, the case is settled once and for all. If, however, the judge dismisses the case, the plaintiff may, depending on the court rules of your particular state, get the chance to refile the claim against you. In most states the judge will dismiss the case "without prejudice," which means it will be taken off the calendar but can be refiled by the plaintiff at a later date. You can, however, ask the judge to dismiss the case "with prejudice." This prohibits the plaintiff from bringing the same suit against you again. Whether or not the judge can grant your request depends partly on how good a case you have and on what the court rules allow concerning defaults and dismissals.

If neither side shows up, the case is usually dismissed without prejudice, but in some states (Colorado and Texas, for example) the defendant automatically defaults.

In some courts the clerk can enter a default judgment if you have enough evidence to establish a simple claim (an unpaid bill, for example) but in most states you will have to appear before the judge, whether you're the one suing or the one being sued. The judge will ask a few simple questions, mostly to make sure that, if you're the plaintiff, you aren't claiming too much. Once assured, the judge will enter a judgment of default.

If you're the defendant, the judge will either dismiss the case or consider the merits of the claim against you on the basis of your evidence alone. A judge is more likely to enter a final decision on your case or to dismiss it with prejudice, if it is clear you are thoroughly prepared and if your witnesses took the trouble to show up.

Usually a default judgment doesn't go into effect until after a grace period of ten to sixty days. This gives the one who missed the hearing time to file a "Motion to Vacate Judgment." The motion asks the judge to erase the default and reschedule the case for a hearing. You can file it simply by asking the clerk's office for the proper form, filling it out and giving it to the clerk.

A judge is unlikely to grant such a motion unless you can establish one of two things: that an emergency made it impossible for you either to attend or to give the court notice by asking for your case to be rescheduled (a "continuance"), or that you were never notified of the hearing ("improper service"). You can file a Motion to Vacate Judgment anytime after the default, but judges generally aren't sympathetic unless you act immediately after you learn about the judgment.

Pretrial Maneuvers

Sometimes the unexpected can happen on the morning of your trial. The other side might decide to settle out of court or at the last minute might ask to reschedule the hearing. If you're a plaintiff, you may find at the last minute that *you* are being sued by your opponent. It is important to know about such pretrial tactics and what to do about them.

Counterclaims

As we've seen, the person you're suing has a right to countersue. In some states, this counterclaim must be filed with the clerk before the trial, but elsewhere it can be made on the morning, or even at the beginning, of the trial.

If you live in a state where counterclaims must be filed in advance, it's worth calling the clerk before trial to see if one has been raised against you. If it has, ask the clerk to read you the reason for the counterclaim. This will allow you to bring to court additional evidence to oppose it.

If the person you're suing counterclaims just before the trial, you have two options. You can rely on your evidence and presentation to show the counterclaim is frivolous, or you can ask for a continuance. Judges almost always grant a continuance when additional evidence is needed to refute an unexpected counterclaim.

The most significant problem with counterclaims is that they sometimes seek more than the dollar limits of the court. In some states this automatically pushes the case into a higher, formal court. If this tactic is used on you, recognize that it's often used to intimidate plaintiffs: the other side may think you'll drop your case rather than take on the trouble and expense of hiring a lawyer and dealing with formal court procedures, delays and other hassles.

In some jurisdictions, a counterclaim over the dollar limit cannot push a case out of small claims court. Unfortunately, only a few courts follow this practice. If your court is not one of them, your only chance of preventing this maneuver—and it's a slim one—is to appeal to the judge. Judges see this maneuver being tried by lawyers in small claims courts all the time. Usually they recognize it as an attempt to prevent you from seeking simple and inexpensive justice. Your only hope is to appeal to the judge's sense of fairness. Respond to the counterclaim by telling your small claims court judge something like this:

> "Your Honor, I think the defendant and his [or her] attorney have made a counterclaim of this size simply because they want to move this case into formal court. They know that the cost of hiring a lawyer to continue this action in a higher court will make it uneconomical for me to pursue my claim. I request that you ask the defendant either to reduce the counterclaim to fit within the limits of this court, to demonstrate the grounds for a counterclaim of this size, or to file a separate suit in civil court."

If the judge is sympathetic, such an appeal might work. If not, you are no longer dealing with a small claims case. Your options at this point are to drop the case, hire a lawyer to handle it in civil court, or try to continue the case yourself in higher court.

The first option may seem to be grossly unfair, but if your claim is for $200 or less, the cost of continuing may be more than you'd recover. The second option is not unreasonable if you think you not only will win your case, but also collect attorneys' fees in the final judgment. The third option may work if you can find a lawyer to coach you on how to use the formal court. Remember, though, that if the other side has a lawyer and some basis for a counterclaim, you could lose not only your case but also end up paying expensive court costs. [1]

---

[1] See *Using a Lawyer* by Kay Ostberg in association with HALT, Random House, 1990, before consulting a lawyer about continuing your case.

Pretrial Settlement

Don't be surprised if the other side offers to settle with you a few days—or even a few minutes—before your case goes to trial. You can almost count on this happening if the other side is represented by a lawyer.

Settlement offers are made when one side recognizes it may not or cannot win in court and decides instead to cut its losses. Whether or not you accept the offer should depend on its size and the strength of your case.

If the offer is made before the trial date, you may decide to accept payment of 75 percent of your claim rather than waste a business day in small claims court. Besides the nuisance of going to court, it's always possible you might not win. And even if you do win, you may not be given all you're claiming. According to Ruhnka and Weller, individuals who sued in consumer cases won, on average, only 68 percent of what they claimed. In landlord-tenant cases, plaintiffs won only slightly more, and in damage suits, they averaged 79 percent of what they sued for.

If the offer is made on the day of the trial, you can probably afford to be more demanding about what you'll settle for. After all, you've already taken the trouble to come to court and it won't be that much more difficult to settle the matter in front of the judge.

If you settle after the clerk's roll call but before you face the judge, the judge may still want to interview both you and your opponent, then enter the settlement in the court record. *Do not leave the courtroom* until you have an opportunity to tell the judge that a settlement has been reached, then ask the judge to note the settlement in your case record.

Should you accept the settlement offer? That depends. If it is made by a lawyer for the other side, you can assume it's a double-barreled strategy. First, if the settlement is less than you sued for, the lawyer can "justify" the fee charged to the client by pointing to the money saved. Second, the lawyer will try to use your refusal as a sign that you did not behave reasonably in pretrial negotiations. If this happens, tell the judge you thought the settlement offer was too low when compared with your documented losses and that you decided to rely on the decision of the judge.

If you do decide to accept the settlement offer, whether from an attorney or directly from the opposing party, be sure to protect yourself. Say you will accept the settlement and drop your suit only if you receive cash or a check for the full agreed amount *before* the trial. Then get the settlement agreement in writing. It should look something like this:

It is agreed by (plaintiff) and (defendant), Plaintiff and Defendant in the case of (plaintiff) vs. (defendant), Docket No. _____, (year) in (name of court) of (location) that the above action will be settled for the sum of ($___).

This sum was received in full by (plaintiff) from (defendant) on (date). In return for this sum, (plaintiff) will notify the court and discontinue the above action.

If the defendant defaults on this agreement, the plaintiff shall have the right to initiate court action to collect both the above sum and the additional costs of collection, including court costs and attorneys' fees.

Signed,

_____

Plaintiff

_____

Defendant

_____

Date

Having a written agreement will be crucial if the other side tries something like stopping payment on a check written on the day of the trial. If this happens, the original elements of your case (loss, liability, and so on) no longer matter. You now have a straightforward contract that the other side has broken. It will be easy to take this document to court and win a judgment. In fact, the costs of hiring a lawyer to do this for you are now covered by the contract.

Continuances

It's fairly easy to get a hearing date postponed, either by mutual consent or by a letter to the court. In most cases, postponements (called "continuances") are arranged well before the trial date, but they can be requested by either side at any point up until the judge renders a decision.

When a continuance is requested during the trial, it is usually because one side needs time to collect further evidence or testimony. When the continuance is requested on the morning of the trial (that is, when you unexpectedly find your name on the calendar's "motion" list), it's probably a stalling tactic. If the other side is represented by a lawyer, you can be fairly sure this is an attempt to complicate matters. If you suspect your opponent is stalling, tell the judge.

At the motion hearing, the other side will first be asked to explain why a continuance is needed, then you will be asked if you object to the continuance. Your best response will be something like this:

> "Your Honor, my telephone number and address are clearly given on both my initial letters of complaint to *(the other side)* and on the Plaintiff's Statement. The defendant has known about this trial date for two weeks. I could have been contacted by telephone or mail at any point before today and would have consented to a postponement. However, I've taken off from work and have gone to some trouble to arrange to be here this morning. Also, I have witnesses here who have taken the trouble to appear in court. I think the other side believes it can get me to drop this case if the number and nuisance of my court appearances can be increased. I ask that we hold the trial now and settle this matter today."

Most judges routinely consent to at least the first request for a continuance. However, the judge will listen to your objections and may well agree with you that the other side's reasons for requesting the continuance are weak.

Arbitration

Eleven states and the District of Columbia have small claims courts that offer arbitration or mediation programs. If you decided to try this option (page 381), you'll be given the opportunity to make this choice just before trial. But remember, the other side must also agree, unless you are suing in a state such as California, which makes arbitration mandatory on the defendant if the plaintiff chooses it. Also, remember that seeking court-sponsored arbitration might deny you any appeal rights.

If previous attempts at arbitration or pretrial settlement have failed, and if you have a solid case, you might as well tell it to the judge. After all, you're already in the courthouse.

CHAPTER

10

THE TRIAL

If you've done a good job collecting the necessary evidence and planning your presentation, the trial will be short and simple. You probably have a good idea of how it works already. Unless your case is first on the docket, you will sit in the courtroom watching other small claims trials until the clerk calls your case. Then you, your opponent and all your witnesses will move to the front of the courtroom and take seats facing the judge.

Usually the clerk or judge begins by reading a summary of the case taken from your Plaintiff's Statement. You'll be sworn in, tell your story and present your evidence. The judge will probably ask you a few questions. Then your witnesses will be sworn in and will give their testimony.

After your witnesses speak, the person you are suing will be sworn in and makes a presentation. The defendants may be allowed to question you or your witnesses to bring out further facts. Then the defendant's witnesses are sworn and testify. You may be allowed to question the defendant or the defendant's witnesses. The judge may ask questions of both sides at any time during the hearing or may wait until everyone has spoken.

Your Appearance

When it's your turn to face the judge, concentrate on your appearance. The trial will last only a few minutes and the evidence on some points may boil down to your word against your opponent's. For this reason, your behavior in court is crucial to your case. Judges call this "demeanor evidence," and they rely upon it to a great extent.

Remember that the judge knows absolutely nothing about you. A judge who has to determine if you behaved reasonably in the events that led to this trial will be guided largely by the impression you make in court. To make the best possible impression, try to follow these basic rules.

1. *Dress neatly.* Judges tend to be fairly conservative. They prefer to see people dressed "properly" for an appearance in court. Gaudy clothing, worn-out jeans, tee-shirts and the like will put you at a disadvantage with many judges.

2. *Stand.* Unless the judge has instructed otherwise, stand whenever you talk to the judge, tell your story or answer questions. Showing respect for the court means showing some respect for the judge.

3. *Be polite.* At all times, address the judge as "Your Honor," and answer "yes" or "no" questions with "Yes, Your Honor," and "No, Your Honor." If a lawyer is an acting judge for the day (a judge *pro tem*), then use "Sir" or "Ma'am." *Never* interrupt a judge, your opponent or a witness. You will have your chance to speak. *Never* argue with a judge. You can emphasize or repeat anything you think is important, but if the judge says the point is irrelevant, accept it and move on to your next point.

4. *Introduce yourself and your case.* If the judge was shuffling through papers when your name or case was called, or if the basis

of your suit wasn't read aloud, introduce yourself and *briefly* describe your case. Don't start reeling off facts until you're sure the judge has focused on the subject at hand.

5. *Be brief.* Stick to the essential facts and let your evidence speak for you.

6. *Be prepared.* If you need to show evidence in support of any assertion you make in your testimony, know how your materials are organized so the judge doesn't have to wait while you fumble through a stack of papers. If you are missing a crucial piece of evidence, be ready to explain its absence.

7. *Never read testimony.* Reading makes your testimony boring and unconvincing to the judge. Don't try to memorize anything. If you are afraid of forgetting important points, make notes or use an outline.

8. *Don't act like a lawyer.* This may be the most important rule of all. Many people sabotage their own cases by using legal terms they don't understand or by performing a ludicrous parody of Perry Mason. If you start acting like a lawyer, the judge may start treating you like one: the natural inclination to help you will disappear, and sympathy may pass to the other side. The first and last legal-sounding term you should utter in a courtroom is "Your Honor."

9. *Listen to the judge.* If the judge tells you to take a few extra minutes and try to settle the case out of court, take the hint. The judge probably means the facts or the law aren't on your side and your best bet is to get what you can through settlement.

10. *Remember your costs.* If you've incurred any special costs in bringing your case to court, be sure to tell the judge. You should specifically state at the end of your presentation that you would like a specified amount of money added to your award for these costs.

The Judgment

After listening to both sides, the judge may discuss the merits of each side's case. Then, depending on the judge and the jurisdiction, the judge will either announce the verdict in court or indicate that both sides will be notified by mail.

Courtroom Verdicts If the judge announces the decision in court—and this is unusual—it will be easier to arrange payment or collection of the award. If you are the one who owes the money, you can either pay the amount in full, arrange a payment plan with the plaintiff or ask the judge to order installment payments. If you pay while still at the courthouse, be sure to get your opponent to sign a "Satisfaction of Judgment" form.

A Satisfaction of Judgment form is usually available from the court clerk's office. If not, you can quickly draft one yourself. It must include the name and district of the court, the names of the plaintiff and defendant and the case number. It should say something like this:

I acknowledge full satisfaction of the judgment in (plaintiff) vs. (defendant), case no. _____, in (name of court) of (location). Satisfaction was executed at (city/county), (state), on (date). The sum of _____ dollars and cents ($_____._____) was received from (defendant) at this time.

                                                                Signature

Judgment Creditor

The Satisfaction of Judgment should be signed by the person who receives the money (the judgment creditor) upon receipt. If you are the one paying, it is important that you get a copy of the Satisfaction of Judgment for yourself, plus one for the court. Filing a copy with the court clerk will prevent your opponent from taking you to court over the same matter again. Keeping a copy could also be important if you later need to clear your credit record.

If you have convinced the judge to allow payment by install-ments, be sure to get a signed Satisfaction of Judgment statement once you make the last payment and file a copy with the court. When you pay on an installment plan, always pay in a way that gives you a record—canceled checks or money orders, for example.

If you win your case, try to collect payment while you're still in the courthouse. It's much easier to do in person just after a verdict than later by telephone or mail. Speak with the defendant in the hallway outside the courtroom. Offer to complete and sign the Satisfaction of Judgment form on the spot and clear the judgment immediately, or make a definite arrangement for payment with the defendant before you leave court. Set a deadline for payment, and promise a Satisfaction of Judgment form in return. It may be easier to arrange if you agree to accept installments.

Verdicts by Mail

In most states, the judge's decision is not announced in court but is sent by mail to both sides. If you receive notice in the mail that you've won, contact the other side immediately and arrange pay-ment. A postcard from the courthouse is not forceful when it comes to encouraging someone to pay, so it's important to act while the authority of the judge is fresh in the defendant's mind. Offer a Satisfaction of Judgment form upon payment in full or at the conclusion of the installment payments, and mention alternative collection procedures if you detect hesitation.

If you were the defendant and are notified that you've lost, you can either pay the amount in full or seek an installment plan. If you can afford only to pay on installments, contact the person who sued you and see if you can arrange a private agreement. Find out how much you'll have to pay per week or month and get an agreement in writing.

If your opponent will not agree to an installment plan and you must have one, ask the judge to order one. Call the court clerk and ask if you must arrange a hearing or if a letter to the judge will suffice. If you must write a letter, be sure to include the name and the docket number of the case, the size of the judgment, and the reason why you can't pay the amount in a lump sum. Say how much you can afford to pay per month and ask that the original order be changed to incorporate this payment schedule. For more information on getting a court-ordered payment plan, speak to the court clerk.

CHAPTER

II

APPEALS

If you feel the judge's verdict was unfair or based on an error, in some states you can appeal your case. The small claims courts of Arizona, Connecticut, Hawaii, Louisiana's City Court, North Dakota, Oregon's District Court, and South Dakota do not permit appeals. California, Massachusetts, New York, Oregon's Justice Court and Rhode Island allow only the defendant to appeal a case. The remaining states, Virgin Islands, Puerto Rico and the District of Columbia permit an appeal by either side, but each state has its own special appeal provisions (see Appendix VI).

Types of Appeals

In more than half the states (including some courts in Georgia, Louisiana, Montana, Oregon and Wyoming), the appeal is *de novo*. This means simply that the first trial is scrapped and the case begins again, from the beginning, in a formal civil court. You will have to present your evidence and witnesses much like you did in small claims court, although the first trial should have taught you how to strengthen your case or presentation. Remember that civil court rules are much more complex than those in small claims court. They involve discovery, formal pleadings and the like. The cost and delay can be considerable.

In the remaining states that allow appeals, the appeal must be based on questions of law, not on the facts of the case. In these states, it's not enough to appeal because you disagree with the judge about the quality of your evidence or the appearance of false testimony. You can only appeal if you can demonstrate that the judge misapplied the law. An example of this would be a consumer case in which a judge failed to recognize the immunity from liability provided by a federal consumer protection statute.

The reasoning behind an appeal of law is usually difficult for nonlawyers to recognize. Further practical problems arise because you'll need a court record. The appeal judge must be able to see the basis for the small claims judge's decision, but, unfortunately, small claims proceedings seldom include making a stenographic or audio recording. Most judges make bench notes during a small claims trial, however, and these are often accepted as a sufficient record. If they are not, the appellate court will either refuse to grant an appeal or order a new trial.

Filing an Appeal

Time is crucial when you are seeking an appeal. In most states, you have only two or three weeks in which to file an appeal of a small claims court decision. If you received notice of the small claims judgment by mail, you may only have a few days before the deadline is past.

To file the appeal, complete a "Notice to Appeal" statement in the court clerk's office. Give the name of your case, the reason for your appeal and the amount of the small claims judgment against you or, if you were the plaintiff, the amount of money you were claiming. You'll have to pay a filing fee of $25 to $100. (Everything is more expensive in formal civil court.) Some courts will require you to post a bond in the amount of the small claims judgment you're appealing to assure that you will pay if you lose a second time.

The bond may also be required to cover such court costs as for a jury or court reporters.

After you've filed and paid the fee, the court will notify the other side and a trial will be scheduled for about a month later. Some districts (as in Iowa, Wyoming and the District of Columbia) have a review court that can reject a groundless appeal without a hearing. In the District of Columbia, fifty-three out of sixty-two appeals from small claims court were refused in 1988. For more information about the appeal procedures in your state, see Appendix VI.

Should You Appeal?

Appeals from small claims to formal civil courts are costly, complicated and risky. If you lose a second time, you will have to pay the original judgment and perhaps the court costs for the second trial.

It is important that you seek some form of legal help before you commit yourself to an appeal. This is especially important if your appeal is on a question of law. You must be sure that you have grounds for an appeal. You will probably have to state those grounds in a legal brief for the appeals judge.

You should seek some sort of legal help even if your appeal is for a new trial. After all, you lost the first time around. If you're going to win in a second trial, you'll need someone's help in organizing and preparing your presentation. Also, appellate judges tend to look upon people who appeal small claims cases as "sore losers." You'll need a significantly better case the second time around if you're to overcome this sort of prejudice.

Appeals from small claims court make sense *only* if a great amount of money is at stake and *only* if you have confirmed that you have a solid basis for an appeal. Otherwise, take the opportunity to cut your losses.

CHAPTER

12

COLLECTING THE AWARD

Unfortunately, winning a judgment in small claims court isn't the end of the matter. You now have to collect what you've won. Sometimes that's not too difficult—you may even get a check from the losing party before leaving the courthouse. Sadly, though, many winners must not only wait to collect what's due but must actively track it down. They soon realize that taking a case through small claims court is not difficult—it's collecting the award that is.

If the appeal period has expired and it's clear that the person the court ordered to pay you the award will not pay willingly, you may have to take additional steps to collect it. Your defendant has turned into a debtor—in legal jargon, your "judgment debtor." Unfortunately, most small claims courts have no established procedures for enforcing their judgments. The small claims clerk will be able to tell you about collection rules for your state, but the task of collecting is yours, not the court's.

Collecting small claims judgments can be troublesome. The procedure is time-consuming and can be complicated and expensive. According to Ruhnka and Weller, two thirds to three fourths of all plaintiffs collect when both sides go to court to contest the case. When the person being sued doesn't show up for court and the plaintiff wins by default, the results are very different. Only one fourth to one half of plaintiffs collect their awards.

If more people knew about the collection options available to them, the success rate could be considerably higher. Because collection procedures are defined both by state law and by the specific practices of the local court and sheriff's office, the following guide must be general. For more specific information, ask your small claims clerk, the clerk of the higher civil court or someone from the sheriff's or marshal's office.

Writ of Execution

To collect any money or property to cover what is owed you, you'll need a court order called a "Writ of Execution." Take your judgment to the small claims clerk to fill out an application for a Writ of Execution. You'll have to pay a small fee, which is recoverable, then wait perhaps a few days for a judge to sign your writ. The writ is the judge's order to a sheriff or marshal to collect any of the debtor's assets needed to satisfy the judgment. It will have an expiration date, usually thirty to ninety days from the date it was signed.

Before it expires, take the writ to the sheriff's or marshal's office in the county where the offices are located. Keep the original and give copies of the writ to the sheriff or marshal, along with payment of a fee for collection. The amount of the fee will depend on the type of asset you're asking the sheriff to collect.

The sheriff or marshal will either give you a form or ask that you write a letter stating your name, the small claims case's name and number, the amount of the judgment, the debtor's name and address and the location and description of the assets you want seized. You may consider claiming the following types of assets:

Automobiles You can ask that a debtor's car be seized and sold at a sheriff's auction. First, contact the Department of Motor Vehicles for your county or state to determine whether your debtor is the registered owner of the car. Also check to see if he or she still owes money on the car. If the debtor has only paid $1,000 on the car, then the debtor's "equity" in the car is $1,000, and you can collect no more than that after an auction. In fact, you'll get less than that, because every state excludes a part of car owner's equity from seizure. Thus, in a state that protects $750 in equity, you'd collect only $250 of the $1,000. Expect the amount of protected equity to be even higher if the car is a "tool of trade" used by the debtor to earn a living. Also, remember that an auction is not likely to bring the full value of the car. After the auction fees and other costs are deducted, there may be little or nothing left for you.

Bank Accounts If you know where the debtor banks, ask the sheriff to go to the bank and empty a debtor's checking or savings account. In some states, you'll have to know the account number. Special provisions may apply if it is a joint account or a business account or if it has any special exemptions. If you do not know where the debtor banks, see "Locating the Debtor's Assets" below.

Business Assets You may have ways of collecting from judgment debtors that are businesses. Besides seizing bank accounts, you can have a sheriff go to the business and empty the cash register, or seize all the money collected during one business day. You cannot have the sheriff seize business property. Such property helps the debtor make a living and is therefore protected against collectors. Basically, that means you can take the cash, but not the cash register.

The cost of hiring someone to collect for you are fairly high, but if you succeed you can be reimbursed for them. Some states have special punitive damages you may collect from a business that ignores a court judgment. Check with the small claims clerk about this.

Personal Property You are permitted to seize some of the person's personal possessions, but in practice this is difficult to do. For one thing, state laws exempt many things from seizure—everything from furniture and clothing to television sets. Further, the property may belong to someone else, for example, a roommate or other creditors who may have a prior claim. For these reasons, sheriffs and marshals dislike seizing personal property and may make you post an attachment bond of $1,000 or more should conflicting claims of ownership arise.

Real Property Real estate may be difficult to seize and sell, but land-owning debtors can easily be pressured into paying. Simply pay the small claims clerk to give you an "Abstract of Judgment" and file this wherever title to the debtor's land is kept—usually the County Records Office. This places a *lien* on the title to the property. The debtor will be unable to sell the land until he or she clears the title by paying you. Of course, you needn't wait until the debtor tries to sell the land. Simply notify the debtor and the bank that holds the mortgage that you have a lien on the property. This usually brings quick results.

Wages Finally, you can have the sheriff or marshal contact the debtor's employer to order that the debtor's wages be garnished. This means that, until the debt is paid off, the employer will have to deduct a percentage from the debtor's paycheck each week and send it to you. Garnishment is not allowed in a few states, and it is usually prohibited when the wages are needed to support a low-income family. For more information on each state's laws governing garnishment of a person's wages, check *Collier on Bankruptcy*[1] at a local law library. It's a ten-volume set with an entire volume dedicated to state exemptions from garnishment.

Locating the Debtor's Assets

So far we have assumed that the judgment debtor has certain assets and that you know where they are located. This is not always the case. If you need more information about the existence or location of assets, you can ask the court to examine the debtor's assets. To do this, ask the clerk for an "Order of Examination of Assets." (As usual, the actual name varies from state to state.) Complete this form and pay a fee. After a judge signs the form, have it delivered to the debtor by personal service. For another fee, a sheriff, marshal or other professional process server should be able to do this for you. All these costs should be recoverable in the end.

If the debtor is properly served, failure to appear in court usually results in being cited for contempt of court. That means a bench

---

[1] *Collier on Bankruptcy*, 15th edition, Mathew Bender, New York, 1979.

warrant will be issued for the debtor's arrest. Given the serious consequences if they don't, most debtors show up this time around. It's probably worth ordering a reluctant debtor to come to court and disclose assets just for the shock value. The debtor may even pay before having to tell all to the judge. If not, the examination will give you a better idea of where the debtor's assets are located.

Often the judge questions the debtor directly, but sometimes dozens of such examinations are in progress in the courtroom at the same time, usually conducted by creditors' lawyers. In this situation, you'll have to question the debtor yourself and report to the judge. Be sure to ask the debtor about all the assets we have discussed and find out where they are located. If the debtor is being evasive, tell the judge. The debtor will be put on the stand for questioning by the judge. Also, ask if the debtor is carrying any cash. You can ask that this be handed over to you in court.

Judgment-Proof Debtors

Sometime a judgment debtor has no job, no income and no assets that can be seized. This sort of debtor is said to be "judgment proof." You have no way to collect a judgment immediately. The other type of judgment-proof debtor is a defendant who moves after a judgment and leaves no forwarding address.

You are most likely to encounter a judgment-proof debtor in default cases. They don't appear in court because they've already moved or know you won't be able to collect from them. However, a small claims judgment is good for five to ten years, and you can have the debtor hauled into court every six months for an examination of assets. The debtor will probably acquire at least some assets over time, and the mere threat of being periodically dragged into court should be an incentive to pay.

Costs After Judgment

Any costs you incurred before the small claims judgment was issued should have been added to your claim when you asked for costs in court. Most costs incurred in trying to collect the judgment can also be collected from the debtor—as long as it is possible to collect anything. In many states, you can ask that these costs be added to the amount ordered collected in the Writ of Execution. Bear in mind that some fees can be collected only *after* you file a collection motion with the judge. You must then collect these fees as if they were a separate judgment. This is unlikely to be worth the effort unless you've spent a considerable sum.

An expensive way of collecting a judgment is to have a collection agency or collection attorney try to collect it for you. Both commonly take a third to half of whatever they manage to collect from the debtor, plus expenses. If you don't have time to track down an elusive debtor or the debtor's assets, you might want to consider this option, but it makes sense only if a lot of money is at stake, if collection has proven too difficult and time-consuming and if you're willing to accept two thirds to half (minus collection costs) of the total judgment.

If you plan to go this route, contact a collection agency. These companies use nonlawyer collectors and have established records of obeying the federal fair practice rules that govern the way debts can be collected. Until recently, collection attorneys were exempt from these rules and were thus able to use unfair, and sometimes unethical collection practices on debtors. Lawyers are no longer exempt from the Fair Debt Collection Practices Act (FDCPA). They are now required to obey the same rules as nonlawyer debt collectors.

The American Collectors Association, Inc., 4040 West 70th Street, Minneapolis, MN 55435, (612) 926-6547, and the Associated Credit Bureaus, Inc., 16211 Park 10 Place, Houston, TX 77084, (713) 492-8155, are trade associations that can tell you how to contact nonlawyer collectors. You can also contact nonlawyer collectors by looking under "collection agencies" in your yellow pages.

If you decide to hire a collection lawyer, ask the court clerk for the names of several in your area and shop for the one who offers a reasonable percentage arrangement and also has a reputation for honesty. Be sure to ask if you'll have to pay a fee if the lawyer doesn't collect anything.

CONCLUSION

Going to court—any court—may not be the best way to resolve your legal difficulties. As we have seen in this book, even when your problem seems to fit the criteria for the small claims court in your state, other methods of resolving your problem may be preferable. Small claims court, however, does offer a reasonably simple, inexpensive and, in most instances, fair way to get a just settlement.

The purpose of this book has been to enable you to make your way through small claims court as an informed and confident consumer, without the need for the services of expensive professionals. If you are involved in a dispute that can be resolved by an award of money, you should now be prepared to take the matter to small claims court.

The truth is that the more people use small claims courts, the more responsive these courts will be to the needs of the public. Already many states have moved to simplify procedures: by distributing brochures and videotapes that explain local rules and processes; by extending court hours to evenings and weekends; by increasing the dollar limit for cases to be brought; by barring attorneys from the courtroom; and by providing alternative dispute resolution programs.

There may, in fact, be an even more significant ripple effect from the use of small claims courts. Perhaps the steps being taken to streamline and increase access to these "people's courts" will some-day also be applied to the higher courts. In that event, justice would be better served.

APPENDIXES

APPENDIX

I

CONSUMER PROTECTION

AGENCIES

Consumer Protection Agencies resolve individual complaints against businesses and educate consumers and businesses about the law. They also provide information about consumer complaints filed against businesses in their area of jurisdiction. Some are operated by the state government, others by local governments.

To file a complaint, call the nearest office listed below and ask if your complaint needs to be in writing and on a particular form or if you can report it over the telephone. Some offices may ask you to come in for an interview. State offices may refer you to a local or county office. The information in this appendix is excerpted from the 1990 edition of the *Consumer's Resource Handbook,* published by the U.S. Office of Consumer Affairs.

Alabama
Consumer Protection Division
Office of Attorney General

11 S. Union St.
Montgomery, AL 36130
(205) 261-7334
(800) 392-5658 (toll free in AL)

Alaska

Consumer Protection Section
Office of Attorney General
1031 W. 4th Ave., Suite 110-B
Anchorage, AK 99501
(907) 279-0428

Arizona

Financial Fraud Division
Office of Attorney General
1275 W. Washington St.
Phoenix, AZ 85007
(602) 542-3702
(800) 352-8431 (toll free in AZ)

Arkansas

Consumer Protection Division
Office of Attorney General
200 Tower Bldg., 4th & Center Sts.
Little Rock, AR 72201
(501) 682-2007
(800) 482-8982 (toll free in AR)

California

Public Inquiry Unit
Office of Attorney General
1515 K St., Suite 511
Sacramento, CA 94244-2550
(916) 322-3360
(800) 952-5225 (toll free in CA)

Consumer Protection Division
Los Angeles City Attorney's Office
200 N. Main St.
1600 City Hall East
Los Angeles, CA 90012
(213) 485-4515

Colorado

Consumer Protection Unit
Office of Attorney General
1525 Sherman St., 3rd Floor
Denver, CO 80203
(303) 866-5167

Connecticut

Department of Consumer Protection
165 Capitol Ave.

Hartford, CT 06106
(203) 566-4999
(800) 842-2649 (toll free in CT)

Delaware

Division of Consumer Affairs
Department of Community Affairs
820 N. French St., 4th Floor
Wilmington, DE 19801
(302) 571-3250

District of Columbia

Department of Consumer &
   Regulatory Affairs
614 H St. NW
Washington, DC 20001
(202) 727-7000

Florida

Division of Consumer Services
218 Mayo Bldg.
Tallahassee, FL 32399
(904) 488-2226
(800) 342-2176 (toll free in FL)

Georgia

Governor's Office of Consumer
   Affairs
2 Martin Luther King, Jr. Dr. SE
Plaza Level, E. Tower
Atlanta, GA 30334
(404) 656-7000
(800) 282-5808 (toll free in GA)

Hawaii

Office of Consumer Protection
828 Fort St. Mall
Honolulu, HI 96812-3767
(808) 548-2560/2540

Idaho

None

Illinois

Consumer Protection Division
Office of Attorney General
100 W. Randolph St., 12th Floor
Chicago, IL 60601
(312) 917-3580

Indiana

Consumer Protection Division
Office of Attorney General
219 State House
Indianapolis, IN 46204
(317) 232-6330
(800) 382-5516 (toll free in IN)

Iowa

Consumer Protection Division
Office of Attorney General
1300 E. Walnut St., 2nd Floor
Des Moines, IA 50319
(515) 281-5926

Kansas

Consumer Protection Division
Office of Attorney General
Kansas Judicial Ctr., 2nd Floor
Topeka, KS 66612
(913) 296-3751
(800) 432-2310 (toll free in KS)

Kentucky

Consumer Protection Division
Office of Attorney General
209 St. Clair St.
Frankfort, KY 40601
(502) 564-2200
(800) 432-9257 (toll free in KY)

Louisiana

Consumer Protection Section
Office of Attorney General
State Capitol Bldg., P.O. Box 94005
Baton Rouge, LA 70804
(504) 342-7013

Maine

Consumer and Antitrust Division
Office of Attorney General
State House Station #6
Augusta, ME 04333
(207) 289-3716 (9:00 A.M.–2:00
P.M.)

Maryland

Consumer Protection Division
Office of Attorney General
7 N. Calvert St., 3rd Floor
Baltimore, MD 21202
(301) 528-8662 (9:00 A.M.–2:00
P.M.)

Massachusetts

Consumer Protection Division
Office of Attorney General
One Ashburton Place, Room 1411
Boston, MA 02108
(617) 727-7780

Michigan

Consumer Protection Division
Office of Attorney General
670 Law Bldg.
Lansing, MI 48913
(517) 373-1140

Minnesota

Office of Consumer Services
Office of Attorney General
117 University Ave.
St. Paul, MN 55155
(612) 296-2331

Mississippi

Consumer Protection Division
Office of Attorney General
P.O. Box 220
Jackson, MS 39205
(601) 359-3680

Missouri

Trade Offense Division
Office of Attorney General
P.O. Box 899
Jefferson City, MO 65102
(314) 751-2616
(800) 392-8222 (toll free in MO)

Montana
Consumer Affairs Unit
Department of Commerce
1424 9th Ave.
Helena, MT 59620
(406) 444-4312

Nebraska
Consumer Protection Division
Department of Justice
2115 State Capitol, P.O. Box 98920
Lincoln, NE 68509
(402) 471-4723

Nevada
Department of Commerce
State Mail Room Complex
Las Vegas, NV 89158
(702) 486-4150

New Hampshire
Consumer Protection and Antitrust
  Division
Office of Attorney General
State House Annex
Concord, NH 03301
(603) 271-3641

New Jersey
Division of Consumer Affairs
1100 Raymond Blvd., Room 504
Newark, NJ 07102
(201) 648-4010

New Mexico
Consumer and Economic Crime
  Division
Office of Attorney General
P.O. Box Drawer 1508
Santa Fe, NM 87504
(505) 872-6910
(800) 432-2070 (toll free in NM)

New York
Consumer Protection Board
99 Washington Ave.
Albany, NY 12210
(518) 474-8583

Consumer Protection Board
250 Broadway, 17th Floor
New York, NY 10007-2593
(212) 587-4908

North Carolina
Consumer Protection Section
Office of Attorney General
P.O. Box 629
Raleigh, NC 27602
(919) 733-7741

North Dakota
Consumer Fraud Division
Office of Attorney General
State Capitol Bldg.
Bismarck, ND 58505
(701) 224-2210
(800) 472-2600 (toll free in ND)

Ohio
Consumer Frauds and Crimes
  Section
Office of Attorney General
30 E. Broad St., 25th Floor
Columbus, OH 43266-0410
(614) 466-4986
(800) 282-0515 (toll free in OH)

Oklahoma
Consumer Affairs
Office of Attorney General
112 State Capitol Bldg.
Oklahoma City, OK 73105
(405) 521-3921

Oregon
Financial Fraud Section
Office of Attorney General
Justice Bldg.
Salem, OR 97310
(503) 378-4320

Pennsylvania
Bureau of Consumer Protection
Office of Attorney General
Strawberry Sq., 14th Floor
Harrisburg, PA 17120

(717) 787-9707
(800) 441-2555 (toll free in PA)

Puerto Rico

Department of Consumer Affairs
Minillas Station
P.O. Box 41059
Santurce, PR 00940
(809) 722-7555

Rhode Island

Consumer Protection Division
Department of Attorney General
72 Pine St.
Providence, RI 02903
(401) 277-2104
(800) 852-7776 (toll free in RI)

South Carolina

Department of Consumer Affairs
P.O. Box 5757
Columbia, SC 29250
(803) 734-9452
(800) 922-1594 (toll free in SC)

South Dakota

Division of Consumer Affairs
Office of Attorney General
State Capitol Bldg.
Pierre, SD 57501
(605) 773-4400

Tennessee

Division of Consumer Affairs
Department of Commerce &
    Insurance
500 James Robertson Pkwy., 5th
    Floor
Nashville, TN 37219
(615) 741-4737
(800) 342-8385 (toll free in TN)

Texas

Consumer Protection Division
Office of Attorney General
Box 12548, Capitol Station
Austin, TX 78711
(512) 463-2070

Utah

Division of Consumer Protection
Department of Business Regulation
160 E. Third South
P. O. Box 45802
Salt Lake City, UT 84145
(801) 530-6601

Vermont

Public Protection Division
Office of Attorney General
109 State St.
Montpelier, VT 05602
(802) 828-3171

Virgin Islands

Department of Licensing and
    Consumer Affairs
Property and Procurement Bldg.
Subbase #1, Room 205
St. Thomas, VI 0801
(809) 774-3130

Virginia

Division of Consumer Counsel
Office of Attorney General
Supreme Court Bldg.
101 N. 8th St.
Richmond, VA 23219
(804) 786-2116

Washington

Consumer and Business Fair Practices
    Division
710-2nd Ave., Suite 1300
Seattle, WA 98104
(206) 464-7744
(800) 551-4636 (toll free in WA)

West Virginia

Consumer Protection Division
Office of Attorney General
812 Quarrier St., 6th Floor
Charleston, WV 25301
(304) 348-8986
(800) 368-8808 (toll free in WV)

Wisconsin
Office of Consumer Protection
Department of Justice
P.O. Box 7856
Madison, WE 53707
(608) 266-1852
(800) 362-8189 (toll free in WI)

Wyoming
Office of Attorney General
123 State Capitol Bldg.
Cheyenne, WY 82002
(307) 777-6286

APPENDIX

II

BETTER BUSINESS BUREAUS

Better Business Bureaus (BBBs) are private dispute-resolution centers funded by local businesses. They attempt to resolve problems between consumers and businesses informally. BBBs accept written complaints and try to get the two sides to reach agreement, through either mediation or arbitration.

BBBs handle problems with contractors, large and small; retailers; auto repair shops; and others. They also publish pamphlets on consumer issues and maintain records of the number of complaints filed against local companies. If you have doubts about any local business, call to ask how many complaints have been filed against it. Also ask about the proper form to use before sending in a complaint. The information in this appendix is excerpted from the 1990 edition of the *Consumer's Resource Handbook,* published by the U.S. Office of Consumer Affairs.

If your state is not listed below, call the national office.

National Headquarters

Council of Better Business Bureaus
4200 Wilson Blvd.
Arlington, VA 22203
(703) 276-0100

Local Bureaus

Alabama
1214 S. 20th St.
Birmingham, AL 35205
(205) 558-2222

P. O. Box 383
Huntsville, AL 35804
(205) 533-1640

707 Van Antwerp Bldg.
Mobile, AL 36602
(205) 433-5494/5495

Commerce St., Suite 810
Montgomery, AL 36104
(205) 262-5606

Alaska
3380 C St., Suite 100
Anchorage, AK 99503
(907) 562-0704

Arizona
4428 N. 12th St.
Phoenix, AZ 85014
(602) 264-1721

50 W. Drachman St., Suite
103
Tucson, AZ 85705
(602) 622-7651 (inquiries)
(602) 622-7654 (complaints)

Arkansas
1415 S. University Ave.
Little Rock, AR 72204
(501) 664-7274

California
705—18th St.
Bakersfield, CA 93301
(805) 322-2074

P.O. Box 970
Colton, CA 92324
(714) 825-7280

6101 Ball Rd., Suite 309
Cypress, CA 90630
(714) 527-0680

5070 N. Sixth, Suite 176
Fresno, CA 93710
(209) 222-8111

510—16th St., Suite 550
Oakland, CA 94612
(415) 839-5900

400 S St.
Sacramento, CA 95814
(916) 443-6843

525 B St., Suite 301
San Diego, CA 92101-4408
(619) 234-0966

33 New Montgomery St.
Tower
San Francisco, CA 94105
(415) 243-9999

1505 Meridian Ave.
San Jose, CA 95125
(408) 978-8700

P.O. Box 294
San Mateo, CA 94401
(415) 347-1251

P.O. Box 746
Santa Barbara, CA 93102
(805) 963-8657

1111 North Center St.
Stockton, CA 95202
(209) 948-4880/4881

Colorado
P.O. Box 7970
Colorado Springs, CO 80933
(719) 636-1155

1780 S. Bellaire, Suite 700
Denver, CO 80222
(303) 758-2100 (inquiries)
(303) 758-2212 (complaints)

1730 S. College Ave., #303
Fort Collins, CO 80525
(303) 484-1348

432 Broadway
Pueblo, CO 81004
(719) 542-6464

Connecticut

2345 Black Rock Tpk.
Fairfield, CT 06430
(203) 374-6161

2080 Silas Deane Hwy.
Rocky Hill, CT 06067-2311
(203) 529-3575

100 S. Turnpike Rd.
Wallingford, CT 06492
(203) 269-2700 (inquiries)
(203) 269-4457 (complaints)

Delaware

P.O. Box 300
Milford, DE 19963
(302) 422-6300 (Kent)
(302) 856-6969 (Sussex)

P.O. Box 5361
Wilmington, DE 19808
(302) 996-9200

District of Columbia

1012 14th St. NW
Washington, DC 20005
(202) 393-8000

Florida

13770—58th St. N., #309
Clearwater, FL 33520
(813) 535-5522

2976-E Cleveland Ave.
Fort Myers, FL 33901
(813) 334-7331/7152
(813) 597-1322 (Naples)
(813) 743-2279 (Port
  Charlotte)

3100 University Blvd. S., #23
Jacksonville, FL 32216
(904) 721-2288

2605 Maitland Center Pkwy.
Maitland, FL 32751-7147
(407) 660-9500

16291 NW 57th Ave.
Miami, FL 33014-6709
(305) 625-0307 (inquiries for
  Dade County)
(305) 625-1302 (complaints
  for Dade County)
(305) 524-2803 (inquiries for
  Broward County)
(305) 527-1643 (complaints
  for Broward County)

250 School Rd., Suite 11-W
New Port Richey, FL 34652
(813) 842-5459

P.O. Box 1511
Pensacola, FL 32597-1511
(904) 433-6111

1950 Port St. Lucie Blvd.,
  #211
Port St. Lucie, FL 34952
(407) 878-2010/337-2083

1111 N. Westshore Blvd.,
  Suite 207
Tampa, FL 33607
(813) 875-6200

2247 Palm Beach Lakes Blvd.,
  #211
West Palm Beach, FL
  33409-3408
(407) 686-2200

Georgia

1319-B Dawson Road
Albany, GA 31707
(912) 883-0744

100 Edgewood Ave., Suite
  1012
Atlanta, GA 30303
(404) 688-4910

P.O. Box 2085
Augusta, GA 30903
(404) 722-1574

P.O. Box 2587
Columbus, GA 31902
(404) 324-0712 (inquiries)
(404) 324-0713 (complaints)

6606 Abercorn St., Suite
    108-C
Savannah, GA 31416
(912) 354-7521

Hawaii
1600 Kapiolani Blvd., Suite
    704
Honolulu, HI 96814
(808) 942-2355

Idaho
409 W. Jefferson
Boise, ID 83702
(208) 342-4649
(208) 467-5547

545 Shoup, Suite 210
Idaho Falls, ID 83402
(208) 523-9754

Illinois
211 W. Wacker Dr.
Chicago, IL 60606
(312) 444-1188 (inquiries)
(312) 346-3313 (complaints)

109 S.W. Jefferson St., #305
Peoria, IL 61602
(309) 673-5194

515 N. Court St.
Rockford, IL 61110
(815) 963-BBB2

Indiana
P.O. Box 405
Elkhart, IN 46515
(219) 262-8996

119 S.E. Fourth St.
Evansville, IN 47708
(812) 422-6879

1203 Webster St.
Fort Wayne, IN 46802
(219) 423-4433

4231 Cleveland St.
Gary, IN 46408
(219) 980-1511/
769-8053/926-5669

Victoria Centre
22 East Washington St.
Indianapolis, IN 46204
(317) 637-0197

320 S. Washington St., #101
Marion, IN 46952
(317) 668-8954/8955

Whitinger Building, Room 150
Muncie, IN 47306
(317) 285-5668

509—85 U.S. #33 North
South Bend, IN 46637
(219) 277-9121

Iowa
2435 Kimberly Road, #110
    North
Bettendorf, IA 52722
(319) 355-6344

1500 Second Avenue SE, #212
Cedar Rapids, IA 52403
(319) 366-5401

615 Insurance Exchange Bldg.
Des Moines, IA 50309
(515) 243-8137

318 Badgerow Bldg.
Siouxland, IA 51101
(712) 252-4501

Kansas
501 Jefferson, Suite 24
Topeka, KS 66607
(913) 232-0455

300 Kaufman Bldg.
Wichita, KS 67202
(316) 263-3146

Kentucky
154 Patchen Dr., Suite 90
Lexington, KY 40502
(606) 268-4128

844 Fourth St.
Louisville, KY 40203
(502) 583-6546

Louisiana
1605 Murray St., Suite 117
Alexandria, LA 71301
(318) 473-4494

2055 Wooddale Blvd.
Baton Rouge, LA 70806
(504) 926-3010

300 Bond St.
Houma, LA 70361
(504) 868-3456

P.O. Box 30297
Lafayette, LA 70593
(318) 234-8341

P.O. Box 1681
Lake Charles, LA 70602
(318) 433-1633

141 De Siard St., Suite 300
Monroe, LA 71201
(318) 387-4600/4601

1539 Jackson Ave.
New Orleans, LA 70130
(504) 581-6222

1401 N. Market St.
Shreveport, LA 71101
(318) 221-8352

Maine
812 Stevens Ave.
Portland, ME 04103
(207) 878-2715

Maryland
2100 Huntingdon Ave.
Baltimore, MD 21211-3215
(301) 347-3990

Massachusetts
Eight Winter St.
Boston, MA 02108
(617) 482-9151 (inquiries)
(617) 482-9190 (complaints)

One Kendall St., Suite 307
Framingham, MA 01701
(508) 872-5585

78 North St., Suite 1
Hyannis, MA 02601
(508) 771-3022

316 Essex St.
Lawrence, MA 01840
(508) 687-7666

106 State Rd., Suite 4
North Dartmouth, MA 02747
(508) 999-6060

293 Bridge St., Suite 324
Springfield, MA 01103
(413) 734-3114

P.O. Box 379
Worcester, MA 01601
(508) 755-2548

Michigan
150 Michigan Ave.
Detroit, MI 48226
(313) 962-7566 (inquiries)
(313) 962-6785 (complaints)

620 Trust Bldg.
Grand Rapids, MI 49503
(616) 774-8236

Minnesota
1745 University Ave.
St. Paul, MN 55104
(612) 646-7700

Mississippi
2917 W. Beach Blvd., #103
Biloxi, MS 39531
(601) 374-2222

105 Fifth St.
Columbus, MS 39701
(601) 327-8594

P.O. Box 390
Jackson, MS 39205-0390
(601) 948-8222

Missouri

306 E. 12th St., Suite 1024
Kansas City, MO 64106
(816) 421-7800

5100 Oakland, Suite 200
St. Louis, MO 63110
(314) 531-3300

205 Park Central East, #509
Springfield, MO 65806
(417) 862-9231

Nebraska

719 N. 48th St.
Lincoln, NE 68504
(402) 467-5261

1613 Farnam St.
Omaha, NE 68102
(402) 346-3033

Nevada

1022 E. Sahara Ave.
Las Vegas, NV 89104
(702) 735-6900/1969

P.O. Box 21269
Reno, NV 89505
(702) 322-0657

New Hampshire

410 S. Main St.
Concord, NH 03301
(603) 224-1991
(800) 852-3757 (toll free in
NH)

New Jersey

34 Park Pl.
Newark, NJ 07102
(201) 642-INFO

Two Forest Ave.
Paramus, NJ 07652
(201) 845-4044

1721 Rte. #37 East
Toms River, NJ 08753
(201) 270-5577

1700 Whitehorse—Hamilton
Square Rd., Suite D5
Trenton, NJ 08690
(609) 588-0808 (Mercer
County)
(201) 536-6306 (Monmouth
County)
(201) 329-6855 (Middlesex,
Somerset, and Hunterdon
counties)

New Mexico

4600-A Montgomery NE,
#200
Albuquerque, NM 87109
(505) 884-0500
(800) 445-1461 (toll free in
NM)

308 N. Locke
Farmington, NM 87401
(505) 326-6501

2407 W. Picacho, Suite B-2
Las Cruces, NM 88005
(505) 524-3130

1210 Luisa St., Suite 5
Santa Fe, NM 87502
(505) 988-3648

New York

346 Delaware Ave.
Buffalo, NY 14202
(716) 856-7180

266 Main St.
Farmingdale, NY 11735
(516) 420-0500

257 Park Ave. South
New York, NY 10010
(212) 533-6200

1122 Sibley Tower
Rochester, NY 14604
(716) 546-6776

100 University Bldg.
Syracuse, NY 13202
(315) 479-6635

120 E. Main St.
Wappinger Falls, NY 12590
(914) 297-6550

30 Glenn St.
White Plains, NY 10603
(914) 428-1230/1231

North Carolina
801 BBB&T Bldg.
Asheville, NC 28801
(704) 253-2392

1130 E. 3rd St., Suite 400
Charlotte, NC 28204
(704) 332-7151
(800) 532-0477 (toll free in
NC)

3608 W. Friendly Ave.
Greensboro, NC 27410
(919) 852-4240/4241/4242

P.O. Box 1882
Hickory, NC 28603
(704) 464-0372

3120 Poplarwood Dr., Suite
101
Raleigh, NC 27604-1080
(919) 872-9240

2110 Cloverdale Ave., #2-B
Winston-Salem, NC 27103
(919) 725-8348

Ohio
P.O. Box 80596
Akron, OH 44308
(216) 253-4590

1434 Cleveland Ave. NW
Canton, OH 44703
(216) 454-9401

898 Walnut St.
Cincinnati, OH 45202
(513) 421-3015

2217 E. 9th St., Suite 200
Cleveland, OH 44115
(216) 241-7678

527 S. High St.
Columbus, OH 43215
(614) 221-6336

40 W. Fourth St., Suite 280
Dayton, OH 45402
(513) 222-5825
(800) 521-8357 (toll free in
OH)

P.O. Box 269
Lima, OH 45802
(419) 223-7010

P.O. Box 1706
Mansfield, OH 44910
(419) 522-1700

425 Jefferson Ave., Suite 909
Toledo, OH 43604
(419) 241-6276

345 N. Market
Wooster, OH 44691
(216) 263-6444

P.O. Box 1495
Youngstown, OH 44501
(216) 744-3111

Oklahoma
17 S. Dewey
Oklahoma City, OK 73102
(405) 239-6860 (inquiries)
(405) 239-6081 (inquiries)
(405) 239-6083 (complaints)

6711 S. Yale, Suite 230
Tulsa, OK 71436
(918) 492-1266

Oregon
601 S.W. Alder St., Suite 615
Portland, OR 97205
(503) 226-3981

Pennsylvania
528 N. New St.
Bethlehem, PA 18018
(215) 866-8780

6 Marion Court
Lancaster, PA 17602
(717) 291-1151
(717) 232-2800 (Harrisburg)
(717) 846-2700 (York County)

P.O. Box 2297
Philadelphia, PA 19103
(215) 496-1000

610 Smithfield St.
Pittsburgh, PA 15222
(412) 456-2700

P.O. Box 993
Scranton, PA 18501
(717) 342-9129

Puerto Rico
G.P.O. Box 70212
San Juan, PR 00936
(809) 756-5400

Rhode Island
Bureau Park
P.O. Box 1300
Warwick, RI 02887-1300
(401) 785-1212 (inquiries)
(401) 785-1213 (complaints)

South Carolina
1830 Bull St.
Columbia, SC 29201
(803) 254-2525

311 Pettigru St.
Greenville, SC 29601
(803) 242-5052

P.O. Box 8603
Myrtle Beach, SC 29578-8603
(803) 448-6100

Tennessee
P.O. Box 1176 TCAS
Blountville, TN 37617
(615) 323-6311

1010 Market St., Suite 200
Chattanooga, TN 37402
(615) 266-6144
(615) 479-6096 (Bradley
   County)
(615) 266-6144 (Whitfield and
   Murray counties)

P.O. 10327
Knoxville, TN 37939-0327
(615) 522-2552/2130/2139

P.O. Box 41406
Memphis, TN 38174-1406
(901) 272-9641

One Commerce Pl., Suite 1830
Nashville, TN 37239
(615) 254-5872

Texas
3300 S. 14th St., Suite 307
Abilene, TX 79605
(915) 691-1533

P.O. Box 1905
Amarillo, TX 79106
(806) 358-6222

1005 American Plaza
Austin, TX 78701
(512) 476-1616

P.O. Box 2988
Beaumont, TX 77704
(409) 835-5348

202 Varisco Bldg.
Bryan, TX 77801
(409) 823-8148/8149

4535 S. Padre Island Dr.
Corpus Christi, TX 78411
(512) 854-2892

2001 Bryan St., Suite 850
Dallas, TX 75201
(214) 220-2000

1910 East Yandell
El Paso, TX 79903
(915) 545-1212/1264

106 West Fifth St.
Fort Worth, TX 76102
(817) 332-7585

2707 N. Loop West, Suite 900
Houston, TX 77008
(713) 868-9500

P.O. Box 1178
Lubbock, TX 79401
(806) 763-0459

P.O. Box 60206
Midland, TX 79711
(915) 563-1880
(800) 592-4433 (toll free in
   TX)

P.O. Box 3366
San Angelo, TX 76902
(915) 653-2318

1800 Northeast Loop 410,
   #400
San Antonio, TX 78217
(512) 828-9441

P.O. Box 6652
Tyler, TX 75711-6652
(214) 581-5704

P.O. Box 7203
Waco, TX 76714-7203
(817) 772-7530

P.O. Box 69
Weslaco, TX 78596
(512) 968-3678

1106 Brook Ave.
Wichita Falls, TX 76301
(817) 723-5526

Utah
385 24th St., Suite 717
Ogden, UT 84401
(801) 399-4701

1588 S. Main
Salt Lake City, UT 84115
(801) 487-4656
(801) 377-2611 (Provo)

Virginia
3608 Tidewater Dr.
Norfolk, VA 23509
(804) 627-5651

701 E. Franklin, Suite 712
Richmond, VA 23219
(804) 648-0016

121 W. Campbell Ave. SW
Roanoke, VA 24011
(703) 342-3455

Washington
127 W. Canal Dr.
Kennewick, WA 99336
(509) 582-0222

2200 Sixth Ave., Suite 828
Seattle, WA 98121-1857
(206) 448-8888

S. 176 Stevens St.
Spokane, WA 99204
(509) 747-1155

P.O. Box 1274
Tacoma, WA 98401
(206) 383-5561

P.O. Box 1584
Yakima, WA 98907
(509) 248-1326

Wisconsin

740 N. Plankinton Ave.
Milwaukee, WI 53202
(414) 273-1600 (inquiries)
(414) 273-0123 (complaints)

Wyoming

BBB/Idaho Falls (Lincoln Park
  and Teton counties)
(208) 523-9754

BBB/Fort Collins (all other
  Wyoming counties)
(800) 873-3222 (toll free)

APPENDIX

III

BANKING RESOURCES

State Banking Authorities

State banking authorities make and enforce the rules that govern state-chartered banks. Most do not handle complaints against finance companies or retail store creditors, but some do. Many will answer basic questions about banking and credit laws, and, if they cannot handle your complaint, will refer you to an agency that can.

If you have a complaint about the way you were treated by a bank, file it with your state's banking authority. Complaints filed with these agencies typically include those about discrimination, illegal rates of interest, and failure to make required disclosures. The information in this appendix is excerpted from the 1990 edition of the *Consumer's Resource Handbook,* published by the U.S. Office of Consumer Affairs.

Alabama
Superintendent of Banks
166 Commerce St., 3rd Floor
Montgomery, AL 36130
(205) 261-3452

Alaska
Director of Banking and Securities
Pouch D
Juneau, AK 99811
(907) 465-2521

Arizona
Superintendent of Banks
3225 N. Central, Suite 815
Phoenix, AZ 85012
(602) 255-4421

Arkansas
Bank Commissioner
323 Center St., Suite 500
Little Rock, AR 72201
(501) 371-1117

California
Superintendent of Banks
235 Montgomery St., Suite 750
San Francisco, CA 94104
(415) 557-3535

Colorado
State Bank Commissioner
First West Plaza, Suite 700
303 W. Colfax
Denver, CO 80204
(303) 866-3131

Connecticut
Banking Commissioner
44 Capitol Ave.
Hartford, CT 06106
(203) 566-4560

Delaware
State Bank Commissioner
P.O. Box 1401
Dover, DE 19903
(302) 736-4235

District of Columbia
Superintendent of Banking and
    Financial Institutions
1350 Pennsylvania Ave. NW., Room
    401
Washington, DC 20004
(202) 727-6365

Florida
State Comptroller
State Capitol Bldg.

Tallahassee, FL 32399
(904) 488-0370

Georgia
Commissioner of Banking and
    Finance
2990 Brandywine Rd., Suite 200
Atlanta, GA 30341
(404) 393-7330

Hawaii
Bank Examiner
P.O. Box 541
Honolulu, HI 96809
(808) 548-7505

Idaho
Director, Department of Finance
700 W. State St., 2nd Floor
Boise, ID 83720
(208) 334-3319

Illinois
Commissioner of Banks and Trust
    Companies
119 S. 5th St., Room 400
Springfield, IL 62701
(217) 785-2837

Indiana
Director, Department of Financial
    Institutions
Indiana State Office Bldg., Room
    1024
Indianapolis, IN 46204
(317) 232-3955

Iowa
Superintendent of Banking
200 E. Grand, Suite 300
Des Moines, IA 50309
(515) 281-4014

Kansas
State Bank Commissioner
700 Jackson St., Suite 300
Topeka, KS 66603
(913) 296-2266

Kentucky
Commissioner of Banking and
 Securities
911 Leawood Dr.
Frankfort, KY 40601
(502) 564-3390

Louisiana
Commissioner of Financial
 Institutions
P.O. Box 94095
Baton Rouge, LA 70804
(504) 925-4660

Maine
Superintendent of Banking
State House Station, #36
Augusta, ME 04333
(207) 289-3231

Maryland
Bank Commissioner
34 Market Pl.
Baltimore, MD 21202
(301) 333-6262

Massachusetts
Commissioner of Banks
100 Cambridge St.
Boston, MA 02202
(617) 727-3120

Michigan
Commissioner, Financial Institutions
 Bureau
P.O. Box 30224
Lansing, MI 48909
(517) 373-3460

Minnesota
Deputy Commissioner of Commerce
500 Metro Square Bldg., 5th Floor
St. Paul, MN 55101
(612) 296-2135

Mississippi
Commissioner, Department of
 Banking and Consumer Finance

P.O. Box 731
Jackson, MS 39205
(601) 359-1031

Missouri
Commissioner of Finance
P.O. Box 716
Jefferson City, MO 65102
(314) 751-3397

Montana
Commissioner of Financial
 Institutions
1424—9th Ave.
Helena, MT 59620
(406) 444-2091

Nebraska
Director of Banking and Finance
301 Centennial Mall S.
Lincoln, NE 68509
(402) 471-2171

Nevada
Commissioner of Financial
 Institutions
406 E. 2nd St.
Carson City, NV 89710
(702) 885-4260

New Hampshire
Bank Commissioner
45 S. Main St.
Concord, NH 03301
(603) 271-3561

New Jersey
Commissioner of Banking
36 W. State St.
Trenton, NJ 08625
(609) 292-3420

New Mexico
Director, Financial Institutions
 Division
Bataan Memorial Bldg., Room 137
Santa Fe, NM 87503
(505) 827-7740

New York
Superintendent of Banks
2 Rector St.
New York, NY 10006
(212) 618-6642

North Carolina
Commissioner of Banks
P.O. Box 29512
Raleigh, NC 27626
(919) 733-3016

North Dakota
Commissioner of Banking and
    Financial Institutions
State Capitol, Room 1301
Bismarck, ND 58505
(701) 224-2256

Ohio
Superintendent of Banks
2 Nationwide Plaza
Columbus, OH 43215
(614) 466-2932

Oklahoma
Bank Commissioner
Malco Bldg.
4100 N. Lincoln Blvd.
Oklahoma City, OK 73105
(405) 521-2783

Oregon
Deputy Administrator, Financial
    Institutions Division
280 Court St. NE
Salem, OR 97310
(503) 378-4140

Pennsylvania
Secretary of Banking
333 Market St., 16th Floor
Harrisburg, PA 17101
(717) 787-6991

Puerto Rico
Commissioner of Banking
P.O. Box S4515

San Juan, PR 00905
(809) 721-5242

Rhode Island
Assistant Director, Banking and
    Securities
100 N. Main St.
Providence, RI 02903
(401) 277-2405

South Carolina
Commissioner of Banking
1026 Sumter St., Room 217
Columbia, SC 29201
(803) 734-1050

South Dakota
Director of Banking and Finance
State Capitol Bldg.
Pierre, SD 57501
(605) 773-2236

Tennessee
Commissioner of Financial
    Institutions
John Sevier Bldg., 4th Floor
Nashville, TN 37219
(615) 741-2236

Texas
Banking Commissioner
2601 N. Lamar
Austin, TX 78705
(512) 479-1200

Utah
Commissioner of Financial
    Institutions
P.O. Box 89
Salt Lake City, UT 84110
(801) 530-6502

Vermont
Commissioner of Banking and
    Insurance
State Office Bldg.
Montpelier, VT 05602
(802) 828-3301

Virgin Islands
Chair, Banking Board
Kongens Garden, #18
P.O. Box 450
St. Thomas, VI 00801
(809) 774-2991

Virginia
Commissioner of Financial
  Institutions
P.O. Box 2-AE
Richmond, VA 23205
(804) 786-3657

Washington
Supervisor of Banking
General Administration Bldg., Room
  219
Olympia, WA 98504
(206) 753-6520

West Virginia
Deputy Commissioner of Banking
State Office Bldg. 3, Suite 311
Charleston, WV 25305
(304) 348-2294

Wisconsin
Commissioner of Banking
P.O. Box 7876
Madison, WI 53707
(608) 266-1621

Wyoming
State Examiner
Herschler Bldg., 4th Floor
Cheyenne, WY 82002
(307) 777-6600

Federal Trade Commission

Contact the Federal Trade Commission (FTC) to file a complaint
of federal credit law violation by a mortgage banker, finance company, or any other nonbank creditor. The FTC has 10 regional
offices, listed below. Call the one nearest you for instructions on
how to file a complaint. Complaints filed with the FTC typically
involve failure by a lender to make required disclosures, discrimination, and illegal terms in a credit contract, such as a waiver of
consumers' rights. The FTC also publishes free pamphlets (in Spanish and English) on the credit laws it enforces.

The FTC investigates appropriate complaints and imposes fines,
but these fines are not used to compensate the aggrieved consumers.
When a settlement can't be reached, the FTC can sue. For more
information about the FTC, see Chapter 6.

FTC National Headquarters
6th and Pennsylvania Aves. NW
Washington, DC 20580
(202) 326-2222

FTC Regional Offices
1718 Peachtree St. NW
Atlanta, GA 30367
(405) 347-4836

10 Causeway St.
Boston, MA 02222
(617) 565-7240

55 E. Monroe St.
Chicago, IL 60603
(312) 353-4423

118 St. Clair Ave.
Cleveland, OH 44114
(216) 522-4210

8303 Elmbrook Dr.
Dallas, TX 75247
(214) 767-7050

1405 Curtis St.
Denver, CO 80202
(303) 844-2271

11000 Wilshire Blvd.
Los Angeles, CA 90024
(213) 209-7890

26 Federal Plaza
New York, NY 10278
(212) 264-1207

901 Market St.
San Francisco, CA 94103
(415) 995-5220

915 Second Ave.
Seattle, WA 98174
(206) 442-4655

Federal Reserve Offices

Your regional Federal Reserve Bank accepts complaints of federal credit law violations by any bank or other financial institution. It refers these complaints within 15 days to the appropriate agency. Although the Federal Reserve Bank's jurisdiction is limited to state-chartered banks that are members of the Federal Reserve System, its enforcement powers extend beyond these institutions, and it can deal with all complaints. Following are the addresses and telephone numbers of the Federal Reserve Bank's national headquarters and its regional offices.

Federal Reserve National Headquarters
Board of Governors of the Federal Reserve System
20th and C Sts. NW
Washington, DC 20551
(202) 452-3000

Federal Reserve Regional Offices
104 Marietta St. NW
Atlanta, GA 30303
(404) 521-8500

600 Atlantic Ave.
Boston, MA 02106
(617) 973-3000

230 S. LaSalle St.
Chicago, IL 60690
(312) 322-5322

1455 E. Sixth St.
Cleveland, OH 44114
(216) 579-2000

400 S. Akard St.
Dallas, TX 75202
(214) 651-6111

925 Grand Ave.
Kansas City, MO 64198
(816) 881-2000

250 Marquette Ave.
Minneapolis, MN 55480
(612) 340-2345

33 Liberty St.
New York, NY 10045
(212) 720-5000

10 Independence Mall
Philadelphia, PA 19106
(215) 574-6000

701 E. Byrd St.
Richmond, VA 23219
(804) 697-8000

101 Market St.
San Francisco, CA 94105
(415) 974-2000

411 Locust St.
St. Louis, MO 63102
(314) 444-8444

APPENDIX

IV

REAL ESTATE
INSPECTION LIST

The U.S. Department of Housing and Urban Development (HUD) (see Appendix II) can direct you to recommended inspectors in your area or supply you with its own printed materials. Whether you decide to hire a professional inspector or not, you should make a personal inspection, making sure to check the following:

Outside

Foundation: Look for holes, cracking, unevenness.

Brickwork: Look for cracks, loose or missing mortar.

Siding: Look for loose, missing, lifting or warping pieces.

Paint: Look for peeling, chipping, blistering, and so on.

Entrance: Examine steps, handrails, posts, and porch flooring for loose or unsafe features.

Windows: Look for cracked or broken glass, holes in screens. Check caulking for cracks and dried or falling-out sections. Are window frames warped, peeling or cracking?

Storm windows: Are they complete? Are they secure? Is the caulking fresh and complete?

Roof: Look for worn or bald spots; ask how old the roof is and whether it is under warranty. Check for missing shingles, tiles or slate, cracked or dried tar. Look for dampness and signs of water damage inside, especially near worn spots.

Gutters: Check for missing sections, gaps, holes in joints, signs of leaks.

Chimney: Look for tilting, loose or missing bricks.

Fences, walls: Look for holes, loose or missing sections, rotted posts.

Garage: Check doors, roof, siding and windows as above.

Driveway: Look for potholes and cracked pavement.

Landscaping: Locate the property line. Are trees, shrubbery and lawn in good shape?

Drainage: Will rain or snow flow away from the house? Do muddy areas indicate possible problems with septic tanks, underground leaks of water, sewage? (Visit during a rain storm if possible.)

Inside

Structure: Jump up and down on the floors. Does the house feel solid? Check support posts and floor supports in basement for looseness, bending, dampness, rot, termites.

Floors: Check for levelness, bowing, movement when you walk.

Walls: Check for major cracks, loose or falling plaster, leaks, stains.

Stairs: Look for loose treads, handrails, posts.

Plumbing: Check pipes and sewer lines for leaks and rust. Flush all toilets. Turn faucets on and off to test waterpressure. Look for clogged or sluggish drains, dripping faucets.

Heating: Is the house heated by warm air, hot water, electricity or steam? What type of fuel is used? How much does it cost to heat? Ask for last year's fuel bills. When was the system last serviced?

Hot water heater: Check for leaks and rust. What is the capacity or "recovery rate?" (This should be at least thirty gallons for a family of four.) How old is the water heater?

Electricity: Does the "service box" use fuses or circuit breakers? Does it look old or new? Look for exposed wires and signs of wear.

Cooling: Is there a cooling and air-conditioning system? What is its age and condition? Is it under warranty? How much did it cost to operate last year? Ask for last year's utility bills.

Storage: Does the home have enough closets? Are they in appropriate locations, including near front and rear entrances? Can you use other areas or rooms for storage?

Windows: Open and close each one. Do they operate easily? Check for broken sash cords, loose or warped frames, locks and latches.

Doors: Do they close properly? Are the locks sound?

Layout: Are the rooms conveniently located? What are the traffic patterns between bedrooms and bathrooms, kitchen and dining area, living room and bathrooms?

Kitchen: What appliances are included (stove, refrigerator, dishwasher, garbage disposal)? Check their age, workability. Is there enough cabinet and counter space? Enough electrical outlets? Leaks under the sink?

Bathrooms: Are there enough for your immediate and anticipated needs? Check for cracks in tiles and leaks. How long does it take to get hot water? Is there a window or fan for proper ventilation?

Living room: Is it large enough for your immediate and anticipated needs? Is there a fireplace? If so, does the damper work? Check for signs of discoloration of walls and fabrics from smoke. Has the chimney been cleaned recently?

Bedrooms: How many are there? Are they large enough for your present and anticipated needs? Does each have a window to the outside (a requirement in some states or countries)? Does each have a large enough closet?

Basement: Check for leaks, dampness, flooding. Is there enough lighting?

Attic: Look for signs of roof leaks. Check insulation. How much is there? Look for signs of nesting by birds, squirrels, other rodents.

APPENDIX

V

HUD OFFICES

The Department of Housing and Urban Development (HUD) is the agency responsible for administering federal programs related to the nation's housing needs. The Fair Housing Office administers the program authorized by the Civil Rights Act of 1968 and is chiefly concerned with housing problems of lower-income and minority groups. The Office of Neighborhoods protects consumer interests in all housing and community development activities and enforces the laws regarding interstate land sales, mobile home safety standards and real estate settlement procedures. For information, publications, advice, referrals or complaints about local housing practices, contact the regional office nearest you.

Region I
(Connecticut, Maine, Massachusetts, New Hampshire, Rhode Island, Vermont)
Department of Housing and Urban Development
10 Causeway St., Room 375
Boston, MA 02222
(617) 565-5234

Region II
(New Jersey, New York, Puerto Rico, Virgin Islands)
Department of Housing and Urban Development
26 Federal Plaza
New York, NY 10287
(212) 264-8053

Region III
(Delaware, Maryland, Pennsylvania,
  Virginia, West Virginia)
Department of Housing and Urban
  Development
Liberty Square Bldg.
105 S. 7th St.
Philadelphia, PA 19106
(215) 597-2560

Region IV
(Alabama, Florida, Georgia, Kentucky,
  Mississippi, North Carolina, South
  Carolina, Tennessee)
Department of Housing and Urban
  Development
Richard B. Russell Federal Building
75 Spring St. SW
Atlanta, GA 30303
(404) 331-5136

Region V
(Illinois, Indiana, Michigan, Min-
  nesota, Ohio, Wisconsin)
Department of Housing and Urban
  Development
526 W. Jackson Blvd.
Chicago, IL 60606
(312) 353-5680

Region VI
(Arkansas, Louisiana, New Mexico,
  Oklahoma, Texas)
Department of Housing and Urban
  Development
1600 Throckmorton
Fort Worth, TX 76113
(817) 885-5401

Region VII
(Iowa, Kansas, Missouri, Nebraska)

Department of Housing and Urban
  Development
Professional Building
1103 Grand Ave.
Kansas City, MO 64106
(816) 374-6432

Region VIII
(Colorado, Montana, North Dakota,
  South Dakota, Utah, Wyoming)
Department of Housing and Urban
  Development
Executive Tower Building
1405 Curtis St.
Denver, CO 80202
(303) 837-4513

Region IX
(Arizona, California, Guam, Hawaii,
  Nevada)
Department of Housing and Urban
  Development
450 Golden Gate Ave.
San Francisco, CA 94102
(415) 556-4752

Region X
(Alaska, Idaho, Oregon, Washington)
Department of Housing and Urban
  Development
Arcade Plaza Building
1321 Second Ave.
Seattle, WA 98101
(206) 442-5414

For General Information
Office of Public Affairs
U.S. Department of Housing and
  Urban Development
451 7th St. SW
Washington, DC 20410
(202) 755-5111

APPENDIX

VI

STATE RULES

This appendix gives some of the special rules that apply to the small claims courts of all fifty states, the District of Columbia, Puerto Rico and the Virgin Islands. All the terms and concepts below are explained in either the text or the glossary. Filing fees are not listed because they vary greatly and change frequently.

All data, except "dollar limits," were compiled in October 1989. The data on dollar limits were compiled in December 1989. Because court rules may change at any time, always check with the clerk of the small claims court to verify the accuracy of the information given for your state.

Additional information on small claims court rules is found under each state's "Special Provisions" section. If that section for your state does not cover a particular rule (for example, the right to a jury trial), you should check with your small claims clerk. Where there is no small claims court or section in a state, check with the clerk of the court named.

Alabama   Small Claims (District Court)

Statutes: Code of Alabama 1986 (amendments to 1989), Title 12, Ch. 12, Sections 31, 70–71; Alabama Rules of Courts; Small Claims Rules.

Dollar Limit: $1,000.

Where to Sue: Where defendant resides or injury occurred. Corporation resides where it does business.

Service: Certified mail, sheriff or court-approved adult.

Hearing Date: Set by court.

Attorneys: Allowed; required for assignees.

Transfer: No provision.

Appeals: By either side for new trial; to Circuit Court within 14 days.

Special Provisions: Limited equitable relief available. Defendant must answer within 14 days or lose by default.

Alaska   Small Claims (District Court)

Statutes: Alaska Statutes 1988 (amendments to 1989), Title 22, Ch. 15, Section 040; District Court Rules of Civil Procedure, Rules 18–22. Alaska Rules of Civil Procedure, Rule 4.

Dollar Limit: $5,000.

Where to Sue: Court nearest defendant's residence or place of employment, or where injury occurred.

Service: Certified or registered mail (binding on defendant who refuses to accept) or peace officer.

Hearing Date: Not less than 15 days from service.

Attorneys: Allowed; required for assignees.

Transfer: Check with clerk of court.

Appeals: By either side for review of law, not facts; to Superior Court within 30 days.

Special Provisions: Equitable relief available. Defendant must file written answer within 20 days of service or lose by default. Arbitration may be ordered in counterclaims for less than $3,000. Court may order installment payments.

Arizona   Small Claims Division (Justice Court)

Statutes: Arizona Revised Statutes 1975 (amendments to 1988), Sections 22.501–523, 22.202 a–e.

Dollar Limit: $1,000.

Where to Sue: Where defendant resides. Intentional torts: where act occurred. To recover personal property: where property is. Contracts: where performance expected. Nonresident defendants: where plaintiff resides. Transient defendants: where found.

Service: Certified or registered mail, sheriff, deputy or court-approved adult.

Hearing Date: Set by court; within 60 days of the filing of the answer.

Attorneys: Not allowed unless both sides agree in writing.

Transfer: If either side requests or if defendant counterclaims for more than $500, case tried under regular civil procedure of court.

Appeals: Not allowed.

Special Provisions: Limited equitable relief available. Defendant must answer within 20 days or lose by default. No discovery. No jury trial. No libel or slander, forcible entry or unlawful detainer, specific performance, prejudgment remedies, injunctions, cases against the state or cases involving ownership of real estate. Right to sue may not be transferred.

Arkansas   Small Claims Division (Municipal Court)

Statutes: Arkansas Code of 1987 (annotated) (amendments to 1989), Title 16.17, Sections 201–210, 218, 601–614; Inferior Court Rules; Constitutions; Arkansas Constitution Amendment 64.

Dollar Limit: $3,000.

Where to Sue: Where defendant resides or injury occurred. Contracts: where performance expected. Corporation resides where it does business.

Service: Certified mail, sheriff or court-approved adult.

Hearing Date: 30–45 days after summons issued.

Attorneys: Not allowed.

Transfer: If attorney appears or if defendant files compulsory counterclaim for more than $3,000, case tried under regular civil procedure of Municipal Court.

Appeals: By either side for new trial; to Circuit Court within 30 days.

Special Provisions: Collection agents and commercial lenders may not sue. Corporations limited to 12 claims a year. Right to sue may not be transferred.

California   Small Claims Division (Justice or Municipal Court)

Statutes: Annotated California Codes, Code of Civil Procedure 1982 (amendments to 1989), Sections 116–117.22.

Dollar Limit: $2,000; $2,500 after Jan. 1, 1991.

Where to Sue: Where defendant resides or injury occurred. Contracts: where performance expected. Consumer contracts: where signed. Corporation resides where it does business.

Service: Certified or registered mail, sheriff or court-approved adult.

Hearing Date: Defendant in county: 10–40 days after summons issued. Defendant outside county: 30–70 days after summons issued.

Attorneys: Not allowed unless attorney represents self.

Transfer: If defendant counterclaims for more than $2,000, counterclaim removed to higher court if judge permits.

Appeals: By defendant only for new trial; to Superior Court within 20 days.

Special Provisions: Equitable relief available. Right to sue may not be transferred. Judge may determine payment schedule. Interpreters available. Small claims advisor available at no cost. Court may order arbitration.

Colorado   Small Claims Division (County Court)

Statutes: Colorado Revised Statutes 1973 (amendments to 1987), Sections 13.6.-401–413; Colorado Rules of Civil Procedure for Small Claims Courts, Rules 501–521.

Dollar Limit: $2,000.

Where to Sue: Where defendant resides or injury occurred. Contracts: for sale of goods, where sold; for debt or installment purchases of personal or household goods, where contract signed; for services, where services were to be performed. Nonresident defendants: where defendant found or plaintiff resides.

Service: Certified mail, sheriff, deputy or court-approved disinterested adult.

Hearing Date: Set by court; at least 21 days after summons issued.

Attorneys: Not allowed unless attorney represents self or as full-time employee of partnership or corporation involved in the case. If attorney appears, other side may also have attorney.

Transfer: If defendant counterclaims for more than $2,000 or wants to use an attorney, case tried under regular civil procedure of court.

Appeals: By either side for review of law, not facts; to District Court within 15 days.

Special Provisions: No equitable relief except nullification of contracts. No jury trial. No libel or slander, forcible entry or detainer, recovery of personal property, specific performance, prejudgment attachment, injunctions or traffic cases. Right to sue may not be transferred. No discovery. Limit of 2 claims a month per plaintiff or 18 claims a year. Referee may be appointed.

Connecticut   Small Claims (Superior Court)

Statutes: Connecticut General Statutes Annotated 1985 (amendments to 1989), Title 51, Section 15; Title 52, Sections 549a–d.

Dollar Limit: $2,000.

Where to Sue: Where defendant resides, does business or where injury occurred. Contracts: where breach occurred or obligation incurred. Landlord-tenant: where premises are located.

Service: Registered or certified mail or sheriff.

Hearing Date: Set by court.

Attorneys: Allowed.

Transfer: If defendant requests and court approves, to regular civil procedure of Superior Court.

Appeals: Not allowed.

Special Provisions: No equitable relief. No libel or slander. Litigants may submit matter to county commissioner for binding decision.

Delaware   No small claims procedure (Justice of the Peace)

Statutes: Delaware Code Annotated 1974 (amendments to 1988), Title 10, Sections 9301–9590.

Dollar Limit: $2,500.

Where to Sue: Any county.

Service: Certified mail, sheriff, deputy or constable.

Hearing Date: Set by court.

Attorneys: Allowed.

Transfer: No provision.

Appeals: By either side for new trial in cases involving more than $5; to Superior Court within 15 days.

Special Provisions: Jury trial available.

District of Columbia Small Claims and Conciliation Branch (Superior Court)

Statutes: District of Columbia Code 1981 (amendments to 1989), Title 11, Sections 1301–1323; Title 16, Sections 3901–3910; Rules for Small Claims and Conciliation.

Dollar Limit: $2,000.

Where to Sue: Only one court in District.

Service: Certified or registered mail, U.S. marshal or court-approved disinterested adult.

Hearing Date: 5–15 days from filing of complaint.

Attorneys: Allowed; required for corporations.

Transfer: If either side requests jury trial, if defendant files counterclaim affecting ownership of real estate, or if court determines interest of justice requires it, case tried under regular civil procedure of court.

Appeals: By either side for review of law, not facts; to Court of Appeals within 3 days.

Special Provisions: No equitable relief. Limited discovery available with court permission. Court may refer cases to arbitration or mediation. Court may order installment payments. Wednesday evening and Saturday morning office hours available.

Florida Summary Procedure (County Court)

Statutes: Florida Rules of Court (1989): Small Claims Rules, Rules 7.010–7.341; Florida Statute Annotated (amendments to 1989), Section 51.011.

Dollar Limit: $2,500.

Where to Sue: Where defendant resides or injury occurred. Contracts: where agreed, if contract provides; where unsecured note was signed or where maker resides; where breach occurred. To recover property: where property is. U.S. corporation resides where it maintains office for customary business. Foreign corporation resides where it has an agent.

Service: Registered mail (Florida residents only), peace officer or court-approved disinterested adult.

Hearing Date: Within 60 days after pretrial conference set by the court.

Attorneys: Allowed; required for collection agents and assignees.

Transfer: If defendant counterclaims for more than $2,500, case tried under regular civil procedure of County Court.

Appeals: By either side for review of law, not facts; to circuit court within 30 days.

Special Provisions: Equitable relief available. Jury trial available. Party represented by attorney is subject to discovery.

Georgia No small claims procedure (Magistrate Court)

Statutes: Georgia Code Annotated 1985 (amendments to 1989), Title 15, Sections 10.1, 10.20, 10.40–137.

Dollar Limit: $5,000.

Where to Sue: Where defendant resides.

Service: Constable or court-approved adult.

Hearing Date: Set by court.

Attorneys: Allowed.

Transfer: If defendant counterclaims for more than $5,000, case tried in appropriate court depending on amount.

Appeals: By either side for new trial; to Superior Court within 30 days.

Special Provisions: Equitable relief available. Defendant must answer within 30 days or lose by default. No jury trial. Court may order installment payments.

Hawaii   Small Claims Division (District Court)

Statutes: Hawaii Revised Statutes 1985 (amendments to 1988), Title 34, Sections 633.27–36.

Dollar Limit: $2,500. Recovery of leased personal property valued less than $1,500 if rent due is less than $2,500. Security deposit disputes: no limit.

Where to Sue: Where defendant resides or where breach or injury occurred.

Service: Certified or registered mail if defendant resides within circuit. Otherwise, by sheriff, deputy, chief of police or court-appointed process server.

Hearing Date: Set by court.

Attorneys: Allowed, except in landlord-tenant cases. Nonattorney may represent party if no fee is charged.

Transfer: If either side requests jury trial or if defendant counterclaims for more than $5,000 and requests a jury trial, case tried in Circuit Court.

Appeals: Not allowed.

Special Provisions: No equitable relief except in landlord-tenant cases, in which jurisdiction is limited to orders to repair, replace, refund, reform and rescind.

Idaho   Small Claims Department (Magistrate's Division of the District Court)

Statutes: Idaho Code 1985 (amendments to 1989), Title 1, Sections 2301–2315.

Dollar Limit: $2,000.

Where to Sue: Where defendant resides or where breach or injury occurred.

Service: Certified or registered mail, sheriff or court-approved adult.

Hearing Date: Set by court; at least 14 days from service.

Attorneys: Not allowed.

Transfer: No provision.

Appeals: By either side for new trial; within 30 days to an "attorney magistrate."

Special Provisions: No jury trial. Right to sue may not be transferred.

Illinois   Small Claims (Circuit Court)

Statutes: Illinois Annotated Statutes 1985 (amendments to 1989), Ch. 110A, Sections 281–289.

Dollar Limit: $2,500.

Where to Sue: Where defendant resides or injury occurred. Contracts: where performance expected.

Service: Registered mail (if defendant resides within county of suit), sheriff or court-approved adult.

Hearing Date: Within 40 days after summons issued.

Attorneys: Allowed; required for corporations.

Transfer: No provision.

Appeals: By either side for review of law, not facts; to Appellate Court within 30 days.

Special Provisions: Cook County has a special *pro se* branch for cases involving less than $1,000. Attorneys not allowed in *pro se* branch. Jury trial available at request of defendant in Cook County and to either side elsewhere. Court may order installment payments. Court may order arbitration.

Indiana   Small Claims Division (Circuit Court)

Statutes: West's Annotated Indiana Code 1983 (amendments to 1988), Title 33, Sections 5-1 to 5-7, 11.6-1-1 to 11.6-1-7, 11.6-4-1 to 11.6-9-5; Indiana Practice; Rules of Procedure (Annotated).

Dollar Limit: $3,000.

Where to Sue: Where defendant resides or injury occurred. Contracts: where obligation incurred or performance expected.

Service: Registered mail; if that fails, sheriff or peace officer.

Hearing Date: Set by court.

Attorneys: Allowed.

Transfer: If defendant requests jury trial, case tried under regular civil procedure of appropriate court.

Appeals: By either side for review of law, not facts; to Court of Appeals within 20 days.

Special Provisions: No equitable relief. No jury trial. Defendant must file written answer within time set by court or lose by default. Court may order installment payments. Evening sessions available.

Iowa   Small Claims (District Court)

Statutes: Iowa Code Annotated 1964 (amendments to 1989), Sections 631.1–17 and Appendix.

Dollar Limit: $2,000.

Where to Sue: Where defendant resides or injury occurred. Contracts: where obligation incurred. Negotiable instruments: where issuer resides. Nonresident defendants: where found. Corporation resides where it has an office or agent.

Service: Certified or registered mail, peace officer or court-approved disinterested adult.

Hearing Date: Defendant must appear within 20 days; hearing set within 5–20 days thereafter.

Attorneys: Allowed.

Transfer: If defendant requests jury trial or counterclaims for more than $2,000 and judge permits, case tried under regular civil procedure of court.

Appeals: By either side for review of law, not facts; to District Court within 20 days.

Special Provisions: No equitable relief. No jury trial. Resident defendants have 20 days and nonresidents have 60 days to answer or lose by default. Written pleadings not required. Court may order installment payments.

Kansas   Small Claims (District Court)

Statutes: Kansas Statutes Annotated 1983 (amendments to 1988), Sections 61.-2701–2713.

Dollar Limit: $1,000.

Where to Sue: Where defendant resides or has a place of business or employment. Corporation resides where it transacts business or maintains registered office or resident agent.

Service: Sheriff, deputy, attorney or court-approved adult.

Hearing Date: Set by court.

Attorneys: Not allowed.

Transfer: If defendant counterclaims for more than $1,000 but less than dollar limit of District Court, judge will decide case or allow defendant to transfer to court of competent jurisdiction.

Appeals: By either side for new trial; to District Court within 10 days.

Special Provisions: Limit of 10 claims a year per plaintiff. Right to sue may not be transferred. No discovery. Collection agents may not sue.

Kentucky   Small Claims Division (District Court)

Statutes: Kentucky Revised Statutes 1986 (amendments to 1988), Ch. 24A.200–360.

Dollar Limit: $1,500.

Where to Sue: Where defendant resides or does business.

Service: Certified or registered mail. If that fails, sheriff or constable.

Hearing Date: 20–40 days from service.

Attorneys: Allowed.

Transfer: If defendant counterclaims for more than $1,500 or requests jury trial or at judge's discretion, case tried under regular civil procedure of District Court or Circuit Court.

Appeals: By either side for review of law, not facts; to Circuit Court within 10 days.

Special Provisions: Limited equitable relief available. Limit of 25 claims a year per plaintiff. Collection agents and lenders of money at interest may not sue. No discovery.

Louisiana   Urban: Small Claims Division (City Court); rural: no small claims procedure (Justice of the Peace)

Statutes: Louisiana Statutes Annotated 1968 (amendments to 1989), Sections 13.5200–5211; Code of Civil Procedure 1961 (amendments to 1989), Articles 4831, 4911–4925.

Dollar Limit: $2,000.

Where to Sue: Where defendant resides. Corporation resides where it has an office or business establishment.

Service: City Court: certified mail, sheriff or constable. Justice of the peace: sheriff or constable.

Hearing Date: Set by court.

Attorneys: Allowed.

Transfer: City Court: if defendant counterclaims for more than $2,000, case tried under regular civil procedure of court. Justice of the Peace: no provision.

Appeals: City Court: not allowed. Justice of the Peace: by either side for new trial; to District Court within 15 days.

Special Provisions: City Court: equitable relief available. No jury trial. Case may be referred to arbitration if both sides consent. Court may order installment payments. Justice of the Peace: no equitable relief. Defendant must answer within 10 days or may lose by default. No cases involving ownership of real estate or family law.

Maine   Small Claims (District Court)

Statutes: Maine Revised Statutes Annotated 1964 (amendments to 1989), Title 14, Sections 1901, 7481–7485; Maine Rules of Small Claims Procedure, Rules 1–18.

Dollar Limit: $1,400.

Where to Sue: Where defendant resides or has a place of business or where transaction occurred. Corporate defendants: where agent resides.

Service: Certified or registered mail, sheriff or court-approved adult.

Hearing Date: Set by court.

Attorneys: Allowed.

Transfer: No removal of small claims to Superior Court allowed.

Appeals: By either side; to Superior Court within 10 days. Plaintiff's appeal will review law, not facts. Defendant's will be a new trial.

Special Provisions: No equitable relief except orders to return, reform, refund, repair, or rescind. No jury trial. Court may order mediation. No cases involving ownership of real estate.

Maryland   Small Claims (District Court)

Statutes: Annotated Code of Maryland 1986 (amendments to 1988), Courts and Judicial Proceedings Article, Section 4-405; Maryland Rules of Civil Procedure, Rule 3-701.

Dollar Limit: $2,500.

Where to Sue: Where defendant resides, has regular business or is employed, or where injury occurred. To recover personal property: where property is. Nonresident individual defendants: any county. Nonresident corporate defendants: where plaintiff resides. Corporation resides where principal office is.

Service: Certified mail, sheriff or any adult (may be an attorney for a party).

Hearing Date: Set by court; at least 60 days from filing of complaint, 90 days for out-of-state defendants.

Attorneys: Allowed.

Transfer: If either side requests jury trial, case tried in Circuit Court. If defendant counterclaims for more than $2,500, case tried under regular civil procedure of court.

Appeals: By either side for new trial; to Circuit Court within 30 days.

Special Provisions: No discovery.

Massachusetts   Small Claims (Boston: Municipal Court; elsewhere: District Court)

Statutes: Annotated Laws of Massachusetts 1986 (amendments to 1989), Ch. 218, Sections 21–25.

Dollar Limit: $1,500 (no limit for property damage caused by motor vehicles).

Where to Sue: Where plaintiff or defendant resides or where defendant has regular business or is employed. Landlord-tenant cases: where property is.
Service: Certified or registered mail.
Hearing Date: Set by court.
Attorneys: Allowed.
Transfer: If defendant requests jury trial or in judge's discretion, case tried under regular civil procedure of appropriate court.
Appeals: By defendant only for new trial; to Superior Court within 10 days.
Special Provisions: No equitable relief. No libel or slander cases. Court may refer cases to mediation if both sides agree.

Michigan   Small Claims Division (District Court)
Statutes: Michigan Statutes Annotated 1986 (amendments to 1989–90), Ch. 27A, Sections 8401–8427.
Dollar Limit: $1,500.
Where to Sue: Where defendant resides or where breach or injury occurred.
Service: Certified mail or disinterested adult.
Hearing Date: 15–45 days from service.
Attorneys: Not allowed.
Transfer: If either side requests or defendant counterclaims for more than $1,500, case tried under regular civil procedure of court.
Appeals: If trial was before District Court magistrate, by either side for new trial; to small claims District Court judge within 7 days. Otherwise, not allowed.
Special Provisions: No equitable relief. Right to sue may not be transferred. No libel or slander, intentional torts or fraud cases. No jury trial. Limit of 5 claims a year per plaintiff. Court may refer cases to mediation or arbitration.

Minnesota   Conciliation Court (County Court)
Statutes: Minnesota Statutes Annotated 1971 (amendments to 1989), Section 487.30; Rules for the Conciliation Court, Rules 1.01–1.26.
Dollar Limit: $3,500.
Where to Sue: Where defendant resides. Automobile accident cases: where occurred. Corporation resides where it has office, resident agent or place of business.
Service: First class mail, sheriff, or court-approved adult.
Hearing Date: Set by court.
Attorneys: Not allowed; required for corporations.
Transfer: By either side on jury demand or if defendant counterclaims for more than $3,500, case tried under regular civil procedure of County Court.
Appeals: By either side for new trial; to regular division of County Court within 20 days.
Special Provisions: No cases involving ownership of real estate. No jury trial. No pretrial attachments or garnishments. Court may order installment payments.

Mississippi   No small claims procedure (justice court)
Statutes: Mississippi Code Annotated 1972 (amendments to 1989), Title 11, Ch. 9, Sections 101–143.

Dollar Limit: $1,000.

Where to Sue: Where defendant resides. Nonresident defendants: where breach or injury occurred.

Service: Sheriff or constable.

Hearing Date: Set by court.

Attorneys: Allowed.

Transfer: No provision.

Appeals: By either side for new trial; to Circuit Court within 10 days.

Special Provisions: Jury trial available.

Missouri Small Claims (Circuit Court)

Statutes: Vernon's Annotated Missouri Statutes 1987 (amendments to 1989), Sections 482.300–365; Missouri Rules of Court, Rules of Practice and Procedure in Small Claims Court, Rules 140–155.

Dollar Limit: $1,500.

Where to Sue: Where defendant resides, where breach or injury occurred or where plaintiff resides and defendant is found. Corporation resides where it has office or agent.

Service: Certified mail.

Hearing Date: Set by court.

Attorneys: Allowed.

Transfer: If defendant files compulsory counterclaim for more than $1,000, case tried under regular civil procedure of court, unless both sides agree not to transfer case.

Appeals: By either side for new trial; to regular Circuit Court judge within 10 days.

Special Provisions: No discovery. No jury trial. Right to sue may not be transferred. Limit of 6 claims a year per plaintiff.

Montana Small Claims (Justice or District Court)

Statutes: Montana Code Annotated 1987 (amendments to 1986), Title 25, Ch. 35, Sections 501–807; Title 25, Ch. 34, Sections 101–404.

Dollar Limit: $2,500.

Where to Sue: Where defendant resides. Contracts: where performance expected.

Service: Sheriff or constable.

Hearing Date: District court: 10–30 days from filing of claim. Justice Court: 10–40 days.

Attorneys: Not allowed, unless all sides represented by attorneys.

Transfer: District Court: no provision. Justice Court: if defendant files notice within 10 days of receipt of complaint, case tried under regular civil procedure of court.

Appeals: District Court: by either side for new trial; to regular District Court procedure within 10 days. Justice Court: By either side for review of law, not facts; to District Court within 10 days.

Special Provisions: Jury trial available to defendant unless counterclaim filed. Right to sue may not be transferred. No personal injury or property damage cases. Limit of 10 claims a year per plaintiff.

Nebraska Small Claims (County Court)
Statutes: Revised Statutes of Nebraska 1943 (amendments to 1988), Title 24, Sections 521–527.
Dollar Limit: $1,500.
Where to Sue: Where defendant or agent resides or does business or where breach or injury occurred. Corporation resides where it does business or has agent.
Service: Certified mail or sheriff.
Hearing Date: Set by court.
Attorneys: Not allowed.
Transfer: If defendant requests jury trial or counterclaim for more than $1,500, case tried under regular civil procedure of court.
Appeals: By either side for new trial; to District Court within 30 days.
Special Provisions: Equitable relief available. Right to sue may not be transferred. Limit of 2 claims a week up to 10 claims a year per plaintiff.

Nevada Small Claims (Justice Court)
Statutes: Nevada Revised Statutes Annotated 1986 (amendments to 1989), Title 6, Sections 73.010–060; Justice Court Rules of Civil Procedure, Ch. XII, Rules 88–100.
Dollar Limit: $2,500.
Where to Sue: Where defendant resides. Corporation resides where it does business or maintains an office.
Service: Certified or registered mail, sheriff, constable or court-approved adult.
Hearing Date: Within 90 days from service.
Attorneys: Allowed.
Transfer: No provision.
Appeals: By either side for review of law, not facts; to District Court within 5 days.
Special Provisions: No equitable relief.

New Hampshire Small Claims (District or Municipal Court)
Statutes: New Hampshire Revised Statutes Annotated 1983 (amendments to 1988), Sections 503:1–10.
Dollar Limit: $2,500.
Where to Sue: Where plaintiff or defendant resides. Nonresident defendants: where breach or injury occurred.
Service: Certified mail, sheriff or constable.
Hearing Date: At least 14 days from service.
Attorneys: Allowed.
Transfer: If either party requests jury trial and claim exceeds $500 or if defendant counterclaims for more than $2,500, case tried in Superior Court.
Appeals: By either side for review of law, not facts; to Supreme Court within 30 days.
Special Provisions: No cases involving ownership of real estate. No jury trial.

New Jersey Division of Small Claims (County District Court)
Statutes: New Jersey Statutes Annotated 1987 (amendments to 1989), Title 2A, Ch. 6, Sections 41–44; County District Court Civil Practice Rules, Rule 6:11.
Dollar Limit: $1,000.

Where to Sue: Where defendant resides. Nonresident defendants: where breach or injury occurred.

Service: Certified mail, sheriff, sergeant at arms or court-approved adult.

Hearing Date: Set by court.

Attorneys: Allowed.

Transfer: If defendant requests jury trial or counterclaims for more than $1,000, case tried under regular civil procedure of Civil Part.

Appeals: By either side for review of law, not facts; to Appellate Division of Superior Court within 45 days.

Special Provisions: Only contract, property damage caused by motor vehicles and landlord-tenant security deposit cases. Right to sue may not be transferred.

New Mexico No small claims procedure (Metropolitan Court or Magistrate Court)

Statutes: New Mexico Statutes 1978 (amendments to 1989), Sections 34.8A.1–9 and 35.3.3–6.

Dollar Limit: $5,000.

Where to Sue: Where plaintiff or defendant resides or where breach or injury occurred. Recovery of property: where property is. Corporation resides where it has an office or agent.

Service: Sheriff or court-approved adult.

Hearing Date: Set by court.

Attorneys: Allowed; required for corporations.

Transfer: No provision.

Appeals: By either side for review of law, not facts; to District Court within 15 days.

Special Provisions: Jury trial available.

New York Small Claims (New York City: Civil Court; Nassau, Suffolk Counties: District Court, except 1st District; other cities: City Court; rural: Justice Court)

Statutes: Consolidated Laws of New York Annotated 1969 (amendments to 1989), Uniform District Court Act, Sections 1801–1814; Uniform Justice Court Act, Sections 1801–1814; N.Y.C. Civil Court Act, Sections 1801–1814; Civil Practice Law and Rules, Section 321(a); N.Y.C. Civil Court Rule 2900.33.

Dollar Limit: $2,000.

Where to Sue: Where defendant resides, is employed or maintains a business office.

Service: Certified or registered mail or court-approved adult.

Hearing Date: Set by court.

Attorneys: Allowed; required for most corporations.

Transfer: Within court's discretion to appropriate court.

Appeals: By defendant only for review of law, not facts, or by plaintiff if "substantial justice" was not done; to County Court or Appellate Terms within 30 days.

Special Provisions: No equitable relief. Nonappealable arbitration available. Corporations and partnerships may not sue. Right to sue may not be transferred. Jury trial available to defendant. Business judgment debtors must pay within 35 days or $100 may be added to judgment. Businesses that fail to pay judgments may face triple damages. No counterclaims allowed in small claims unless within the dollar limit.

North Carolina   Small Claims (Magistrate Court)
Statutes: General Statutes of North Carolina 1986 (amendments to 1988), Ch. 7A, Sections 210–232.
Dollar Limit: $2,000.
Where to Sue: Where defendant resides. Corporation resides where it has place of business.
Service: Certified or registered mail, sheriff or court-approved adult.
Hearing Date: Within 30 days of filing claim.
Attorneys: Allowed.
Transfer: No provision.
Appeals: By either side for new trial; to District Court within 10 days.
Special Provisions: No equitable relief except enforcement of liens. No counterclaims allowed in small claims unless within the dollar limit.

North Dakota   Small Claims (County Court)
Statutes: North Dakota Century Code Annotated 1974 (amendments to 1989), Title 27, Sections 08.1–01 to 1–08.
Dollar Limit: $2,000.
Where to Sue: Where defendant resides. Corporation resides where it does business or where breach or injury occurred.
Service: Certified mail or court-approved adult.
Hearing Date: 10–30 days from service.
Attorneys: Allowed.
Transfer: If defendant requests, case tried under regular civil procedure of court.
Appeals: Not allowed.
Special Provisions: No equitable relief except to cancel agreements obtained by fraud or misrepresentation. No jury trial. Right to sue may not be transferred. No prejudgment attachment. Plaintiff's withdrawal of case results in dismissal with prejudice.

Ohio   Small Claims Division (County or Municipal Court)
Statutes: Page's Ohio Revised Code Annotated 1983 (amendments to 1989), Title 19, Ch. 1925, Sections .01–.17; Ohio Rules of Civil Procedure.
Dollar Limit: $1,000.
Where to Sue: Where defendant resides, has a place of business or where breach or injury occurred. Nonresident defendants: where plaintiff resides. Corporation resides where it has principal place of business or an agent.
Service: Certified mail, sheriff, bailiff or court-approved adult.
Hearing Date: 15–40 days from filing of complaint.
Attorneys: Allowed. A corporation may proceed through an officer or employee, but may not cross-examine, argue or advocate except through attorney.
Transfer: If either side requests, if defendant counterclaims for more than $1,500, or at court's discretion, case tried under regular civil procedure of appropriate court.

Appeals: By either side for review of law, not facts; to Court of Appeals within 30 days.

Special Provisions: No equitable relief. No jury trial. No discovery. No libel or slander cases. Right to sue may not be transferred. Limit of 24 claims a year per plaintiff. Court may order arbitration. Mediation is available in some jursidictions.

Oklahoma   Small Claims Division (District Court)

Statutes: Oklahoma Statutes Annotated 1980 (amendments to 1989), Title 12, Sections 1751–1771.

Dollar Limit: $2,500.

Where to Sue: Where defendant resides, debt arose or contract signed. Damage to land or buildings: where property is. Corporations: where principal office is, where officer resides, where any codefendant is sued or where injury occurred. Nonresident corporations: where property or debts are due, where agent is found, where any codefendant is sued, where injury occurred or where plaintiff resides.

Service: Certified mail, sheriff or court-approved adult.

Hearing Date: 10–30 days from filing of complaint.

Attorneys: Allowed.

Transfer: If defendant counterclaims for more than $2,500 or if court grants defendant's request, case tried under regular civil procedure of court.

Appeals: By either side for review of law, not facts; to Supreme Court within 30 days.

Special Provisions: Cases only to recover money, personal property or debt-payment distribution to several creditors. No libel or slander cases. Jury trial available. Collection agents may not sue. Right to sue may not be transferred.

Oregon   Small Claims (District or Justice Court)

Statutes: Oregon Revised Statutes 1988 (amendments to 1989), Sections 46.010–760; Sections 55.011–140.

Dollar Limit: $2,500.

Where to Sue: Where defendant resides or is found or where injury occurred. Contracts: where performance expected.

Service: Certified mail, sheriff, constable or court-approved adult.

Hearing Date: District Court: set by court. Justice Court: 5–10 days from service.

Attorneys: Not allowed unless court consents.

Transfer: If defendant counterclaims for more than $2,500 or either side requests jury trial, case goes to mandatory nonbinding arbitration in District Court. If still dissatisfied, case tried in District Court.

Appeals: District Court: not allowed. Justice Court: by defendant or counter-defendant for new trial; to circuit court within 10 days.

Special Provisions: Plaintiff must attest to good faith efforts to collect before filing claim. In District Court, defendant must answer within 14 days or lose by default. Cases may be referred to mediation or arbitration.

Pennsylvania   No small claims procedure (Philadelphia: Municipal Court; elsewhere: District Justice Court)
Statutes: Pennsylvania Statutes Annotated 1981 (amendments to 1989), Title 42, Sections 1511–1516; Rules of Civil Procedure Governing District Justices, Rules 201–325; Philadelphia Municipal Rules of Civil Practice, Rules 101–134.
Dollar Limit: Municipal Court: $5,000; District Justice Court: $4,000.
Where to Sue: Where defendant resides or is found or where breach or injury occurred. Corporation resides where it has principal place of business.
Service: Certified or registered mail, sheriff or court-approved adult.
Hearing Date: Municipal Court: set by court. District Justice Court: 12–60 days from service.
Attorneys: Allowed; required for corporations, except when corporation is defendant and claim is for less than $1,000.
Transfer: Municipal Court: if defendant counterclaims for more than $5,000, case tried in Court of Common Pleas. District Justice Court: no provision.
Appeals: By either side for new trial; to court of common pleas within 30 days.
Special Provisions: District Justice Court: no cases involving ownership of real estate; court may order installment payments; court may order arbitration. Municipal Court: no jury trial. If defendant appeals, any part of plaintiff's previously waived claim for more than $5,000 may be considered on appeal.

Puerto Rico   No small claims procedure (District Court)
Statutes: Laws of Puerto Rico Annotated 1983 (amendments to 1988), Title 32, Appendix III, Rule 60.
Dollar Limit: $2,000.
Where to Sue: Where defendant resides. Corporation resides where it does business or where obligation incurred.
Service: By clerk's written notice.
Hearing Date: Set by court.
Attorneys: Allowed.
Transfer: No provision.
Appeals: By either side for review of law, not facts; to Superior Court within 10 days.
Special Provisions: No personal injury or property damage cases. Defendant must file written answer at or before the hearing. Court may order installment payments. All pleadings must be in Spanish, or Spanish translations must be provided.

Rhode Island   Small Claims (District Court)
Statutes: General Laws of Rhode Island 1985 (amendments to 1988), Title 10, Ch. 16, Sections 1–16.
Dollar Limit: $1,500.
Where to Sue: Where either side resides. Corporation resides where it does business.
Service: Certified or registered mail (binding on defendant who refuses to accept), sheriff, deputy, constable or court-approved adult.
Hearing Date: Set by court.

Attorneys: Allowed; required for corporations, except close and family corporations with less than $1 million in assets.

Transfer: If defendant counterclaims for more than $1,500, case tried under regular civil procedure of District Court.

Appeals: By defendant only for new trial; to Superior Court within 2 days.

Special Provisions: No personal injury or property damage cases. Court may order installment payments.

South Carolina No small claims procedure (Magistrate Court)

Statutes: Code of Laws of South Carolina 1976 (amendments to 1989), Title 22, Ch. 3, Sections 10–320; Administrative and Procedural Rules for Magistrate's Court, Rules 1–19.

Dollar Limit: $2,500; none in landlord-tenant cases.

Where to Sue: Where defendant resides. Nonresident defendants: where plaintiff designates. To recover personal property: where property is. Corporation resides where it does business.

Service: Certified or registered mail, sheriff, deputy, attorney in case or court-approved disinterested adult.

Hearing Date: Set by court.

Attorneys: Allowed.

Transfer: If defendant counterclaims for more than $2,500, case tried under regular civil procedure of appropriate court.

Appeals: By either side for review of law, not facts; to Circuit Court within 30 days.

Special Provisions: Jury trial available. Defendant must answer within 20 days (30 days if claim for less than $25) or lose by default. No cases for more than $100 against the state and no cases involving ownership of real estate.

South Dakota Small Claims Division (Circuit or Magistrate Court)

Statutes: South Dakota Compiled Laws Annotated 1984 (amendments to 1989), Title 15, Ch. 39, Sections 45–78.

Dollar Limit: $2,000.

Where to Sue: Where defendant resides or injury occurred. Corporation resides where it does business.

Service: Certified or registered mail; if that fails, sheriff or court-approved adult.

Hearing Date: Set by court.

Attorneys: Allowed.

Transfer: If defendant requests jury trial at least 2 days before hearing, to regular civil procedure of appropriate court.

Appeals: Not allowed.

Special Provisions: No libel or slander cases. Court may order installment payments. Defendant must answer at least 2 days before hearing or lose by default.

Tennessee No small claims procedure (Court of General Sessions or Justice Court)

Statutes: Tennessee Code Annotated 1980 (amendments to 1988), Title 16, Ch. 15, Sections 501–713.

Dollar Limit: $10,000; in counties of more than 700,000 population, $15,000.

No limit in eviction cases or to recover specific personal property, except $25,000 limit for alternative money judgments in personal property cases in counties of less than 700,000 population.
Where to Sue: Where defendant resides or is found or where injury occurred. To recover personal property: where property is. Corporation resides where it maintains an office.
Service: Certified mail, sheriff, deputy or constable.
Hearing Date: Set by court.
Attorneys: Allowed.
Transfer: No provision.
Appeals: By either side for new trial; to Circuit Court within 10 days.
Special Provisions: Equitable relief limited to restraining orders. No jury trial. No formal pleadings required.

Texas   Small Claims (Justice Court)
Statutes: Texas Code Annotated 1988 (amendments to 1989), Government Code, Sections 28.001–055; Texas Rules of Civil Procedure.
Dollar Limit: $2,500.
Where to Sue: Where defendant resides. Contracts: where performance expected.
Service: Certified mail, sheriff, constable or court-approved adult.
Hearing Date: Set by court.
Attorneys: Allowed.
Transfer: No provision.
Appeals: By either side for claims of more than $20; to Constitutional County Court or County Court at law within 10 days.
Special Provisions: No equitable relief. Jury trial available if requested at least 1 day before trial. Right to sue may not be transferred. Collection agents and commercial lenders may not sue.

Utah   Small Claims (Circuit or Justice Court)
Statutes: Utah Code Annotated 1953 (amendments to 1989), Sections 78.6.1–15.
Dollar Limit: $1,000.
Where to Sue: Where defendant resides or where breach or injury occurred.
Service: Sheriff, deputy, constable or disinterested adult.
Hearing Date: Set by court.
Attorneys: Allowed.
Transfer: No provision.
Appeals: By either side for new trial; to Circuit Court within 10 days.
Special Provisions: No jury trial. Right to sue may not be transferred. Evening sessions available.

Vermont   Small Claims (District Court)
Statutes: Vermont Statutes Annotated 1973 (amendments to 1989), Title 12, Sections 405, 5531–5538.
Dollar Limit: $2,000.
Where to Sue: Where either side resides or where breach or injury occurred.
Service: First-class mail or sheriff.

Hearing Date: Set by court.

Attorneys: Allowed.

Transfer: If defendant requests jury trial, to regular civil procedure of court.

Appeals: By either side for review of law, not facts; to Superior Court within 30 days.

Special Provisions: No equitable relief. Defendant must file written answer within 20 days or lose by default. Defendant may counterclaim (not involving third parties outside court's jurisdiction) for more than $2,000, but court may not award more than $2,000; defendant may later sue in separate action for the difference. Defendant may request jury trial. No libel or slander cases.

Virgin Islands   Small Claims (Territorial Court)

Statutes: Virgin Islands Code Annotated 1979 (amendments to 1989), Title 4, Ch. 3, Sections 32–33; Title 5, Ch. 7, Sections 111–112; Title 5, Ch. 9, Sections 141–142 and Appendices IV and VII.

Dollar Limit: $2,000.

Where to Sue: Where defendant resides or where breach or injury occurred.

Service: Registered mail, marshal or court-approved adult.

Hearing Date: 5–15 days from service.

Attorneys: Not allowed.

Transfer: If either side requests jury trial or defendant counterclaims for more than $2,000 and court permits, case tried under regular civil procedure of court.

Appeals: By either side for review of law, not facts; to United States District Court within 10 days.

Special Provisions: Pretrial conciliation encouraged. Court may order installment payments. No jury trial.

Virginia   No small claims procedure (General District Court)

Statutes: Code of Virginia 1982 (amendments to 1989), Sections 16.1.76–113 and 122.1–122.7.

Dollar Limit: $7,000.

Where to Sue: Where defendant resides, is employed or regularly transacts business, or where breach or injury occurred. To recover property: where property is.

Service: Sheriff or court-approved adult.

Hearing Date: Set by court.

Attorneys: Allowed.

Transfer: If defendant counterclaims for more than $1,000 and requests transfer, case tried in Circuit Court.

Appeals: By either side for new trial on claims more than $50; to Circuit Court within 10 days.

Special Provisions: The General District Court in Fairfax has a small claims division, through 1990. It will probably be continued. Any Virginia resident may file a claim. Court operates on Fridays, has a $1,000 limit and does not allow attorneys.

Washington   Small Claims Department (District Court)

Statutes: Revised Code of Washington Annotated 1962 (amendments to 1989), Title 12, Sections 40.010–120.

Dollar Limit: $2,000.

Where to Sue: Where defendant resides. Corporation resides where it does business or has an office.

Service: Certified or registered mail, sheriff, deputy, constable or disinterested adult.

Hearing Date: Set by court.

Attorneys: Not allowed unless court consents.

Transfer: If plaintiff is a corporation represented by an attorney and defendant requests transfer, case tried under regular civil procedure of court.

Appeals: By side that requests small claims court jurisdiction when the amount is more than $1,000 or by defendant when the amount is more than $100; for new trial, to Superior Court within 14 days.

Special Provisions: No equitable relief. Counterclaims for more than $2,000 must be filed separately in appropriate court.

West Virginia   No small claims procedure (Magistrate Court)

Statutes: West Virginia Code 1986 (amendments to 1989), Ch. 50, Sections 1.1–6.3; Ch. 56, Sections 1.1, 1.2.

Dollar Limit: $3,000.

Where to Sue: Where defendant resides or where injury occurred.
Contracts: where breach occurred. Property insurance claims: where property is. Nonresident defendants: where plaintiff resides or where defendant has property or debts due. Corporation resides where it has principal office or where chief officer resides. Nonresident U.S. corporate defendants: where corporation does business or where plaintiff resides.

Service: Sheriff; if that fails, any credible disinterested adult or attorney in case.

Hearing Date: Defendant has 20 days to appear (5 days in eviction cases). Trial date set after defendant notifies court of intention to defend against claim.

Attorneys: Allowed; required for collection agents.

Transfer: Claims less than $300: if both sides consent, case tried in Circuit Court. Claims more than $300: if either side requests, case tried in Circuit Court.

Appeals: By either side for new trial; to circuit court within 20 days.

Special Provisions: No equitable relief. Jury trial available on claim of $20. Defendant must answer within 20 days or lose by default. No libel or slander, ownership of real estate, foreclosure of real estate liens, false imprisonment or eminent domain cases. Claims against the state must be brought in the Court of Claims at the State Capitol.

Wisconsin   Small Claims (Circuit Court)

Statutes: Wisconsin Statutes Annotated 1981 (amendments to 1989), Sections 799.01–45.

Dollar Limit: $2,000; none in eviction cases.

Where to Sue: Where defendant resides or does substantial business or where breach or injury occurred. Consumer credit claims: where customer resides, collateral is or document signed. Corporation resides where it has principal office or where it does business.

Service: Certified or registered mail, any disinterested adult resident.

Hearing Date: 8–30 days after summons issued (5–30 days in eviction cases).

Attorneys: Allowed; required for assignees.

Transfer: If either side requests jury trial or if defendant files compulsory counter-claim for more than $2,000, case tried under regular civil procedure of court.

Appeals: By either side for review of law, not facts; to Court of Appeals within 45 days (15 days in eviction cases).

Special Provisions: Prevailing party may be awarded attorney fees up to $100 on judgments more than $1,000. Jury trial available. Evening and Saturday sessions available.

Wyoming   Small Claims (County or Justice of the Peace Court)

Statutes: Wyoming Statutes Annotated 1977 (amendments to 1989), Sections 1.5.101–108 and 1.21.201–205; Rules of Civil Procedure for Justice of the Peace Courts, Rules 1–8.

Dollar Limit: $2,000.

Where to Sue: Where defendant resides or is found. Corporation resides where it has principal place of business. Nonresident defendants: where breach or injury occurred.

Service: Certified or registered mail, sheriff, deputy, deputized process server or court-approved adult.

Hearing Date: 3–12 days from service.

Attorneys: Allowed.

Transfer: No provision.

Appeals: By either side for review of law, not facts; to District Court within 10 days.

Special Provisions: Jury trial available. No formal pleadings required.

APPENDIX
VII

ALTERNATIVE RESOURCES

As discussed in Chapter 2, small claims courts may not accurately address or provide the best solution to every small claims dispute that occurs. This appendix lists a variety of out-of-court alternatives for resolving disputes. Some of the information in this and later appendices is excerpted from the 1990 edition of the *Consumer's Resource Handbook,* published by the U.S. Office of Consumer Affairs.

Consumer Information

Consumer Information Center
Pueblo, CO 81009

PRIVATE CONSUMER ACTION AGENCIES (CAAs)

Consumer Federation of America
1424 16th St. NW, Suite 604
Washington, DC 20036
(202) 387-6121

National Consumers League
815 15th St. NW, Suite 516

Washington, DC 20005
(202) 639-8140

Call for Action National Center
3400 Idaho Ave. NW
Washington, DC 20016
(202) 537-0585

CONSUMER ACTION PANELS (CAPs)

Auto Action Program
    (AUTOCAP)
8400 Westpark Dr.
McLean, VA 22102
(703) 821-7144

Major Appliance Consumer Action
    Panel (MACAP)
20 N. Wacker Dr.
Chicago, IL 60606
(312) 984-5858

Trade Associations

American Apparel Manufacturers
    Association
2500 Wilson Blvd., Suite 301
Arlington, VA 22201
(703) 524-1864

American Automobile Association
8111 Gatehouse Rd., Suite 535
Falls Church, VA 22047
(703) 222-6446

American Collectors Association
4040 W. 70th St.
Minneapolis, MN 55435
(612) 926-6547

American Council of Life Insurance
1001 Pennsylvania Ave. NW
Washington, DC 20004-2599
(Written inquiries only)

American Health Care Association
1201 L St. NW
Washington, DC 20005
(202) 842-4444

American Hotel and Motel
    Association
1201 New York Ave., Suite 600
Washington, DC 20005
(Written inquiries only)

American Society of Travel Agents,
    Inc.
P.O. Box 23992
Washington, DC 20026
(703) 739-2782

Better Hearing Institute
P.O. Box 1840

Washington, DC 20013
(703) 642-0580
(800) Ear-Well (toll free nationwide)

Blue Cross/Blue Shield Association
655 15th St. NW, Suite 350
Washington, DC 20005
(202) 626-4780

Carpet and Rug Institute
1155 Connecticut Ave., Suite 500
Washington, DC 20036
(Written inquiries only)

Cemetery Consumer Service Council
P.O. Box 3574
Washington, DC 20007
(703) 379-6426
(Handles complaints about cemetery
    practices)

Direct Mail Marketing Association
6 E. 43rd St.
New York, NY 10017
(Written inquiries only; complaints
    about junk mail)

Electronic Industries Association
2001 Eye St. NW
Washington, DC 20006
(202) 457-4900

Funeral Service Consumer
    Arbitration Program
11121 W. Oklahoma Ave.
Milwaukee, WI 53227
(414) 541-2500
(Offered by the National Funeral
    Directors Association)

International Fabricare Institute
12251 Tech Rd.
Silver Spring, MD 20904
(301) 622-1900
(Dry-cleaning complaints)

Mail Order Action Line
6 E. 43rd St.
New York, NY 10017
(Written inquiries only; complaints
about mail-order and telephone
solicitation companies)

Mail Preference Service
P.O. Box 3861
Grand Central Station
New York, NY 10163
(Written inquiries only; Will remove
your name from a direct-mail list)

National Association of Home
Builders
15th and M Sts. NW
Washington, DC 20005
(202) 822-0409
(Coordinates "Home Owners
Warranty" [HOW] program)

National Association of Personnel
Consultants
3133 Mt. Vernon Ave.
Alexandria, VA 22303
(703) 684-0180
(Arbitrates consumer complaints with
employment agencies, recruiting
firms and temporary help services)

National Association of Professional
Insurance Agents
400 N. Washington St.
Alexandria, VA 22314
(703) 836-9340

National Association of Securities
Dealers
33 Whitehall St., 10th Floor
New York, NY 10004
(212) 858-4000
(Operates arbitration program for
conflicts between investors and
broker members)

National Foundation for Consumer
Credit
8701 Georgia Ave., Suite 507
Silver Spring, MD 20910
(301) 589-5600

National Home Study Council
1601 18th St. NW
Washington, DC 20009
(Written inquiries only: information
about home study correspondence
schools)

Pharmaceutical Manufacturers
Association
1100 15th St. NW, Suite 900
Washington, DC 20005
(202) 835-3468

Toy Manufacturers of America
200 5th Ave.
New York, NY 10010
(212) 675-1141

Alternative Dispute Resolution Resources

American Arbitration Association
(National Office)
140 W. 51st St., 10th Floor
New York, NY 10020
(212) 661-4451

American Bar Association
Standing Committee on Dispute
Resolution

1800 M St. NW
Washington, DC 20036
(202) 331-2258

Better Business Bureau
AUTOLINE
4200 Wilson Blvd., Suite 800
Arlington, VA 22203
(703) 276-0100

Center for Public Resources
366 Madison Ave.
New York, NY 10017
(212) 949-6490

Federal Mediation and Conciliation
   Service
2100 K St. NW

Washington, DC 20037
(202) 543-5320

Society of Professionals in Dispute
   Resolution
1730 Rhode Island Ave. NW, Suite
   909
Washington, DC 20036
(202) 833-2188

BETTER BUSINESS BUREAUS (BBBS)

Better Business Bureaus are nonprofit organizations sponsored by local businesses. They offer a variety of consumer services. For example, they can provide consumer education materials, answer consumer questions, mediate and arbitrate complaints, and provide general information on consumer complaint records of companies. This list includes the local BBBs in the United States. The national headquarters can give you the addresses for BBBs in Canada and Israel.

National Headquarters

Council of Better Business
Bureaus
4200 Wilson Blvd.
Arlington, VA 22203
(703) 276-0100

Local Bureaus

Alabama

1214 S. 20th St.
Birmingham, AL 35205
(205) 558-2222

P.O. Box 383
Huntsville, AL 35804
(205) 533-1640

707 Van Antwerp Bldg.
Mobile, AL 36602
(205) 433-5494/5495

Commerce St., Suite 810
Montgomery, AL 36104
(205) 262-5606

Alaska

3380 C St., Suite 100
Anchorage, AK 99503
(907) 562-0704

Arizona

4428 N. 12th St.
Phoenix, AZ 85014
(602) 264-1721

50 W. Drachman St., Suite 103
Tucson, AZ 85705
(602) 622-7651 (inquiries)
(602) 622-7654 (complaints)

Arkansas

1415 S. University Ave.
Little Rock, AR 72204
(501) 664-7274

California

705—18th St.
Bakersfield, CA 93301
(805) 322-2074

P.O. Box 970
Colton, CA 92324
(714) 825-7280

6101 Ball Rd., Suite 309
Cypress, CA 90630
(714) 527-0680

5070 N. Sixth, Suite 176
Fresno, CA 93710
(209) 222-8111

510—16th St., Suite 550
Oakland, CA 94612
(415) 839-5900

400 S St.
Sacramento, CA 95814
(916) 443-6843

525 B St., Suite 301
San Diego, CA 92101-4408
(619) 234-0966

33 New Montgomery St. Tower
San Francisco, CA 94105
(415) 243-9999

1505 Meridian Ave.
San Jose, CA 95125
(408) 978-8700

P.O. Box 294
San Mateo, CA 94401
(415) 347-1251

P.O. Box 746
Santa Barbara, CA 93102
(805) 963-8657

1111 North Center St.
Stockton, CA 95202
(209) 948-4880, 4881

Colorado

P.O. Box 7970
Colorado Springs, CO 80933
(719) 636-1155

1780 S. Bellaire, Suite 700
Denver, CO 80222
(303) 758-2100 (inquiries)
(303) 758-2212 (complaints)

1730 S. College Ave., #303
Fort Collins, CO 80525
(303) 484-1348

432 Broadway
Pueblo, CO 81004
(719) 542-6464

Connecticut

2345 Black Rock Tpk.
Fairfield, CT 06430
(203) 374-6161

2080 Silas Deane Hwy.
Rocky Hill, CT 06067-2311
(203) 529-3575

100 S. Turnpike Rd.
Wallingford, CT 06492
(203) 269-2700 (inquiries)
(203) 269-4457 (complaints)

Delaware

P.O. Box 300
Milford, DE 19963
(302) 422-6300 (Kent)
(302) 856-6969 (Sussex)

P.O. Box 5361
Wilmington, DE 19808
(302) 996-9200

District of Columbia

1012 14th St. NW
Washington, DC 20005
(202) 393-8000

Florida

13770—58th St. N., #309
Clearwater, FL 33520
(813) 535-5522

2976-E Cleveland Ave.
Fort Myers, FL 33901
(813) 334-7331/7152
(813) 597-1322 (Naples)
(813) 743-2279 (Port Charlotte)

3100 University Blvd. S., #23
Jacksonville, FL 32216
(904) 721-2288

2605 Maitland Center Pkwy.
Maitland, FL 32751-7147
(407) 660-9500

16291 N.W. 57th Ave.
Miami, FL 33014-6709

(305) 625-0307 (inquiries for Dade County)
(305) 625-1302 (complaints for Dade County)
(305) 524-2803 (inquiries for Broward County)
(305) 527-1643 (complaints for Broward County)

250 School Rd., Suite 11-W
New Port Richey, FL 34652
(813) 842-5459

P.O. Box 1511
Pensacola, FL 32597-1511
(904) 433-6111

1950 Port St. Lucie Blvd., #211
Port St. Lucie, FL 34952
(407) 878-2010/337-2083

1111 N. Westshore Blvd., Suite 207
Tampa, FL 33607
(813) 875-6200

2247 Palm Beach Lakes Blvd., #211
West Palm Beach, FL 33409-3408
(407) 686-2200

Georgia

1319-B Dawson Road
Albany, GA 31707
(912) 883-0744

100 Edgewood Ave.,
Suite 1012
Atlanta, GA 30303
(404) 688-4910

P.O. Box 2085
Augusta, GA 30903
(404) 722-1574

P.O. Box 2587
Columbus, GA 31902
(404) 324-0712 (inquiries)
(404) 324-0713 (complaints)

6606 Abercorn St., Suite 108-C
Savannah, GA 31416
(912) 354-7521

Hawaii

1600 Kapiolani Blvd., Suite 704
Honolulu, HI 96814
(808) 942-2355

Idaho

409 W. Jefferson
Boise, ID 83702
(208) 342-4649
(208) 467-5547

545 Shoup, Suite 210
Idaho Falls, ID 83402
(208) 523-9754

Illinois

211 W. Wacker Dr.
Chicago, IL 60606
(312) 444-1188 (inquiries)
(312) 346-3313 (complaints)

109 S.W. Jefferson St., #305
Peoria, IL 61602
(309) 673-5194

515 N. Court St.
Rockford, IL 61110
(815) 963-BBB2

Indiana

P.O. Box 405
Elkhart, IN 46515
(219) 262-8996

119 S.E. Fourth St.
Evansville, IN 47708
(812) 422-6879

1203 Webster St.
Fort Wayne, IN 46802
(219) 423-4433

4231 Cleveland St.
Gary, IN 46408
(219) 980-1511/769-8053/926-5669

Victoria Centre
22 East Washington St.
Indianapolis, IN 46204
(317) 637-0197

320 S. Washington St., #101
Marion, IN 46952
(317) 668-8954/8955

Whitinger Building, Room 150
Muncie, IN 47306
(317) 285-5668

509—85 U.S. #33 North
South Bend, IN 46637
(219) 277-9121

Iowa

2435 Kimberly Road, #110 North
Bettendorf, IA 52722
(319) 355-6344

1500 Second Avenue SE, #212
Cedar Rapids, IA 52403
(319) 366-5401

615 Insurance Exchange Bldg.
Des Moines, IA 50309
(515) 243-8137

318 Badgerow Bldg.
Siouxland, IA 51101
(712) 252-4501

Kansas

501 Jefferson, Suite 24
Topeka, KS 66607
(913) 232-0455

300 Kaufman Bldg.
Wichita, KS 67202
(316) 263-3146

Kentucky

154 Patchen Dr., Suite 90
Lexington, KY 40502
(606) 268-4128

844 Fourth St.
Louisville, KY 40203
(502) 583-6546

Louisiana

1605 Murray St., Suite 117
Alexandria, LA 71301
(318) 473-4494

2055 Wooddale Blvd.
Baton Rouge, LA 70806
(504) 926-3010

300 Bond St.
Houma, LA 70361
(504) 868-3456

P.O. Box 30297
Lafayette, LA 70593
(318) 234-8341

P.O. Box 1681
Lake Charles, LA 70602
(318) 433-1633

141 De Siard St., Suite 300
Monroe, LA 71201
(318) 387-4600, 4601

1539 Jackson Ave.
New Orleans, LA 70130
(504) 581-6222

1401 N. Market St.
Shreveport, LA 71101
(318) 221-8352

Maine

812 Stevens Ave.
Portland, ME 04103
(207) 878-2715

Maryland

2100 Huntingdon Ave.
Baltimore, MD 21211-3215
(301) 347-3990

Massachusetts

Eight Winter St.
Boston, MA 02108
(617) 482-9151 (inquiries)
(617) 482-9190 (complaints)

One Kendall St., Suite 307
Framingham, MA 01701
(508) 872-5585

78 North St., Suite 1
Hyannis, MA 02601
(508) 771-3022

316 Essex St.
Lawrence, MA 01840
(508) 687-7666

106 State Rd., Suite 4
North Dartmouth, MA 02747
(508) 999-6060

293 Bridge St., Suite 324
Springfield, MA 01103
(413) 734-3114

P.O. Box 379
Worcester, MA 01601
(508) 755-2548

Michigan

150 Michigan Ave.
Detroit, MI 48226
(313) 962-7566 (inquiries)
(313) 962-6785 (complaints)

620 Trust Bldg.
Grand Rapids, MI 49503
(616) 774-8236

Minnesota

1745 University Ave.
St. Paul, MN 55104
(612) 646-7700

Mississippi

2917 W. Beach Blvd., #103
Biloxi, MS 39531
(601) 374-2222

105 Fifth St.
Columbus, MS 39701
(601) 327-8594

P.O. Box 390
Jackson, MS 39205-0390
(601) 948-8222

Missouri

306 E. 12th St., Suite 1024
Kansas City, MO 64106
(816) 421-7800

5100 Oakland, Suite 200
St. Louis, MO 63110
(314) 531-3300

205 Park Central East, #509
Springfield, MO 65806
(417) 862-9231

Nebraska

719 N. 48th St.
Lincoln, NE 68504
(402) 467-5261

1613 Farnam St.
Omaha, NE 68102
(402) 346-3033

Nevada

1022 E. Sahara Ave.
Las Vegas, NV 89104
(702) 735-6900/1969

P.O. Box 21269
Reno, NV 89505
(702) 322-0657

New Hampshire

410 S. Main St.
Concord, NH 03301
(603) 224-1991
(800) 852-3757 (toll free in NH)

New Jersey

34 Park Pl.
Newark, NJ 07102
(201) 642-INFO

Two Forest Ave.
Paramus, NJ 07652
(201) 845-4044

1721 Rte. #37 East
Toms River, NJ 08753
(201) 270-5577

1700 Whitehorse—Hamilton Square
Trenton, NJ 08690
(609) 588-0808 (Mercer County)
(201) 536-6306 (Monmouth
   County)
(201) 329-6855
(Middlesex, Somerset and Hunterdon
   counties)

New Mexico

4600-A Montgomery NE, #200
Albuquerque, NM 87109
(505) 884-0500
(800) 445-1461 (toll free in NM)

308 N. Locke
Farmington, NM 87401
(505) 326-6501

2407 W. Picacho, Suite B-2
Las Cruces, NM 88005
(505) 524-3130

1210 Luisa St., Suite 5
Santa Fe, NM 87502
(505) 988-3648

New York

346 Delaware Ave.
Buffalo, NY 14202
(716) 856-7180

266 Main St.
Farmingdale, NY 11735
(516) 420-0500

257 Park Ave. South
New York, NY 10010
(212) 533-6200

1122 Sibley Tower
Rochester, NY 14604
(716) 546-6776

100 University Bldg.
Syracuse, NY 13202
(315) 479-6635

120 E. Main St.
Wappinger Falls, NY 12590
(914) 297-6550

30 Glenn St.
White Plains, NY 10603
(914) 428-1230/1231

North Carolina

801 BBB&T Bldg.
Asheville, NC 28801
(704) 253-2392

1130 E. 3rd St., Suite 400
Charlotte, NC 28204
(704) 332-7151
(800) 532-0477 (toll free in NC)

3608 W. Friendly Ave.
Greensboro, NC 27410
(919) 852-4240/4241/4242

P.O. Box 1882
Hickory, NC 28603
(704) 464-0372

3120 Poplarwood Dr., Suite 101
Raleigh, NC 27604-1080
(919) 872-9240

2110 Cloverdale Ave., #2-B
Winston-Salem, NC 27103
(919) 725-8348

Ohio

P.O. Box 80596
Akron, OH 44308
(216) 253-4590

1434 Cleveland Ave. NW
Canton, OH 44703
(216) 454-9401

898 Walnut St.
Cincinnati, OH 45202
(513) 421-3015

2217 E. 9th St., Suite 200
Cleveland, OH 44115
(216) 241-7678

527 S. High St.
Columbus, OH 43215
(614) 221-6336

40 W. Fourth St., #1250, Suite 280
Dayton, OH 45402
(513) 222-5825
(800) 521-8357 (toll free in OH)

P.O. Box 269
Lima, OH 45802
(419) 223-7010

P.O. Box 1706
Mansfield, OH 44910
(419) 522-1700

425 Jefferson Ave., Suite 909
Toledo, OH 43604
(419) 241-6276

345 N. Market
Wooster, OH 44691
(216) 263-6444

P.O. Box 1495
Youngstown, OH 44501
(216) 744-3111

Oklahoma

17 S. Dewey
Oklahoma City, OK 73102
(405) 239-6860 (inquiries)
(405) 239-6081 (inquiries)
(405) 239-6083 (complaints)

6711 S. Yale, Suite 230
Tulsa, OK 71436
(918) 492-1266

Oregon

601 S.W. Alder St., Suite 615
Portland, OR 97205
(503) 226-3981

Pennsylvania

528 N. New St.
Bethlehem, PA 18018
(215) 866-8780

6 Marion Court
Lancaster, PA 17602
(717) 291-1151
(717) 232-2800 (Harrisburg)
(717) 846-2700 (York
  County)

P.O. Box 2297
Philadelphia, PA 19103
(215) 496-1000

610 Smithfield St.
Pittsburgh, PA 15222
(412) 456-2700

P.O. Box 993
Scranton, PA 18501
(717) 342-9129

Puerto Rico

G.P.O. Box 70212
San Juan, PR 00936
(809) 756-5400

Rhode Island

Bureau Park
P.O. Box 1300
Warwick, RI 02887-1300
(401) 785-1212 (inquiries)
(401) 785-1213 (complaints)

South Carolina

1830 Bull St.
Columbia, SC 29201
(803) 254-2525

311 Pettigru St.
Greenville, SC 29601
(803) 242-5052

P.O. Box 8603
Myrtle Beach, SC 29578-8603
(803) 448-6100

Tennessee

P.O. Box 1176 TCAS
Blountville, TN 37617
(615) 323-6311

1010 Market St., Suite 200
Chattanooga, TN 37402
(615) 266-6144
(615) 479-6096 (Bradley County)
(615) 266-6144 (Whitfield and Murray counties)

P.O. 10327
Knoxville, TN 37939-0327
(615) 522-2552/2130/2139

P.O. Box 41406
Memphis, TN 38174-1406
(901) 272-9641

One Commerce Pl., Suite 1830
Nashville, TN 37239
(615) 254-5872

Texas

3300 S. 14th St., Suite 307
Abilene, TX 79605
(915) 691-1533

P.O. Box 1905
Amarillo, TX 79106
(806) 358-6222

1005 American Plaza
Austin, TX 78701
(512) 476-1616

P.O. Box 2988
Beaumont, TX 77704
(409) 835-5348

202 Varisco Bldg.
Bryan, TX 77801
(409) 823-8148/8149

4535 S. Padre Island Dr.
Corpus Christi, TX 78411
(512) 854-2892

2001 Bryan St., Suite 850
Dallas, TX 75201
(214) 220-2000

1910 East Yandell
El Paso, TX 79903
(915) 545-1212/1264

106 West Fifth St.
Fort Worth, TX 76102
(817) 332-7585

2707 N. Loop West, Suite 900
Houston, TX 77008
(713) 868-9500

P.O. Box 1178
Lubbock, TX 79401
(806) 763-0459

P.O. Box 60206
Midland, TX 79711
(915) 563-1880
(800) 592-4433 (toll free in TX)

P.O. Box 3366
San Angelo, TX 76902-3366
(915) 653-2318

1800 Northeast Loop 410, #400
San Antonio, TX 78217
(512) 828-9441

P.O. Box 6652
Tyler, TX 75711-6652
(214) 581-5704

P.O. Box 7203
Waco, TX 76714-7203
(817) 772-7530

P.O. Box 69
Weslaco, TX 78596
(512) 968-3678

1106 Brook Ave.
Wichita Falls, TX 76301
(817) 723-5526

Utah

385 24th St., Suite 717
Ogden, UT 84401
(801) 399-4701

1588 S. Main
Salt Lake City, UT 84115
(801) 487-4656
(801) 377-2611 (Provo)

Virginia

3608 Tidewater Dr.
Norfolk, VA 23509
(804) 627-5651

701 E. Franklin, Suite 712
Richmond, VA 23219
(804) 648-0016

121 W. Campbell Ave. SW
Roanoke, VA 24011
(703) 342-3455

Washington

127 W. Canal Dr.
Kennewick, WA 99336
(509) 582-0222

2200 Sixth Ave., Suite 828
Seattle, WA 98121-1857
(206) 448-8888

S. 176 Stevens St.
Spokane, WA 99204
(509) 747-1155

P.O. Box 1274
Tacoma, WA 98401
(206) 383-5561

P.O. Box 1584
Yakima, WA 98907
(509) 248-1326

Wisconsin

740 N. Plankinton Ave.
Milwaukee, WI 53202

(414) 273-1600 (inquiries)
(414) 273-0123
(complaints)

Wyoming

BBB/Idaho Falls (Lincoln Park and
Teton counties)
(208) 523-9754

BBB/Fort Collins (all other Wyoming
counties)
(800) 873-3222 (toll free)

APPENDIX

VIII

STATE CONSUMER ACTION AGENCIES

This appendix lists state consumer action agencies. If you do not live in or close to the city listed for your state, call the state office or the toll-free number to get a local office referral. Most offices distribute consumer information pamphlets and resolve complaints through mediation or arbitration.

Alabama

Consumer Protection Division
Office of Attorney General
11 S. Union St.
Montgomery, AL 36130
(205) 261-7334
(800) 392-5658 (toll free in AL)

Alaska

Consumer Protection Section
Office of Attorney General

1031 W. 4th Ave., Suite 110-B
Anchorage, AK 99501
(907) 279-0428

Arizona

Financial Fraud Division
Office of Attorney General
1275 W. Washington St.
Phoenix, AZ 85007
(602) 542-3702
(800) 352-8431 (toll free in AZ)

Arkansas

Consumer Protection Division
Office of Attorney General
200 Tower Bldg., 4th & Center Sts.
Little Rock, AR 72201
(501) 682-2007
(800) 482-8982 (toll free in AR)

California

Public Inquiry Unit
Office of Attorney General
1515 K St., Suite 511
Sacramento, CA 94244-2550
(916) 322-3360
(800) 952-5225 (toll free in CA)

Consumer Protection Division
Los Angeles City Attorney's Office
200 N. Main St.
1600 City Hall East
Los Angeles, CA 90012
(213) 485-4515

Colorado

Consumer Protection Unit
Office of Attorney General
1525 Sherman St., 3rd Floor
Denver, CO 80203
(303) 866-5167

Connecticut

Department of Consumer Protection
165 Capitol Ave.
Hartford, CT 06106
(203) 566-4999
(800) 842-2649 (toll free in CT)

Delaware

Division of Consumer Affairs
Department of Community Affairs
820 N. French St., 4th Floor
Wilmington, DE 19801
(302) 571-3250

District of Columbia

Department of Consumer & Regula-
    tory Affairs

614 H St. NW
Washington, DC 20001
(202) 727-7000

Florida

Division of Consumer Services
218 Mayo Bldg.
Tallahassee, FL 32399
(904) 488-2226
(800) 342-2176 (toll free in FL)

Georgia

Governor's Office of Consumer Affairs
2 Martin Luther King, Jr. Dr. SE
Plaza Level, E. Tower
Atlanta, GA 30334
(404) 656-7000
(800) 282-5808 (toll free in GA)

Hawaii

Office of Consumer Protection
828 Fort St. Mall
Honolulu, HI 96812-3767
(808) 548-2560/2540

Idaho

None

Illinois

Consumer Protection Division
Office of Attorney General
100 W. Randolph St., 12th Floor
Chicago, IL 60601
(312) 917-3580

Indiana

Consumer Protection Division
Office of Attorney General
219 State House
Indianapolis, IN 46204
(317) 232-6330
(800) 382-5516 (toll free in IN)

Iowa

Consumer Protection Division
Office of Attorney General
1300 E. Walnut St., 2nd Floor

Des Moines, IA 50319
(515) 281-5926

Kansas

Consumer Protection Division
Office of Attorney General
Kansas Judicial Ctr., 2nd Floor
Topeka, KS 66612
(913) 296-3751
(800) 432-2310 (toll free in KS)

Kentucky

Consumer Protection Division
Office of Attorney General
209 St. Clair St.
Frankfort, KY 40601
(502) 564-2200
(800) 432-9257 (toll free in KY)

Louisiana

Consumer Protection Section
Office of Attorney General
State Capitol Bldg., P.O. Box 94005
Baton Rouge, LA 70804
(504) 342-7013

Maine

Consumer and Antitrust Division
Office of Attorney General
State House Station #6
Augusta, ME 04333
(207) 289-3716 (9 A.M.–1 P.M.)

Maryland

Consumer Protection Division
Office of Attorney General
7 N. Calvert St., 3rd Floor
Baltimore, MD 21202
(301) 528-8662 (9 A.M.–2 P.M.)

Massachusetts

Consumer Protection Division
Office of Attorney General
One Ashburton Place, Room 1411
Boston, MA 02108
(617) 727-7780

Michigan

Consumer Protection Division
Office of Attorney General
670 Law Bldg.
Lansing, MI 48913
(517) 373-1140

Minnesota

Office of Consumer Services
Office of Attorney General
117 University Ave.
St. Paul, MN 55155
(612) 296-2331

Mississippi

Consumer Protection Division
Office of Attorney General
P.O. Box 220
Jackson, MS 39205
(601) 359-3680

Missouri

Trade Offense Division
Office of Attorney General
P.O. Box 899
Jefferson City, MO 65102
(314) 751-2616
(800) 392-8222 (toll free in MO)

Montana

Consumer Affairs Unit
Department of Commerce
1424 9th Ave.
Helena, MT 59620
(406) 444-4312

Nebraska

Consumer Protection Division
Department of Justice
2115 State Capitol, P.O. Box 98920
Lincoln, NE 68509
(402) 471-4723

Nevada

Department of Commerce
State Mail Room Complex

Las Vegas, NV 89158
(702) 486-4150

New Hampshire

Consumer Protection and Antitrust
   Division
Office of Attorney General
State House Annex
Concord, NH 03301
(603) 271-3641

New Jersey

Division of Consumer Affairs
1100 Raymond Blvd., Room 504
Newark, NJ 07102
(201) 648-4010

New Mexico

Consumer and Economic Crime Division
Office of Attorney General
P.O. Box Drawer 1508
Santa Fe, NM 87504
(505) 872-6910
(800) 432-2070 (toll free in NM)

New York

Consumer Protection Board
99 Washington Ave.
Albany, NY 12210
(518) 474-8583

Consumer Protection Board
250 Broadway, 17th Floor
New York, NY 10007-2593
(212) 587-4908

North Carolina

Consumer Protection Section
Office of Attorney General
P.O. Box 629
Raleigh, NC 27602
(919) 733-7741

North Dakota

Consumer Fraud Division
Office of Attorney General
State Capitol Bldg.

Bismarck, ND 58505
(701) 224-2210
(800) 472-2600 (toll free in ND)

Ohio

Consumer Frauds and Crimes Section
Office of Attorney General
30 E. Broad St., 25th Floor
Columbus, OH 43266-0410
(614) 466-4986
(800) 282-0515 (toll free in OH)

Oklahoma

Consumer Affairs
Office of Attorney General
112 State Capitol Bldg.
Oklahoma City, OK 73105
(405) 521-3921

Oregon

Financial Fraud Section
Office of Attorney General
Justice Bldg.
Salem, OR 97310
(503) 378-4320

Pennsylvania

Bureau of Consumer Protection
Office of Attorney General
Strawberry Sq., 14th Floor
Harrisburg, PA 17120
(717) 787-9707
(800) 441-2555 (toll free in PA)

Puerto Rico

Department of Consumer Affairs
Minillas Station
P.O. Box 41059
Santurce, PR 00940
(809) 722-7555

Rhode Island

Consumer Protection Division
Department of Attorney General
72 Pine St.
Providence, RI 02903

(401) 277-2104
(800) 852-7776 (toll free in RI)

South Carolina

Department of Consumer Affairs
P.O. Box 5757
Columbia, SC 29250
(803) 734-9452
(800) 922-1594 (toll free in SC)

South Dakota

Division of Consumer Affairs
Office of Attorney General
State Capitol Bldg.
Pierre, SD 57501
(605) 773-4400

Tennessee

Division of Consumer Affairs
Department of Commerce & Insurance
500 James Robertson Pkwy., 5th Floor
Nashville, TN 37219
(615) 741-4737
(800) 342-8385 (toll free in TN)

Texas

Consumer Protection Division
Office of Attorney General
Box 12548, Capitol Station
Austin, TX 78711
(512) 463-2070

Utah

Division of Consumer Protection
Department of Business Regulation
160 E. Third South
P.O. Box 45802
Salt Lake City, UT 84145
(801) 530-6601

Vermont

Public Protection Division
Office of Attorney General
109 State St.
Montpelier, VT 05602
(802) 828-3171

Virgin Islands

Department of Licensing and Consumer Affairs
Property and Procurement Bldg.
Subbase #1, Room 205
St. Thomas, VI 0801
(809) 774-3130

Virginia

Division of Consumer Counsel
Office of Attorney General
Supreme Court Bldg.
101 N. 8th St.
Richmond, VA 23219
(804) 786-2116

Washington

Consumer and Business Fair Practices Division
710 2nd Ave., Suite 1300
Seattle, WA 98104
(206) 464-7744
(800) 551-4636 (toll free in WA)

West Virginia

Consumer Protection Division
Office of Attorney General
812 Quarrier St., 6th Floor
Charleston, WV 25301
(304) 348-8986
(800) 368-8808 (toll free in WV)

Wisconsin

Office of Consumer Protection
Department of Justice
P.O. Box 7856
Madison, WI 53707
(608) 266-1852
(800) 362-8189 (toll free in WI)

Wyoming

Office of Attorney General
123 State Capitol Bldg.
Cheyenne, WY 82002
(307) 777-6286

APPENDIX

IX

BIBLIOGRAPHY— EVERYDAY CONTRACTS

This bibliography of form books and books about general contract law should be used to supplement the resources listed in each part. Some books are written for lawyers and law students, others for nonlawyers. Many include a variety of forms with do-it-yourself instructions.

Form books should be used with some caution. Their sample forms will probably have to be adjusted to your particular situation. In any event, be sure you understand all parts of a sample form before using any of it.

The Complete Legal Kit, by the Consumer Law Foundation. Running Press, 125 S. 22nd St., Philadelphia, PA 19103. (215) 567-5080. 1988. 164 pages. $17.95.
Self-help book with over 150 ready-to-use tear-out forms. Covers employment, leases, credit, assignments, and loans, among other subjects, all in plain language.

Contracts, by Gordon D. Schaber and Claude D. Rohwer. Nutshell Series, West Publishing Co., P.O. Box 43526, St. Paul, MN 55164. (612) 228-2500. 1984. 425 pages. $10.95.

Written for law students by law professors; covers contract theory as it would be taught to first-year students. Complete, easy-to-read (although not in plain language) discussion of all contract theory, but more than you may ever need.

Everyday Legal Forms, by Irving J. Sloan. Oceana Group, 75 Main St., Dobbs Ferry, NY 10522. (914) 693-1320. 1984. 146 pages. $8.50. Thirty-four legal forms for business agreements, domestic relations, real estate, estate planning (including wills and trusts), powers of attorney, and promissory notes, among others. Covers protection needed in common legal transactions and background of forms in the book.

How To Avoid Lawyers, by Don Biggs. Garland Press, 136 Madison Ave., New York, NY 10016. (212) 686-7492. 1989. 1,000 pages. $27.95.

Basic reference tool, perfect for do-it-yourselfers. Overview of most everyday law, including real estate, domestic law, and probate, plus hundreds of forms, including powers of attorney and promissory notes.

Instant Legal Forms, by Ralph E. Troisi. Tab Books, Blue Ridge Summit, PA 17294. (717) 794-2191. 1989. 305 pages. $15.95.

Book of easy-to-use forms, including rental agreement, deed, promissory note, home-improvement contract, and living will.

Legal Agreements in Plain English, by Joel D. Joseph and Jeffrey Hiller. Contemporary Books, Inc., 180 N. Michigan Ave., Chicago, IL 60601. (312) 782-9181. 1982. 136 pages. $9.95.

Principles, definitions, and forms for conducting basic legal business. Agreements with simple explanations and tear-out contracts. Includes setting up a business, separation and divorce, loans, wills, home improvements, and buying, renting, or selling a home.

The Legal Forms Kit. Homestead Publishing Co., 4455 Torrance Blvd., Torrance, CA 90503. (213) 214-3559. 1987. 320 pages. $41.95. Forms for almost every legal topic with plain-language explanations for each. Topics include real estate, credit and collections, employment, loans and debts, small businesses and partnerships, among others.

Make Your Own Contract, by Stephen Elias. Nolo Press, 950 Parker St., Berkeley, CA 94710. (415) 549-1976. 1987. 208 pages. $12.95.

Detailed workbook for writing your own contract in plain language. Includes many variations of forms, plus warnings and tips.

Personal Lawyer. Bloc Publishing Co., 800 S.W. 37th Ave., Suite 765, Coral Gables, FL 33134. (800) 888-2562. 1988. $50.

IBM computer program of five do-it-yourself forms: will, power of attorney, statement of guardianship, promissory note, and lease. Question-and-answer format to complete user's personalized form.

The Power of Attorney Book, by Dennis Clifford. Nolo Press, 950 Parker St., Berkeley, CA 94710. (415) 549-1976. 1988. 280 pages. $17.95.

All forms and instructions to create your own conventional or durable power of attorney as well as advice on when and how to delegate authority over your health and personal affairs.

Sign Here, by Mari W. Privette. Doubleday and Co., 501 Franklin Ave., Garden City, NY 11530. (212) 765-6500. 1985. 297 pages. $9.95. Easy-to-use book that explains contract terms, requirements, and remedies, and includes sample contracts and a complete glossary. In question-and-answer form, includes insurance, marriage and divorce, real estate warranties, and credit.

What You Should Know about Contracts, by Robert A. Farmer. Simon and Schuster, 1230 Ave. of the Americas, New York, NY 10020. (212) 698-7000. 1979 (out of print). 189 pages. $3.95.

Good, clear, plain-language discussion of contract basics, including offer and acceptance, consideration, defenses, and breach of contract. Also sample contracts and short glossary. No longer in bookstores.

APPENDIX

X

BIBLIOGRAPHY— REAL ESTATE

All America's Real Estate Book, by Carolyn Janik and Ruth Rejnis. Penguin Group, 40 W. 23rd St., New York, NY 10010. 1985. $14.95.
Exhaustive source of information on all aspects of buying, selling, renting and moving.

Barron's Real Estate Handbook, by Jack C. Harris and Jack Friedman. Barron's Educational Series, 250 Wireless Blvd., Hauppauge, NY 11788. 1988. $19.95.
Glossary of real estate and financial terms with chapters on buying, selling and careers in real estate. Extensive bibliography.

The Common-Sense Guide to Successful Real Estate Negotiation, by Peter G. Miller and Douglas M. Bregman. Harper and Row Publishers, 10 E. 53rd St., New York, NY 10022. 1987. $16.95.
Strategies for buying and selling house without an agent. Information you need easy to find with small sections and index. Sample contracts and forms throughout.

The Common-Sense Mortgage—How to Cut the Cost of Home Ownership by $100,000 or More, by Peter G. Miller. Harper and Row Publishers, 10 E. 53rd St., New York, NY 10022. 1987. $7.95.
Well-reviewed do-it-yourself book on mortgages and finances. Includes extensive index and list of relevant questions to ask.

543

The Complete Book of Homebuying, by Michael Sumichrast and Ronald C. Shafer. Bantam Books, 666 5th Ave., New York, NY 10103. 1987. $4.95.

Pros and cons of buying new versus older homes, doing home improvements and selling property on your own. Financing and tax information.

The Complete Guide to Real Estate Loans, by Andrew James McLean. Contemporary Books, 180 N. Michigan Ave, Chicago, IL 60601. 1983. $6.95.

Covers most major topics, but in a rather cursory manner. Large print and many charts make it easy to read, but there is not much information in this 116-page book.

The Complete Homebuyers Kit, by Edith Lank. Longman Financial Service, 520 N. Dearborn St., Chicago, IL 60610-4975. 1989. $14.95.

Thorough book on all aspects of home buying including tips on choosing agent, financing purchase, comparing properties and negotiating contract. Includes mortgage rate charts.

The Complete Homesellers Kit, by Edith Lank. Longman Financial Service, 520 N. Dearborn St., Chicago, IL 60610-4975. 1988. $14.95.

Useful comparisons on whether you should sell on your own or with an agent. Includes tips on negotiating sales contracts, fixing up homes and taxes. Glossary.

The Complete House Inspection Book, by Don Frederickson. Fawcett Columbine, Ballantine Books, 201 E. 50th St., New York, NY 10022. 1988. $9.95.

Thorough evaluation from author, former plumber, electrician, builder and inspector, of all parts and possible defects in a home. Encourages making your own evaluations.

The Deeds Book: How to Transfer Title to California Real Estate, by Mary Randolph. Nolo Press, 950 Parker St., Berkeley, CA 94710. 1987. $15.95.

Step-by-step guide to changing property title in California. Includes tear-out forms.

The Field Guide to Home Buying in America, by Stephen Pollan, Mark Levine, and Michael Pollan. Simon and Schuster, 1230 Avenue of the Americas, New York, NY 10020. 1988. $8.95.

Authors cover every possible question from thinking about buying to moving in.

First Home Buying Guide, by H. L. Kibbey. Panoply Press, Inc., P.O. Box 1885, Lake Oswego, OR 97035. 1988. $8.95.

Useful guide for first-time home buyers on how to find a home, work with agent, get loan approved and close deal.

For Sale By Owner: All the Contracts and Instructions Necessary to Sell Your Own California House, by George Devine. Nolo Press, 950 Parker St., Berkeley, CA 94710. 1987. $24.95.

Home-selling tips for California residents. Includes glossary and tear-out contracts and forms.

Home Buyers: Lambs to Slaughter, by Sloan Bashinsky, Menasha Ridge Press, Route 3, Box 450 HB, Hillsborough, NC 27278. 1984. $12.95.

Short, complete look at real estate "game." Describes your allies and opponents, contains table of how to figure monthly mortgage costs.

How to Buy a Home While You Can Still Afford To, by Michael C. Murphy. Sterling Publications Co., 387 Park Ave. South, New York, NY 10016. 1989. $7.95.
Tips on finding mortgage, using short-term loans, computing tax advantages. Includes worksheets.

How to Buy a House, Condo or Co-op, by Michael C. Thomsett. Consumer Report Books, 51 E. 42nd St., New York, NY 10017. 1987. $12.00.
For first- and second-time home buyers; information includes locating property, negotiating prices, closing deals. Index and glossary.

How to Buy a House When You Are Cash Poor, by Vanessa A. Bush. Contemporary Books, 180 N. Michigan Ave., Chicago, IL 60601. 1986. $4.95.
Evaluates various mortgage systems and ways of financing home purchase. Lists areas of house essential to inspect before buying.

How to Buy Your Home in 90 Days, by Marc Stephen Garrison. Doubleday Publishing Co., 666 5th Ave., New York, NY 10103. 1989. $12.95.
Tips for novice on financing, dealing with brokers, negotiating best possible price and closing deal. Includes amortization schedules and glossary.

How to Sell Your House Without a Broker, by Harley Bjelland. Cornerstone Library, 1230 Avenue of the Americas, New York, NY 10020. 1979. $3.95.
Fairly complete synopsis of what is involved in a sale including cleaning house, writing advertisements, financing and moving.

Making Mortgages Work for You, by Robert Irwin. McGraw-Hill Book Co., 1221 Avenue of the Americas, New York, NY 10020. 1987. $12.95.
Major financing options in well-organized and easy-to-read fashion. Lengthy appendix helps determine how much money to spend under variety of interest rates.

The New Real Estate Game, by Hollis Norton. Contemporary Books, 180 N. Michigan Ave., Chicago, IL 60601. 1987. $17.95.
Tips on how to get financing, buy and sell properties, renovate and juggle tax laws to your financial advantage.

Nothing Down, by Robert G. Allen. Simon and Schuster, 1230 Avenue of the Americas, New York, NY 10020. 1984. $19.95.
For the real estate investor, offers creative financing tips if you have little or no money to put down and information on how to manage properties.

101 Easy Ways to Make Your Home Sell Faster, by Barbara Jane Hall. Ballantine Books, 201 E. 50th St., New York, NY 10022. 1985. $4.95.
How to present your home in best possible light to prospective buyers, including interior decoration.

Power Real Estate Negotiations, by William H. Pivar and Richard W. Post. Longman Financial Services, 520 N. Dearborn St., Chicago, IL 60610-4975. 1990. $19.95.
Useful resource for investors and real estate professionals. Covers general negotiating strategies for every aspect of buying and selling property.

Selling Your Home Sweet Home: A Practical Survival Guide for Selling Your Home, by Sloan Bashinsky. Monarch Press, 1230 Avenue of the Americas, New York, NY 10020. 1985. $12.95.

With innovative ways to get the highest price for your house, this book will help you deal with professionals, prepare your house, set a price, finance, negotiate and more. Ethical codes, regulatory agencies and a sample grievance complaint form included.

The Single Person's Home-Buying Handbook, by Kristelle L. Petersen. Hawthorn/ Dutton, 2 Park Ave., New York, NY 10016. 1980. $6.95 (Out of print.) Useful information for single people, emphasizing legal concerns and protections still useful but should be supplemented with more recent information on financing and tax considerations. Index and glossary.

Sonny Bloch's Inside Real Estate, by H. I. Sonny Bloch and Grace Lichtenstein. Weidenfeld and Nicolson, 10 East 53rd St., New York, NY 10022. 1987. $18.95. Role of both seller and buyer in each side of real estate transaction. Glossary and amortization tables included.

Sonny Bloch's 171 Ways to Make Money in Real Estate, by Sonny Bloch and Grace Lichtenstein. Prentice-Hall Press, 15 Columbus Circle, New York, NY 10023. 1989. $19.95. Step-by-step instructions through every phase of investment process. Includes sample contracts, rental and purchase agreements, financial portfolios and more.

Top Dollar for Your Property, by James E. A. Lumley. John Wiley and Sons, 605 Third Ave., New York, NY 10158-0012. 1988. $12.95. Good guide to all aspects of selling your home. Well-organized and easy to read.

Webster's New World Illustrated Encyclopedic Dictionary of Real Estate, by Jerome S. Gross. Simon and Schuster, One Gulf and Western Plaza, New York, NY 10023. 1987. $12.95. Includes complete dictionary of terms, portfolio of forms, list of organizations, amortization schedule, and National Association of Realtors Code of Ethics.

APPENDIX
XI

BIBLIOGRAPHY—
SMALL CLAIMS COURT

Collect Your Court Judgment, by Gini Graham Scott, Stephen Elias and Lisa Goldoftas. Nolo Press, 950 Parker St., Berkeley, CA 94710. 1988 (1st Ed.). $24.95.
Guide to collecting court judgments in California—whether from small claims, municipal or superior court. Step-by-step instructions and forms used to collect judgments from a debtor's bank accounts, wages, business receipts, real estate and other assets.

Everybody's Guide to Small Claims Court, by Ralph Warner. Nolo Press, 950 Parker St., Berkeley, CA 94710. 1987 (national 3rd Ed.). $14.95.
Step-by-step "how-to" book illustrated with true-to-life examples. Sample forms for New York and California's small claims courts included along with information compiled in 1987 for all fifty states is also included.

Everybody's Guide to Small Claims Court, by Ralph Warner. Nolo Press, 950 Parker St., Berkeley, CA 94710. 1987 (California 7th Ed.). $14.95.
Specifically for California residents, with much of the same information, examples and California forms in national edition.

How You Can Sue Without Hiring a Lawyer, by John Striker and Andrew Shapiro. Simon and Schuster, 1230 6th Ave., New York, NY. 10020. 1981. (Out of print.)
Attorneys John Striker and Andrew Shapiro advise you to defer to or consult

with lawyers often. Nevertheless, this helpful book devotes equal space to describing process and applying it to wide variety of legal problems.

Inexpensive Justice: Self Representation in the Small Claims Court, by Robert L. Spurrier, Jr. Associated Faculty Press, Inc., Route 100, Millwood, NY. 10546. 1983. $12.95.

Excellent but expensive resource book. Its fewer than 100 pages can be read in one sitting. Does not include information on mediation or arbitration.

Small Claims Court Guide for Washington, by Donald D. Stuart. Self-Counsel Press Inc., 1303 N. Northgate Way, Seattle, WA, 98133. 1989 (2d Ed.). $8.95. Useful guide for residents of Washington with instructions on successfully filing or defending a case in small claims court, appealing a decision and collecting your judgment. Twenty-one sample forms used in Washington's small claims court.

Sue the B*st*rds: The Victim's Handbook Newly Revised and Updated, by Douglas Matthews. Arbor House Publishing Co., 235 E. 45th St. New York, NY. 10017. 1981. (Out of print.)228

Although text written in 1973, book still offers useful tips but because laws governing small claims courts change frequently, the state rules appendices, most recently revised in 1981, are no longer up to date. Available only through local libraries and law libraries.

The People's Court: How to Tell It to the Judge, by Harvey Levin, William Morrow & Co., 105 Madison Ave., New York, NY 18016. $4.95. 1985.

Impressive array of cases from television courtroom of Judge Joseph Wapner's *People's Court.* Cases bear catchy names like "The Munched-on Mailman" and "Looking for Love in All the Wrong Places." Particularly helpful is Levin's explanation of how Judge Wapner arrives at his decisions.

APPENDIX

XII

GLOSSARY

The following defines terms used throughout this book. Italicized terms are defined in other entries of this glossary.

Abstract of title Condensed history of *title* to property that includes the chain of ownership and a record of all *liens,* taxes or other *encumbrances* that may affect the title.

Acceleration The process by which a lender, such as a bank, makes the entire amount of a loan due and requests that it be paid at once. Usually triggered by the borrower's *default.*

Acceleration clause Clause in a loan agreement that gives the lender the right to demand full payment on the remaining balance of the loan if certain events occur.

Acceptance Agreement to a contract *offer* on the terms presented. An acceptance can be verbal, written, or an action, such as the payment of money. Once accepted, a contract is created.

Accounts receivable Money that is owed.

Addendum Attachment to a *contract.* It is often placed on an additional sheet of paper and referred to in the main contract document. Also called a rider.

Adjustable-rate mortgage (ARM) Mortgage whose interest rate fluctuates depending on a previously agreed-upon *index.*

Agent   Someone who acts on behalf of another. In real estate, agents work for buyers and sellers, called *principals (1)*.

Amortization   System of loan repayment whereby *principal (2)* and *interest* are calculated for the life of the loan and the interest is based on the declining balance of the principal.

Amortization schedule   A schedule of equal payments over a specified period to pay off both a debt and the *interest* on that debt. This is provided by a lender, such as a bank, when someone takes out a loan.

Annual percentage rate (APR)   The *interest* for each year of a loan, expressed as a percentage of the money borrowed.

Answer   *Defendant's* formal written statement of defense against the *plaintiff's* complaint in a lawsuit. The answer addresses the truth or falsity of the plaintiff's claims and can include a *counterclaim*.

Appeal   Request that a higher court review the decision of a lower court to correct errors in the application of law or procedure.

Appraisal   Assessment of the value of a piece of property as of a specified date, usually made by an expert in the field.

Arbitration   Method of settling disputes in which the two sides submit arguments to a neutral third party or panel, which makes a decision after listening to both sides and considering the evidence.

Assessed value   Value of a piece of property as set by the government for taxation.

Assignee   Person to whom a right or interest is given or transferred. In small claims court, a party to a lawsuit may decide to transfer his or her right or interest in that lawsuit to another person (the assignee).

Assignment   Formally giving someone a right or obligation.

Assumable mortgage   Loan that can be taken over by another party, such as a future buyer. One benefit of the arrangement is that, if the interest rate of the original loan is lower than the current prevailing rates, its transfer to the new buyer results in substantial savings.

Attachment   Method by which real or *personal property* is legally taken by a creditor and held pending the outcome of a lawsuit over a debt.

Attorney in fact   The person designated in a power of attorney to handle the affairs of the person making the power of attorney.

Balloon mortgage   *Mortgage* that is paid back in a few low payments and one very large payment at the end of the mortgage.

Bankruptcy   A procedure rescheduling or canceling a person's debts. Typically, a court seizes all of a person's assets and disburses them among creditors. A small amount, an "exemption," is reserved by the court for the individual— once the individual has been officially discharged of all debts. Under some forms of bankruptcy, the individual must pay back a percentage of those debts afterward, as decided by the court.

Binder   "Agreement to agree" signed by buyer and seller. It states the agreed-upon price for the property and forbids the seller to contract with other buyers.

Bond   A monetary guarantee that should a contractor fail to perform a contract fully, compensation will be awarded up to the bond's limit.

Breach   Reason for suing based on failure to live up to a legally binding promise.

Breach of contract   Reason for suing based on failure to live up to a legally binding promise, such as a real estate *contract*.

Bylaws   Governing document of a *condominium* or *cooperative* association.

Cap   Limit on interest rates or individual payment rates for loans.

Certificate of title   Document stating that the seller has a good and *marketable title*.

Chain of title   List of owners of a piece of property. It is checked each time a home is sold to ensure that full and total ownership was transferred at each sale.

Class action   Lawsuit brought by one or more individuals on behalf of a larger group of individuals in the same legal situation.

Clear and conspicuous   A phrase used to describe how the important parts of a lending contract must appear so that the borrower will notice them, as required by the *Truth in Lending Act*. The costs of credit (for purposes of comparison), as well as the loan's significant benefits, obligations, and restrictions, must all be "clear and conspicuous" on the contract.

Closing   Formal meeting of all those involved in the sale of real estate to exchange documents and money and execute the final deal.

Closing agent   Person who oversees the *closing* process. This may be one already involved in the transaction, such as a title insurance representative or one of the *agents* of the buyer or seller.

Collateral   Something of value provisionally given to the lender during the life of the loan. In the event of *default*, it can be seized and sold by the lender.

Collection   A method of obtaining debts owed.

Commission   Fixed percentage of a price paid to others (e.g., a *real estate* or *mortgage broker*) for an agreed-upon service.

Commitment fee   One-time fee paid by a buyer to a lender to bind the lender to the loan. It usually equals 1%, or one *point*, of the loan amount.

Common area   That part of a *condominium* or *cooperative* that is shared and used by all residents and paid for from the general fees charged to all unit owners.

Compulsory counterclaim   *Counterclaim* in which the *defendant*'s claim against the *plaintiff* arises out of the same transaction or occurrence as in the original complaint. The defendant must file a counterclaim in that lawsuit or forever be barred from raising that claim in a separate lawsuit.

Condominium   Form of property ownership in which individuals own and control their own units and share the costs of the *common areas* with other unit owners.

Confession of judgment   A clause that allows the lender to appoint a lawyer on the borrower's behalf in order to get a court *judgment* on a debt without notifying the borrower. The Credit Practices Rule makes this provision illegal in consumer loans.

Conflict of laws   The body of laws a court uses to decide whether its own previous rulings or those of some other court related to the case are to be used in a specific case.

Conforming mortgage   Mortgage that conforms to the standards set by the secondary mortgage market, those who buy loans from primary lenders.

Conservator   A person or corporation appointed by a court to handle the affairs or property of another who is unable to do so because of *incapacity* or being under the age of majority.

Consideration   Something of value each side gives up in order to make a contract valid. Usually in the form of money-for-goods, this may also be a promise or service.

Contingency   Provision in a real estate *contract* that makes a buyer's offer to purchase dependent on certain events or terms.

Continuance   Postponement of a legal proceeding or deadline.

Contract   Binding agreement between two parties who have willingly exchanged something of value, called the consideration.

Conversion   Change of type of ownership of a property to a *condominium* or *cooperative*. This change is regulated by state or local law.

Convey   To transfer property to another.

Conveyance   An exchange of two things, usually used when referring to land transactions.

Cooperative   Form of pooled property ownership in which individuals own shares of stock in a cooperative association that owns the property; shareholders are given control over their individual units.

Cosigner   One who adds his or her signature to the loan of another and thereby assumes equal responsibility for payments on that loan.

Counterclaim   Claim made by a *defendant* in a civil lawsuit that, in effect, sues the *plaintiff* (see *Permissive counterclaim* and *Compulsory counterclaim*).

Counteroffer   An invitation to exchange promises and enter into a contract, thereby canceling an earlier *offer* by the other side in the prospective contract. The counteroffer must be accepted to make a contract.

Credit bureau   Company that maintains records of consumers' credit history for potential creditors, who pay a fee for the report.

Credit history   A history of credits used, loans paid, and outstanding debts owed by an individual.

Credit report   A document that shows all or part of a person's *credit history*.

Creditworthiness   An evaluation of whether a person should be granted a loan or a line of credit, made at the discretion of the bank or other lender organization.

Crossclaim   Claim litigated by codefendants or coplaintiffs against each other and not against persons on the opposite side of the lawsuit.

Damages   Amount of money or other relief requested by a plaintiff in a lawsuit.

Deed   Formal representation of ownership of a piece of property.

Deed of trust   Loan made by a lender to a buyer for the purchase of real estate.

Default   Declaration by a lender that a borrower has failed to make scheduled payments on a loan, thereby enabling the lender to seize the property or other *collateral*.

Default judgment   Decision in favor of the *plaintiff* because the *defendant* failed to respond to the plaintiff's complaint within the time required by law, or failed to appear in court on the scheduled date of the hearing or trial.

Defendant   Person against whom a legal action is filed.

Deposition   Out-of-court process of taking the sworn testimony of a witness. This is usually done by a lawyer with a lawyer from the other side being permitted to attend or participate. The purpose is to disclose relevant information so that each side can evaluate its case before going to trial and decide whether to pursue the claim or settle out of court.

Detainer   Holding a person against his or her will, or keeping a person from goods or land he or she legally owns.

Disclosures   Affirmative statement made to ensure certain information is communicated. Lenders are required by the *Truth in Lending Act* to make certain disclosures to their customers.

Discount points   See *Points.*

Discount rate   The *interest* rate charged by the *Federal Reserve Board* to its member banks.

Discovery   Before-trial formal and informal exchange of information between the sides in a lawsuit. Two types of discovery are *interrogatories* and *depositions.*

Down payment   That part of the purchase price given to a seller at the time of *closing,* over and above the amount of the loan.

Due on sale clause   Clause in a *mortgage* agreement that requires the balance to be paid in full when the property or *collateral* is sold. This clause forbids the *mortgage* from being *assumable.*

Duress   Unlawful pressure on a person to do something she or he would not voluntarily do. A contract shown to have been made under duress will be declared invalid.

Earnest money   Also called a deposit. Money given by the buyer to the seller at the signing of the *binder* to demonstrate good faith.

Easement   Right to have a limited, specified use of someone else's property.

Eminent domain   Government's power to take private property for public use simply by paying for it.

Encumbrance   Anything that affects *title* to property, such as a *lien* or *mortgage.*

Equitable title   Form of ownership that is transferred when the papers are signed but actual possession is delayed. With it, responsibility for the property passes to the new owner.

Equity (Real Estate)   Value of that part of real estate an owner has actually paid for and owns. Often it refers to that part of the total *mortgage* payments already paid, excluding *interest,* taxes and other fees plus the down payment and any appreciated value.

Equity (Small Claims Court)   Principles of fairness and justice. In small claims courts that allow "equitable relief," judges are allowed to order a party to do something other than payment of money damages (see *Rescission, Restitution, Reformation* and *Specific performance*).

Escrow   Money placed in a separate account to be used in previously agreed-to circumstances and released when certain conditions are met. Escrow money is often used to pay tax and insurance bills on property during the life of a *mortgage*.

Exclusive listing contract   Agreement between a seller and *real estate broker* giving the broker the sole right to locate buyers for the listed property.

Excused counterperformance   A *remedy* for a broken contract whereby, if one side fails to live up to its side of the agreement, the other may not be obligated to live up to its side.

Federal Reserve Board   A 13-member board appointed by the president and approved by Congress. It regulates both banks in the United States and the entire U.S. monetary system. (Complaints about banks that are members of the Federal Reserve System should be made here.)

Federal Trade Commission   A commission appointed by the president responsible for regulating trade practices, including those of finance companies. (Problems concerning nonbank loans—e.g., department store credit—should be reported to the FTC.)

Fee simple   Absolute and total ownership of a piece of property.

Fee tail   Ownership of a piece of property that can be transferred only to one's familial heirs. A centuries-old form of ownership now not permitted in many states.

FHA loan   Loan backed by the government and made to individuals who meet certain criteria.

Fiduciary duty   Legal obligation to represent the best interests of another.

Finance charge   *Interest* and other added fees, in addition to the cost of goods or services, to be paid when a purchase is made in installments; usually must be stated as an *annual percentage rate*.

Fixture   Any object firmly attached to a piece of real estate that cannot easily be removed. Fixtures are transferred with property unless otherwise specified.

Fixed-rate mortgage   *Mortgage* for which the rate of *interest* remains the same for the life of the mortgage.

Forcible entry and detainer   Court proceeding that restores land or property to one who is wrongfully kept out or deprived of legal possession.

Foreclosure   Process by which property offered as security for a loan is sold to pay off the debt if the borrower is unable to pay.

Fraud   Intentional deception, grounds for canceling a contract. Also a defense to breaching a contract.

Garnishment   Legal proceeding in which a debtor's wages, property, money or credits are taken to satisfy payment of a debt or *judgment*.

GI loan   See *VA loan*.

Gift letter   Statement required by a lender of loan applicants who are receiving money from another person to make a *down payment* on a *mortgage*.

Grace period   Short period, usually ten to fifteen days after a *mortgage* payment is due, during which the borrower will be assessed no late charge or additional *interest*.

Graduated-rate mortgage   *Mortgage* whose payments increase each year for a number of years and then level off.

Grantee   Purchaser of real estate.

Grantor   Seller of real estate.

Guardian   See *Conservator*.

Homeowner's insurance   Insurance designed to protect homeowners from losses caused by fire, theft, and so on. Some lenders require that this be purchased before they approve the loan.

Housing code   State or local regulations that mandate sanitary and technical requirements that must be met before a residence can be occupied.

Implied warranty of habitability   The legal obligation of a landlord to provide tenants with livable, safe, and sanitary housing.

Incapacity   A declaration by a court that a person is unable to handle his or her own affairs because of a mental or physical condition.

Index   Listing of figures against which the *interest* rate is measured for *mortgages*.

Injunction   Judge's order to do or to refrain from doing a specified thing. For example, a court might issue an injunction ordering a landlord to restore heat to a tenant's apartment even though the tenant's rent is overdue.

Inspection   Formal process of examining a piece of property and its *fixtures* to determine whether it meets a buyer's needs.

Interest   Payment the lender receives for lending the money. Payment of interest creates no *equity*.

Interrogatory   Form of *discovery* in which written questions posed by one side in a lawsuit require written responses under oath by the other.

Joint tenancy with a right of survivorship   Form of ownership in which property is equally shared by all owners and is automatically transferred to the surviving owners if one owner dies.

Judgment   Final decision announced or written by a judge about the rights and claims of each side in a lawsuit.

Judgment creditor   Person to whom money is owed after a court's *judgment*.

Judgment debtor   Person who owes money after a court's *judgment*.

Libel   False or malicious written statements that injure a person's reputation, business or property rights.

Lien   Legal claim to hold or sell property as security for a debt.

Life estate   Ownership in a piece of property for one's lifetime only. The holder of a life estate has no power to leave it to anyone in a will. That power remains with the person who gives the property to the holder of the life estate.

Liquidity   The ease with which assets may be converted to cash; the amount of a person's assets in a state of cash or near cash (as in a bank's savings account).

Listing contract   Agreement made with a *real estate broker* by a seller giving the broker the right to locate a buyer.

Loan officer   Lender's employee who coordinates all of the loan processes from initial application through *closing*.

Loan principal   The amount of money borrowed, as contrasted with *interest* to be paid on that amount.

Marketable title   *Title* to property that is free from all *liens, encumbrances* and defects.

Market value   Value a property would command if sold on the open market.

Material terms   The essential details that define each side's rights and obligations under a contract.

Mechanic's lien   Legal claim by a service person to hold or sell property as security for a debt.

Mediation   Informal alternative to suing in which both sides to a dispute meet with a neutral third party (mediator) to negotiate a resolution. The resolution is usually put into a written agreement that is signed by both sides.

Mortgage   Formal document a home buyer signs pledging the property as security for the payment of the loan taken out to buy it.

Mortgage banker   Professional who controls the investment for certain funds and locates borrowers to use those funds.

Mortgage broker   Professional who matches borrowers with *mortgage opportunities.*

Mortgage servicing company   Company hired by a lender to handle all the administrative aspects of *mortgage* repayment.

Multiple listing service   Arrangement by which *real estate brokers* share through a computer listing the right to sell a property that has been exclusively listed with them. The broker who had the original right to sell receives a portion of the *commission* if one or the others finds a buyer.

Negative amortization   Decline in owner *equity* that occurs when the *interest* rate on a mortgage has risen so high that loan payments no longer are large enough to cover the interest due. This results in an increase at each payment period in the *principal (2)* that is owed.

Negotiable   Something that can be exchanged for cash, such as a check or promissory note.

Negotiable instrument   Signed document containing an unconditional promise to pay an exact sum of money on demand or at a specified time. It must be marked, payable "to the order of" or "to the bearer." Examples are checks, notes and certificates of deposit.

Notary public   One who has finished a course of study and is licensed by the state to verify the legitimacy of documents signed in his or her presence.

Note   Written, signed document in which a borrower acknowledges a debt and promises payment.

Notice of default   A written notice by one side in an agreement to the second stating that the contract has been *breached* and reclaiming whatever benefits the second party gained by the contract.

Offer   An invitation to make a contract or to exchange promises. (See also *Counteroffer.*)

Open listing   Arrangement by which a *real estate broker* or *agent* has a nonexclusive right to sell a property. Open listings may be given to several brokers or agents. Only the one that sells the home is entitled to a *commission.*

Order   Written command by a judge or court clerk describing a decision of the court, directing or forbidding an action, or issuing the final ruling of the court in a case.

Origination fee   One-time charge by a lender for processing the loan papers. It usually amounts to 1% of total loan. It is paid at closing as a part of the *points.*

Payable on demand An item payable within a reasonable time after it is requested (e.g., a note or loan payable on demand may be requested at any time).

Performance The completion of one side of an agreement or contract; carrying out one's end of a bargain.

Permissive counterclaim *Counterclaim* in which the *defendant's* claim against the *plaintiff* is unrelated to the claims stated in the original complaint. It is "permissive" in that if the defendant doesn't counterclaim, he or she may still bring an individual lawsuit.

Personal property All property other than land and *fixtures.*

Plaintiff Person who files a lawsuit against another.

Pleading Making a formal written statement of the claims or defenses of each side in a lawsuit.

Points Fee a lender collects for making a loan, paid by the buyer, seller, or both. It includes both loan *origination* and *commitment fees.* Each point equals 1% of the loan amount.

Prejudgment detainer Court *order* to hold property or personal goods until a final court decision is made.

Prepayment A payment before a sum is due.

Prepayment penalty Charge that penalizes a borrower who pays off a loan earlier than required by the terms of the loan.

Prime rate *Interest* banks charge their best customers.

Principal (1) Person for whom an *agent* acts. (2) That part of every *mortgage* payment that pays the cost of the home, excluding *interest* and fees. Payment of this builds *equity.*

Private mortgage insurance Insurance required by some lenders, especially when the *down payment* is low. It ensures against loss if the borrower is unable to pay.

Probate Legal process of proving a will and making the distribution of a deceased person's assets as described in the will.

Prorate To allocate respective shares of an obligation among parties or over time.

Quasi-contract A court award of money for work already done before the contract was broken. A *remedy* for *breach* of contract.

Quiet enjoyment A common-law requirement that landlords who rent residences guarantee peace and quiet to tenants.

Quitclaim deed *Deed* that transfers to another the ownership one has in a property, even if that ownership is none or encumbered. Usually used to transfer property between family members.

Real estate broker Individual licensed to engage in the business of providing ready, willing and qualified buyers for sellers of property, a service for which a *commission* is paid by the seller. A "Realtor" is a real estate broker who belongs to the National Association of Realtors. (Also see *Mortgage broker.*)

Real property Land and all that is affixed to it.

Receivership proceedings A court action during which either money or property of one party is put under the control of an outside, responsible party, called a receiver.

Redlining Discrimination against members of minority groups by refusing to make loans for home purchases in neighborhoods or communities populated by members of those groups. It is forbidden by federal law.

Refinancing Process of paying back one loan with the proceeds of a new one. This is often done to get a better *interest* rate and usually involves payment of *closing* costs.

Reformation Equitable remedy in which a court rewrites, corrects or amends a written agreement to conform with the original intent of the parties to that agreement.224

Release A legal document that relieves someone of an obligation or potential obligation.

Remedy The means by which someone is compensated for an injury. Types of remedies include restitution, *damages,* and *specific performance.* Also, a penalty to prevent the breaking of a contract.

Rescission Equitable remedy in which a court cancels a contract. For instance, if a judge finds that a contract is unfair or fraudulent, he or she may decide to cancel (rescind) the contract and act as if it had never existed.

Restitution Equitable remedy in which something is ordered given back or made good on. For instance, a judge may order that a *plaintiff* be put back in the financial position he or she was in before entering a contract.

Restrictive covenant "House rule" about what residents of a given area may or may not do with their property.

Revocable trust Property held by one party for the sake and benefit of a second but that can be taken back by the second party.

Rider See *Addendum.*

Right of survivorship Right to inherit all property held as a co-owner.

Second mortgage New *mortgage* based on the *equity* in an existing mortgage.

Secured loan A loan in which the lender holds an interest in property of the borrower to assure that the loan will be paid.

Security interest Rights a creditor has to a borrower's *collateral* if the borrower *defaults* on a loan.

Service Delivery of a legal document by an officially authorized person to meet formal requirements of the applicable laws and assure that the person being sued is formally notified about the lawsuit or other legal action.

Settlement Process by which all documents are signed and placed in order and all participants in a real estate purchase are required to keep their respective promises. Also called the *closing.*

Slander False or malicious oral statements that injure a person's reputation, business or property rights.

Specific performance Equitable *remedy* in which a court requires a party to do something. For example, a judge may order that a one-of-a-kind object be returned to its original owner.

Statute of frauds State law that specifies what contracts must be in writing to be considered legal and enforceable.

Statute of limitations   Law that sets a deadline for filing a lawsuit. This varies from state to state and with the basis of the lawsuit.

Steering   Discriminatory act of leading minority-group members away from neighborhoods not populated by members of that group. It is forbidden by federal law.

Sublease   Rental of a rented tenancy to a third party, in effect turning the first renter into a landlord. The original renter remains liable to the original landlord for the terms of the lease.

Substantial performance   Completion of a project sufficiently to warrant payment for all service, less the amount not completed.

Successors   Persons who take over the rights, responsibilities, or property of another.

Survey   Detailed measurement map of a property, made by a licensed surveyor. Lenders often require a survey as a condition for making a loan.

Title   Official representation of ownership that is transferred when a home is sold. Title can be "held" in the name of one or more persons.

Title insurance   Insurance against damages should any claims later be found in the *title*. This is paid for by the buyer. Lenders often require that additional coverage also be purchased for them.

Title search   Review of the *chain of title* by a professional to discover whether any defects, *liens* or *encumbrances* exist.

Transfer   Procedure by which a *defendant* can have a case moved to a higher court.

Transfer tax   State or local tax to be paid whenever property is transferred from one owner to another. Local custom determines who pays this tax.

Truth in Lending Act   Federal law that requires certain *disclosures* to be made to all those who apply for a loan.

Unconscionability   An unreasonable and challengeable provision in a contract that results from unequal bargaining power between the parties, such as when one side is forced by a take-it-or-leave-it proposal to accept the unreasonable provision. A court may strike down the unconscionable clause but uphold the rest of the contract.

Variable-rate mortgage   See *Adjustable-rate mortgage.*

Variance   Approved exception to *zoning* laws and regulations.

VA loan   Government-backed loan available to individuals who have served in active duty in the military.

Venue   Place where a case may be tried. A court may have the power to take a case within a wide geographic area, but the proper venue for the case may be one place within that area.

Waiver   A purposeful, voluntary surrender of a known right.

Waiver of exemption   A clause in a loan agreement that waives a borrower's legal right to restrict a court's seizure of personal property if the borrower *defaults.*

Walk-through   Final cursory *inspection* of a piece of property a buyer is about to purchase. Often done the day before *closing* and not by a professional.

Warranty   Guarantee by the seller that the condition of what is being transferred is exactly as described.

Writ of attachment A judge's order to seize persons or property in order to bring them under court control to pay off a court *judgment*.

Writ of execution Court *order* allowing a sheriff, marshal or other official to collect money or property owed by the *judgment debtor*.

Zoning Land-designation system that sets aside certain areas for certain uses. It usually permits *variances* in areas where a requested type of development is not permitted.

INDEX

About the Authors

George Milko is the Director of Education for HALT. He is the author of *Real Estate,* co-author of *After the Crash: An Information Kit for Victims of Airline Disasters,* and editor of *Alternative Compensation Strategies: Creating No Lawsuit Options to the Tort System.* Mr. Milko received his J.D. in 1983 from the National Law Center at George Washington University. He is a member of the District of Columbia Bar.

Kay Ostberg is the Deputy Director of HALT. She is the author of *Using a Lawyer, Probate, Directory of Lawyers Who Sue Lawyers,* and the "Attorney Discipline National Survey and Report." Ms. Ostberg received her J.D. in 1983 from the National Law Center at George Washington University. She is a member of the National Federation of Paralegal Associations Advisory Board.

Theresa Meehan Rudy is a program specialist with HALT—An Organization of Americans For Legal Reform. She has contributed to HALT's library of educational materials as author of *Fee Arbitration: Model Rules and Commentary* and as a coauthor of *Everyday Contracts: Protecting Your Rights.* Ms. Rudy also serves as a lay arbitrator for the District of Columbia Bar's fee arbitration program. She holds a B.A., cum laude, from the University of Massachusetts, Amherst.

MECA LICENSE AGREEMENT — HYATT LEGAL SERVICES' HOME LAWYER

Plain Language License

Carefully read all the terms and conditions of this agreement before opening this package. By opening this package, you agree to become bound by the terms and conditions of this agreement as a complete and exclusive statement of your agreement with us. If you do not agree to these terms and conditions, return the unopened disk package and other components of this product to the place of purchase and you will receive a full refund.

About This Product and Your Rights

This product (disks, manual, etc.) is protected by United States copyright laws. You are not allowed to make copies of the product for anyone else or for more than one computer. You may make a copy for your own safekeeping (back-up).

OverDrive Systems, Inc. and MECA Software, Inc. guarantee that the disks will be free of defects, but do not make any other warranties. If you find a disk is defective, we will replace it during the first 90 days. Send us the bad disks and your receipt for the Product and we'll send you a new disk or refund your money. This agreement is controlled by Ohio law.

THIS WARRANTY IS IN PLACE OF ALL OTHER WARRANTIES. OVERDRIVE SYSTEMS, INC. AND MECA SOFTWARE, INC. MAKE NO OTHER WARRANTIES OF ANY KIND, EITHER EXPRESS OR IMPLIED, INCLUDING WITHOUT LIMITATION ANY WARRANTY OF MERCHANTABILITY OR FITNESS FOR A PARTICULAR PURPOSE. OVERDRIVE SYSTEMS, INC. AND MECA SOFTWARE, INC. ARE NOT LIABLE FOR ANY INCIDENTAL OR CONSEQUENTIAL DAMAGES ARISING FROM YOUR USE OR INABILITY TO USE THE PROGRAM. OVERDRIVE SYSTEMS, INC.'S AND MECA SOFTWARE, INC.'S LIABILITY IN NO EVENT SHALL EXCEED THE AMOUNT YOU PAID FOR THE PROGRAM.

The documents included in this product can be used to handle the simple legal matters encountered by the typical family in everyday life. This product provides examples and prompts — in plain, simple English — to enable you to create a will, power of attorney or other documents suitable for your needs.

Your use of this product does not create an attorney-client relationship between you and Hyatt Legal Services, MECA Software, Inc. or OverDrive Systems, Inc. You may need a lawyer for your particular matter. It is your right and option to consult with one.

Be aware that laws and procedures do vary from state to state and may change. They may also be interpreted differently and by different people. Furthermore, there is no way to identify that you fully understand the reasons for the questions asked, that you have accurately followed the directions provided or that the result you intend can or will be met by the documents you find in this product. As a result, neither Hyatt Legal Services, OverDrive Systems, Inc nor MECA Software, Inc. guarantees or warrants that the documents created with this program will be valid at the time you use them, will lead to the result you desire or will carry out your intentions. Neither Hyatt Legal Services, OverDrive Systems, Inc. nor MECA Software, Inc. accepts any responsibility or liability for a document which is incorrectly used or inaccurately completed.

These documents are to be used only by you for personal legal matters. Our aim is to assist you to "do it yourself." Recognize, however, that if you do not understand the effect of the document you choose, or if you are confused by any of the document's provisions, you should consult with an attorney in your state for assistance and advice. Discussing your concerns with an attorney may be essential to your full understanding of your rights and options. Toward that end, a list of state-sponsored attorney referral programs is enclosed in this package for your reference. This list is provided for your convenience and is not intended to be an endorsement of the product by these Bar Associations.

If you have any questions regarding this Agreement, please contact MECA Software, Inc. at 55 Walls Drive, P.O. Box 912, Fairfield, CT 06430-0912.